THE NEW LITERACIES

The New Literacies

Multiple Perspectives on Research and Practice

Edited by
Elizabeth A. Baker

Foreword by Donald J. Leu

THE GUILFORD PRESS
New York   London

© 2010 The Guilford Press
A Division of Guilford Publications, Inc.
72 Spring Street, New York, NY 10012
www.guilford.com

Printed in the United States of America

This book is printed on acid-free paper.

Last digit is print number: 9   8   7   6   5   4   3   2   1

Library of Congress Cataloging-in-Publication Data

The new literacies : multiple perspectives on research and practice / edited by
Elizabeth A. Baker, foreword by Donald J. Leu.
   p. cm.
  Includes bibliographical references and index.
  ISBN 978-1-60623-604-8 (pbk.: alk. paper) — ISBN 978-1-60623-605-5
(hardcover: alk. paper)
   1. Technological literacy.   2. Computers and literacy.   3. Educational
technology.   4. Education—Effect of technological innovations
on.   5. Students—Effect of technological innovations on.   I. Baker, Elizabeth
A.   II. Leu, Donald J.
  LC149.5.N48 2010
  372.3′4—dc22

2010002476

About the Editor

Elizabeth A. Baker, EdD, is Associate Professor of Literacy Studies in the Department of Learning, Teaching, and Curriculum at the University of Missouri, where she teaches graduate seminars on new literacies, theoretical foundations of literacy, and qualitative research methods. Her research interests include the nature of literacy in digital environments, multimedia case-based instruction in teacher education, classroom websites used to support literacy development, and theoretical groundings of new literacies. Dr. Baker has published research reports in such journals as the *Journal of Literacy Research, Journal of Reading Education, Reading and Writing Quarterly, Reading Research and Instruction, National Reading Conference Yearbook, Reading Online, Journal of Educational Multimedia and Hypermedia, Journal of Technology and Teacher Education, Computers in Schools,* and *Learning and Leading with Technology.* She is the creator and host of the *Voice of Literacy* podcast, produced in collaboration with *Reading Research Quarterly* and the *Journal of Literacy Research,* and is codeveloper and principal investigator of "ChALK, Children as Literacy Kases."

Contributors

Peggy Albers, PhD, Department of Middle and Secondary Education and Instructional Technology, Georgia State University, Atlanta, Georgia

Elizabeth A. Baker, EdD, Department of Learning, Teaching, and Curriculum, University of Missouri, Columbia, Missouri

Kelly Chandler-Olcott, EdD, Reading and Language Arts Center, Syracuse University, Syracuse, New York

Anne Cloonan, PhD, School of Education, Deakin University, Melbourne, Australia

Kristin Conradi, PhD Cand., Department of Curriculum, Instruction, and Special Education, University of Virginia, Charlottesville, Virginia

Bill Cope, PhD, Department of Educational Policy Studies, University of Illinois at Urbana–Champaign, Champaign, Illinois

James Paul Gee, PhD, Division of Learning, Technology, and Psychology in Education, Arizona State University, Tempe, Arizona

Barbara J. Guzzetti, PhD, Division of Learning, Technology, and Psychology in Education, Arizona State University, Tempe, Arizona

Jerome C. Harste, PhD, Department of Literacy, Culture, and Language Education, Indiana University, Bloomington, Indiana

Douglas K. Hartman, PhD, Department of Teacher Education and Department of Educational Psychology, Michigan State University, East Lansing, Michigan

Ted S. Hasselbring, PhD, Department of Special Education, Peabody College, Vanderbilt University, Nashville, Tennessee

Mary Kalantzis, PhD, Department of Curriculum and Instruction, University of Illinois at Urbana–Champaign, Champaign, Illinois

Sohrob Kazerounian, PhD Cand., Department of Cognitive and Neural Systems, Boston University, Boston, Massachusetts

Linda D. Labbo, PhD, Department of Language and Literacy Education, University of Georgia, Athens, Georgia

Elizabeth Lewis, PhD, Department of Education, Dickinson College, Carlisle, Pennsylvania

Michael C. McKenna, PhD, Department of Curriculum, Instruction, and Special Education, University of Virginia, Charlottesville, Virginia

Larry Mikulecky, PhD, Department of Literacy, Culture, and Language Education, Indiana University, Bloomington, Indiana

Paul Mark Morsink, MA, Department of Counseling, Educational Psychology, and Special Education, Michigan State University, East Lansing, Michigan

P. David Pearson, PhD, Department of Language and Literacy, Society and Culture, University of California, Berkeley, Berkeley, California

Mary S. Rozendal, PhD, EnCourage Institute for Teaching and Learning, Grandville, Michigan

Tammy Ryan, PhD, School of Education, Jacksonville University, Jacksonville, Florida

Alex W. Storer, PhD Cand., Department of Cognitive and Neural Systems, Boston University, Boston, Massachusetts

Diane H. Tracey, EdD, Department of Communication Sciences, Kean University, Union, New Jersey

Vivian Vasquez, EdD, School of Education, Teaching, and Health, American University, Washington, DC

Jinjie Zheng, MS, MA, Department of Counseling, Educational Psychology, and Special Education, Michigan State University, East Lansing, Michigan

Foreword

The Internet changes everything, doesn't it? It has rapidly become the defining medium for information, reading, communication, culture, and learning in the 21st century (International Reading Association, 2009; Organization for Economic Co-operation and Development, n.d.; Partnership for 21st Century Skills, 2006). In short, it is a powerful new context for literacy. Ultimately, the Internet is likely to influence our lives more profoundly than any other aspect of the 21st century.

Prompted by the Internet, other information and communication technologies, and an expanded conception of literacy, many are beginning to see new literacies in the new social practices, new technologies, and new skills required for success in contemporary life (Lankshear & Knobel, 2006; Leander, 2008; Street, 2003). Holding us back, however, is a lack of clarity about what exactly these "new literacies" are. It is a term that has come to mean many different things to many different people. Unless this construct is defined more precisely, we will eventually cast it aside. It will fail to be useful to the research community in helping us to study and eventually understand the changes we are experiencing.

The book you hold in your hands (I wonder how soon this phrase will begin to sound archaic and strange to the ear?) allows you to participate in the important dialogue that is currently taking place in the research community as we seek to define this important new concept. What is "new" about literacy? Why should we consider it "new"? What are the implications for both research and practice as we consider new conceptions of literacy? Or is anything indeed really "new"? Elizabeth Baker and her colleagues are to be congratulated for exploring an issue that is so central to our field in such an accessible fashion. They continue an important conversation that will be important to understanding the expanded range of social, cognitive, and cultural practices that define our literate lives today.

The beauty of this volume is the breadth of thinking it includes, as scholars consider new literacies from an impressively diverse set of perspectives. Because the construct is so wonderfully rich and complex, the best way to develop new literacies theory is to expand the conversation, not narrow it. Baker and her colleagues understand this fundamental point. In the following chapters you will see new literacies considered from the point of view of new technologies being used to support the development of more traditional literacies, and you will also see new literacies considered from multiple sociocultural perspectives, a multiliteracies perspective, feminist perspectives, and cognitive perspectives. The voices in this collection are compelling and provocative.

New literacies theory appears to be developing on two levels: upper case (New Literacies) and lower case (new literacies) (Leu, O'Byrne, Zawilinski, McVerry, & Everett-Cocapardo, 2009). *New Literacies*, as the broader, more inclusive concept, benefits from work taking place in the multiple lower-case dimensions of *new literacies*. The diversity of voices and perspectives in new literacies work is an important advantage, not a limitation, and Baker and her colleagues perfectly demonstrate the power of this approach. Their important work enables the broader, and largely incomplete, theory of New Literacies to benefit from the richness and power of these multiple perspectives.

Lower-case theories often explore a specific area of new literacies, such as the semiotics of early literacy acquisition (Labbo & Ryan, Chapter 5). They also explore specific contexts such as workplace literacy (Mikulecky, Chapter 10) or specific populations such as struggling readers (Hasselbring, Chapter 2) or teachers (Vasquez, Harste, & Albers, Chapter 12). They also explore the issue from alternative frameworks such as sociocultural perspectives of literacy and technology (Gee, Chapter 8; Chandler-Olcott & Lewis, Chapter 9), a multiliteracies perspective (Kalantzis, Cope, & Cloonan, Chapter 4), feminist perspectives (Guzzetti, Chapter 11), behaviorist and constructivist perspectives (McKenna & Conradi, Chapter 3), cognitive processes (Tracey, Storer, & Kazerounian, Chapter 6), or cognitive conceptions (Hartman, Morsink, & Zheng, Chapter 7). Each body of work contributes to the larger, continually changing theory of New Literacies.

What defines this broader theory of New Literacies? A recent review (Coiro, Knobel, Lankshear, & Leu, 2008) concludes that most lower-case perspectives of new literacies share four common elements that define the larger theory of New Literacies:

1. New Literacies include the new skills, strategies, dispositions, and social practices that are required by new technologies for information and communication.
2. New Literacies are central to full participation in a global community.
3. New Literacies regularly change as their defining technologies change.
4. New Literacies are multifaceted and our understanding of them benefits from multiple points of view.

As work at the lower levels continues, it will add new dimension and depth to our understanding of the larger construct of new literacies.

Baker and her colleagues encourage us not to narrow down the definition of new literacies, but rather to expand it so that we might better understand it. Our field will gain greatly from the decision Baker and her colleagues have made to invite many voices into this conversation. By doing so, we build the most complete and comprehensive understanding of the changes taking place in literacy today, taking advantage of the power of the many, not the limitation of the few.

DONALD J. LEU, PhD
Neag Endowed Chair in Literacy and Technology
University of Connecticut

REFERENCES

Coiro, J., Knobel, M., Lankshear, C., & Leu, D. J. (2008). Central issues in new literacies and new literacies research. In J. Coiro, M. Knobel, C. Lankshear, & D. J. Leu (Eds.), *Handbook of research on new literacies* (1–22). Mahwah, NJ: Erlbaum.

International Reading Association. (2009). *IRA position statement on new literacies and 21st century technologies.* Newark, DE: Author.

Lankshear, C., & Knobel, M. (2006). *New literacies* (2nd ed.). Maidenhead, UK: Open University Press.

Leander, K. M. (2008). Toward a connective ethnography of online/offline literacy networks. In J. Coiro, M. Knobel, C. Lankshear, & D. Leu (Eds.), *Handbook of research on new literacies* (pp. 33–66). Mahwah, NJ: Erlbaum.

Leu, D. J., O'Byrne, W. I., Zawilinski, L., McVerry, J. G., & Everett-Cocapardo, H. (2009). Expanding the new literacies conversation. *Educational Researcher, 38*, 264–269.

Organization for Economic Co-operation and Development. (n.d.). *The OECD programme for international student assessment.* Retrieved August 15, 2007, from *www.oecd.org/dataoecd/51/27/37474503.pdf.*

Partnership for 21st Century Skills. (2006). *Are they really ready for work?: Employers' perspectives on the basic knowledge and applied skills of new entrants to the 21st century U.S. workforce.* Report written in collaboration with the Conference Board, Corporate Voices for Working Families, the Partnership for 21st Century Skills, and the Society for Human Resource Management. Retrieved December 9, 2006, from *www.21stcenturyskills.org/documents/FINAL_REPORT_PDF9-29-06.pdf.*

Street, B. (2003). What's new in new literacy studies? *Current Issues in Comparative Education, 5*(2), 1–14.

Thorne, S. L. (2008). Computer-mediated communication. In N. Hornberger & N. Van Duesen-Scholl (Eds.), *Encyclopedia of language and education* (Vol. 4, 2nd ed., pp. 325–336). New York: Springer/Kluwer.

Acknowledgments

It has been said that no one is an island. This is certainly the case in my life and in my endeavors to serve as editor of and contributing author to this book. During this project, it has been a great pleasure to work with a wide array of extremely talented and insightful scholars. The contributing authors, reviewers, and staff at The Guilford Press have worked tirelessly, diligently, and expertly to create this volume.

A number of competent reviewers provided detailed and thoughtful feedback to the authors and helped each author consider ways to improve his or her contributions. They are Shannon Cuff, Danielle Johnson, Karyn Knox, Paul Mark Morsink, Mary S. Rozendal, Jill Smith, and M. Juanita Willingham. This volume is greatly improved by their insights.

I thank Chris Jennison, Craig Thomas, and Anna Nelson of The Guilford Press for their gracious support and guidance throughout the process of creating this book. From submitting the prospectus to working through the "bumps in the road" to completing the final book, these collaborators have been there for me with quick replies and pertinent insights.

Finally, I thank my friends and family. They graciously asked about this project, willingly listened to updates, and eagerly shared in my excitement as each chapter was crafted. I dedicate this volume to my parents, Maude D. Baker and Walter Baker, Jr., for their love, support, and steadfastness. They have always supported my pursuits and encouraged me to become all I could be. Their lives attest to a love that always protects, always trusts, always hopes, always perseveres—and never fails (see I Corinthians 13:7-8). They are active demonstrations of the power and importance of love, compassion, and kindness, which they selflessly share with all.

Contents

CHAPTER 1

Theoretical Perspectives and Literacy Studies
An Exploration of Roles and Insights

ELIZABETH A. BAKER
P. DAVID PEARSON
MARY S. ROZENDAL

It has been said that perspective is everything. No two people come away from the same experience with the same impressions. In 2002 Jack Nicholson earned an award for best actor in a *drama*. For his acceptance speech he commented that he did not deserve the award because he thought the film was a *comedy*. He concluded his acting must have been lacking if the awards committee thought the film was a drama. Perspective likely played a role in how the audience perceived the genre of this film. Or perhaps the boundaries between the allegedly distinct categories of drama and comedy are more permeable than literary conventions would suggest.

Understanding of literacy is also influenced by perspective. Perspective changes how we define literacy, the skills we consider to be paramount to literacy acquisition, the environmental factors we deem necessary to support literacy development, and how we assess literacy abilities. For decades, scholars have explored literacy from multiple perspectives.

Each perspective has contributed to our current understandings of literacy. Some commonly invoked perspectives are: behavioral, neurological, linguistic, psycholinguistic, semiotic, cognitive, sociocultural, feminist, and critical (Alexander & Fox, 2004; Pearson & Stephens, 1994). Within each of these perspectives there exists an opportunity to bring new insight into this thing we call literacy; across these sensibilities, we have the opportunity to broaden our conception and understanding of it. Some of these perspectives come with a long history while others bring the naïvely wonderful freshness of intellectual infancy.

Those who consider literacy to be an artifact of the culture (sociocultural perspective) argue that the nature of literacy is changing. They argue that literacy changes as culture changes. For example, a few decades ago people were considered literate if they could read a familiar text and answer a literal question (e.g., "What color is Little Red Riding Hood's hood?"). Even earlier, say 150 years ago, they were considered literate if they could read and write their whole names. Technology has ushered in new literacy skills needed to succeed in today's (and tomorrow's) cultures. There are new literacies, ones not needed 50, 20, even 5 years ago. Consider the skills needed to effectively communicate such technologies as text messaging, e-mail, Facebook, Google, YouTube, and Second Life. Leu (2006) made a striking point about online technologies. He stated, "The Internet is a reading and literacy issue, not a technology issue" (p. 6). In other words, the skills required to proficiently communicate with technology requires traditional as well as new reading and writing skills. How often do we see the literacy skills associated with reading and writing with communication technologies represented in our school curricula? If our schools continue to limit the literacy curriculum to reading and writing traditional, alphabetic, printed texts, then our children will be well prepared for 1950 but ill prepared for 2050. A few of the more curmudgeonly in the field, such as P. David Pearson in this authorship team, might question the cognitive uniqueness of these new literacies, but that does not stop, or even slow down, their march onto the center stage of literacy. And even David admits that if they don't prompt cognitively distinct processes, they provide a unique context that prompts significant accommodations and adaptations to the cognitive processes involved.

The purpose of this book is to gain insights into new literacies from multiple perspectives. In fact, some of the perspectives represented in this book may not perceive the need to consider new literacies—rather, they see technology as a tool for reading and writing more or less traditional, alphabetic, printed texts (see Chapters 2 and 3). Others argue that readers and writers carry some traditional print-centric literacy skills when making sense of digital texts but that they invoke new skills as well. Specifically, they argue that reading and writing with technology requires traditional as well as new cognitive processes (see Chapters 6 and 7). Yet others question the very nature of literacy as a verbocentric (word-based) communication system. They emphasize the semiotic character of all literacy practices and incorporate all of the multiple sign systems of multimedia (see Chapters 4 and 5). As stated above, other scholars contend that literacy changes as culture changes. Thus because our culture uses technologies as text messaging, e-mail, Google, Facebook, YouTube, and Second Life, we need to prepare children to read and write fluently with these and other such communication systems (see Chapters 8, 9, and 10). Scholars drawing on additional perspectives focus on who is empowered and disempowered—who gets constructed as powerful and who as powerless—by the ways we help our populace engage in technology-based communications (see Chapters 11 and 12). Finally, new perspectives may shed new light on the phenomena of reading and writing with technology (see Chapter 13).

The field of literacy has benefited from a long, rich, and diverse history of perspectives. In this book, we do not claim that one perspective or set of perspectives is superior to another. Instead, we privilege the unique contribution that each brings to the table of literacy understanding. When Don Leu (2006) was president of the National Reading Conference he challenged all literacy researchers, from all theoretical perspectives, to examine the integration of literacy and technology. He argued that all literacy researchers should be investigating new literacies; in fact even the allegedly old literacies were transforming themselves into the "new." This text is intended to provide groundwork for such efforts. It is both an invitation to researchers from multiple perspectives to explore new literacies as well as a potential model for future researchers to explore new literacies. We also hope it provides a model for teachers, principals, superintendents, and policymakers, one that will enable them to see how literacy and technology can be integrated in different ways, for different purposes, and with different outcomes. In this book, we, as well as the contributing authors, attempt to help all who are interested in literacy to make sense of the complexities of being literate in today's technology-rich cultures.

PERSPECTIVES AND THEORIES: DEFINITIONS AND METAPHORS

Because the driving concept of this book is to demonstrate that a range of theoretical perspectives fosters a rich and nuanced understanding of literacy, we elaborate on what is meant by the terms *perspectives* and *theories*. A variety of definitions and metaphors are useful.

Perspective: Definitions and Metaphors

Perspectives are points of view. An old adage that demonstrates multiple perspectives is the story of the blind men and the elephant. When each are asked to describe the elephant, the blind man who is feeling a leg says the elephant is round and rough like the trunk of a large tree. The blind man feeling the trunk of the elephant says the elephant is wiggly and supple like a fat snake. The blind man feeling the ear says the elephant is thin and malleable like a fan. Literacy, like the elephant, is large and complex. Throughout the decades, due to differing perspectives, many have disagreed about the basic components of reading and writing. In this book we encourage readers to consider the role of divergent perspectives. While you may not agree with every perspective, we believe it is valuable to understand your own perspective(s) as well as the perspectives that others may take. Perhaps listening to and valuing divergent perspectives will help you better understand the complexities of literacy.

Just as the blind men describing the elephant brought different perspectives to understanding same phenomenon, literacy researchers, teachers, and policymakers commonly value a range of perspectives when it comes to understanding the reading and writing process—how it can be developed, acquired, taught, learned, and assessed. We contend that one perspective is not superior to another. Rather, they each reveal important information and insight that can help us grasp the complexities of literacy. We hope this book helps you understand the values and interests of a range of literacy researchers who have different perspectives toward reading and writing.

Theories: Definitions and Metaphors

As an undergraduate student, elementary school teacher, and master's student I (E. A. B.) was not interested in what different theories said about reading and writing acquisition, development, or instruction. When I heard people mention theories of reading and writing my eyes would glaze over. I just wanted to know what worked for my students and be given time and resources to use those methods. I did not realize the value of theories. However, I was a user of theory, whether I knew it or not. As a professor, I have more respect for theory and how it can be used to guide practice. Not surprisingly, I commonly find that my undergraduate and master's students have the same reaction I had to discussions of theories. Strauss and Corbin (1998) describe a research method called *grounded theory*. They state that the value of theory is that it explains where something came from and helps us to predict where it might go. For example, the theory of evolution attempts to explain where the range of species on earth came from and predict what they might become. Given rich descriptions and systematic categorizations of animal species, scientists have been able to generate a theory of the evolution of species. They posit that for living creatures to survive the elements of earth they have adapted and evolved across extended periods of time. They will likely continue to evolve and adapt. The theory of evolution helps us understand where different species may have come from and predict how they may continue to change.

Similarly, in this book the authors use theories to grapple with explanations for how humans make sense of text—how they read and write. They use theories to understand the infrastructure of reading and writing. They use theories to understand how various pedagogies support literacy acquisition and development. These theories are based on rich descriptions and systematic categorizations.

Theoretical Perspectives: So What?

Given these definitions and metaphors for *perspectives* and *theories*, the next question is one of significance—why should these notions be significant to teachers, graduate students, and researchers? We argue that teachers use theories, whether they know it or not. Their actions reveal their theories, even those that are only implicit in their work. For example, if a teacher isolates the sounds of words and drills children on sound–symbol relationships, she is utilizing behavioral learning theory that assumes that component skills of reading are picked up along an assembly line. Specifically, her actions are supported by the stimulus–response theories of Thorndike (1898) and Skinner (1974). A student can be drilled on the symbols *c-a-t*, such that when he sees these symbols he says the word *cat*. The stimuli are the letters *c-a-t*. The response is "cat." The teacher may not know that her actions are rooted in stimulus–response theory—but they are. They are tacit and implicit; they underlie and motivate her actions.

The Utility of Theories: The Role of Theories for Teachers

For several decades, the literacy community has recognized that a primary factor that makes a difference in children's literacy acquisition and development is the teacher. The First-Grade Studies (Bond & Dykstra, 1967; Readence & Barone, 1997) revealed that teachers can be effective *and* ineffective when using explicit isolated phonics instruction. Teachers can be effective *and* ineffective when using whole-word reading instruction (e.g., *Dick and Jane*). In other words, it is not the use of a particular teaching method that makes the difference—it is the teacher that makes the difference. This raises a pertinent question: What do effective teachers do that sets them apart from the ordinary? In 1987 Schön published a seminal book entitled *Educating the Reflective Practitioner*. Schön contends that a significant characteristic that differentiates effective teachers from less effective teachers is their ability to reflect. In other words, effective teachers tend to evaluate their own teaching. They think about what helped their students learn that day and what did not. They identify what worked and what did not. Shulman (1992) contends that practice does *not* make perfect—rather, thinking about, evaluating, and changing practice accordingly is what makes perfect.

Some have argued that teachers who understand a range of theoretical perspectives and their pedagogical implications are more empowered to be reflective than those who do not (Pressley, Wharton-McDonald, Raphael, Bogner, & Roehrig, 2002; Risko et al., 2008). An analogy from cooking helps to explain how theory improves practice in teaching. An expert chef understands what the ingredients of a cake contribute to the cake by using principles of chemistry. The amateur does not. If a cake comes out of the oven flat, the amateur must make a "guess" about how to correct the recipe. Next time, the amateur may try more flour, or a higher oven temperature, or a smaller pan. The master understands the theoretical explanation of the ingredients and is therefore empowered to make more informed decisions about the next cake. The amateur is limited to guessing. Similarly, the teacher who understands a range of literacy theories (explanations for reading and writing acquisition, development, and pedagogy) is more empowered to be reflective about what literacy skills to teach and how to teach them. Herein, theories make us smarter about our practice and thereby increase the likelihood that our instructional decisions will be effective.

The Usefulness of Theories to Those Who Consume and Conduct Research: The Role of Theories in Research

Research tries to answer questions. Questions emerge from values and beliefs. What are some questions you asked today? Why did you ask them? You must have thought the questions were worth asking. You valued the answer for some reason. For the first time, I (E. A. B.) recently traveled to Savannah, Georgia. I asked a tour guide, "Why is this city named Savannah?" I am interested in history. I am interested in learning how civilizations came to be the way they are. So I asked, "Why is the city named Savannah?" Those traveling with me did not think to ask this question. They were more interested in asking, "Where is a good place for lunch and how do we get there?" Their questions demonstrate another set of values: quenching hunger, sampling local cuisine. (For those interested, Savannah is thought to be a Native American term for grassy plain. The Olde Pink House now serves not only dinner but also lunch—and it is fabulous.) In the same way, research questions reveal a set of underlying beliefs and values. If you ask which teaching method causes students to have the highest standardized test results in communication arts you believe in a direct cause–effect relationship between teaching method and standardized measures of literacy. If you ask about the characteristics of classrooms in which children perform well on standardized measures you believe there is something in the environment that has an impact. This something could be teaching methods, but it could be social interactions between the teacher and student, or it could be a complex set of interactions among a range of factors in the milieu. The first question values an understanding of the cause–effect of a particular factor (teaching method). The second question values an understanding of the complexities of the social context of a classroom.

Researchers benefit from understanding the values, beliefs, and assumptions inherent in their research questions. This allows them to "stand on the shoulders of the giants" who came before them. For example, if a researcher knows that her questions are rooted in the beliefs and values of evolution, then she is able to address both the immediate questions she asked as well as the basic assumptions of evolution.

Her findings might corroborate current conceptions of evolution, shift them a bit, or even refute them. The theoretical implications are then significant to all who use evolutionary theory to understand how living creatures came to be the way they are. In the literacy world, if researchers know their question aligns well with behaviorism or sociocognitive theory they are better able to explain the significance of their questions. In addition, they are better prepared to refine, refute, or reposition the theories on which their questions are based. Thus theory is important to researchers because, among other reasons, (1) it helps them formulate questions and (2) it helps them confirm, expand, and disconfirm assumptions of theories others may use.

Teachers, graduate students, policymakers, and researchers are consumers of research. Thus it is important for them to understand the range of theoretical perspectives taken toward literacy. Their understandings allow them to examine research and consider whether it aligns with the beliefs and values they deem worthwhile. They can examine research and consider the possibility of changing their own beliefs and values in light of new findings. For example, as a teacher, graduate student, policymaker, or researcher you may have beliefs and values that align well with a sociocultural perspective of literacy; you may believe that the nature of literacy is shaped by the culture in which it is enacted. You may encounter a research article that examines literacy from a critical perspective—one that considers who gets privileged and who gets marginalized by a particular literacy practice. You can either assimilate the new research and find a way to make it fit your sociocultural schema or you may decide that your sociocultural schema requires major restructuring (what Piaget called accommodation) in order to take this new research into account. Both acts—the assimilation (strained though it might be) and the accommodation—influence your theoretical perspective on literacy research.

Understanding a range of theoretical perspectives toward literacy is important for both consumers and producers of research, be they teachers, graduate students, university faculty, or policymakers. This book is neither an apology nor an exposé of one or more theoretical perspectives; instead, it attempts to persuade all readers that a range of perspectives can inform, broaden, and even deepen our understanding of any particular phenomenon, including the phenomenon addressed in this book, new literacies. To begin that process we provide a broad overview of the subsequent chapters and then leave it to our contributing authors to unpack and deepen these perspectives in more vivid detail.

THEORETICAL PERSPECTIVE TOWARDS LITERACY

Multiple theoretical perspectives have brought us to our current understanding of literacy (Alexander & Fox, 2004; Kucer, 2005; Pearson & Stephens, 1994; Ruddell & Unrau, 2004; Tracey & Morrow, 2006). To examine new literacies, we have selected a handful of perspectives to explain in more detail; that's the rest of the book. In this overview chapter, we can do little more than describe the historic contributions of these perspectives. Our overview is hopelessly simplified (as overviews are destined to be), but we hope it provides an advance organizer of sorts—to provide you, our readers, with a basic feel for the similarities and differences among the perspectives.

Each perspective embodies a wide swath of inquiry. We asked the contributing authors to explain what their perspective means to them and what aspects (lenses and tools) of their perspective they use to understand the integration of literacy and technology. To complicate things (in the good sense), we provide readers with multiple chapters from each perspective. This reflects what we know to true—that within a given perspective, uniformity is the exception, not the rule. While these chapters in no way capture the rich traditions of each perspective we hope they give readers an appreciation for the range of insights each one brings to new literacies.

Our overview begins with a set of perspectives referred to as behavioral (see Chapters 2 and 3). Next, we showcase perspectives based on theories of semiotics and multiliteracies (see Chapters 4 and 5). Cognitive perspectives are the next set of theories, presented in Chapters 6 and 7. Sociocultural theories provide the foundation for Chapters 8, 9, and 10. Critical and feminist perspectives, represented in Chapters 11 and 12, use poststructuralist theoretical perspectives to understand new literacies. Finally, in Chapter 13 new perspectives are proposed that may reveal fresh insights and seek to inspire dialogue regarding new perspectives into the complexities involved in the integration of literacy and technology.

Behavioral Perspectives

Generally speaking, a basic tenet of this family of perspectives is that written words are simply a man-made code. Thus learning to read is a matter of cracking the code. When I (E. A. B.) was a child, my friends and I would invent codes. Only those who held the key to which symbols represented which sounds were able to make sense of the messages. We commonly begged our mothers for cereals that included secret decoder rings in the box. Similarly, studies that examine literacy as a visual perception process share this basic tenet: children simply need to learn the code. When a child can make the correct sounds represented in a written word, then he can hear the word and make a match between the written and oral word. Thus a pedagogical implication and another basic tenet of this perspective is that an effective way to help children learn the code is to focus on the code itself. There are two variants of this approach. In the alphabetic version, teachers need to isolate sounds (phonemes) and help children make matches between the sounds and their symbols (grapheme). This is the cipher, the code-cracking part. The more fluent a child becomes with making this match, the easier it is to decode words. In the second variant, what scholars have come to call the "whole-word" approach to teaching reading (e.g., *Dick and Jane*), the orthographic or visual unit is the written word and the phonological unit is the spoken word. Under either variation of this approach, the assumption is that once the match of visual stimulus (the letter or the written word) to auditory response (the phoneme or the spoken word) is mastered, then and only then can a child make sense of phrases, sentences, paragraphs, and stories (see Gray, Artley, & Arbuthnot, 1951; Chall, 1967; Flesch, 1955).

Such methods align with theories of behaviorism (Skinner, 1974; Watson, 1913) that define learning in terms of stimulus–response and operant conditioning. Behaviorists contend that learning cannot be observed. We cannot crack open your head and see what you learn. The only way to ascertain learning is by observation of behaviors. A teacher can observe how well students make matches between the phoneme and grapheme for the letter *A*. A teacher can reward them for correct matches and thereby enhance their motivation to learn the code.

Learning can be broken down into basic units of objective truth. There are right and wrong answers when making correct matches to the code. For example, the correct reading of *h-o-u-s-e* is *house*, not *home*. The match a child makes between phoneme and grapheme can readily be ascertained as right or wrong. Teachers are encouraged to write "objectives" in their lesson plans that define learning in terms of behaviors. Assessment can focus on children's abilities to accurately match the sound to the symbol. Assessment measures can highlight specific areas of the code with which a particular child struggles. Additional practice can remediate this child's abilities to match the grapheme with the phoneme. Specifically, the child who incorrectly says, "home" when the written word is *h-o-u-s-e*, can be evaluated for his ability to decode words with *o-u-s* as well as make sense of medial letters. Difficulties with reading are defined in terms of difficulty with perception (e.g., dyslexia studies). Given additional practice with the specific aspects of perception that one lacks will enhance one's ability to break the code. In turn, this will foster the ability to read. Chapters 2 (Hasselbring) and 3 (McKenna & Conradi) in this volume utilize behavioral constructs to discuss insights into the integration of literacy and technology.

Semiotic and Multiliteracies Perspectives

In contrast with these behavioral perspectives, which examine reading and writing in terms of the alphabetic code, are semiotic, multiliteracies perspectives that examine reading and writing with sign systems in general—not just with the alphabet. Semiotics is the study of sign systems (Eco, 1976; Peirce, 1934; Saussure, 2006). Semioticians explore how meaning is constructed and associated with signs. Peircian semiotics is known for exploring and understanding three types of particular signs—indexes, icons, and symbols. *Indexes* are signs that indicate or imply something else. For example, a bullet hole is a sign that implies that a gun was fired in the vicinity. *Icons* refer to signs that stand for something else and usually contain an imaginal clue to the referent. For example, my computer has an icon of a trashcan. It is not an actual trashcan. It simply represents a trashcan, and as an icon, it resembles what it represents. *Symbols* are signs that represent ideas or concepts. For example, an American flag can be a symbol of patriotism. The meaning represented by a flag is so highly esteemed that various times in our history, you could be arrested for burning or desecrating this symbol. The flag is not actually patriotism, but it can and does represent patriotism. Symbols gain their semiotic value, their meaning, only through experiences as enacted through cultural practices. In contrast to the trashcan, there is nothing in the symbol, the sign, of the flag to denote patriotism, but cultural practices have conspired to create a strong connection to things patriotic. Another symbol germane to this discussion is orthography, the letters and shapes of the written word. Alphabetic text is used to represent oral words that represent concepts. It is no accident that we commonly talk about symbol–sound correspondences when we describe decoding instruction.

Semioticians examine how meaning gets assigned to indexes, icons, and symbols. Specifically, they examine signs, the entities they represent, and their interpretants (the persons making sense of the signs). Herein, a semiotic perspective allows literacy researchers to explore alphabetic and nonalphabetic symbols to ask questions about how they are used to make and exchange meaning. In addition, a semiotic perspective can be used to understand nonverbal meanings—how they are captured, conveyed, and interpreted. Surprisingly, one of the most well-studied, at least from a semiotic perspective, areas of literacy is emergent literacy (see Baker & Rowe, 2008; Harste, 1994; Rowe, 1994). Given a semiotic perspective, researchers are able to explore the underlying communicative intent of preschool children's compositions. The semiotic lens transforms what appear to be scribbles and drawings into meaning-laden artifacts. Semiotics allows us to understand how meaning is assigned to these nonalphabetic communications and how, over time, young writers transfer the meaning-making intentions to graphosemantic (match between letters and meanings) concepts. While a semiotic view of preschoolers' "scribbles" has been advocated for a while, using this broader view of literacy for older children and adults is much newer and being readily advocated by those who examine the integration of literacy and technology (e.g., Cope & Kalantzis, 2000; Kress, 2003).

In a study of the nature of literacy in our technological world, I (E. A. B.) found a semiotic perspective to be fundamental to understanding reading and writing digital texts (Baker, 2001). From a semiotic perspective, I asked, if we continue to limit literacy instruction to the ability to read and write alphabetic text, are we preparing our children for the past instead of the future? If making sense of a topic includes the multimedia offered on the Internet (e.g., Wikipedia, YouTube, Google, podcasts, CNN/ireport) then literacy includes the ability to read and write with not only alphabetic sign systems but also video (with embedded narrations, accompanying music, sound effects), animations, photos, illustrations, and the like. Notice that a semiotic perspective can apply to diverse activities—from understanding preschoolers' "scribbles" to making sense of the complexities of reading and writing with multimedia-based technologies. Widespread recognition of literacy as a semiotic system is gaining official as well as academic status. The International Reading Association (2009) advocates the expansion of literacy curricula to include multimedia. However, the pressures of high-stakes testing seem to reify a behavioral, isolated, verbocentric, alphabetic conception of reading and writing. In Chapters 4 (Kalantzis, Cope, & Cloonan) and

5 (Labbo & Ryan) in this volume you will read much more about multimodality, multiliteracies, and the use of multiple sign systems readily used to read and write with technology. While these chapters purposely examine new literacies from semiotic, multiliteracies perspectives, many of the remaining chapters in the book also embrace and view literacy as a semiotic, multiliteracies activity.

Cognitive Perspectives

In contrast with behaviorists who contend that learning can only be ascertained through observation of behaviors, cognitive psychologists examine and theorize about thinking; they assume something is happening inside that black box called the brain. One of the key functions in cognitive psychology is to invent structures and processes that explain the nature of the thinking that must have gone on to produce the language and action in which humans engage. For example, cognitive psychologists have advanced the conceptualization of thinking in terms of *schema* (Anderson & Pearson, 1984; Rumelhart, 1980; see Chapters 6 and 7, this volume). Knowledge, even in our memory, is viewed as a rich network of schemas connected to one another through a rich and expansive array of connections driven by experience. For example, you may have a node of memory, schema, for *cat*. When you encounter a new cat, you ascertain its qualities and determine whether this new cat is indeed a cat (e.g., it contains all of the features you have stored with your cat schema—fur, meows, independence), some other feline, some other animal, or an entirely different entity. If you determine it is a cat but has qualities you did not store in your schema for cat (e.g., hairless), then you alter the structure of your schema to accommodate these new data. Schema theory is significant to understanding reading and writing because it helps us see how different readers commonly interpret the meanings of text differently. We all have different schema because we all have different experiences. Thus what we read will mean different things depending on our individual schema.

The hindsight of history tells us that these cognitive perspectives influenced classroom practice as well as research as it unfolded through the decades of the '70s, '80s, and '90s. Teachers asked children to brainstorm about topics before they read about the topic. So if they were going to read a story in which a grandmother was a primary character they might brainstorm what they knew about grandmothers. The idea was that children would understand and remember the stories and articles better if they activated and/or constructed related schema prior to reading. Teachers also sought ways to increase children's background knowledge. Instead of reading about photosynthesis they might grow plants in the classroom in various light conditions. Herein, children build their schema and ability to comprehend related texts. Educators eschewed standardized tests (which have difficulty taking background knowledge and inevitable interpretive differences into account) in favor of more open versions of assessment, such as constructed response, performance assessment, and demonstrations of competence through portfolios and exhibitions.

Another legacy of the cognitive revolution was the notion of metacognition, awareness of one's own thinking (Flavell, 1979, 1987) along with a set of comprehension strategies (Baker & Brown, 1984; Garner, 1987; Pressley, 2002) that could be used to "fix up" comprehension after our metacognitive detectors told us something had gone awry. While behaviorists contend that we cannot see what is learned, only the result of learning that is evident in behaviors, cognitive psychologists attempt to assess thought processes directly by asking students to "think out loud" about their inner struggles while reading or writing. Pedagogically, this means that teachers can explain to children how they personally think through a passage of reading and how they think through composing. Children can then emulate these thought processes. What behaviorists conceptualize as skills that are separable entities to be taught and practiced until students are fluent and automatic, cognitive psychologists conceptualize as strategies to be taught in context and scaffolded until students reach independence (Baker & Brown, 1984; Bruner, 1978; Palincsar, 1986). For example, if a teacher notices that a student or group of children struggle with words that have a vowel–consonant–e pattern (VCe; e.g., *-ade, -ode, -ide, -ede*) she might call them aside and read through a story while telling the students her thought process whenever she encounters VCe words. She gradually releases the responsibility (Pearson & Gallagher, 1983) to the students as they attempt to make sense of these words. They emulate her metacognition and even share their own metacognition. Herein, appropriate decoding of VCe words is not a skill to be taught in isolation for automaticity but a strategic thought process that is scaffolded while reading authentic texts for real purposes. This notion of scaffolding and gradual release is even more prominent in comprehension instruction.

A wide range of insights about reading and writing can be gleaned from a cognitive perspective; in this volume, Chapters 6 and 7 give a flavor for how these insights inform conceptions of new literacies. Specifically, Chapter 6 (Tracey, Storer, & Kazerounian) examines new literacies in terms of narrative theories, box and pointer models, computational models, and cognitive neuroscience. Chapter 7 (Hartman, Morsink, & Zheng) details the cognitive complexities of reading and writing from print to pixels.

Sociocultural Perspectives

A sociocultural perspective examines literacy as an artifact of culture. From this perspective, the nature of literacy changes as culture changes. Resnick and Resnick (1977) recount how expectations for reading in Europe and the United States in the late 1600s involved mastering a range of religious texts. If you could orally read these familiar texts you were considered to be literate. By the mid 1700s reading was limited to mostly familiar texts and not intended as an activity for learning. By the early 1900s literacy was operationally defined as getting the gist of newspaper articles and following simple written directions. Researchers in the sociocultural tradition also demonstrate that etic (outsider) perspectives construct literacy differently from emic (insider) perspectives. For example, Heath (1983) examined the culture of literacy in two Appalachian communities. She then contrasted these practices with the expectations these children faced in their classrooms. While schools saw these Appalachian children as illiterate, Heath's work showed that the literacies of their home culture were simply not the same as the literacies of the school culture. In other words, the culturally sophisticated literacy practices of this community was simply not aligned with (or privileged in) those of the broader culture. Similarly, Moll (1992) examined the tension between the literacy practices of Latino children and those of the schools they attended. Leu (2000) goes as far as to claim that literacy is deictic (i.e., its meaning requires reference to the context in which it is used); for Leu, the nature of literacy changes so readily that what was literacy a moment ago has already changed in the present moment.

    In 2001 I (E. A. B.) published a study of what, at the time, was considered to be a technology-rich classroom (more computers in the room than students, one Internet connection, scanners, video cameras, printers) from a sociocultural perspective (Baker, 2001). My question was, what is the nature of literacy in this setting? Four characteristics emerged. First, literacy was *semiotic*. Students read (gained meaning) from alphabetic text as well as photos, graphs, illustrations, and video (with musical accompaniment and narration). Furthermore, they wrote (expressed themselves) by using multiple sign systems such as PowerPoint presentations that incorporated alphabetic text with photos, narration, video, graphs, and the like. Second, literacy was *public*. Reading and writing in this classroom were not private activities. Students walked past one another's computers, read each other's screens, and discussed their work in passing as well as by invitation. If they chose to post their work to the Internet, students also had a worldwide audience. They were no longer limited to the teacher as their primary audience (see Baker, Rozendal, & Whitenack, 2000). Third, literacy was *transitory*. The products that the students read and wrote were in constant flux, more dynamic than fixed or static, more situated than generic. The websites they used today may be different or even nonexistent tomorrow (e.g., content posted to Wikipedia). In addition, they were able to update their publications months after they presented them to the class, handed them into the teacher, or posted them to the Web. They were not limited to a publication being "done" and fixed forever, like a butterfly pinned to cardboard in a collection. Finally, literacy was *product oriented*, but in the positive sense of creating artifacts to communicate to specific audiences or "reading" artifacts to learn specific concepts. In some ways, this product orientation incorporates other important characteristics of authentic communication. For example, students did not read for their own, individual, isolated pleasure. They read to engage in conversations (*public nature*), albeit asynchronous, with classmates and other audience members. Reading resulted in products that would communicate what interested them. Because these products were all about conveying meaning, they had an inherent *semiotic* character. As they discussed their readings with others, students commonly chose to improve both the content and the presentation of their compositions (*transitory and provisional nature*). This study is useful to demonstrate the focus of the sociocultural perspective. Literacy was shaped by the culture of a technology-rich fourth-grade classroom that used technology to find and share information and insights.

Given a sociocultural perspective, focus shifts from individual cognition to cultural norms. In her book regarding literacy and identity in Second Life with avatars, Thomas (2007) states, "With every new form of community, children are participating in new forms of literacy" (p. 182). In Chapter 8 of this volume, Gee examines literacy as a sociocognitive practice by melding the concepts of literacy as a cognitive and cultural practice. In Chapter 9, Chandler-Olcott and Lewis use the metaphor of scrapbooking for examining new literacies from a sociocultural perspective. In Chapter 10, Mikulecky reveals the reading and writing skills required in current workplaces. He then highlights the role of schools in preparing children for a workplace that requires proficient technology-based reading and writing skills.

Critical and Feminist Perspectives

Critical theorists (Foucault, 1980; Freire, 1970; Giroux, 1991) and feminist theorists (Connell, 1987; Stanley & Wise, 1993; Thorne, 1993) travel further down the contextual pathway than do sociocultural theorists. They expand the notion of context beyond the social and the cultural to include historical, political, and economic forces (Siegel & Fernandez, 2000; Tracey & Morrow, 2006). These forces are viewed as influential in shaping our perspectives, ideologies, and cultural practices. Thus it is not only how we view a particular situation that is determined by external forces; our assumptions, our actions, and our evaluation of the consequences of those actions are all shaped by these forces. Freire, a Brazilian philosopher and educator, is noted for his work in Brazil, in which he examined how schools reified social stratification so as to maintain the economic status quo. In other words, Freire argued that the literacy instruction in Brazil was designed to keep workers in their place. He based this argument on his ability to help 300 illiterate adults become literate within 45 days. Similarly, feminist theory examines the disenfranchisement, marginalization, and underrepresentation of women.

For any given cultural practice or action (including speech acts), the questions to ask are:

- Whose interests are served by this point of view, perspective, or practice?
- Who benefits by its existence?

For any text, oral or written or imaginal, we can ask, who (or whose perspective) is represented, who is marginalized, and who is just plain absent? What we think, say, and do is inherently "interested" and shaped by these powerful external forces. What matters about a given text (again, broadly defined) or action is its assumptions (where does it come from?) and its consequences (what does it do? to whom?).

Critical and feminist theories are markedly different from the other perspectives in their focus on power, power relationships, and a call to activism for equality. In Chapter 11, Guzzetti situates her discussion of new literacies by drawing on gender schema theory, feminist sociology, feminist poststructuralist theory, and cyberfeminist theory. In Chapter 12, Vasquez, Harste, and Albers describe a summer workshop in which they worked with a group of teachers to make multimedia presentations about a social issue within their communities. They take a critical perspective toward the workshop and the multimedia compositions the teachers created.

NEW LITERACIES FROM MULTIPLE PERSPECTIVES

When the call for chapters was issued, contributing authors were asked to take on a specific perspective (e.g., behavioral, semiotic, multiliteracies, cognitive, sociocultural, feminist, or critical) and respond to several prompts:

- Define your theoretical perspective toward literacy. Situate yourself within the context of the perspective you are taking.
- From your perspective,

  - What does it mean to integrate literacy and technology?
  - What is the nature of literacy in technological environments?
  - How would you define new literacies?
  - What research needs to be done to understand the integration of literacy and technology?
  - What are the implications for classroom instruction?
  - What are the implications for policymakers?

In the resulting chapters, the authors discuss reading and writing with skills-based software, text messaging, e-mail, fan fiction, zines, anime, Facebook, YouTube, Second Life, and the like. It is our hope that by asking authors to unpack their particular perspectives and by providing more than one "take" on each perspective that we provide a broader understanding of what it does mean and might mean to integrate technology and literacy. These chapters, written from these widely varying perspectives, indeed reveal that reading and writing are complex, rich, multifaceted, nuanced phenomena. We hope that this collection will facilitate ongoing discussions, research, and policies that advance our understanding and practice of literacy in our technology-rich culture and global economy.

REFERENCES

Alexander, P. A., & Fox, E. (2004). A historical perspective on reading research and practice. In R. B. Ruddell & N. J. Unrau (Eds.), *Theoretical models and processes of reading* (5th ed., pp. 33–68). Newark, DE: International Reading Association.

Anderson, R. C., & Pearson, P. D. (1984). A schema-theoretic view of basic processes in reading comprehension. In P. D. Pearson (Ed.), *Handbook of reading research* (pp. 255–291). White Plains, NY: Longman.

Baker, E. A. (2001). The nature of literacy in a technology rich classroom. *Reading Research and Instruction, 40*(2), 153–179.

Baker, E. A., & Rowe, D. W. (2008, September 15). Preschool writing. *Voice of Literacy.* Podcast retrieved from *www.voiceofliteracy.org/posts/26532.*

Baker, E. A., Rozendal, M., & Whitenack, J. (2000). Audience awareness in a technology rich elementary classroom. *Journal of Literacy Research, 32* (3), 395–419.

Baker, L., & Brown, A. L. (1984). Metacognitive skills and reading. In P. D. Pearson, M. Kamil, R. Barr, & P. Mosenthal (Eds.), *Handbook of reading research* (Vol. I, pp. 353–394). White Plains, NY: Longman.

Bond, G. L., & Dykstra, R. (1967). The cooperative research program in first-grade reading instruction. *Reading Research Quarterly, 2,* 5–142.

Bruner, J. S. (1978). The role of dialogue in language acquisition. In A. Sinclair, R. J. Jarvelle, & W. J. M. Leveet (Eds.), *The child's conception of language.* New York: Springer.

Chall, J. S. (1967). *Learning to read: The great debate.* New York: McGraw-Hill.

Connell, B. W. (1987). *Gender and power.* Stanford, CA: Stanford University Press.

Cope, B., & Kalantzis, M. (Eds.). (2000). *Multiliteracies: Literacy learning and the design of social futures.* New York: Routledge.

Eco, U. (1976). *A theory of semiotics.* London: Macmillan.

Flavell, J. H. (1979). Metacognition and cognitive monitoring: A new area of cognitive-developmental inquiry. *American Psychologist, 34,* 906–911.

Flavell, J. H. (1987). Speculations about the nature and development of metacognition. In F. E. Weinert & R. H. Kluwe (Eds.), *Metacognition, motivation and understanding* (pp. 21–29). Hillsdale, NJ: Erlbaum.

Flesch, R. (1955). *Why Johnny can't read—and what you can do about it.* New York: Harper & Brothers.

Foucault, M. (1980). *Power/knowledge: Selected interviews and other writings (1972–1977)* (C. Gordon, L. Marshall, J. Mepham, & K. Soper, Trans.). New York: Pantheon Books.

Freire, P. (1970). *Pedagogy of the oppressed.* New York: Continuum.

Garner, R. (1987). *Metacognition and reading comprehension.* Norwood, NJ: Ablex.

Giroux, H. (Ed.). (1991). *Modernism, postmodernism, and feminism: Rethinking the boundaries of educational discourse.* Albany, NY: State University of New York Press.

Gray, W. S., Artley, A. S., & Arbuthnot, M. H. (1951). *The new fun with Dick and Jane.* Chicago: Foresman.

Harste, J. (1994). Literacy as curricular conversations about knowledge, inquiry, and morality. In R. Ruddell, M. Ruddell, & H. Singer (Eds.), *Theoretical models and processes of reading* (4th ed., pp. 1220–1242). Newark, DE: International Reading Association.

Heath, S. B. (1983). *Ways with words.* London: Cambridge University Press.

International Reading Association. (2009). *New literacies and 21st-century technologies: A position statement of the International Reading Association.* Retrieved September 15, 2009, from *www.reading.org/General/AboutIRA/PositionStatements/21stCenturyLiteracies.aspx.*

Kress, G. (2003). *Literacy in the new media age.* New York: Routledge.

Kucer, S. B. (2005). *Dimensions of literacy: A conceptual base for teaching reading and writing in school settings* (2nd ed.). Mahwah, NJ: Erlbaum.

Leu, D. J., Jr. (2000). Literacy and technology: Deictic consequences for literacy education in an information age. In M. L. Kamil, P. Mosenthal, P. D. Pearson, & R. Barr (Eds.), *Handbook of reading research* (Vol. 3, pp. 743–770). Mahwah, NJ: Erlbaum.

Leu, D. J., Jr. (2006). New literacies, reading research, and the challenges of change: A deictic perspective. In J. V Hoffman, D. L. Schallert, C. M. Fairbanks, J. Worthy, & B. Maloch (Eds). *Fifty-fifth National Reading Conference Yearbook* (pp. 1–20). Oak Creek, WI: National Reading Conference.

Moll, L. C. (1992). Literacy research in community and classrooms: A sociocultural approach. In R. Beach, J. L. Green, M. L. Kamil, & T. Shanahan (Eds.), *Multidisciplinary perspectives on literacy research* (pp. 179–207). Urbana, IL: National Council of Teachers of English.

Palincsar, A. S. (1986). The role of dialogue in providing scaffolded instruction. *Educational Psychologist, 21,* 73–98.

Pearson, P. D., & Gallagher, M. C. (1983). The instruction of reading comprehension. *Contemporary Educational Psychology, 8,* 317–344.

Pearson, P. D., & Stephens, D. (1994). Learning about literacy: A 30-year journey. In R. B. Ruddell, M. R. Ruddell, & H. Singer (Eds.), *Theoretical models and processes of reading* (4th ed., pp. 22–42). Newark, DE: International Reading Association.

Peirce, C. S. (1934). *Collected papers: Volume V. Pragmatism and pragmaticism.* Cambridge, MA: Harvard University Press.

Pressley, M. (2002). Metacognition and self-regulated comprehension. In A. E. Farstrup & S. Samuels (Eds.), *What research has to say about reading instruction* (pp. 291–309). Newark, DE: International Reading Association.

Pressley, M., Wharton-McDonald, R., Raphael, L. M., Bogner, K., & Roehrig, A. (2002). Exemplary first-grade teaching. In B. M. Taylor & P. D. Pearson (Eds.), *Teaching reading: Effective schools, accomplished teachers* (pp. 73–88). Mahwah, NJ: Erlbaum.

Readence, J. E., & Barone, D. M. (Eds.). (1997). Revisiting the first-grade studies: The importance of literacy history [Special issue]. *Reading Research Quarterly, 32*(4).

Resnick, D. P., & Resnick, L. B. (1977). The nature of literacy: An historical exploration. *Harvard Educational Review, 47,* 370–385.

Risko, V. J., Roller, C. M., Cummins, C., Bean, R. M., Block, C., Anders, P. L., et al. (2008). A critical analysis of research on reading teacher education. *Reading Research Quarterly, 43*(3), 252–288.

Rowe, D. W. (1994). *Preschoolers as authors: Literacy learning in the social world of the classroom.* Cresskill, NJ: Hampton Press.

Ruddell, R. B., & Unrau, N. J. (Eds.). (2004). *Theoretical models and processes of reading* (5th ed.). Newark, DE: International Reading Association.

Rumelhart, D. E. (1980). Schemata: The building blocks of cognition. In R. J. Spiro, B. C. Bruce, & W. F. Brewer (Eds.), *Theoretical issues in reading comprehension: Perspectives from cognitive psychology, linguistics, artificial intelligence, and education* (pp. 33–58). Hillsdale, NJ: Erlbaum.

Saussure, F. (2006). *Writings in general linguistics.* Oxford, UK: Oxford University Press.

Schön, D. A. (1987). *Educating the reflective practitioner: Toward a new design for teaching and learning in the professions.* San Francisco: Jossey-Bass.

Shulman, L. (1992). Toward a pedagogy of cases. In J. Shulman (Ed.), *Case methods in teacher education* (pp. 1–30). New York: Teachers College Press.

Siegel, M., & Fernandez, S. L. (2000). Critical approaches. In M. L. Kamil, P. B. Mosenthal, P. D. Pearson, & R. Barr (Eds.), *Handbook of reading research* (Vol. 3, pp. 141–151). Mahwah, NJ: Erlbaum.

Skinner, B. F. (1974). *About behaviorism.* New York: Knopf.

Stanley, L., & Wise, S. (1993). *Breaking out again: Feminist ontology and epistemology.* New York: Routledge.

Strauss, A., & Corbin, J. (1998). *Basics of qualitative research: Techniques and procedures for developing grounded theory* (2nd ed.). Thousand Oaks, CA: Sage.

Thomas, A. (2007). *Youth online: Identity and literacy in the digital age.* New York: Lang.

Thorndike, E. L. (1898). Animal intelligence: An experimental study of the associative processes in animals. *Psychological Review Monograph Supplement, 2*(8), 1–109.

Thorne, B. (1993). *Gender play: Girls and boys in school.* New Brunswick, NJ: Rutgers University Press.

Tracey, D. H., & Morrow, L. M. (2006). *Lenses on reading: An introduction to theories and models.* New York: Guilford Press.

Watson, J. B. (1913). Psychology as the behaviorist views it. *Psychological Review, 20,* 158–177.

CHAPTER 2

Reading Proficiency, the Struggling Reader, and the Role of Technology

TED S. HASSELBRING

Reading proficiency has historically been valued as *the* fundamental enabling competency in public education in the minds of parents, educators, and the general public. If students cannot read, they are often challenged in all other academic areas. Furthermore, they may be denied the opportunity for advanced coursework or the pursuit of lifelong learning. Although humans are "hardwired" for oral language, learning to read often takes extreme effort on the part of the learner in order to reach any level of proficiency. For many struggling students, learning to read is the most difficult cognitive challenge they are ever asked to undertake. And for many students who struggle, the process of learning to read must continue into the middle grades, high school, and beyond.

Despite the dedication and expertise of so many educational professionals, the data on older readers indicate that too many of our nation's students are failing to reach a proficient level in the literacy skills they need for success in school and life. According to the 2007 National Assessment of Educational Progress (NAEP), just one-third of public school fourth graders and less than one-third of eighth graders read at or above grade level (Lee, Grigg, & Donahue, 2007).

Research suggests that many of the older struggling readers who perform poorly on the NAEP are students who lack foundational reading skills at the word level. Difficulties with word-level reading become increasingly problematic as students get older. Problems with decoding and sight word fluency result in poor comprehension and lower motivation (Snow, Burns, & Griffin, 1998), and as texts become increasingly advanced with each grade, struggling readers fall further and further behind. Recent studies of older struggling readers showed that more than 60% of the students performed at very low levels on basic word-reading skills (Hock, Deshler, Marquis, & Brasseur, 2005; Leach, Scarborough, & Rescorla, 2003; Torgesen et al., 2007). This finding was especially evident in urban schools.

Explanations for the problems exhibited by older struggling readers vary, and different explanations pertain to individual students. Much research, however, suggests that their decoding skills prove insufficient as words become more phonologically and morphologically complex. In fact, Juel (1991) reported that some older students have never learned to decode. In primary grades, they appeared to be successful readers by relying on memorization of words. However, faced with more challenging material, they could not manage with memorized words alone. In her seminal work on beginning readers, Adams (1990) states, "Without phonics, readers' only recourse would be to rote memorize their way to literacy. But there are just too many words to make that a hopeful strategy" (p. 410).

Wagner (2008) reinforces the notion that many older struggling readers lack the foundational, decoding, and morphological skills necessary to progress in the face of increasingly challenging texts. He suggests that these students:

- Lack conceptual understanding of the alphabetic principle.
- Know some but not all of the decoding elements they need to progress.
- Lack automaticity in word recognition.
- Lack strategies for unlocking unfamiliar words.

Because of the above factors, these students tend to skip words, misread words, and spend a significant amount of time and mental energy identifying words when reading. This is unfortunate, because research clearly shows that the mastery of any complex domain (such as reading) depends on the ability to perform the subprocesses of that domain with speed and accuracy while consciously carrying out other higher-level cognitive tasks (Bloom, 1986; Hasselbring, Goin, & Bransford, 1987; LaBerge & Samuels, 1974).

BUILDING WORD-LEVEL AUTOMATICITY

Although word-level automaticity by itself is not sufficient to make older struggling readers proficient, clearly it is a prerequisite for proficiency (Moats, Furry, & Brownell, 1998). Shaywitz (2003) argues that word-level automaticity is developed over time as follows:

> In reading, students first learn the alphabetic principle and use this to decode words, often very laboriously. Through repeated trials, the student will develop a "neural model" of the word and no longer relies on the use of the alphabetic principle. The more times the student reads the word correctly the stronger the neural pathway becomes and fluency increases. (p. 189)

Shaywitz's description of how students build word-level automaticity is consistent with the development of expertise in other domains, that is, sufficient time to practice skills to a high level of speed and accuracy. In their classic study of expertise in chess, Simon and Chase (1973) observed that nobody had attained the level of an international chess master (grandmaster) "with less than about a decade's intense preparation with the game" (p. 402). Simon and Chase's "10–year rule" is supported by data from a wide range of domains: music, mathematics, swimming, tennis, and long-distance running (Ericsson, Krampe, & Tesch-Romer, 1993).

Stanovitch (1986) describes the deleterious effect that the lack of "word reading" practice has on beginning readers in his description of the "Matthew effect." When children fail at early reading, they begin to dislike reading and avoid practice. They read less than their classmates who are stronger readers. And when children who are struggling do not receive adequate remediation, they read less—and learn less from reading—than children who are reading. As a consequence, they do not gain vocabulary, background knowledge, and information about how reading material is structured. In short, the word-rich get richer, while the word-poor get poorer—the Matthew effect.

Clearly, to learn any complex subject it is necessary to be realistic about the amount of time it takes. However, it takes more than just time.

A considerable amount is known about variables that affect learning. For example, learning is most effective when people engage in what Ericsson et al. (1993) call "deliberate practice." Ericsson and his colleagues studied the role of deliberate practice in the acquisition of expert performance in a variety of domains and found that the one consistent factor in building expert performance, apart from innate ability and individual differences, was the amount and type of practice. Deliberate practice differs from simple "drill and practice" in that it involves activities that are explicitly intended to improve performance, that reach for objectives just beyond one's level of competence, provides feedback on results, and involves high levels of repetition. The evidence is clear—the highest performers in any field are those who devote the most hours to "deliberate practice."

DELIBERATE PRACTICE AND THE ROLE OF TECHNOLOGY

Practice at many levels is the key to the kingdom in reading. Maryanne Wolf (2007) eloquently describes the importance of practice as restructuring occurs in the young brain as follows: "Becoming virtually automatic does not happen overnight and is not a characteristic of either a novice bird-watcher or a young novice reader. These circuits and pathways are created through hundreds or, in the case of some children with reading difficulties like dyslexia, thousands of exposures to letters and words" (p. 14). So, the obvious question must be asked: How do we provide struggling readers with the necessary amount of deliberate practice in order to get them to the point of automaticity? There is ample evidence that many struggling readers are not getting the amount of deliberate practice necessary to develop high levels of word-level automaticity. Furthermore, it is unrealistic to expect that teachers are able to provide the high level of deliberate practice that struggling readers need. Indeed, this is a poor use of teacher time when we have technologies that can provide more and better practice opportunities at a fraction of the cost.

Rapidly advancing technology offers a powerful way to scale up instruction and deliberate practice for large numbers of struggling readers. Bransford, Brown, and Cocking (1999) point out that several reviews of the literature on technology and learning support the great potential of technology to enhance student achievement when used appropriately. The key is the "appropriate use" of technology. We have known from more than 20 years of research in math and reading that when technology is used in ways that support the principles of deliberate practice, even struggling students can reach high levels of automaticity and fluency (Cognition and Technology Group at Vanderbilt, 1996; Dede, 1998; Hasselbring et al., 1987; Panel on Educational Technology, 1997).

AUTOMATICITY, FLUENCY, AND MEMORY

Although automaticity and fluency are often used interchangeably, in this discussion we will distinguish between the two. Automaticity can be defined as the ability to perform a skill without having to devote much conscious effort to the task. In reading, this would be characterized as fast, accurate, and effortless word recognition. Fluency, on the other hand, involves not only automatic word identification but also the application of appropriate prosodic features (rhythm, intonation, and phrasing) at the phrase, sentence, and text levels.

Generally speaking, automaticity is necessary for fluency. That is, the automatic recall of information is necessary for the fluent performance in most any academic domain. Expert-level performance in reading requires that relevant information be stored in long-term memory and retrieved accurately and quickly without conscious effort when needed (Shaywitz, 2003). Thus the retrieval of information with speed and accuracy first requires that it be stored in memory.

Stages and Types of Memory

Today, neuroscientists generally agree that there are three types of memory: immediate memory and working memory for temporary interactions (short-term memory), and long-term memory for permanent storage.

Immediate Memory

Immediate memory is one of the two temporary memories where we put information very briefly until a decision is made about what to do with it. Generally, information is held in immediate memory for up to 30 seconds before it is either moved on to working memory or the information is dropped out of the memory system and is forgotten.

Working Memory

The working memory is the place where conscious information processing occurs. When information is in working memory it generally
requires our focused attention. Working memory can only handle a few
items at a time. For students between the ages of 5 and 14, the capacity of working memory generally ranges from three to seven items. For
adults, the range is generally five to nine items (Miller, 1956), and this
remains constant throughout adulthood.

The amount of time that items remain in working memory varies based on the perceived value of the information; typically, this can
range from a few minutes to several days. However, for most preado-
lescents the time is more likely 5 to 10 minutes. Most adolescents and
adults can generally process information intently for 10 to 20 minutes
before fatigue sets in. For information to become permanent, it must be
moved from working memory to long-term memory.

Long-Term Memory

Long-term memory allows us to retain information in a permanent form
for months, years, or for a lifetime. Retention of information occurs
when it is preserved in such a way that we can locate and retrieve it accurately in the future. This process of moving information to long-term
storage is inexact and influenced by such factors as length and type
of rehearsal and the meaningfulness of the information to be stored.
However, storing information in long-term memory is unlikely to occur
without deliberate practice.

FLUENCY AND AUTOMATICITY
THROUGH SYSTEMATIC TEACHING WITH TECHNOLOGY

Beginning in 1984, my colleague Laura Goin and I began experiment-
ing with computer technology for the purpose of developing automaticity in students with learning disabilities. We called our approach FASTT,
which stood for Fluency and Automaticity through Systematic Teaching
with Technology.

The goal of our FASTT model was to help learners move information out of working memory and into long-term memory as effectively
and efficiently as possible. The rationale for the FASTT model is that

because all human beings have a limited capacity for information processing (working memory), increasing the speed and accuracy with which information is retrieved from long-term storage can enhance human information processing. People's abilities to retrieve relevant knowledge and information can vary from being "effortful" to "relatively effortless" to "automatic" (Cohen, Dunbar, & McClelland, 1990). Fluency is important to expertise because effortless processing places fewer demands on working memory (Miller, 1956). Because the amount of information a person can attend to at any one time is limited, ease of processing some aspects of a task gives a person more capacity to attend to other, often more important, aspects of the task (Binder, Haughton, & Bateman, 2002; LaBerge & Samuels, 1974; Schneider & Shiffrin, 1985). For example, novice readers whose ability to decode words is not yet automatic are unable to devote attention to the task of understanding what they are reading (LaBerge & Samuels, 1974). Similarly, students who rely on finger counting to calculate the sum to an addition problem have difficulty in higher-level tasks such as multiple-digit addition and addition of fractions because of attention overload. Fluency development is critical to helping students attain proficiency in higher-level academic tasks.

The FASTT model is delivered via computer and consists of a specific set of instructional procedures designed to be used in conjunction with each other to develop the automatic recall of information for all learners. The instructional procedures include:

1. Assessment of the learner's current level of accuracy and speed.
2. Use of a small instruction set that is to be stored in long-term memory.
3. Use of an expanding recall presentation structure.
4. Use of a stringent and controlled response time.
5. Use of corrective feedback when errors occur.
6. Practice of only the information stored in long-term memory.

The following sections describe each of these instructional procedures.

Assessment of the Learner's Current Level of Automaticity

The FASTT model requires that before instruction can be provided, a learner's level of accuracy and speed must be assessed in the target domain (e.g., phonic elements, sight words, spelling words, math facts). The assessment typically consists of presenting the learner with a stimulus that requires a response and then measuring the accuracy as well as the response latency for the item. For example, in assessing the speed and accuracy of phonic elements, a list of nonsense words could be presented on the computer screen and a target word could be pronounced to the student. The student would then click on what he believes to be the correct word as quickly as possible and the computer would measure the accuracy as well as the time it took the learner to select the word. To increase the accuracy of the latency data, "keyboarding time" or "mousing time" is determined and then factored out of the total response time.

Once response latencies are determined for each correct response, they are compared to a predetermined criterion, and the stimulus items are either considered "automatic" or "nonautomatic." The automatic and nonautomatic stimuli must be determined since the FASTT model treats them differently. In addition, analysis of the incorrect responses can provide diagnostic data to further inform instruction.

Use of a Small Instruction Set That Is to Be Stored in Long-Term Memory

The FASTT model requires that any set of information that is not already considered automatic be "chunked" into small sets. A chunk is a small unit of information such as a word or a phonic element like *ing*. This chunking is based on the fact that the information to be stored in long-term memory must first be held in "working memory," which has limited capacity (Miller, 1956). Thus information to be stored in long-term memory must be presented in small chunks, or else working memory will be overloaded and will not be moved to long-term memory. The FASTT model requires that information not be presented in chunks larger than five.

Use of an Expanding Recall Presentation Structure

Learning and memory are generally improved by rehearsal. However, not all rehearsal is equally beneficial. The effectiveness of repetition-type rehearsal depends in part on its temporal distribution.

Studies of the effects of the timing of rehearsal for learning and retention have a long history. The positive effects of "spaced" rather than "massed" practice were first recognized as early as 1885 when the German psychologist Hermann Ebbinghaus found that spaced learning

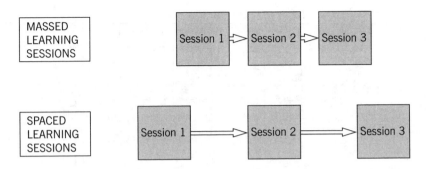

FIGURE 2.1. Massed versus distributed practice.

sessions produced higher retrieval scores than massed learning sessions, when the total time spent learning was kept constant for both learning conditions (see Figure 2.1). Over the next century, Ebbinghaus's findings were repeatedly confirmed and extended.

Until 1978, most studies of spaced learning involved the use of uniformly spaced distributed learning sessions. However, Landauer and Bjork (1978) discovered that learning is often more efficient if the time interval between retrieval sessions is steadily increased for successive sessions. This strategy is known as "expanding retrieval practice" (see Figure 2.2). For example, the first retrieval attempt might be made after a 1–second interval, the second retrieval after 2 seconds, the third after 4 seconds, and so on.

The FASTT model has built on the Landauer and Bjork research and has incorporated a modified form of "expanding retrieval practice" called "expanding recall." In this model, targeted information to be stored in long-term memory is presented for rehearsal and interspersed with already stored information. The stored information serves as the temporal expander, yet presents very little additional cognitive load, allowing the learner to focus on the new information to be learned (see Figure 2.3).

As depicted in Figure 2.3, the presentation of the chunks of target information to be stored in long-term memory are interspersed

FIGURE 2.2. Expanded retrieval practice.

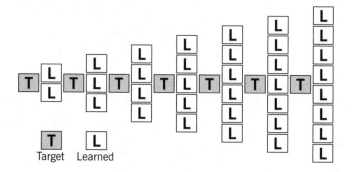

FIGURE 2.3. FASTT expanding recall model.

with information that has already been stored successfully in long-term memory.

Use of a Stringent and Controlled Response Time

The FASTT model requires the learner to respond to a stimulus within a finite amount of time where stored information in the learner's memory must be retrieved in order to provide a correct response (e.g., click on the correct answer). If the response is correct and within the allowable cutoff time a new stimulus is presented. However, if the response is incorrect or over the allowable cutoff time the learner is provided with corrective feedback as described below.

Use of Corrective Feedback When Errors Occur

The FASTT model requires that any incorrect response to a stimulus be immediately corrected using "imitation plus modeling" feedback and then requires a correct response from the learner before a new stimulus is presented. For example, if the student is asked to spell the word *America* and there is an error the following sequence would occur:

The student spells the word: Amereca
Computer feedback: "No, you spelled America like this": Amereca
"America is spelled like this": America [with animation, the *e* turns to an *i*].
"Now, you spell it correctly."

Following the corrective feedback, the learner is again presented with the stimulus that was just corrected.

Practice of Only Information Stored in Long-Term Memory

The practice of information recently moved to long-term storage is necessary to make it permanent. The old adage of "practice makes perfect" is not quite accurate. Actually, "practice makes permanent." Once the FASTT model determines that information has been moved to long-term storage based on the accuracy and speed of response, that information is presented to the learner in a drill-and-practice format where stimuli are presented multiple times requiring a learner response. The purpose of this rehearsal is to strengthen neural pathways and reduce response latencies. The more opportunities the learner has to respond, the stronger the neural pathway becomes. Thus in the FASTT model, practice is structured so that the most recent items moved to long-term storage get the most practice. This ensures that the pathways are strengthened and accurate recall occurs.

EFFECTIVENESS OF THE FASTT MODEL AT THE PHONEME LEVEL

While the need for adolescent reading intervention programs that teach the most foundational reading skills is apparent, there is little substantive research on computer-delivered reading interventions at the phonological decoding level for this age group (Baker & Slavin, 2008; Slavin, Cheung, Groff, & Lake, 2008). The effectiveness of the FASTT model for developing automaticity has been demonstrated in several domains, including math, spelling, and sight words. Most recently, we have applied the FASTT model to developing automaticity at the phoneme level. What follows is a description of a recent pilot study where we tested the FASTT model with high school special-needs students who were lacking phonological decoding skills.

Study Participants and Implementation

The pilot was conducted in a large metropolitan high school in the southeastern United States. More than 4,500 students were enrolled in the school and a majority (91%) of the students were Hispanic, 5% were white, 3% were African American, 1% were Asian, and less than 1% were American Indian/Alaskan Native. Forty percent qualified for free or reduced-price lunch. On average, 67% graduated from high school every year. Nine percent of the student body was composed of English language learners and 13% were students with special needs. The school performed below the district average in reading. Only 32% were proficient in reading as determined by the state exam, and only 49% were making reading gains (National Center for Education Statistics, 2008). For this study, eight students, ranging from 17 to 20 years old, were selected from the Special Diploma class to participate in the pilot study. The selected students were in great need of intensive reading support, as evidenced by their low performance on the Scholastic Reading Inventory (SRI). Four of these students performed at the lowest range of the SRI, receiving a score of Beginning Reader (BR), one student received a score of 247 lexiles, two students scored between 300 and 410 lexiles, and one student received a score of 587 lexiles. For comparison purposes, expected SRI scores for third graders at the 50th, 75th, and 95th percentiles are 550 lexiles, 715 lexiles, and 945 lexiles, respectively (Scholastic, 2006).

All students had been diagnosed with special needs. Five of the eight students were English as a second language (ESL) students. One student had lived in the United States and attended an English-speaking school for only one year prior to this study; one student came to the United States and began learning English in elementary school; the other six students had attended U.S. schools since kindergarten. These students voiced an interest in a variety of post–high school activities, including joining the Navy and working in computer graphics, the food industry, and camera technology. All of the students agreed to participate in the formative research because they were interested in improving their reading skills.

The classroom teacher worked with us to create a schedule that allowed us to work one-on-one with the eight students during their reading period. Piloting the FASTT prototype with a small group allowed us to test the prototype's scope and sequence and to determine whether the instructional interface and the application of the FASTT model increased the accuracy and fluency of the students' phonological decoding and word recognition.

We worked with the students individually over a 3–month period. The students participated in a median of 19 sessions and each received approximately 200 minutes of computer instruction. During this time each student received the FASTT computerized instruction and practice on short vowels, single consonants, consonant blends, and consonant digraphs.

Data Collection and Measures

We used two subtests from the Woodcock–Johnson Reading Mastery Test (WRMT; Woodcock, McGrew, & Mather, 2001): the Word Attack and Passage Comprehension subtests—to measure the growth of phonological and comprehension skills.

Findings

As shown in Figures 2.4 and 2.5, students began the program with grade equivalents no higher than second grade on the Word Attack and no higher than early third grade on the Passage Comprehension. The participants had very limited decoding skills and any reading that was accomplished was done by relying solely on whole-word recognition or "word-calling" methods. Figure 2.4 shows that four students gained at least one grade equivalent (GE) during the 3–month period and, on average, the students gained 0.95 GEs on the Word Attack subtest. Figure 2.5 shows that all of the students increased their GEs on the Passage Comprehension subtest between pretest and posttest. Five students gained at least one GE during the 3–month period. On average, the eight students gained 1.15 GEs on the Passage Comprehension section.

In addition to their gains on the Woodcock–Johnson subtests, students in the program reported that the program helped them improve their reading skills. Interestingly, the teacher also reported that the FASTT prototype helped her to better identify her students' specific areas of weakness in reading, allowing her to tailor her instruction accordingly.

Conclusion

The findings from the pilot study support that the use of the FASTT model results in increased accuracy and fluency of adolescent students' phonological decoding and word-recognition abilities. This formative research allowed us to further enhance the prototype and carry out

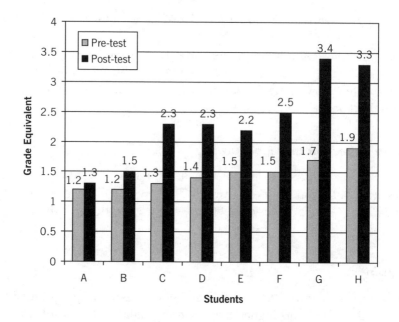

FIGURE 2.4. Individual student gains on the Woodcock–Johnson Word Attack Subtest (pre- and postgrade equivalents).

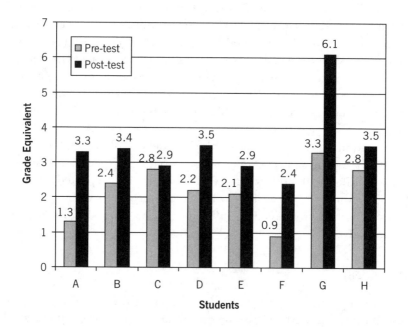

FIGURE 2.5. Individual student gains on the Woodcock–Johnson Passage Comprehension Subtest (pre- and posttest equivalents).

additional classroom testing and evaluation. This work has led to a new and innovative fundamental reading skills program entitled System 44, published by Scholastic. We believe that System 44 will lead to significant improvement in the fundamental reading skills and reading fluency for the most struggling readers. Furthermore, this work demonstrates the effectiveness of using computer-based intervention for struggling readers in grades 3 and above.

IMPLICATIONS FOR CLASSROOM INSTRUCTION

It is no secret that America's schools have struggled for decades to build reading proficiency in all students. For too long, large numbers of students have failed to develop proficiency in the alphabetic principle and word-level reading, which has led to low levels of fluency and comprehension. It's been estimated that more than 3,000 students drop out of school each day, often because of reading problems.

The demand placed on teachers to make every student a proficient reader represents an almost Herculean feat. Teachers are faced with students having very different needs, developmental levels, and backgrounds, making it necessary to provide individualized instruction in classrooms with 20 or more students. In reality it's virtually impossible for teachers to provide that level of instruction. Furthermore, students require vastly different amounts of instruction and rehearsal in order to reach proficiency. Finally, teachers are often forced to move through a packed curriculum even when they know some students have not mastered the previous skills.

Perhaps the only way to meet the individual needs of struggling readers is to call on technology to provide the additional instruction and deliberate practice that will lead to proficiency. Without the use of technology it will be difficult to meet the needs of the millions of struggling students in our schools today. With technology, teachers have another tool to support instruction and give students the instruction and practice they need to have some hope of becoming proficient readers. To make this a reality, instruction leaders must make teachers aware of the technology options available and make these technologies and the training to use them available. Until we provide teachers with the tools to address the problems they face every day we will continue to have students who fail to become proficient readers.

IMPLICATIONS FOR POLICYMAKERS

While many instructional leaders and policymakers have embraced the use of technology for reading instruction, many others have not. It's hard to ignore the evidence showing the positive impact that some technology-based programs have had on reading achievement (Slavin et al., 2008). Clearly, there are many examples where technology has been used to help the most struggling readers and to turn around failing schools and even districts (White, Haslam, & Hewes, 2006). It is the job of instructional leaders and policymakers to provide all students with the most powerful instruction possible. Instructional leaders and policymakers can no longer ignore the evidence that demonstrates how technology can help many struggling readers overcome their reading difficulties and become proficient readers.

Today we know much about how technology can help teach students who have never experienced reading success: however, there is much more to learn. As technology continues to advance we are constantly challenged to learn how to incorporate these new technologies into reading instruction. Technology continues to become more ubiquitous and transparent in our daily lives. Devices like the iPod are found in virtually every student's pocket and provide enormous opportunity for delivering instruction anytime and anyplace. Amazon's Kindle continues to evolve into a device that may be useful for supporting and instructing struggling readers outside of the school environment. Much more research and development must take place to move these evolving technologies to the next level for meeting the learning needs of the millions of students who need additional support in reading. Policymakers must support a research and development environment that allows researchers to evolve these promising technologies into useful tools for students and teachers alike. Although technology can't be expected to solve all of the problems we face around reading today, it does provide us with another tool in the fight against reading failure. We must continue the quest to evolve these technologies.

REFERENCES

Adams, M. J. (1990). *Beginning to read: Thinking and learning about print.* Cambridge, MA: MIT Press.
Baker, E. A., & Slavin, R. (2008, October 6). Effective middle and high school

reading programs. *Voice of Literacy*. Podcast retrieved from *www.voiceoflit-eracy.org/posts/27155*.

Binder, C., Haughton, E., & Bateman, B. (2002). Fluency: Achieving true mastery in the learning process. *Professional Papers in Special Education*. University of Virginia Curry School of Special Education (*curry.edschool.virginia.edu/go/specialed/papers*).

Bloom, B. (1986). Automaticity: The hands and feet of genius. *Educational Leadership, 43*(5), 70–77.

Bransford, J., Brown, A., & Cocking, R. (1999). *How people learn: Brain, mind, experience, and school*. Washington, DC: National Academy Press.

Cognition and Technology Group at Vanderbilt. (1996). Looking at technology in context: A framework for understanding technology and education research. In D. C. Berliner & R. C. Calfee (Eds.), *The handbook of educational psychology* (pp. 807–840). New York: Macmillan.

Cohen, J. D., Dunbar, K., & McClelland, J. L. (1990). On the control of automatic processes: A parallel distributed processing account of the Stroop effect. *Psychological Review, 97*, 332–361.

Dede, C. (Ed.). (1998). Introduction. In *Association for Supervision and Curriculum Development (ASCD) Yearbook: Learning with technology* (pp. v–x). Alexandria, VA: Association for Supervision and Curriculum Development.

Ericsson, K., Krampe, R. T., & Tesch-Romer, C. (1993). *Psychological Review, 100*(3), 363–406.

Hasselbring, T. S., Goin, L. I., & Bransford, J. D. (1987). Effective mathematics instruction: Developing automaticity. *Teaching Exceptional Children, 19*(3), 30–33.

Hock, M. F., Deshler, D. D., Marquis, J., & Brasseur, I. (2005). *Reading component skills of adolescents attending urban schools*. Lawrence: University of Kansas Center for Research on Learning.

Juel, C. (1991). Beginning reading. In R. Barr, M. L. Kamil, P. B. Mosenthal, & P. D. Pearson (Eds.), *Handbook of reading research* (Vol. 2, pp. 759–788). New York: Longman.

LaBerge, D., & Samuels, S. J. (1974). Toward a theory of automatic information processing in reading. *Cognitive Psychology, 6*(2), 293–322.

Landauer, T. K., & Bjork, R. A. (1978). Optimum rehearsal patterns and name learning. In M. M. Gruneberg, P. E. Morris, & R. N. Sykes (Eds.), *Practical aspects of memory* (pp. 625–632). London: Academic Press.

Leach, J. M., Scarborough, H. S., & Rescorla, L. (2003). Late-emerging reading disabilities. *Journal of Educational Psychology, 95*(2), 211–224.

Lee, J., Grigg, W., & Donahue, P. (2007). *The Nation's Report Card: Reading 2007*. Washington, DC: National Center for Education Statistics, Institute for Education Sciences, U.S. Department of Education.

Miller, G. A. (1956). The magical number seven, plus or minus two: Some limits on our capacity for processing information. *Psychological Review, 63,* 81–97.

Moats, L. C., Furry, A. R., & Brownell, N. (1998). *Learning to read: Components of beginning reading instruction, K–8.* Sacramento, CA: Comprehensive Reading Learning Center.

National Center for Education Statistics. (2008). Retrieved August 1, 2008, from *nces.ed.gov.*

President's Committee of Advisors on Science and Technology, Panel on Educational Technology. (1997). *Report to the president on the use of technology to strengthen K–12 education in the United States.* Washington, DC: Author. Available online at *www.ostp.gov/PCAST/k-12ed.html.*

Schneider, W., & Shiffrin, R. M. (1985). Categorization (restructuring) and automatization: Two separable factors. *Psychological Review, 92*(33), 424–428.

Scholastic, Inc. (2006). *Scholastic Reading Inventory: Educator's guide.* New York: Scholastic.

Shaywitz, S. (2003). *Overcoming dyslexia: A new and complete science-based program for reading problems at any level.* New York: Knopf.

Simon, H. A., & Chase, W. G. (1973). Skill in chess. *American Scientist, 61,* 394–403.

Slavin, R. E., Cheung, A., Groff, C., & Lake, C. (2008). Effective reading programs for middle and high schools: A best evidence synthesis. *Reading Research Quarterly, 43*(3), 290–322.

Snow, C. E., Burns, M. S., & Griffin, P. (Eds.). (1998). *Preventing reading difficulties in young children.* Washington, DC: National Academy Press.

Stanovich, K. E. (1986). Matthew effects in reading: Some consequences of individual differences in the acquisition of literacy. *Reading Research Quarterly, 21,* 360–407.

Torgesen, J. K., Houston, D. D., Rissman, L. M., Decker, S. M., Roberts, G., Vaughn, S., et al. (2007). *Academic literacy instruction for adolescents: A guidance document from the Center on Instruction.* Portsmouth, NH: RMC Research Corporation, Center on Instruction.

Wagner, R. (2008). *Learning to read: The importance of assessing phonological decoding skills and sight-word knowledge.* New York: Scholastic.

White, R. N., Haslam, M. B., & Hewes, G. M. (2006). *Improving student literacy in the Phoenix Union High School District 2003–04 and 2004–05: Final report.* Washington, DC: Policy Studies Associates.

Wolf, M. (2007). *Proust and the squid: The story and science of the reading brain.* New York: Harper.

Woodcock, R. W., McGrew, K. S., & Mather, N. (2001). *Woodcock–Johnson III Test of Achievement.* Itasca, IL: Riverside.

CHAPTER 3

Can Behaviorist and Constructivist Applications Coexist in the New Literacies?

MICHAEL C. McKENNA
KRISTIN CONRADI

In the closing decades of the 20th century, the behaviorist perspective that had grounded the study of reading gave way first to the information-processing perspectives of cognitive psychology and later to the tenets of constructivism (Gance, 2002). Constructivist approaches, which stress social interaction and divergent thinking, came to be seen as superior to each of these perspectives. Cognitive processing involves the interaction of modular components (the lexicon, word decoding, etc.) and is therefore viewed as accurate but narrow, ignoring the role of motivation and multiple perspectives. Constructivists view behaviorist notions, which stress reinforcement, practice, and convergence, as still less acceptable. It is hardly surprising that the behaviorist and constructivist orientations have grounded technology applications that are quite different in structure and purpose. We argue, however, that these two perspectives can at times coexist in mutually reinforcing instructional environments made possible by the new literacies of the Internet. That is to say, the emerging literacy applications made possible by technology (e.g., gaming, blogging, website navigation) can accommodate both perspectives if properly designed. Constructivist approaches to literacy champion higher-order thinking but also require basic skills that are not readily acquired through such approaches. The same digital environments that make the new literacies *possible* also hold the key to making them *accessible* to individuals whose basic skills are inadequate.

These three perspectives have both theoretical and pedagogical stances, and it is important to maintain this distinction. During the advent of cognitive psychology in the 1970s, behaviorists had long harbored a "black box" notion of mental processes, proscribing the use of models that might illuminate these invisible processes and relying exclusively on observed behaviors (Friedenberg & Silverman, 2005). Cognitive psychologists, in their advocacy of information-processing models, blamed behaviorists for limiting advances in our understanding of these processes during much of the 20th century (Rayner & Pollatsek, 1989). Indeed, the very term *behaviorism* acquired a negative connotation that led research journals associated with literacy and language to rename themselves in order to escape the possibility that their orientation might be misperceived. The *Journal of Reading Behavior* became the *Journal of Literacy Research* and the *Journal of Verbal Learning and Verbal Behavior* became *Memory and Cognition*. Our take on this era is that instructional practices based on the *pedagogical* stance of behaviorism were similarly shunned by educators who, in our view, overextended the reaction against the *theoretical* stance of behaviorism. Although we do not consider ourselves behaviorists, we nevertheless recognize that its lessons for instruction can be valuable, especially when used in tandem with other approaches, such as those embraced by constructivists. We acknowledge at the outset of this chapter that some readers may find this contention hard to accept. We ask only that they weigh our position objectively and appreciate that the questions we raise are ultimately empirical.

A BRIEF HISTORY OF BEHAVIORIST AND CONSTRUCTIVIST APPLICATIONS

Although machines were used in reading instruction as early as 1809 (Lockee, Moore, & Burton, 2004), the advent of technology in American classrooms coincided with the rise of behaviorism. Decades before computers would enter classrooms, the notion of teaching machines became the focus of experimentation, primarily for the purpose of test administration (Pressey, 1926). The simplicity of these devices was well suited to the behavior analyses that reduced complex processes to simple components that could be introduced, modeled, and reinforced. Skinner (1954) heralded the potential of mechanization. Using fourth-grade math instruction as an example, he listed key problems in traditional instruction that might be solved through machines. These include children's fear of teacher displeasure, the delay between a student's behavior and feedback from a teacher, infrequency of receiving feedback at all, and "the lack of a skillful program which moves forward through a series of progressive approximations to the final complex behavior desired" (p. 91).

During the 1960s, still two decades prior to the use of computers in schools, programmed instruction arose as a print-based medium and employed principles that technology would later embrace. Programmed instruction involved a behavior analysis of the desired skill set. A decision was made about how the instruction should be formatted, followed by "the sequencing of content and the construction of programmed sequences, called frames" (Lockee et al., 2004, p. 549). An assessment system was set up both to determine where to start and to gauge subsequent progress. Many structures were implemented, but the most important variations were between linear and branching systems. In the former, a student works to the point of proficiency in a single series of progressively more challenging skills. In the latter, a student's responses might occasionally trigger alternative pathways preprogrammed to foster proficiency.

The format of instruction was informed by the process–product research that led to the explicit instruction model. This model championed clear objectives, the use of carefully developed examples, continuous monitoring of student progress, and a movement from guided to independent practice of skills (e.g., Rosenshine, 1986). Explicit instruction was also called direct instruction, and a commercial reading program bearing this name is still widely used. Speaking about this program, but generalizing to any similarly structured system of instruction, Becker and Carnine (1981) identified the importance of shifting from simple to complex contexts, from massed to distributed practice, from prompts to no prompts, and from immediate to delayed feedback.

By the time computers had become commonplace in schools in the late 1980s, it was natural to employ these ideas in the creation of software. Although not purely behaviorist, the approaches used were

remarkably close to the principles espoused by Skinner. They had gar-
nered an impressive body of effectiveness research, mirroring earlier
studies that provided support for behaviorist approaches (Burton,
Moore, & Magliaro, 2004; Silver-Pacuilla, Ruedel, & Mistrett, 2004). Of
course, another reason for behaviorist computer applications lay in the
limitations of the new technologies. By today's standards the processing speed, text and graphics resolution, and available memory of the
first generation of microcomputers can only be described as primitive.
It is nonetheless important to note that improvements in technology, far
from ushering out behaviorist software, have led to products with higher
appeal. An example is Simon Sounds It Out, by Don Johnson, Inc., in
which research-based approaches to phonics instruction are coupled
with rapid feedback and adaptive instruction made possible through
continuous monitoring (see Figure 3.1.).

In the late 1980s, improved hardware made more sophisticated
software applications possible. The creation of hypertext and hypermedia environments, such as Culture 1.1, by Cultural Resources, Inc. (see
Blanchard & Rottenberg, 1990), constituted a departure from behaviorist applications. Early simulations, like The Oregon Trail, produced
by the Minnesota Educational Computing Consortium, invited student

FIGURE 3.1. Screen shot from Simon Sounds It Out. Reprinted with permission from Don Johnston, Inc.

collaboration in a problem-focused environment. However, as much as these new applications fostered exploration, they largely fell short of supporting constructivist approaches in which numerous resources are made available in problem-focused activities.

Nevertheless, they foreshadowed later applications that shifted control of the environment from designer to learner. Instead of focusing on controlling the learner's behavior, constructivist "learning environments aim now at enhancing cognitive and metacognitive processes" (Lowyck, 2002, p. 201). A key to such enhancement in constructivist pedagogies is social collaboration organized around a common purpose. "The principle of collaborative learning," Harasim (2006) asserts, "may be the single most important factor for online networked learning, since it is this principle which provides the strong socioaffective and cognitive power of learning on the Web" (p. 84). Important distinctions between behaviorist and constructivist approaches are summarized in Table 3.1. The characteristics of the latter have made it necessary to wait on technological improvements in order to be realized. It remained for the Internet to present a setting in which these characteristics could flourish.

PARALLEL TRAJECTORIES

The development of the Internet, including large-scale access to it in school settings, developed over an interval in which behaviorism was largely abandoned in favor of cognitive psychology and, eventually, constructivism. These changing psychological orientations were essentially independent of the growth of the Internet, although the parallels are interesting. The advent of microcomputers in the 1980s made available

TABLE 3.1. Contrasting Qualities of Behaviorist and Constructivist Approaches to Learning

Behaviorism	Constructivism
Designer control	Learner control
Objective centered	Problem centered
Skills emphasis	Strategy emphasis
Convergent outcomes	Divergent outcomes
Decomposition of complex tasks	Holistic approaches to complex tasks

technology that was offline, slow, and simple. It was, however, well suited to behaviorist software focusing on basic literacy skills. The Internet, in tandem with faster, more mobile, and more powerful hardware, is well suited to more complex literacy activity that takes such a variety of forms that reference to it is now in the plural.

Does this mean that these new literacies are inherently constructivist? Gance (2002) contends "that technology can be used to support constructivism but is neither inherent in it nor necessary for it" (n.p.). We agree. The Internet makes many approaches to instruction possible, including those grounded in behaviorism. Websites like *starfall.com*, for example, embody skills-based approaches that look very much like programmed learning. Although there is an inherent "tension between explicit instruction and constructivism" (McKenna, 2006, p. xv), the Internet has proved sufficiently large that applications of each type can find a home.

The roles technology can play in learning depend on the role of the learner. As a general principle, we suggest that these roles vary with respect to control. Environments in which the software largely controls the learning experiences differ considerably from those in which students are in control. Long before the Internet, Taylor (1980) described three functions for computers in the classroom: the computer as a tutor, the computer as a tool, and the computer as a tutee. Taylor's description of the tutor role reflects the use of computers from a behaviorist perspective. "The computer presents some subject material, the student responds, the computer evaluates the response, and, from the results of the evaluation, determines what to present next" (p. 3). This process is essentially the same as the progression, championed by Skinner (1954), through successive stages leading to ideal performance. Computers are used as tools, Taylor maintained, when they are used in order to accomplish some task; currently, computers are used as tools when students engage in word-processing, research, and graphical representations. Such uses conform to our notions of constructivist learning. Computers fill the role of tutee when the perspectives of teacher and learner are in effect reversed. The learner "teaches" the computer in order to transform it into a better tool. At present, such "instruction" might involve the creation of macros, the addition of terms to a dictionary, the embedding of formulas into an Excel spreadsheet, and so forth. This role, too, supports constructivist learning. As tool and tutee, computers have the potential to help realize the goal of such learning.

CAN BEHAVIORIST AND CONSTRUCTIVIST APPROACHES COEXIST?

We contend that behaviorist and constructivist pedagogies, notwithstanding their diametric opposition, not only can but must coexist in the Internet era. Our contention is based principally on two reasons. The first is the inappropriateness of constructivism in meeting the needs of some readers. The second is its inappropriateness in teaching some proficiencies.

Constructivist learning is not well suited to children who struggle with decoding and fluency. This is because reading occurs in a limited resource system in which attention devoted to word recognition detracts from the cognitive resources available to comprehend (LaBerge & Samuels, 1974). Although it might be argued that constructivist approaches involving discovery learning can be applied in teaching children how to decode words, the goal is to foster a set of skills that are convergent and not subject to multiple interpretation and that must be learned to the point of automaticity through practice and reinforcement. Given this reality, it is hardly surprising that research has supported explicit, systematic instruction in word recognition (National Institute of Child Health and Human Development, 2000), instruction that is of a distinctly behaviorist character.

Although supported text can, to some extent, compensate for word-recognition deficiencies in digital environments (Anderson-Inman & Horney, 1998), the use of what the first author has called electronic scaffolds (McKenna, 1998) requires determination and focus. When such supports are available in Internet settings, learners still may founder. Dillon and Jobst (2005) argue that there is an irony here in that, although hypermedia environments like the Internet no doubt facilitate "learning complex or ill-structured material" (p. 571), such an environment may be detrimental to struggling learners who find the unconstrained options mazelike and confusing. Duke, Schmar-Dobler, and Zhang (2006) have accordingly called for further study of this issue since it lacks a true counterpart in print-based comprehension research.

All readers need to be able to apply basic skills automatically for optimal learning to occur. This principle is true of print and digital environments alike. The road to automaticity is, however, an arduous one for many readers. Because fluent, automatic word recognition is a prerequisite for constructivist learning (Eagleton & Dobler, 2007), it seems sensible to pursue the shortest route to this goal, and that route entails systematic, explicit instruction for many learners (National Institute of Child Health and Human Development, 2000). It is hardly surprising that a recent survey of teachers revealed a preference for behaviorist software among primary-grade instructors (Niederhauser & Stoddart, 2001). These teachers, after all, bear the principal responsibility for teaching children how to decode and are cognizant of their students' limitations and instructional needs. Older readers who struggle with decoding are also positioned to benefit from such instruction, and research has begun to substantiate their response to what are essentially behaviorist interventions (Scammacca et al., 2007).

We speculate that technology can best be used in three overlapping phases. The first entails systematic, adaptive, skills-based instruction with roots in behaviorism. The second involves constructivist applications in which decoding and other deficits are supported through electronic scaffolds. The third embraces constructivist learning without the need for such supports. These phases are described in Figure 3.2. Although this figure provides a useful organizer, we do not mean to suggest that these phases should occur in strict sequence, with the completion of each one a prerequisite to the next. Instead, we advocate a gradual release model, the ultimate goal of which is the integrated and strategic application of skills for authentic purposes. Figure 3.3 represents this model. Over time, technology applications will exhibit fewer behaviorist characteristics as they approach a constructivist ideal. Electronic scaffolds (McKenna, 1998), like their use in conventional print-

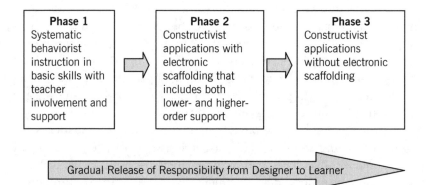

FIGURE 3.2. Three-phase model of a behaviorist-to-constructivist transition.

FIGURE 3.3. Gradual transition from behaviorist to constructivist applications.

based settings (e.g., Bruner, 1960), will be removed as the need for them diminishes.

Research provides a few lessons for the first of these phases, although questions remain. It is undeniable that well-crafted behaviorist software applications embody essential features of effective practice. These include curricular coherence in the form of logical sequencing; rapid feedback provided to students; progress monitoring; delineation of skills instruction into small, achievable steps; and a progression from guided to independent practice. The apparent desirability of incorporating these characteristics into digital applications has an unfortunate downside, however. The necessity that students be actively engaged can prove elusive, especially when teachers assume that the software possesses design features that assure such engagement. Coiro et al. (2003) reviewed the research on the effectiveness of integrated learning systems, which are built on behaviorist assumptions and often tout a leave-everything-to-us capacity. Findings have generally been disappointing, and have been marked by an initial novelty effect followed almost inevitably by disengagement as lesson formats are repeated again and again (see also Slavin, 1990). A subsequent investigation of a particular integrated learning system, the Waterford Early Reading Program, contrasted its use with conventional instruction and found no advantage for the software (Paterson, Henry, O'Quin, Ceprano, & Blue, 2003). Waterford comprises a variety of activities designed to foster phonics, phonological awareness, and oral language, but a common thread is a child's gradual progress through carefully sequenced skills, the repetition of activities until mastery is achieved, and positive reinforcement of successful skill attainment.

The effectiveness of integrated learning systems with struggling young readers is less clear. A replication of the Waterford study by Cassady and Smith (2005) found that children at risk of not learning to read proficiently benefited significantly more from the Waterford Program than from conventional instruction. However, a subsequent investigation of Waterford and several other computerized reading (and math) interventions revealed no advantage for Waterford or any of the other programs (Dynarski et al., 2007). We suspect that much depends on how the software is implemented and in particular on what assumptions teachers make about that level of teacher involvement that may be needed for optimal results. Blok, Oostdam, Otter, and Overmaat (2002) reported a small effect size ($d = 0.19$) for computer-assisted instruction in beginning reading, and, although they cautioned that the studies varied in quality, we suspect that the manner in which such software is implemented influences the impact on learning. It is on the basis of this line of inquiry that we suggest close teacher involvement even in the initial phase of instruction.

An important distinction must be made between our three-phase model and the original behaviorist intentions. Skinner and others envisioned a gradual progression of tasks from simple to complex. According to this view, even the most sophisticated tasks can be delineated into simpler versions, each of which can be taught to mastery using behaviorist techniques. We find it difficult to conceptualize how this progression can be made to apply to constructivist aims, because the end goal of instruction varies with the learner. One approach might entail a series of problems and tasks in which the constraints are successively lifted so that learners could become accustomed to constructivist explorations in simpler and less confusing settings. Such a series would, of course, be neither fish nor fowl but represent a useful transition. Our notion of electronic scaffolds in Phase 2 therefore applies not only to low-level, decoding-oriented skills but to higher-order processes such as navigating and inferring. It is for this reason that we suggest a transition based on the nature of the skills we wish our students to acquire. When the end goal is limited to automatic word recognition in context, a simple-to-complex progression not only makes sense but is well supported by research and theory (McKenna & Stahl, 2009). Comprehension, however, has not yielded to attempts to delineate it into a progression of stages. Just as in research, methods must match questions; in software design, the pedagogical orientation must match the objectives. Paris (2005) offered a useful distinction between constrained and unconstrained skills. Learning a particular letter–sound correspondence is an example of a constrained skill, one that can be taught to mastery. A comprehension strategy such as prediction, on the other hand, can never be totally mastered because the texts in which it must be applied will grow more demanding over time. Behaviorist approaches are less appropriate for unconstrained skills.

TOWARD UNIFIED SYSTEMS OF READING INSTRUCTION THROUGH TECHNOLOGY

The Internet provides an ideal platform for the research and development of instructional systems that wed behaviorist and constructivist approaches. Such systems should be grounded on several assumptions based on previous inquiry:

1. The system must include an active role for the teacher in all three phases, but particularly in the first, during which the danger of overrelying on the software is greatest.
2. The system should provide a series of constrained constructivist tasks that progress in complexity during Phase 2.
3. The system should monitor student progress to ensure that students move through the three phases at an appropriate pace.

We suggest that present-day applications make possible the kind of sophisticated electronic scaffolding that the first two phases require. Two examples are improvements in voice recognition (Adams, 2006) and the successful development of intelligent tutoring systems (Van Lehn et al., 2007). Such developments now facilitate far more sophisticated interaction between learner and machine. It remains for applications developed independently of one another to be merged into comprehensive systems in which behaviorist and constructivist components play their respective parts.

EXAMPLE OF A COMPREHENSIVE SYSTEM

How might such a system work in the real-life context of a classroom? Step into Ms. Young's fourth-grade classroom, where technology plays an active and seamless role in instruction. Most of her students have acquired a full range of decoding skills and can read with adequate fluency. They have also been schooled on the process of using digital resources to solve problems, although their acquaintance has been gradual, involving a limited range of such resources applied to problems with somewhat convergent solutions.

To begin a unit on ancient Rome, Ms. Young uses a student response system to assess students' prior knowledge of the topic. As she poses multiple-choice questions, Ms. Young's students record their responses using hand-held clickers. Immediately, a graph of students' responses appears on the SmartBoard in the front of the room. Scanning the graph, Ms. Young initiates discussion to correct misconceptions about each question before moving on to the next one.

Then, in order to preteach key vocabulary before reading, Ms. Young shows students a clip from the movie *Gladiator* on YouTube. As they watch, Ms. Young draws students' attention to images of a chariot, a temple, and an oracle. Afterwards, students hypothesize definitions for the words based on the video clip. To confirm their hunches, students consult online dictionaries. Finally, the class constructs student-friendly definitions of the key vocabulary using concept and schema maps found on Kidspiration software.

Before students move into collaborative groups at workstations, Ms. Young introduces students to a program that will help them hone their writing skills. This computer application reinforces instruction Ms. Young's students have already received on sentence combining. Using the software and knowing they will be writing a report soon, students practice identifying and creating effective complex sentences. The software, like the German prototype, *Die Satzfee,* (Sentence Fairy), offers students the opportunities to combine sentences, reconstruct stories, and manipulate word order, all with the simple click of a mouse (see Harbusch, Hsova, Koch, & Kühner, 2008).

Next, students begin reading and researching about ancient Rome on the Internet. They have expressed interest in one of several problems posed by Ms. Young, such as how the Romans managed to bring to the city large quantities of fresh water from the mountains. Students in each group decide which sites to visit to find out how the Romans resolved the problem, which information to collect at each site, and how to integrate the information into a PowerPoint to be shared later with their classmates. As they work, Ms. Young moves from group to group, offering help and hints, simplifying wordings and defining terms where necessary, and encouraging the children to think creatively. She wants them not only to discover how the Romans addressed the problems the groups have selected but also to critique the solution.

Within the limits of their prior knowledge and vocabulary, these students are well prepared to engage in constructivist problem solving using the Internet as a resource. With the scaffolding provided by Ms. Young, they will apply skills in strategic ways, in preparation for future learning experiences that may involve working alone and without teacher scaffolding.

The Challenge of Serving Children at Risk

How many fourth graders would succeed in this environment? We stipulated that most of Ms. Young's students had attained fluency, but if her classroom were representative of the American population, at least a quarter would lack the basic skills needed for fourth-grade work (National Assessment of Educational Progress, 2007). It is unlikely they would be able to take part productively in the constructivist activities we have described, however much scaffolding Ms. Young might provide. We argue that they would require a different set of experiences, characterized by instruction that is guided by assessments.

Depending on the extent of a student's proficiency, this instruction might be grounded in behaviorist notions of skill acquisition. A comprehensive technology system might provide content related to the unit on ancient Rome, incidentally teaching facts while the main agenda is the development of word-recognition proficiency. Ms. Young's whole-class background building will have benefited struggling students as well, and the aligned content will give them information to share when the class reconvenes. Ms. Young will need to support these children's as well as their abler classmates' work in constructivist contexts. She must not buy in to the myth that computer-based lower-order skill instruction requires no teacher supervision. Obviously, the dovetailing of Internet projects and basic skill instruction would require a coordinated effort, orchestrated across themes and grade levels and no doubt aligned with state standards.

To illustrate how such a system might work, consider first the case of Craig, a fourth grader with strong oral language and decoding skills, but whose sight vocabulary is weak and whose fluency is consequently below benchmark levels. Craig has been able to participate in whole-class activities, but his lack of fluency hinders his work on an Internet project. Ms. Young activates a text-to-speech software application that will enable Craig to hear the pronunciation of any word he selects. She makes clear that he is expected to read the text he accesses in order to complete the tasks required by the project, but she tells him that he may listen to any of the words he wishes. The project provides Craig with the opportunity to engage in constructivist learning about ancient Rome. Such learning may include navigating Web pages that combine text, graphics, and video and that offer multiple pathways for exploration. At the same time, the word pronunciation feature embeds a dimension that is essentially behaviorist. Each time Craig clicks on a word to hear it pronounced a look–say association is strengthened. By accessing a word repeatedly, a stimulus–response connection (visual to auditory) is established, and it will endure after the electronic scaffold is no longer available (McKenna, Reinking, & Bradley, 2003).

In Craig's case, the merger of constructivist and behaviorist software applications is simultaneous. Because he accesses pronunciations on a need-to-know basis and because the pronunciations are provided quickly, the process of acquiring sight words is minimally intrusive. In other cases, however, the merger of applications may need to be sequential. Consider Allison, Craig's classmate. Allison shares Craig's strong oral language background and, like Craig, she is also dysfluent. Unlike Craig, however, her fluency problems can be traced to weak decoding skills. Without considerable assistance, she would be unable to engage in the same project activities. There are several possible approaches to scaffolding her through behaviorist applications. One is to provide her with access to the same point-and-click pronunciations used by Craig. This approach would enable her to read the text required by the project, but research suggests that it would not improve her decoding (McKenna et al., 2003). Another approach is to embed "mini-lessons" on decoding. These would pop up whenever she accesses the pronunciation of a word containing phonics elements she does not yet grasp. For example, assume that upon encountering the sentence, "The Romans had a zest for life," she clicks on the word *zest*. She does not hear the pronunciation immediately. Instead, the word *best* temporarily appears above *zest* and a voice says, "Let's see, if *b-e-s-t* is *best*, then *z-e-s-t* must be [pause] *zest*!" These embedded lessons are fully contextualized, but they have not resulted in increased decoding proficiency (McKenna et al., 2003). A shortcoming is that, brief though they are, such mini-lessons disrupt the process of constructing meaning and split a child's focus between two very different types of learning. We believe that a better means of helping a child like Allison would be to provide her with behaviorist instruction in advance of the project activities. Software applications would isolate words that will appear in the Internet texts and tailor lessons around these words. These lessons would involve practice and reinforcement of general decoding principles, but they would also prepare Allison for the specific words when she encounters them online. She may still access the pronunciations if need be, and doing so will contribute to her ability to recognize the words on sight, but the acquisition of decoding skills will be addressed in advance.

Finally, consider Lauren, a classmate of Craig and Allison but one with a very different profile. Lauren is quite fluent. She has a strong sight vocabulary and has learned decoding skills to the point at which she can apply them almost automatically to unfamiliar words. Lauren's problem is that she possesses a modest listening vocabulary, which frequently impairs her comprehension. There are several approaches to assisting her by means of behaviorist software. One is to precede the Internet project with activities designed to preteach words essential to an understanding of specific Web content. These activities would provide practice and reinforcement, and they would prescribe and deliver additional work as needed until mastery was exhibited. This approach is parallel to the one we have recommended for Allison. That is, the skills work would precede the constructivist learning that such work would facilitate. An alternative is to equip the Internet text with mouse-over glossary entries. For example, when Lauren encounters the sentence, "The Romans had a zest for life," she has no difficulty pronouncing the word *zest*, but she does not know what it means. When she moves the cursor over the word, a simple synonym appears as the word is highlighted. As soon as she moves the cursor away, the support disappears. Both approaches have their advantages, and the former is well supported by research in print environments (e.g., Stahl & Nagy, 2005).

The Challenge of Serving Younger Children

Those of Ms. Young's students who are ready to engage in the collaborative constructivist activities that ground the new literacies of the Internet have acquired a complex array of skills and strategies. They did not develop them overnight. What role might technology have played in preparing the children for this high-level application? Given the dismal history of integrated learning systems, it is tempting to assign technology applications only a minor role in the long process of fostering skill development. We are optimistic, however, that a new generation of such systems can overcome the well-documented shortcomings of the past. In our optimal comprehensive system, learning basic skills would involve a variety of formats, continuous teacher involvement, intelligent tutoring, and new methods of interaction, such as voice recognition. Over time, children would move seamlessly into higher-level tasks that entail collaboration and problem solving. Along the way, electronic scaffolds like pronunciations on demand and mouse-over glossary entries would supplement teacher support as children progress to more conceptually demanding learning contexts. Such a system would be designed to take them as efficiently as possible through the first two phases we have described so that they can flourish in the third.

BACK TO EARTH: CONFRONTING THE REALITIES OF PRODUCT DEVELOPMENT

It is one thing to propose a comprehensive system of technology applications that will prepare children for, and eventually engage them in, the new literacies of the Internet. It is quite another to actualize such a system, for in fact the obstacles are formidable. There are at least three methods of approach, each with its own advantages and drawbacks. One is for practitioners to build such a system using existing software and websites, cobbling them together into something resembling an integrated system. The resulting patchwork would be relatively inexpensive, to be sure, but probably incoherent as well. Another approach is for commercial developers to produce components that are research based in design and field tested in actual classrooms. Stafford, Miller, and Ollivierre (2006) detail the process that software developers typically follow in product development. It is painstaking and costly, and it does not always result in effective applications. As research continues to inform the creation of such products, however, and as hardware innovations continue to offer more engaging possibilities for design, the advent of improved components seems nearly certain. A major challenge for practitioners at the classroom, school, or district level would lie in linking the components into a comprehensive system. A third approach would entail a single commercial developer undertaking such a system, an endeavor involving not only the development of each component but also the creation of a coordinated assessment system capable of tracking the process of individual children, prescribing instructional activities, suggesting small-group configurations, generating reports, and formatively adapting to student performance. This option would arguably lead to the best system, but at the highest cost. It is questionable whether a commercial developer would be likely to invest the resources needed to see it through.

We have no doubts that sophisticated systems can and will be developed in the near future, allowing for a seamless and integrated use of technology in our classrooms. This, in turn, will enable teachers both to differentiate according to the varying needs of their students and to cultivate critical thinking and problem-solving skills in students, giving way ultimately to learning environments that foster collaboration as well as independent thinking. Such learning environments are already being realized in the classrooms of many teachers, such as our hypothetical Ms. Young, but their prevalence will be constrained by the availability of software and teachers' awareness about how best to use it.

REFERENCES

Adams, M. J. (2006). The promise of automatic speech recognition for fostering literacy growth in children and adults. In M. C. McKenna, L. D. Labbo, R. D. Kieffer, & D. Reinking, (Eds.), *International handbook of literacy and technology* (Vol. 2, pp. 109–128). Mahwah, NJ: Erlbaum.

Anderson-Inman, L., & Horney, M. A. (1998). Transforming text for at-risk readers. In D. Reinking, M. C. McKenna, L. D. Labbo, & R. D. Kieffer (Eds.), *Handbook of literacy and technology: Transformations in a post-typographic world* (pp. 15–44). Mahwah, NJ: Erlbaum.

Becker, W. C., & Carnine, D. W. (1981). Direct instruction: A behavior theory model for comprehensive educational intervention with the disadvantaged. In S. W. Bijou & R. Ruiz (Eds.), *Behavior modification: Contributions to education* (pp. 145–210). Hillsdale, NJ: Erlbaum.

Blanchard, J. S., & Rottenberg, C. J. (1990). Hypertext and hypermedia: Discovering and creating meaningful learning environments. *The Reading Teacher, 43*, 656–661.

Blok, H., Oostdam, R., Otter, M. E., & Overmaat, M. (2002). Computer-assisted instruction in support of beginning reading instruction: A review. *Review of Educational Research, 72*, 101–130.

Bruner, J. S. (1960). *The process of education.* New York: Vintage Books.

Burton, J. K., Moore, D. M., & Magliaro, S. G. (2004). Behaviorism and instructional technology. In D. H. Jonassen (Ed.), *Handbook of research on educational communications and technology* (2nd ed., pp. 3–36). Mahwah, NJ: Erlbaum.

Cassady, J. C., & Smith, L. L. (2005). The impact of a structured integrated learning system on first-grade students' reading gains. *Reading and Writing Quarterly, 21,* 361–376.

Coiro, J., Leu, D. J., Jr., Kinzer, C. K., Labbo, L., Teale, W., Bergman, L., et al. (2003, December). *A review of research on literacy and technology: Replicating and extending the NRP subcommittee report on computer technology and reading instruction.* Paper presented at the 53rd annual meeting of the National Reading Conference, Scottsdale, AZ.

Dillon, A., & Jobst, J. (2005). Multimedia learning with hypermedia. In R. E. Mayer (Ed.), *The Cambridge handbook of multimedia learning* (pp. 569–588). Cambridge, UK: Cambridge University Press.

Duke, N., Schmar-Dobler, E., & Zhang, S. (2006). Comprehension and technology. In M. C. McKenna, L. D. Labbo, R. D. Kieffer, & D. Reinking, (Eds.), *International handbook of literacy and technology* (Vol. 2, pp. 317–326). Mahwah, NJ: Erlbaum.

Dynarski, M., Agodini, R., Heaviside, S., Novak, T., Carey, N. Campuzano, L., et al. (2007). *Effectiveness of reading and mathematics software products: Findings from the first student cohort: Report to Congress.* Washington, DC: U.S. Department of Education. Retrieved November 1, 2008, from *ies.ed.gov/ ncee/pdf/20074005.pdf.*

Eagleton, M. B., & Dobler, E. (2007). *Reading the Web: Strategies for Internet inquiry.* New York: Guilford Press.

Friedenberg, J. D., & Silverman, G. (2005). *Cognitive science: An introduction to the study of mind.* Thousand Oaks, CA: Sage.

Gance, S. (2002). Are constructivism and computer-based learning environments incompatible? *Journal of the Association for History and Computing, 5*(2). Retrieved October 10, 2008, from *mcel.pacificu.edu/jahc/2002/ issue1/k-12/gance/.*

Harasim, L. (2006). A history of e-learning: Shift happens. In J. Weiss, J. Nolan, J. Hunsinger, & P. Trifonas (Eds.), *The international handbook of virtual learning environments* (Vol. 1, pp. 59–94). Dordrecht, the Netherlands: Springer.

Harbusch, K., Itsova, G., Koch, U., & Kühner, C. (2008). The Sentence Fairy: A natural-language generation system to support children's essay writing. *Computer Assisted Language Learning, 21,* 339–352.

LaBerge, D., & Samuels, S. J. (1974). Toward a theory of automatic information processing in reading. *Cognitive Psychology, 6,* 293–323.

Lockee, B., Moore, D. M., & Burton, J. (2004). Foundations of programmed instruction. In D. H. Jonassen (Ed.), *Handbook of research on educational communications and technology* (2nd ed., pp. 545–569). Mahwah, NJ: Erlbaum.

Lowyck, J. (2002). Pedagogical design. In H. H. Adelsberger, B. Collis, & J. M. Pawlowski (Eds.), *Handbook on information technologies for education and training* (pp. 199–217). Heidelberg, Germany: Springer.

McKenna, M. C. (1998). Electronic texts and the transformation of beginning reading. In D. Reinking, M. C. McKenna, L. D. Labbo, & R. D. Kieffer (Eds.), *Handbook of literacy and technology: Transformations in a posttypographic world* (pp. 45–59). Hillsdale, NJ: Erlbaum.

McKenna, M. C. (2006). Introduction: Trends and trajectories of literacy and technology in the new millennium. In M. C. McKenna, L. D. Labbo, R. D. Kieffer, & D. Reinking (Eds.), *International handbook of literacy and technology* (Vol. 2, pp. xi-xviii). Mahwah, NJ: Erlbaum.

McKenna, M. C., Reinking, D., & Bradley, B. A. (2003). The effects of electronic trade books on the decoding growth of beginning readers. In R. Malatesha Joshi, C. K. Leong, & B. L. J. Kaczmarek (Eds.), *Literacy acquisition: The role of phonology, morphology, and orthography* (pp. 193–202). Amsterdam, The Netherlands: IOS Press.

McKenna, M. C., & Stahl, K. A. D. (2009). *Assessment for reading instruction* (2nd ed). New York: Guilford Press.

National Assessment of Educational Progress. (2007). *The nation's report card.* Retrieved December 20, 2008, from *nces.ed.gov/nationsreportcard/reading_2007.*

National Institute of Child Health and Human Development. (2000). *Report of the National Reading Panel. Teaching children to read: An evidence-based assessment of the scientific research literature on reading and its implications for reading instruction* (NIH Publication No. 00-4769). Washington, DC: U.S. Government Printing Office.

Niederhauser, D. S., & Stoddart, T. (2001). Teachers' instructional perspectives and use of educational software. *Teaching and Teacher Education, 17,* 15–31.

Paris, S. G. (2005). Reinterpreting the development of reading skills. *Reading Research Quarterly, 40,* 184–202.

Paterson, W. A., Henry, J. J., O'Quin, K., Ceprano, M. A., & Blue, E. V. (2003). Investigating the effectiveness of an integrated learning system on early emergent readers. *Reading Research Quarterly, 38,* 172–207.

Pressey, S. L. (1926). A simple apparatus which gives tests and scores—and teaches. *School and Society, 23*(586), 373–376.

Rayner, K., & Pollatsek, A. (1989). *The psychology of reading.* Mahwah, NJ: Erlbaum.

Rosenshine, B. V. (1986). Synthesis of research on explicit teaching. *Educational Leadership, 43*(7), 60–69.

Scammacca, N., Roberts, G., Vaughn, S., Edmonds, M., Wexler, J., Reutebuch, C. K., et al. (2007). *Interventions for adolescent struggling readers: A meta-analysis with implications for practice.* Portsmouth, NH: RMC Research Corporation, Center on Instruction. Retrieved December 23, 2009, from *www.centeroninstruction.org/.*

Silver-Pacuilla, H., Ruedel, K., & Mistrett, S. (2004). *A review of technology-based approaches for reading instruction: Tools for researchers and vendors.* Washington, DC: National Center for Technology Innovation. Retrieved October 10, 2008, from *www.nationaltechcenter.org/matrix/docs/AReviewTechnology-BasedApproaches_final.pdf.*

Skinner, B. F. (1954). The science of learning and the art of teaching. *Harvard Educational Review, 24,* 86–97.

Slavin, R. E. (1990). IBM's Writing to Read: Is it right for reading? *Phi Delta Kappan, 72,* 214–216.

Stafford, B., Miller, L., & Ollivierre, M. (2006). A science-based development and implementation model for online and CD-ROM curriculum programs. In M. C. McKenna, L. D. Labbo, R. D. Kieffer, & D. Reinking, (Eds.), *International handbook of literacy and technology* (Vol. 2, pp. 163–178). Mahwah, NJ: Erlbaum.

Stahl, S. A., & Nagy, W. E. (2005). *Teaching word meanings.* Mahwah, NJ: Erlbaum.

Taylor, R. P. (1980). Introduction. In R. P. Taylor (Ed.), *The computer in the school: Tutor, tool, tutee* (pp. 1–10). New York: Teachers College Press.

Van Lehn, K., Graesser, A. C., Jackson, G. T., Jordan, P., Olney, A., & Rose, C. P. (2007). When are tutorial dialogues more effective than reading? *Cognitive Science, 31,* 3–62.

CHAPTER 4

A Multiliteracies Perspective on the New Literacies

MARY KALANTZIS
BILL COPE
ANNE CLOONAN

The new communications environment of the 21st century offers unprecedented opportunities for multimodal meaning making, a transformed dynamics of social agency and divergence of discourses. Multiliteracies theory presents a set of educationally useable conceptual schemas and suggestions for an expanded repertoire of literacy practices as a response to these opportunities (Cope & Kalantzis, 2000a). The following discusses the theory and case study of a collaborative application of a set of schemas to address contemporary issues in multiliteracies pedagogy (Cloonan, 2008a).

TECHNOLOGY AND LITERACY IN THE NEW COMMUNICATIONS CONTEXT

It has become commonplace to observe that communication in the 21st century is no longer limited to print-based forms of literacy, and that to be effective participants in today's society, young people need to become capable and competent users of both print and other forms of meaning enabled by new technologies. Meaning making in the digital communications environment of the 21st century is being transformed. Sound, written language, still images, and moving images can all be made, stored, and distributed through the same media because they can all be reduced to a common platform that is the code of the digital world. The proliferation of new communications technologies has shifted capacity for combining representational modes in a wide range of sites, from technical specialists to contemporary students' households and classrooms. This is the basis for the ubiquitous spread of multimodality, or the capacity to mix modes. Meaning is made in ways that are increasingly multimodal—in which linguistic modes of meaning interface with other modes of meaning such as visual, audio, gestural, tactile, and spatial patterns of meaning (New London Group, 1996, 2000).

While traditional print-based forms of literacy continue to dominate school curriculum, pedagogy, and assessment, in their out-of-school lives students are increasingly participating in online worlds and other forms of digital culture. These experiences are transforming students' expectations of and orientations toward texts, literacy, and pedagogy. Learners' eager adoption of practices using new technologies presents challenges to traditional school-based teaching and learning relationships, pedagogies, and curricula.

Educational responses to digitization are complex and often contradictory. Digital creation and access to media are becoming as ubiquitous as the telephone and the radio were in earlier times, and projects such as One Laptop Per Child or the "hundred-dollar laptop" promise multimedia digital access for students even in the poorest countries (*laptop.org*). Claims that the new digital media and the Internet will change the face of education, however, are counterpointed by data on student access, indicating that a "digital divide" is apparent between those who can afford technology and broadband, and those who can't.

New school practices as a result of digitization are varied. One kind of response to the new media is the rush to adopt. In that rush, we have seen new media brought into the classroom, as if the medium itself was the message. Instead of writing stories longhand on a piece of paper, students type them on a word processor, or a blog, or put together a film. While there's something new in such practices, the relationships of knowledge and pedagogy have not necessarily changed in any significant way.

At the level of government and administrative reframing of education, there have been policies which advocate digital or ICT literacy

(European Commission, 2008; Ministerial Council on Education, Employment, Training and Youth Affairs, 2007), but these often stop short of advising on teaching related to digital *meaning-making* practices.

In educational practice, responses have included attempts to mechanize learning using digital technologies. For example, students have been provided with devices that look like a remote control. When the teacher asks a question, instead of having just one student answering, all the students answer by pressing a button on their remote. In this way, the teacher gets a picture of what every learner knows, not just the child who answers first. Activities have been presented in the form of "digital learning objects." Instead of content knowledge such as the phases of the moon represented as a sequence of drawings on the page of a book, students can perform rotations in a Flash animation and can interact with an image (pushing it with a mouse). Put a number of these activities together into a "learning management system," and students can be assigned work, access that work, participate in online class "discussions" and have their work scored. For their apparent novelty, these examples are called e-learning. What was done through language in a traditional classroom now involves a computer. However, they do not always involve *pedagogical* innovation.

These devices and activities are, at face value, new to education. Schools have collected together new resources, teachers have learned new strategies, and students have engaged in new types of activity as a part of their school-based experiences. But often they are not that new in the sense that they are instructional or epistemological breakthroughs. The use of a range of devices produced by the new media does not necessarily mean new learning. Traditional educational institutions have an enormous capacity to assimilate new forms without fully exploiting their affordances. Rather, they deploy them in a "makeover" manner (Lankshear, Snyder, & Green 2000; Neville, 2008). That is teachers all too often selectively use them as another way of doing what is not much more than conventional in terms of both teaching and learning.

New is a dynamic term when used in relation to digitized technologies and associated practices. At the time of writing, new examples of these include social networking tools such as Facebook; film and music dissemination tools such as YouTube, and social tools for knowledge and inquiry, such as wikis. These are influencing culture, community, and citizenship, as well as what constitutes literacy. More meaningfully "new" is the revolutionary aspect of the digital affordances insofar as they affect the manufacturing of textual design and explosive divergence of discourses. Coupled with the march to multimodality is a profound "shift in the balance of agency" (Kalantzis & Cope, 2008) in which we are increasingly required to be users, players, creators, and discerning consumers rather than the spectators, delegates, audiences, or quiescent consumers of an earlier time. In the digitized world, unidirectionality has been joined not only by relationships of "bidirectionality" (Kress, 2003) in users' interactions with textual designs but by complex, shifting, multifarious networks of social, political, professional, learner, and other affinity communities.

In the creation of space for agency, the new media also supply channels for differences to represent themselves. New media provide avenues for divergence rather than homogeneity. The logic of mass production (big-production TV; long-print-run books) has been joined by the logic of mass customization (tens of thousands of widely divergent messages in YouTube; books where a print run of one costs the same per unit as a print run of 10 or 10,000). Through social software such as wikis, knowledge and culture become more fluid, contestable, and open. As communities diverge—as they develop discourses specific to professions, peer groups, interests, and affinities—discourses become less mutually intelligible, and more effort is required for cross-cultural communication.

The development of literate abilities across the breadth of each new emerging technology is increasingly a more challenging goal. Literacy in the new communications environment is more productively approached by considering the broader affordances of the new digital communications technology for the production of different modes of meaning and their multimodal combinations. This is more important than mastery of particular literacy routines or software tools.

A MULTILITERACIES PERSPECTIVE: DEVELOPING A NEW AGENDA FOR LITERACY PEDAGOGY

Notwithstanding the gradual adoption of new media tools in the classroom, teaching practices continue in the main to reflect an old agenda for literacy—one that focuses on monomodal print literacy, driven in part by system-mandated literacy policies and assessment regimes. A broader and more relevant agenda for literacy pedagogy requires a rethinking of what constitutes literacy for the 21st century. This includes ongoing professional learning that engages teachers in reflections of their own practices and the pedagogical influences that determine their instructional choices.

The term *multiliteracies* was coined by the New London Group, an international group of educators who met in the mid-1990s to consider the current state of literacy pedagogy. This group was brought together by the two of the authors of this chapter, Mary Kalantzis and Bill Cope. The outcome of the meeting (in New London, New Hampshire) was a jointly authored paper, "A Pedagogy of Multiliteracies: Designing Social Futures," which was subsequently published in the *Harvard Educational Review*, and a book, *Multiliteracies: Literacy Learning and the Design of Social Futures.*

Since that time we have researched the effectiveness of the emergent multiliteracies theoretical frameworks in various educational settings across the globe. The case study discussed in this chapter is drawn from one such collaboration (Cloonan, 2008a). The theory and practice of multiliteracies was used in the following case study to engage teachers and students with the affordances of the digital communications environment in a number of classroom contexts. It involved the introduction and tracking of teachers' and learners' adoption of the affordances of multimodal meaning making. The case study tracked levels of learner engagement and transformation as well as the degree to which learner differences were accommodated in the learning experiences that were created. The starting point for the case study was the multiliteracies position that two aspects of language use were affected by the changing communications environment: the variability of meaning making in different cultural, social, or professional contexts, and the nature and impact of new communications technologies. It was also a base assumption that contemporary literacy pedagogy needs to engage diverse, multilayered learners' identities so as to experience belonging and transformation in their capacities and subjectivities (New London Group, 1996, 2000).

Multimodality

Traditionally, literacy teaching has confined itself to the forms of written language, with an emphasis on reading print. The new media, however, mix modes more powerfully than was culturally the norm and even technically possible in the earlier modernity dominated by the printed page. In the original multiliteracies work, becoming "multiliterate" was conceived as students developing proficiency in a range of meaning-making modes: linguistic, visual, audio, gestural, spatial, and multimodal designs, with multimodal being a combination of the other modes. Through the theorizations and curriculum experimentations of the past 10 years, we have reconfigured the range of possible modalities. We have separated written and oral language as fundamentally different modes, added a tactile mode, and redefined the contents and scope of the other modes, as follows:

- *Written language:* writing (representing meaning to another) and reading (representing meaning to oneself)—handwriting, the printed page, the screen.
- *Oral language:* live or recorded speech (representing meaning to another); listening (representing meaning to oneself).
- *Visual representation:* still or moving image, sculpture, craft (representing meaning to another); view, vista, scene, perspective (representing meaning to oneself).
- *Audio representation:* music, ambient sounds, noises, alerts (representing meaning to another); hearing, listening (representing meaning to oneself).
- *Tactile representation:* touch, smell and taste; the representation to oneself of bodily sensations and feelings or representations to others that "touch" them bodily. Forms of tactile representation include kinesthesia, physical contact, skin sensations (heat/cold, texture, pressure), grasp, manipulable objects, artefacts, cooking and eating, and aromas.
- *Gestural representation:* movements of the hands and arms, expressions of the face, eye movements and gaze, demeanors of the body, gait, clothing and fashion, hairstyle, dance, action sequences, timing, frequency, ceremony and ritual. Here, gesture is understood broadly and metaphorically as a physical act of signing (as in "a gesture to . . . "), rather than the narrower literal meaning of hand and arm movement. Representation to oneself may take the form of feelings and emotions or rehearsing action sequences in one's mind's eye.
- *Spatial representation:* proximity, spacing, layout, interpersonal distance, territoriality, architecture/building, streetscape, cityscape, landscape.

Different modes have the capacity to express similar kinds of meanings in alternate ways; the representational potentials that are unique unto themselves. Between the various modes, however, there are inherently different or incommensurate affordances as well parallel aspects of the representational jobs they do.

On the side of parallelism, a visual grammar can explain the ways in which images work like language. Action expressed by verbs in sentences may be represented in images by vectors. Locative prepositions in language are like foregrounding or backgrounding in images. Comparatives in language are like sizing and placement in images. The given and the new of English clause structures are like left/right placement in images (in the cultures of left-to-right viewing, at least), and the real/ideal in language is like top/down placement in images. The process of shifting between modes and re-representing the same thing from one mode to another is called synesthesia. Representational parallels make synesthesia possible. (A note: transmediation operates at the level of medium—printed book, video, performance etc.; synesthesia operates at the level of mode. Media are intrinsically multimodal, and the peculiarities of a medium defined by its specific mix of modes.)

Children have natural synesthetic capacities, and rather than build upon and extend these, traditional school literacy has, over a period of time, separated them off, to the extent even of creating different subjects or disciplines, literacy in one cell of the class timetable and art in another. Synesthesia is integral to representation. In a very ordinary, material sense, our bodily sensations are holistically integrated, even if the focus of our meaning-making attentions in any particular moment might be one particular mode. Gestures may come with sound; images and text sit side by side on pages; architectural spaces are labeled with written signs. Much of our everyday representational experience is intrinsically multimodal. Some modes are naturally close to others, so close, in fact, that the one easily melds into the others in the multimodal actualities of everyday meaning. Written language is closely connected to the visual in its use of spacing, layout, and typography. Spoken language is closely associated with the audio mode in the use of intonation, inflection, pitch, tempo, and pause. Gesture may need to be planned or rehearsed, either in inner speech (talking to oneself), or by visualization.

The different modes of meaning are, however, not simply parallel. Meaning expressed in one mode cannot be directly and completely translated into another. The movie can never be the same as the novel. The image can never do the same thing as the description of a scene in language. Parallelism allows the same thing to be depicted in different modes, but the meaning is never quite the same. Writing (along the line, sentence by sentence, paragraph by paragraph, one page after the next) sequences elements in time and so favors the genre of narrative. Image collocates elements according to the logic of simultaneous space, and so favors the genre of display. Writing's intrinsic temporality orients it to causality: image to location. Written language is open to a wide range of possible visualizations (is the movie how you visualized things when you were reading the book?). The words have to be filled in with visual meaning. Visuals, however, require that the viewer create order (time, causation, purpose, effect) by arranging elements that are already visually complete. Reading and viewing, in other words, require different kinds of imagination and different kinds of transformational effort in the re-representation of their meanings to oneself. They are fundamentally different ways of knowing and learning the world.

This paradoxical mix of parallelism and incommensurability between modalities is what makes addressing multimodality integral to the pedagogy of multiliteracies. Synesthesia is a pedagogical resource that makes for powerful learning in a number of ways. Some learners may be more comfortable in one mode than another. This may be their preferred mode of representation—what comes to them easiest, what they're good at, the mode in which they best express the world to themselves and themselves to the world. One student may prefer to conceive a project as a list of instructions; another as a flow diagram. Parallelism of modes means that you can do a lot of the same things in one mode that you can do in the next, so a pedagogy that restricts learning to one artificially segregated mode will favor some types of learners over others. It also means that the starting point for meaning in one mode may be a way of extending one's representational repertoire by shifting from favored modes to less comfortable ones. If the words don't make sense, the diagram might, and then the words start to make sense. But the incommensurability of modes works pedagogically, too. The words make sense because the picture conveys meaning that words could never (quite or in a completely satisfactory way) do. Conscious mode switching makes for more powerful learning.

Changes in the contemporary communications environment add urgency to the call to deploy multimodality consciously in learning and for developing a metalanguage to teach about the design features (i.e., grammars) of other modes in addition to language. Contemporary websites are full of written text, but the logic of their reading is more like the syntax of the visual than that of the written language. Reading the screen requires considerable navigational effort (see Hartman, Mor-sink, & Zheng, Chapter 7, this volume). Today's screens are designed for many viewing paths, allowing for diverse interests and subjectivities among viewers, and the reading path they choose will reflect the consid-erable design effort a viewer has put into their reading. In fact, the com-monsense semantics is telling—"readers" of books have become "users" now that they are on the Web. Nor is this the only shift happening on the Web—printed pages more and more resemble screens. The mix of image, caption, list, and breakout box is such that the reading paths of the image are now to be found on the page—the science textbook, the glossy magazine, the contemporary newspaper, or the instruction manual, for instance. And where writing is found, visual supports allow a simplified syntax for the writing itself, in the form, for instance, of a decreasing clausal complexity. This decreasing complexity of writing, however, is accompanied by an increasingly complex multimodality.

For every shift in the direction of the visual in the new communica-tions environment, however, there are other returns to writing—e-mail, text messaging, and blogging, for instance. None of these, however, are simply returns. They all express new forms of multimodality—the use of icon in text messaging and the juxtaposition of image in MMS (sending images with text), the layout of blog pages and e-mail messages, and the trend in all of these new forms of writing to move away from the grammar of the mode of writing to the grammar of the mode of speaking. Then there's the deep paradox of the "semantic web" in which images, sound, and text are only discoverable if they are labeled. The semantic web of the presently emerging Internet is built on a kind of multimodal gram-mar ("structural and semantic markup," semantic schemas or ontolo-gies) by way of running commentary on the images, sound, and writing it labels. Written language is becoming more closely intertwined with the other modes, and in some respects is becoming more like them.

Design

Using the concept of *design* (instead of the more static word *grammar*), multiliteracies theory offers a reconceptualization of what constitutes literacy education in the light of the increasing multimodality of texts. Multiliteracies regards any meaning-making activity as a matter of design involving three elements: available designs, designing, and the redesigned. Together these three elements emphasize the fact that meaning making is an active and dynamic process, and not something governed by static rules. In the multiliteracies pedagogical framework, students are positioned as designers who draw on available designs— existing design elements that can be linguistic (written and oral), visual, audio, tactile, gestural, spatial, or multimodal. Students deploy modes of meaning in their designing by harnessing available designs to make meaning for their own purposes. They produce redesigned or trans- formations of meaning, which then become available designs for other meaning-makers to draw upon.

Two key aspects of the notion of design distinguish it from the approaches to teaching language conventions taken by many earlier tra- ditions of literacy pedagogy: variability and agency. Traditional gram- mar instruction, for example, is taught to a single sociolinguistic end: the official, standard or high forms of the national language. The issue of language variability was rarely part of the teaching process. And always closely linked to this issue of variability is the issue of agency. The lifeworld language experiences students brought to learning traditional grammars were irrelevant at best, as the aim was to induct students into the standard written form. School was about the reproduction of received cultural and linguistic forms.

The *design* notion takes the opposite tack on both of these issues: the starting point is language variation—the different accents, regis- ters and dialects that serve different purposes in different social con- texts and for different social groups. The key issues of language use are agency and divergence—the ways in which every act of language draws on disparate language resources and remakes the world into a form that it has never quite taken before. The reality of language is not simply the reproduction of regularized patterns and conventions. It is also a matter of intertextuality, hybridity, and language as the basis of cultural change. In this sense, language is both an already designed resource and the ground of designs for social futures.

In multiliteracies pedagogy all forms of representation, including language, are regarded as dynamic processes of transformation rather than processes of reproduction. That is, students are not simply replica- tors of representational conventions. Their meaning-making resources may be found in representational forms, patterned in familiar and thus recognizable ways. However, they rework these forms. Students don't simply use what they have been given; they are fully makers and remak- ers of signs and transformers of meaning.

Language has sophisticated frameworks for interpreting, describ- ing, and creating available print texts. Ways of describing and comparing how meaning is constructed within isolated and combined modes of available linguistic, visual, gestural, audio, and spatial designs of meaning are required. This requires a metalanguage that is accessible to students and able to be generated by teachers and students in various teaching contexts. We have proposed the consideration of five dimensions of meaning making—representational, social, organizational, contextual, and ideological—across modes of meaning in the development of a multimodal metalanguage (Cope & Kalantzis, 2000b). In order to promote a generative metalanguage in individual and multiple modes of meaning, specific questions can be addressed to the modes, as follows:

- *Representational meaning*, which is explored through the question "What do the meanings refer to?" (relating to the participants represented and the being and acting the meanings represent). This dimension prompts a consideration of who and what the design represents and what's happening in the design.
- *Social meaning*, which is explored through the question "How do the meanings connect the persons they involve?" (relating to the roles of participants in the communication of meaning; the commitment the producer has to the message, interactivity, and relations between participants and processes). This dimension prompts consideration of the way meaning connects/relates to the producer and the recipient.
- *Organizational meaning*, which is explored through the question "How do the meanings hang together?" (relating to mode of communication, medium, delivery, cohesion, and composition). This dimension prompts consideration of the composition or shape of the organization of the meaning.
- *Contextual meaning*, which is explored through the question "How do the meanings fit into the larger world of meaning?" (relating to reference, cross-reference, and discourse). This prompts consideration of the context of the meaning and how context and meaning interrelate.
- *Ideological meaning*, which is explored through the question "Whose interests are the meanings skewed to serve?" (drawing attention to the possible motivations of the creator and consequent positioning of receiver). Secondary questions relate to indications of interests, attributions of truth value and affinity, space for readership, deception by omission if not commission, and types of transformation.

Such questions are not the basis for rules of correct usage that students might learn. Rather, they constitute the framework for the development of a contrastive metalanguage. They are tools that learners can use for interpreting and creating meaning, to assess the reasons why particular design choices are made in particular cultural and situational contexts. They are a heuristic by means of which students can describe and account for design variations. The dimensions offer students a way of thinking about how patterns of meaning are the product of different contexts—particularly in the changing contexts created by new communications technologies.

The aim is to design learning experiences through which learners develop strategies for reading the new and unfamiliar in whatever form they may manifest themselves. Instead of simply telling of authoritative designs, questions are asked of design, or the relation of meaning form to meaning function. In addressing these questions, learners may be able draw on various metalanguages describing the forms of contemporary meaning—professional and specialist, for instance—and from these construct their own frames of functional explanation.

Pedagogy

The pedagogical implications of rethinking meaning making as more dynamically designed are enormous. In the old literacy, learners were passive recipients or at best agents of reproduction of received, sanctioned, and authoritative representational forms. The logic of literacy pedagogy was one that made it an instrument of social design that buttressed a regime of apparent stability and uniformity. But literacy teaching is not only about skills and competence; it is aimed a creating a kind of person, an active designer of meaning, with a sensibility open to differences, change, and innovation. A pedagogy of multiliteracies requires that the role of agency in the meaning-making process be recognized, and in that recognition it seeks to create a more productive, relevant, innovative, creative, and even, perhaps, emancipatory pedagogy. The logic of multiliteracies recognizes that meaning making is an active, transformative process, and a pedagogy based on that recognition is more likely to open up paths to a world of change and diversity.

Such a transformative pedagogy is, we would argue, based both on a realistic view of contemporary society (how does schooling offer cultural and material access to its institutions of power?) and on an emancipatory view of possible paths to improvement in our human futures (how can we make a better, more equal, less humanly and environmentally damaging world?). Or, insofar as these two goals might at times be at odds, a transformative pedagogy could be used to support either view. Then it is up to the learners to make of the pedagogy what they will, be that a sensible conservatism (sensible for being realistic about the contemporary forces of technology, globalization, and cultural change) or an emancipatory view that aims to make a future different from the present by addressing its crises of poverty, environment, cultural difference, and existential meaning.

A pedagogy of multiliteracies identifies four major dimensions of pedagogy that we originally called situated practice, overt instruction, critical framing, and transformed practice. In applying these ideas to curriculum realities over the past decade, we have refined these ideas and reframed them into the more immediately recognizable pedagogical acts or "knowledge processes" (Kalantzis & Cope, 2005). Considered to be problematic when deployed in isolation, when used in combination the four aspects of the multiliteracies pedagogy represent four ways of knowing, four "takes" on processing meaning. These pedagogical orientations or knowledge processes are not a pedagogy in the singular or a sequence to be followed. Rather, they are a map of the range of pedagogical moves that may prompt teachers to extend their pedagogical repertoires:

■ *Experiencing.* Human cognition is situated. It is contextual. Meanings are grounded in the real-world of patterns of experience, action, and subjective interest. Students have in- and out-of-school experiences. They encounter familiar and unfamiliar texts and experiences. Experiencing takes two forms. "Experiencing the known" involves reflecting on one's own experiences, interests, perspectives, familiar forms of expression, and ways of representing the world in one's own understanding. In this regard, learners bring their own diverse knowledge, experiences, interests, and life texts to the learning situation. "Experiencing the new" entails observing or reading the unfamiliar, immersion in new situations and texts, reading new texts, or collecting new data. Learners are exposed to new information, experiences, and texts within a zone of intelligibility and safety sufficiently close to their own realities to be somewhat meaningful in the first instance, yet potentially transformative as the learner moves into new domains of action and meaning.

■ *Conceptualizing.* Students are involved in processing specialized, disciplinary, and deep knowledges based on the distinctive concepts and theories typical of those developed by expert communities of practice. Conceptualizing is not a matter of teacherly or textbook telling based on legacy academic disciplines, but a knowledge process in which the learners become active conceptualizers, making the tacit explicit and generalizing from the particular. "Conceptualizing by naming" involves drawing distinctions of similarity and difference, categorizing, and naming. Here, learners give abstract names to things and develop concepts. "Conceptualizing by theorizing" means making generalizations and putting the key terms together into interpretative frameworks. Learners build mental models, abstract frameworks, and transferable disciplinary schemas. In the same pedagogical territory, didactic pedagogy would lay out disciplinary schemas for the learners to acquire (the rules of literacy). Conceptualizing requires that learners be active concept- and theory-makers. It also requires shunting between the experiential and the conceptual.

■ *Analyzing.* Powerful learning also entails a certain kind of critical capacity. In a pedagogical context "critical" can mean to be functionally analytical or to be evaluative with respect to relationships of power. Analyzing involves both of these kinds of knowledge processes. "Analyzing functionally" includes processes of reasoning, drawing inferential and deductive conclusions, establishing functional relations (such as between cause and effect), and analyzing logical and textual connections. Learners explore causes and effects, develop chains of reasoning, and explain patterns in text. "Analyzing critically" involves evaluation of your own and other people's perspectives, interests, and motives. In these knowledge processes, learners interrogate the interests behind a meaning or an action, as well as their own processes of thinking.

■ *Applying.* "Applying appropriately" entails the application of knowledge and understandings to the complex diversity of real-world situations and testing their validity. By these means, learners do something in predictable and expected ways in a "real-world" situation or a situation that simulates the real world. "Applying creatively" involves making an intervention in the world that is innovative and creative and that brings to bear the learner's interests, experiences, and aspirations. This is a process of remaking the world with fresh and creative forms of action and perception. Learners do something that expresses or affects the world in new way, or that transfers their previous knowledge into a new setting. This can take many forms, bringing new experiential, conceptual, or critical knowledge back to bear on the experiential world.

A pedagogy of multiliteracies allows alternative starting points for learning (what the learner perceives to be worth learning, what engages the particularities of their identity). It allows for alternative forms of engagement (the varied experiences that need to be brought to bear on the learning, the different conceptual bents of learners, the different analytical perspectives the learner may have on the nature of cause, effect, and human interest, and the different settings in which they may apply or enact their knowledge). It allows for divergent learning orientations (e.g., preferences for particular emphases in knowledge making and patterns of engagement). It allows for different modalities in meaning making, embracing alternative expressive potentials for different learners, and promoting synesthesia as a learning strategy. And it reflects a rebalancing of agency in the recognition of active "design" and inherent learning potentials in the representational process: every meaning draws on resources of the already designed world of representation; each meaning-maker designs the world afresh in a way that is always uniquely transformative of found meanings, and then leaves a representational trace to be found by others and transformed once again. Finally, a transformative pedagogy allows for alternative pathways and comparable destination points in learning. The measure of success of transformative pedagogy is equally high-performance learning outcomes that can produce comparable social effects for learners in terms of material rewards and socially ascribed status.

Using the heuristic of the different pedagogical orientations to reflect on their practice, teachers may find themselves to have been unreflectively caught in the rut of one or just a few of the knowledge processes, or in knowledge processes that do not in practice align with the stated goals of learning. It is useful to be able to unpack the range of possible knowledge processes in order to decide and justify what's appropriate for a subject or a learner, to track learner inputs and outputs, and in order to extend the pedagogical repertoires of teachers and the knowledge repertoires of learners. A pedagogy of multiliteracies suggests a broader range of knowledge processes be used, and that more powerful learning arises from moving backwards and forward between different knowledge processes in an explicit and purposeful way.

In the last decade, there has been increasing recognition of the need to integrate the first two of the pedagogical processes, experiencing and conceptualizing. At least in many English-medium countries, the "reading wars" between phonics and whole language' have been replaced by an emphasis on balanced literacy. But the critical literacy implied by analyzing has had less uptake in either of its meanings, perhaps because of its latent possibility of arousing controversies. Applying in the sense of transformed practice has also faced greater barriers. Educational reforms supporting economic competition offer statements about the importance of fostering entrepreneurship, creativity, and problem posing as well as problem solving—all forms of transformative applying. Intervening to effect such changes requires overcoming resistance to change and opening up entrenched didactic teaching practices, which in some contexts are exacerbated by large class sizes. In such cases, any opening up must not to simply be to didactic teaching's opposite, that is, a "progressive" overreliance on experiencing, but to a repertoire of the four learning processes for students and complementary teaching strategies for teachers.

CASE STUDY: A COLLABORATIVE PRACTICAL APPLICATION OF MULTILITERACIES SCHEMAS

The previous section discusses seven modes in which meaning making can be designed (oral and written language, visual, audio, tactile, gestural, and spatial representation); five dimensions of these modes that can be considered when interpreting and creating designs (representational, social, organizational, contextual, and ideological); and four major dimensions of pedagogy (experiencing, conceptualizing, analyzing, and applying knowledge processes) that can be deployed to map teachers' pedagogical choices. These three aspects of multiliteracies theory can be productively conceptualized as frameworks or schemas for multimodal meaning making and pedagogical repertoires that address learner engagement, diversity, and transformation. Three key schemas emanating from multiliteracies theory—a multimodal schema, a dimensions of meaning schema, and a pedagogical knowledge processes schema were deployed in analyzing shifts in teachers' literacy pedagogy choices.

Following is a case study discussion of a teacher who renewed her classroom literacy teaching practices as a consequence of engaging with the multimodal schema and the pedagogical knowledge processes schema within the context of a professional learning project. Recognizing the powerful influence of the teacher on student outcomes (Hattie, 2003), and using the prism of the three multiliteracies schemas referred to above, this study sought to investigate teacher learning as a means for influencing print-based literacy pedagogies to incorporate multimodality literacy practices. The case study is included to illustrate the impact of teacher engagement with multiliteracies schemas on literacy pedagogy.

The study took place in the context of an Australian state government education sector in 2003 and involved literacy teachers of students ages 5–10. The teachers were drawn from government schools—one in an inner-city suburb of a capital city, the other from a semirural town. Both schools had a high proportion of students from low socioeconomic backgrounds. The teachers' classroom experience ranged between 8 and 25 years.

The teacher described in this chapter was a participant in a project that sought to support teachers' professional learning and classroom application of multimodal pedagogies through engagement with theoretically influenced schemas (Cloonan, 2005a, 2005b, 2008a, 2008b). The teachers engaged in participatory action research (Carr & Kemmis, 1986) forming a community of practice (Wenger, 1999), which sought to develop classroom responses that were cognizant of multimodal shifts in contemporary communication. The teachers agreed to undertake sustained and reflective engagement with multiliteracies schemas over an 8-month period. These were specific to their individual teaching contexts. During this time, each teacher undertook two sequences of teaching, with 62 lessons analyzed. Following is an illustration of one case study participant's professional learning journey.

Professional Learning, Multimodality, and Website Design

A preschool and primary educator with more than 20 years' experience, at the time of the research Pip (a pseudonym) had recently returned to the semirural school involved in this study after a 3-year placement in an ICT/literacy consultancy position in a regional education office. The school is situated 200 kilometers east of the state capital city and has a population of approximately 240 students, many from families experiencing socioeconomic disadvantage. The main forms of industry open to the community are agricultural or agriculture-related (sales, agistment, haulage), with a well-represented "trucking community."

Pip's ICT and literacy expertise had been deployed by the region in the conduct of initiatives to encourage the use of ICT across the cur-

riculum. Pip was also a regional literacy trainer responsible for training school-based coordinators. She was very confident with and eager
to incorporate technology into literacy learning. Pip's school-based
responsibilities included teaching a years 3 and 4 class (students ages
8–10); school literacy and numeracy coordination involved Pip in supporting the professional learning of other teachers at her school.

Despite expertise and access to professional learning in the regional
position, Pip had only a limited and superficial understanding of multiliteracies. Early in the project, Pip described perceptions of multiliteracies as

> "a term that's been around a long time and I guess I'd heard about
> it . . . my initial understanding was probably the changing nature of
> literacy, particularly now with e-mail, mobile phones, and SMS mes-
> sages, how that's changed . . . I really didn't know anything about,
> or hadn't considered the multimodal nature of the learning."

While Pip was aware of the connection between multiliteracies
and technology, these connections did not initially extend to the multimodal schema. Pip's starting point was an amalgam of her own and her
students' personal interests and her need to engage a diverse group of
learners, of when 19 out of 28 students were boys. In her words:

> "As a way of connecting to them and making their learning more
> meaningful to them and engaging them and motivating them,
> technology and computers was a fantastic link, but linking it to
> what they already knew. I just felt [technology] was a way of engag-
> ing particularly all those boys and it just hooked in so well with the
> multimodal . . . I've felt [technology] was a tool that engages chil-
> dren and particularly boys because it's so hands on."

Prior to commencing work in this project, Pip's students' school-
related experiences with computers were mainly for "publishing" handwritten work. Pip wanted to change students' view of computer usage,
encouraging them, for example, to compose, research, save and change,
download, upload, and use a range of programs. During her participation in the professional learning research project, Pip designed two
sequences of lessons, influenced by her engagement with the multiliteracies schemas (see Table 4.1). The first teaching sequence involved the

TABLE 4.1. Pip's Multimodal Emphasis, Lesson Focus, and Deployment of Pedagogical Knowledge Processes

Lesson	Multimodal emphasis and lesson focus	Pedagogical knowledge process
Teaching sequence 1		
1	*Linguistic* and visual: Concept map knowledge of websites	Experiencing the known
2	*Linguistic:* Personal details	Experiencing the known
3	*Linguistic* and visual: Listening and responding to website stories	Experiencing the new
4	*Linguistic* and visual: Navigating websites	Conceptualizing by naming
5	*Visual:* Website features	Conceptualizing by naming
6	*Visual:* Structure and layout of website	Conceptualizing by theorizing
7	*Visual* and linguistic: Features of a search engine	Analyzing functionally
8	*Linguistic:* Writing about a "passion"	Analyzing functionally
9	*Linguistic:* Researching for information on websites	Analyzing functionally
10	*Visual* and linguistic: Critiquing features on websites	Analyzing critically
11	*Linguistic* and visual: Critiquing features on websites	Analyzing critically
12	*Linguistic* and visual: Comparing websites and books	Applying appropriately
13	*Visual,* linguistic (and audio): Publishing profiles	Applying creatively
14	*Linguistic,* visual (and audio): Publishing and presenting projects	Applying creatively

(cont.)

TABLE 4.1. *(cont.)*

Lesson	Multimodal emphasis and lesson focus	Pedagogical knowledge process
Teaching sequence 2		
15	*Linguistic* and visual: Reading print newspapers	Experiencing the known
16	*Visual* and linguistic (and audio): Reading online newspapers	Experiencing the new
17	*Linguistic*, visual (and audio): Naming newspaper features	Conceptualizing by naming
18	*Visual* and linguistic (and audio): Print and online comparisons	Conceptualizing by theorizing
19	*Linguistic*, visual (and audio): Print and online functions	Analyzing functionally
20	*Linguistic:* Consideration of audience preferences	Analyzing critically
21	*Linguistic* and visual: Creation of class newspaper	Applying appropriately
22	*Visual* and linguistic: Creation of class newspaper	Applying creatively

Note. The predominant mode of focus is shown in *italics.*

exploration and researching of personal passions and the creation of a class website. The second teaching sequence involved the exploration and creation of online and print newspapers. The emphasis of teaching sequence 1 was mainly on linguistic meaning-making resources and their interplay with the visual in online and print-based environments.

Comparison of data from the two teaching sequences in Table 4.1 shows that in teaching sequence 1 the impact of the multimodal schema on Pip's documented classroom practices was limited to expanding oral and written linguistic literacy teaching to include visual meaning-making resources. Pip displayed skill in teaching *through* and *about* the linguistic and visual modes. This skill became more pronounced over the two teaching sequences.

Individually and in combination in teaching sequence 1, Pip addressed the linguistic and visual modes within the context of a study of Web design involving the students in developing personal profiles and interest-based "passion projects" on topics such as dancing or trucks. Teaching about the audio mode was limited to inserting effects into PowerPoint presentations. A strong focus on teaching *about* the linguistic remained apparent (writing concept maps, personal profiles, writing about a passion, reading an author's website and writing an author profile in lessons 1–3 and 8), as well as *through* the linguistic such as researching for information on the Internet in lessons 4 and 9.

Pip's early deployment of the visual mode was to teach *through* the visual, for example to use the visual incidentally to show knowledge of websites in the lesson focused on writing concept maps (lesson 1), and to use the visual features of a website as a means to listening to an author read stories (lesson 3). Pip's teaching *about* the visual indicated recognition of the visual as a mode of meaning making with specific design (grammatical metalanguage) characteristics (lessons 5 and 6), an influence of the multimodal schema on her professional learning. Later in the sequence Pip addressed the meaning-making affordances of both the linguistic and the visual, teaching through and about them (lessons 9–14), incidentally incorporating the audio for presenting information but not teaching *about* it (lessons 13 and 14).

In teaching sequence 2, an exploration of print and online newspapers, Pip continued to emphasize teaching *about* both the linguistic and visual within the contexts of newspapers. Teaching incorporated the learners' prior knowledge of linguistic and visual knowledge of newspapers (lessons 15 and 16); the linguistic, visual, and audio features of newspapers, including concepts such as mastheads, datelines, bylines, captions, and photographs (lessons 17 and 18); comparisons of print and online newspapers, including design structure and its relation to purposes and audiences (lessons 19 and 20); and the creation of a class newspaper involving design of mastheads, logos, bar codes, prices, interviewing, genre selection, and reporting (lesson 21). While teaching of the audio mode was increasingly incorporated, it was still not taught *about*.

A juxtaposition of emphasis between the two modes, linguistic and visual, was evident as Pip emphasized one mode and then the other, exploring them individually and their intermodal relations. Teaching addressed audio only as a means for delivering linguistic information in online newspapers, or linguistic *through* audio. Pip did not address the gestural, tactile, and spatial modes of meaning in these teaching sequences.

The theoretical input provided by the multimodal schema, consideration of students' disengagement with writing, and personal interest and expertise, influenced Pip's decision to explore and create websites and newspapers. In the course of classroom action, the shift from print-based texts to the Web environment led to a focus on the visual as well as the linguistic mode, and in particular on the organizational dimension of meaning. The multimodal schema had an evident impact on Pip's literacy teaching. Her heightened awareness of a wider range of meaning-making resources other than linguistic and their designs (i.e., dynamic grammar) was evident in teaching that focused on aspects of the visual in the interpreting, analysis, and construction of Web resources. The result, in turn, was an expansion of students' capacities to articulate and deploy visual and linguistic aspects of websites.

Pip was a digital native (Prensky, 2001), with well-developed technological knowledge. Engagement with the multimodal schema allowed her to reflect on her professional growth in terms of becoming more explicit, analytical, and purposeful in the use of a greater variety of meaning-making modes, as shown in the following excerpt:

> "I was always aware of the range of learning needs, I guess, and learning styles within the classroom, but actually looking at the way the children bring meaning. I've had to reflect on that a lot more . . . I'm more strategically planning for those particular purposes; looking at the multimodality and the way children learn has been really powerful for me as a teacher."

Pip included multimodality into her teaching as a means of both supporting traditional print literacy learning outcomes and as a way of catering to diverse students through multiple entry points for making meaning (van Haren, 2007).

Comparison of data from the two teaching sequences shows how Pip's relatively confident and purposeful teaching of modes through deployment of a range of appropriate pedagogical choices was fine-tuned in teaching sequence 2: a study of print and online newspapers (see Table 4.2). Pip emphasized the pedagogical knowledge process of analysis in teaching sequence 1, reflecting the usefulness of this knowledge process in exploring the newness of the visual as a meaning-making resource. In both teaching sequences, Pip deployed all of the pedagogical knowledge processes in an effective way to address the learning goals in either the linguistic and/or the visual mode. Teaching

TABLE 4.2. Pip's Deployment of "Pedagogical Knowledge Processes" in Two Teaching Sequences

	Experiencing	Conceptualizing	Analyzing	Applying
Teaching sequence 1	21%	21%	37%	21%
Teaching sequence 2	25%	25%	25%	25%

sequence 2, which placed a greater focus on the visual as a meaning-making mode in its own right as well as in a secondary capacity in teaching the linguistic, also saw each of the pedagogical knowledge processes deployed in the teaching of each mode.

For example, Pip's deployment of the pedagogical knowledge process of experiencing, used in teaching sequence 1 to address the linguistic mode, was expanded in teaching sequence 2 to address the teaching of linguistic and visual modes and, to a lesser extent, the audio in print and online newspapers (lessons 15 and 16). Deployment of the pedagogical knowledge process of conceptualizing, used mainly in teaching sequence 1 to name and theorize about the linguistic mode in website features, was, in teaching sequence 2, deployed in naming and theorizing about the multimodal realization of online and print newspapers, specifically the linguistic and visual modes (lessons 17 and 18). The metalanguage that emerged to describe the design characteristics (dynamic grammars) of each of the meaning making modes that were used was emphasized in an ongoing way and documented through the development of a class glossary.

The pedagogical knowledge process of analysis, predominantly deployed in teaching sequence 1 to address the linguistic mode but with a lesser emphasis on the visual, was similarly deployed in teaching sequence 2 to focus on linguistic functions, and to a lesser extent the visual and audio modes (lesson 19), as well as audience preferences through the linguistic mode (lesson 20).

The pedagogical knowledge process of applying, deployed in teaching sequence 1 to emphasize the linguistic but with a lesser emphasis on the visual in the publication and presentation of personal profiles and passion projects on a class website, was deployed in teaching sequence 2 in addressing both the linguistic and visual modes in creating a newspaper (lessons 21 and 22). In Pip's case, teaching sequence 2 showed a fine-tuning of emphasis between the teaching of the linguistic and visual. Teaching in both teaching sequences was tightly focused on students' literacy development, encouraging traditional literacies of reading and writing in the online environment enabled by technology, with the visual increasingly treated as a mode of meaning in its own right.

CONCLUSIONS

In considering the deployment of schemas emanating from multiliteracies theory in research collaborations with educators, a number of conclusions can be drawn. Through engagement with the multimodal schema teachers can become more explicit about their teaching of mode and multimodality. The multimodal schema can prompt teachers to design teaching that addresses different modes of meaning and directs them to engage with deep grammatical knowledge of modes and multimodality. The multimodal schema provides a scaffold for teaching multimodality and a language with which to discuss such teaching.

The multimodal schema can also expand teacher perception of the modes of meaning that need to be addressed as literacy resources. Examples of teaching multimodality, teaching through multimodality, and teaching about multimodality were evident in teachers' pedagogy. Teaching the linguistic mode remains the predominant concern of literacy teachers; however, a new appreciation of the meaning-making affordances of modes other than the linguistic is apparent. Modes previously positioned as extralinguistic, auxiliary, or as belonging to another part of the curriculum (such as the arts) became elements seen to be fundamental parts of teaching literacy.

However, in relation to nonlinguistic modes of meaning, teachers feel themselves to be on more substantial theoretical ground teaching the visual mode than they do in teaching the other nonlinguistic modes, where they appear to feel ill at ease. So although the multimodal schema can develop teacher awareness of previously overlooked meaning-making affordances of modes other than linguistic, and this awareness has resulted in teaching that emphasizes particular modes of meaning or aspects of intermodal relationships, it is clear that research and professional learning programs will have to target the acceptance of the lesser-used modes. The dimensions of meaning schema has been shown to be a useful analytical tool in revealing patterns in multimodality teaching choices and a lack of explicit teacher expertise in deploying a functional metalanguage for different modes of meaning making (Cloonan, 2008b). It holds great potential as a stimulus for a teacher-generated metalanguage of multimodality.

The pedagogical knowledge processes schema has been shown to be influential in scaffolding the purposeful deployment, articulation, and reflection of pedagogical choices related to multimodal literacy teaching. Teachers' engagement with the pedagogical knowledge processes schema reveals habitual practices and preferences in teaching and learning, such as a disinclination to deploy specialized multimodal metalanguage with all students. The co-deployment of the pedagogical knowledge processes schema combined with the multimodal schema and the dimensions of meaning schema needs to be further explored in promotion of reflective literacy professional learning and practice.

Teacher engagement with theory has positive implications for practice, particularly in the context of participatory research relationships. Teacher disposition plays a demonstrated role in the efficacy of professional development and the design and delivery of student learning experiences. However, membership of and accountability to a professional learning community, to a sense of team, an interdependent collegiality between team members, has had a positive impact on the quality of teaching. Participatory action research methodology has been found to empower teacher learning through engagement with theory, the undertaking of context-specific enactments, the collective production and examination of data, and subsequent reframing of practice.

Finally, literacy teachers work within a framework of literacy policy directives. Literacy policies can work as both constraining and enabling mechanisms in supporting teacher professional learning and performance and learner performance. Literacy policy directives require a flexible orientation to their implementation to ensure that they enable teachers to interpret policy appropriately within given contexts and to be free to innovate and respond to the needs of their learners in a rapidly changing environment.

Given that print-alphabetic literacy in English remains the dominant understanding of the term *literacy* within many education department policies, the emerging multimodal literacies remain theoretically, and in practice, elusive to many teachers currently in classrooms. Future literacy policy needs to be developed that explicitly advises on the teaching, learning, and assessment of multimodal meaning making, helping teachers to gain a firmer grasp of theories of multimodal design.

ACKNOWLEDGMENTS

The empirical components of this chapter are drawn from Anne Cloonan's doctoral thesis, supervised by Mary Kalantzis. Theoretical sections of this text rework Cope and Kalantzis's most recent update of the multiliteracies agenda (Cope & Kalantzis, 2009).

REFERENCES

Carr, W., & Kemmis, S. (1986). *Becoming critical: Education, knowledge and action research* (3rd ed.). London: Falmer Press.

Cloonan, A. (2005a). Professional learning and enacting theory (or trying to be a lifelong/lifewide teacher-learner while hanging on to your sanity). In M. Kalantzis & B. Cope (Eds.), *Learning by design* (pp. 217–330). Melbourne: Victorian Schools Innovation.

Cloonan, A. (2005b). *Injecting early years teaching with a strong dose of multiliteracies.* Paper presented at the Pleasurable Learning, Passionate Teaching, Provocative Debates, Broadbeach, Queensland, Australia.

Cloonan, A. (2008a). Multimodality pedagogies: A multiliteracies approach. *The International Journal of Learning, 15,* 159–168.

Cloonan, A. (2008b). *The professional learning of teachers: A case study of multiliteracies teaching in the early years of schooling.* Unpublished doctoral dissertation, RMIT University, Melbourne, Australia.

Cope, B., & Kalantzis, M. (Eds.). (2000a). *Multiliteracies: Literacy learning and the design of social futures.* London: Routledge.

Cope, B., & Kalantzis, M. (2000b). Designs for social futures. In B. Cope & M. Kalantzis (Eds.), *Multiliteracies: Literacy learning and the design of social futures* (pp. 203–234). London: Routledge.

Cope, B., & Kalantzis, M. (2009). Multiliteracies: New literacies, new learning. *Pedagogies: An International Journal, 4,* 164–195.

European Commission. (2008). *Digital Literacy European Commission working paper and recommendations from Digital Literacy High-Level Expert Group.* Retrieved December 11, 2008, from *ec.europa.eu/information_society/eeurope/i2010/index_en.htm.*

Hattie, J. (2003, October). *Teachers make a difference: What is the research evidence?* Paper presented at the Building Teacher Quality Research Conference, Melbourne, Australia.

Kalantzis, M., & Cope, B. (2005). *Learning by design.* Melbourne: Victorian Schools Innovation Commission.

Kalantzis, M., & Cope, B. (2008). Digital communications, multimodality and diversity : Towards a pedagogy of multiliteracies. *Scientia Paedagogica Experimentalis, 45,* 15–50.

Kress, G. (2003). *Literacy in the new media age.* London: Routledge.

Lankshear, C., Snyder, I., & Green, B. (2000). *Teachers and techno-literacy: Managing literacy and technology and learning in schools.* Sydney: Allen & Unwin.

Ministerial Council on Education, Employment, Training and Youth Affairs (MCEETYA). (2007). *National assessment program—ICT literacy years 6 and 10 Report 2005.* Canberra, Australia: Ministerial Council on Education, Employment, Training and Youth Affairs (MCEETYA).

Neville, M. (2008). *Teaching multimodal literacy using the learning by design approach to pedagogy: Case studies from selected Queensland schools.* Melbourne: Common Ground.

New London Group. (1996). A pedagogy of multiliteracies: Designing social futures. *Harvard Educational Review, 66,* 60–92.

New London Group. (2000). A pedagogy of multiliteracies: Designing social futures. In B. Cope & M. Kalantzis (Eds.), *Multiliteracies: Literacy learning and the design of social futures* (pp. 182–202). Melbourne: Macmillan.

Prensky, M. (2001). Digital natives, digital immigrants. *On the Horizon, 9*(5).

van Haren, R. (2007). *Diversity and the learning by design approach to pedagogy.* Unpublished Master's thesis. Melbourne: The Royal Melbourne Institute of Technology University.

Wenger, E. (1999). *Communities of practice: Learning, meaning, and identity.* Cambridge: Cambridge University Press.

CHAPTER 5

Traversing the "Literacies" Landscape
A Semiotic Perspective on Early Literacy Acquisition and Digital Literacies Instruction

LINDA D. LABBO
TAMMY RYAN

Technology plays a significant role in all aspects of American life today, and this role will only increase in the future. The potential benefits of technology for young children's learning and development are well documented (Wright & Shade, 1994). As technology becomes easier to use and early childhood software proliferates, young children's use of technology becomes more widespread. Therefore, early childhood educators have a responsibility to critically examine the impact of technology on children and be prepared to use technology to benefit children.
—International Reading Association and National Association for the Education of Young Children (1998)

The future is not a result of choices among alternative paths offered by the present, but a place that is created—created first in the mind and will, created next in activity. The future is not some place we are going to, but one we are creating. The paths are not to be found, but made, and the activity of making them changes both the maker and the destination.
—Schaar (n.d.)

The literacy landscape for children of yesterday was a fairly simple one to traverse. Traversals refer to "movement from one object to another through a relationship between them" (see Sedris Technologies, 2007). Traditional literacy materials of the home, the classroom, and the workplace of yesterday consisted primarily of paper, pencils, pens, books, and all things print related. Thus when children traversed different social and learning spaces, the movement was fluid and synergistic. Literacy functions at school complemented literacy functions at home (e.g., book reading, letter writing).

The literacy landscape for young children of today consists of a complex continuum and juxtaposition of print-based and computer-related interactive multimedia. Lemke (1993, 2004) explains that today's different institutional and cultural sites involve unique ideological spaces that entail specific genres, media, discourses, and registers. Thus when children of today attempt to traverse different social and learning spaces, the movement may be dysfunctional and disruptive. Institutions of today, such as home, workplace, and classroom, are often separated by differing communicative technologies, purposes, and functions. Children gain specific types of "capital"—abilities, identities, and even status—in different cultural and institutional locations. Thus a child who has a computer-rich home life and a computer-poor classroom life is likely to find her capital of technology expertise unwelcome in a school setting.

The purpose of this chapter is to explore computer use in the earliest grades by uncovering the semiotic nature of young children's traditional and *electronic symbol making*. Electronic symbol making refers to the conceptual processes, strategies, and knowledge that young children develop when they use creativity programs that include expressive tools and multimedia symbol systems for various inter- and intrapersonal purposes in homes or in classroom computer center settings (Labbo & Kuhn, 1998). While delving into the semiotics of young children's computer-related symbol making, we briefly offer observations about literacy and computer-related literacies, present relevant research, and provide an example of how a teacher helped young children culminate meanings along their daily traversals across the landscape of the various institutional and cultural worlds of home, community, and school.

LITERACY AND COMPUTER-RELATED LITERACIES

Computers are present in the homes and classrooms of young children across America, and it is crucial that educators figure out what to do with them. Sometime between the ages of 2 and 3, most youngsters develop the ability to understand that moving a computer mouse causes actions on the monitor. For example, the Kaiser Family Foundation (2003) study ("Zero to Six: Electronic Media in the Lives of Infants,

Toddlers and Preschoolers") reported that 31% of infants to 3-year-olds have used a computer. The percentage increases to 70% between 4 and 6 years of age. It's worth noting that the largest group of new users of the Internet in 2001–2002 was 2- to 5-year-old children (U.S. Department of Education, 2003). Children who consistently access computers in various settings have occasions for accruing technological and media-related capital.

"Computer and Internet Use by Children and Adolescents in 2001" (U.S. Department of Education, 2004) indicates that, for children attending nursery school, 67% used computers and 23% accessed the Internet. For those attending kindergarten, 80% used computers and 32% used the Internet. As promising as these statistics are, many disadvantaged children remain caught in a subtle digital divide. The most recent divide, the gap between the "parent know-hows"—those who have access and know how to support computer use by their young children—and the "parent know-nots"—those who have access but do not use it to consistently support computer use by their young children, is a noteworthy economic and educational issue (Neuman & Celano, 2006). In addition, at least 50% of veteran and new teachers identify themselves as educational technology novices, and only 42% of new teachers recently stated that they feel that they are well prepared to use computers for instruction (Office of Social and Economic Data Analysis, 2003). Thus, both veteran and new teachers need support to become technologically literate.

It is clear that people who grapple with sorting out the appropriate role for computers in early childhood education care deeply about children's welfare and curricular issues. At the heart of most considerations about computer use are strongly held beliefs about what constitutes developmentally appropriate practice. Thus some teachers view the presence of computers in the earliest grades as a "benign addition" (Cuban, 2001, p. 67), that is, a rather nondescript and frequently underused supplemental resource for more traditional literacy instruction materials. In such classrooms where the benign view is taken, the computers may never be turned on or even put to effective use. In some classrooms, the computer may be treated as a stand-alone device, a tool children have access to for entertainment after print-based work is completed.

Alarmists, such as author Jane Healy (2000), view computers in the early grades as wasteful because of the "mindless or rote-level technology [that is] without substantive, interpersonal learning experiences"

(p. 172). Healy provides dire scenarios that compare a wired-up child (e.g., one who wears headphones while sitting in an isolated computer center in the corner) to the free child (e.g., one who is playing in an outdoor setting). Educators who wonder about developmentally appropriate practice focus on what children learn *from* a computer (Goldberg & Sherwood, 1983). Learning from a computer suggests a focus on short-term and specific learning objectives in which the computer *delivers* instruction. From this perspective, the computer is a device that is passive and essentially neutral in regard to specific learning objectives (Clarke, 1988), providing small-scale advantages, such as immediate feedback and rote-level individualized instruction. Research guided by this focus tends to be behaviorist or atheoretical.

Others, who are perhaps more optimistic, think of the computer as a constructive device, one that simply requires thoughtful integration into the classroom curriculum. Proponents expect technology to transform literacy instruction (Reinking, McKenna, Labbo, & Kieffer, 1998), introduce children to new literacies skills (Leu & Kinzer, 2003), and prepare children for their personal and professional futures (Leu, & Kinzer, 2000). Computers are social places where children gather information, assemble knowledge, generate knowledge, represent knowledge, communicate with others, and publish for authentic online audiences. From this perspective, the computer is an integral part of classroom life and the focus is on what might be learned *with* (Clements, 1994; Haughland, 1992) a computer, with the computer features, interactivity, and multimedia feedback scaffolding learning (cf. Salomon, Perkins, & Globerson, 1991) in an intelligently sensed zone of proximal development (Vygotsky, 1978).

The beliefs of educators, theorists, and researchers rest squarely upon good intentions, a fairly shallow research base, and assumptions about the nature of work children do with computers. In light of the lack of consensus among early childhood stakeholders, the recent and ongoing investment in placing computers in early-grade classrooms, and the potential misuse of technologies, it is essential to seek insights into the semiotic nature of young children's traditional and computer-related literacy development.

Learning with a computer implies incidental outcomes in which the computer fundamentally shapes orientations to learning, content, and semiotic meaning-making tasks. The computer's advantages over other modes of instruction are considered more specifically in terms of the broader cognitive or social dimensions of learning. Research guided by this focus is more likely to be grounded in sociocultural or sociocognitive theoretical perspectives.

For more than a decade, researchers and theorists who sought to understand how young children emerge as makers, inventors, and users of sign systems have drawn from a semiotic perspective to understand the production and use of meaningful sign systems and symbols (Crenshaw, 1985; Halliday, 1978; Harste, Woodward, & Burke, 1984; Rowe, 1994; Wells, 1993). Suhor (1992) explained that semiotics, the study of signs, involves three types of signs:

1. Symbols—signs that bear an arbitrary relationship to what they stand for (e.g., the word "apple" by convention stands for the fruit we identify with the word).
2. Icons—signs that resemble what they stand for (e.g., a painting of an apple looks like the fruit it represents).
3. Indexes—signs that are indicators of a fact or condition (e.g., a chest pain can indicate heartburn; smoke usually indicates fire). . . . Ideas are signs, too, since they represent entities as defined in one's culture. (p. 228)

Some researchers who have focused on early writing development have noted that preschool children frequently negotiate several sign systems as they make meaning with graphic symbols (Dyson, 1988; Harste et al., 1984; Rowe, 1994; Sulzby, 1989) and found that children make a distinction among modes of symbolic use (e.g., oral language, written language, and drawing) as they communicate (Dyson, 1991). For instance, when writing with paper and pencil preschool children move fluidly between writing and drawing in an effort to make their meanings public (Harste et al., 1984).

Prekindergarten and kindergarten classrooms at the beginning of the 21st century include designated spaces and sanctioned times for children to thoughtfully and playfully explore various ways of making meaning that include but also go beyond print-based literacies. For example, in most classrooms teachers provide 3-, 4-, and 5-year-old children with brushes, paper, tempera paint, and easels so they can explore creative expression as they make painted pictures in art centers. Teachers also invite children who cannot yet spell conventionally to use pencils to write their names with scribbles or crooked lines of random letters to sign up for a turn in various centers. Most recently in a growing number of classroom computer centers, youngsters who cannot yet read conventionally fill computer screens with a convergence of digital symbols that include letters, numbers, squiggly lines, clip art, animation, video clips, narrated text, and sound effects. In all of these instances, children are using expressive tools and available symbol systems to make meaning for various academic and personal purposes.

RELEVANT RESEARCH

Research suggests that computer technologies do indeed support young children's writing ability. From an emergent literacy perspective and utilizing a process writing approach, word-processing and other software aimed at creative expression do indeed support composing, writing, and publishing. Emergent literacy, with an emphasis on natural experimentation and hypotheses about writing (Teale & Sulzby, 1989), aligns well with computer technologies and multimedia tools.

Multimedia Composing

Labbo (1996) noted that kindergarten children who worked independently at computer center to produce stories with pictures, icons, drawings, painting, and text on screen achieved cognitive growth, development of literacy insights, and child-initiated collaborations. They solved problems and made hypotheses about meaning making while composing. Multimedia tools scaffolded children's exploration of symbolic representations. Students also gained traditional skills, such as letter recognition, directionality, punctuation, and sound–symbol correspondence (see also Bangert-Drowns, 1989; Rosengrant, 1988). Lomangino, Nicholson, and Sulzby (1999) have also documented how children begin to form connections cognitively among writing, print, and symbol making when using computers.

Word-Processing Programs

Cochran-Smith (1991) suggested that word processing programs allow children to engage in more sophisticated writing processes than when writing with paper and pencil. Children select from a variety of icons, letter stamps, music, and animations to negotiate and communicate meaning. Word processing with a computer helps students overcome difficulties of print production and facilitates physical manipulations and revision of text without rewriting or recopying text, tasks that are sometimes laborious and counterproductive for primary-grade children. Word processing with electronic tools increases the amount of children's metacognitive self-guiding talk, revisions, lexical density, and cohesiveness (e.g., Jones & Pellegrini, 1996).

Traditional literacy development is also fostered through a process approach to writing (Calkins, 1983; Graves, 1983) as children are encouraged to brainstorm, draft, revise, and publish their work. Preschoolers who playfully write with word processors exhibit an ability to brainstorm, collect thoughts, and generate ideas for a topic before writing (Lehr, Levin, Dehart, & Comeaux, 1987). Children who have access to revising tools tend to gain the insight that computer screens make print changeable and thus appropriate for revision. Students are freer to manipulate and refine text and ideas (Labbo & Kuhn, 1998). Notably, Kahn (1997) found that children who wrote with a computer shifted their focus from producing perfectly printed text to one of audience awareness (e.g., sharing information and focusing on a specific topic).

Research from a Semiotic Perspective

From a semiotic perspective, it is clear that many youngsters who cannot yet read and write conventionally are making good use of the informal tools of expression and accessible symbol systems they see on the computer screen to make meaning for various purposes. Symbol systems include various sets of communicative and culturally realized expressions (Eco, 1976, 1990; Gillan, 1982; Goodman, 1976; Lemke, 1993). Of the three foundational areas of semiotic language systems (semantics, pragmatics, and syntactics), semantics is the area that delves into the meanings of signs. Thus the focus is on exploring the meaning of gestures within a cultural context, words or sentences in various types of communications, paintings, and combinations across sign systems (Suhor, 1992). A semiotic perspective that focuses on learning that occurs when children create meaning on a computer screen provides insight into youngsters' development of schemata for literacy. Salomon (1970) notes the wide range of cognitive skills required in the production and reception of multimedia messages. For example, multimedia and creativity programs such as KidPix Studio Deluxe (Hickman, 1994) contain a hodgepodge of expressive tools that invite constructive exploration and constructivist Piagetian foundation (Piaget, 1962) for developmentally appropriate practice. Developmentally appropriate creativity programs allow youngsters to move freely between artistic tools (e.g., drawing pencil, clip art icons, paintbrush), word-processing tools (e.g., letter stamps, pencil writing, cutting, pasting, erasing, keyboard typing), and multimedia tools (e.g., sound effects, voice narration, animation, music, transitions).

Studying a classroom of children for an academic year, Labbo (1996) found that 5-year-olds adopted various stances toward their computer work. They focused on the computer screen as a location for accomplishing various types of work and play. Thus the metaphor of "screenland" was employed to describe the types of stances children took toward their computer interactions. Children approached the screen as a *stage* location for sociodramatic play by moving icons around, supplying role-playing dialogue, and engaging in retelling of favorite stories. At other times they approached the screen as a *playground* location for creating visual jokes, such as a child who collaborated with a peer to draw a picture of his sister and push an icon of an ice-cream cone up her nose—an action that was accompanied by much laughter and immediate erasure of the picture. Children also approached the screen as a *canvas* (using artistic tools and symbols to create drippy, painted-looking works of art) and as *paper* (using literacy/print tools to create lists, notes, get-well cards, stories, and reports).

It is worth noting that kindergarten children studied engaged in semiotic processes of depictive, transformative, and typographic symbol making. *Depictive symbolism* refers to a child's creation or selection of a graphic icon as a culturally recognizable sign that denotes established concepts or ideas. For example, a child pastes a stamp icon of a chair and states, "This is a chair and people sit on it." *Transformative symbolism* refers to the activity of selecting a graphic symbol as a placeholder for another graphic symbol or as a symbol from another symbol system (e.g., a child pastes a stamp of a shoe and says, "This is my spaceship"). This is similar to the motion of a child selecting a block from the block center and using it like a telephone receiver to make pretend calls. Typographic symbolism refers to the use of letters or special effects to represent ideas linguistically, or as an extension of speech. In these instances, a child types a string of letters such as *HKEROD48* and states, "I like to play with Juanito."

Relevant to the topic of this chapter is the intersection of young children's talk, symbols selected, computer tools, and operations carried out in the process of electronic symbol making. Indeed, rather than focusing on the development of any one of the literacy skills—listening, speaking, reading, writing—multimedia symbols converge on the computer screen in ways that foster all of the language arts and literacy skills simultaneously and symbiotically. In most instances, children orchestrate meaning making that is intended to be inter- or intrapersonal. Interpersonal symbol making is routinely depictive in the sense that it is intended to express meaning that is recognizable by others. Thus when one child wanted to entertain a peer in a playground scenario, he made a visually graphic joke that communicated pushing an ice-cream cone up a sibling's nose. The oral explanation and resulting laughter demonstrated that the shared meaning making was interpersonal. The resulting quick erasure demonstrated that both children understood the likelihood that the teacher would not sanction this type of joke in the classroom environment—a cultural index that was brought about when the teacher looked with disapproval at the eruption of off-task laughter from across the room. Intrapersonal meaning making, which occurred within the child through onscreen explorations, constructions, and verbalizations, did not have to signify in instantly recognizable ways to others. Thus it was acceptable to utilize a clip art icon of a shoe to represent a spaceship. No one else was socially engaged in making meaning, so an idiosyncratic symbol was acceptable.

Over the course of the year, young children began to seek a convergence of symbol systems that were intended to server inter- and intrapersonal purposes. For example, graphically *abstract symbolism* combined onscreen graphics with multimedia effects. In these instances, a child draws concentric circles that pulsate on screen, adds a sound effect of wooshing and states, "Spaceships go *wooooosssssshhhh* through space." When children showcased work that was graphically abstract, they took great care to explain what the abstract symbols meant. As such, other children who witnessed the explanation within the classroom routine of computer share time began to appropriate the same symbols in their own onscreen artwork, stories, or play. Children who generated graphically abstract symbolism began with an intrapersonal exploration of meaning making whereby computer tools and special effects served as thinking stimuli. When given further oral explanation in a social setting, the symbols became stable signs and accepted referents for meaning making that were adopted within the classroom culture.

Analysis of data related to children's electronic symbol making with KidPix Studio Deluxe (e.g., discourse while working at the computer center, videotapes of children's onscreen interactions, videotape and printouts of children's computer work through various stages of completion, and informal interviews) result in insights into conceptual knowledge 4- and 5-year-old children gain about electronic symbol making (Labbo, 1996) and notions of new or digital literacy. Young children learn:

- Computers have symbol-making tools that allow one to accomplish personal and public communicative goals.
- Computers allow one to retrieve completed or in-progress work.
- Computer screens are repositories of symbols and symbol-making tools.
- Computers are devices for composing, printing, and publishing.
- Computers are used to transact business.
- Computers are used for playing and creating art.
- Computers include symbols and signs that aid memory.
- Making meaning on a computer screen involves dependable action schemes (e.g., cutting, pasting, importing clip art).
- Computers offer a variety of multimedia and symbolic forms.
- Computers help one combine or select the appropriate symbol systems to meet specific communicative purposes. (Labbo & Kuhn, 1998)

Furthermore, it is clear that the computer screen displays features, tools, symbols, and symbol systems that converge in unique ways to support young children's development of meaning-making processes that employ all of the language arts. The computer serves as a thinking partner that scaffolds young children's intrapersonal meaning-making processes. When the classroom teacher allows children to share their computer work during a show-and-tell time, the process of meaning making becomes interpersonal as others appropriate and utilize symbols in their own work. Thus knowledge is generated and signs become adopted in ways that are meaningful within a classroom culture.

AN EXAMPLE: HOW A TEACHER HELPED KINDERGARTEN CHILDREN CULMINATE MEANINGS ACROSS DAILY TRAVERSALS

Digital cameras, classroom computers, and KidPix became the multimedia tools one classroom teacher used to help kindergarten students culminate meanings across daily traversals between home and school. To illustrate the teacher's traversing of literacies landscapes, we drew from Moll, Amanti, Neff, and Gonzales's (1992) concept of funds of knowledge. Moll and his colleagues noted the value of understanding, celebrating, and incorporating Latino families' areas of interest and expertise into the classroom curriculum. Thus teachers learned to celebrate, embrace, and include the talents of Latino households within the curriculum. Their work illustrates how to capitalize on children's complete resources and repertoires of cultural knowledge. We also drew from our own work on the Digital Language Experience Approach (D-LEA; Labbo, Eakle, & Montero, 2002; Labbo, Love, & Ryan, 2007) to sort out how to incorporate digital photography into literacy instruction. D-LEA is a computer-enhanced version of a traditional language experience approach (Stauffer, 1970). Language experiences—occasions for children to participate in and then dictate stories about classroom experiences—are enhanced when digital photographs are used to create a tangible record of the experience. For example, when teachers snap digital photos of students' activities, children have a visual resource that elicits rich oral language and serves as a memory link. In addition, multimedia features of creativity software, applications that include tools for drawing, selecting graphics, importing photographs, adding sound, utilizing speech synthesis, and writing on the same computer screen, offer unique support for young children's efforts to compose stories (Labbo, 1996; Lomangino et al., 1999).

It is also worth noting that teachers can use D-LEA to suit the literacy learning needs of students of various abilities. For example, some children will benefit if they serve as a photographer for their own experience (Turbill, 2003). In these instances, children determine the focus of their D-LEA project, take selected photographs, organize and compose their thoughts with creativity software (e.g., KidPix), presentation applications (e.g., PowerPoint), or word-processing programs (e.g., Microsoft Word). Thus teachers may adapt the procedures to meet the literacy learning needs of emerging, beginning, or fluent readers.

The teacher, Ms. Thomas (a psuedonym), participated in a 2-year project (see Allen, 2007) aimed to make connections between children's in- and out-of-school lives, the Photographs of Local Knowledge Sources (PhOLKS) group was funded with a small Spencer Foundation grant. Ms. Thomas invited her 5-year-old students to take one-use digital cameras home to photograph what was important to them in their homes and neighborhoods. She accomplished the project in four steps:

(1) preparation; (2) photography and writing; (3) learning from photographs; and (4) sharing the photograph essay stories.

Preparation

Ms. Thomas read aloud photographic essay books such as *My Painted House, My Friendly Chicken, and Me* (Angelou, 1994) and *Daddy and Me: A Photo Story of Arthur Ashe and His Daughter* (Moutoussamy-Ashe, 1993). Students talked about the role that photographs and narrative played together in telling the stories. Ms. Thomas also created a D-LEA with the children about daily routines. She took photographs of circle time, center time, lunchtime, recess, and so on. She imported the digital photographs into KidPix and invited different small groups of children to dictate sentences that explained the activities. The teacher then printed out hard copies of the book for the classroom library as well as copies to be sent home. Many of the discussions centered on the notion of visual literacy, that is, juxtaposing text with photographs on the screen in aesthetically pleasing and relevant ways.

Photography and Writing

At least three children took digital cameras home for 3 days at a time until all the children in class had had a turn. Each camera had the capacity for 27 photographs. Each child had permission to take nine photographs. Ms. Thomas invited parents to take photos of children doing household chores. As soon as the camera was filled, Ms. Thomas took them to a photo processor to have the images placed on a CD-ROM as well as printed out. Printed copies of the photographs were sent home with invitations to parents, caregivers, and children to provide narrative accounts, creating a photo essay of things they valued at home and in their neighborhoods. Parents wrote by describing what "they" saw in the photographs. They wrote memories, poetry, letters, and personal accounts (Allen et al., 2002). Family members proudly assembled their photographic essays into photo albums.

Learning from Photographs

Ms. Thomas and her teaching assistant, as well as other members of the project team, viewed and re-viewed the photo albums. One of the teachers in the group, Ms. Piha, voiced a sentiment shared by many of us: "It was like going from house to house. . . . I have a very wide range of children—economically, educationally, ethnically—and every single one of them has a very unique life, a very rich life outside of my class-room, and [sometimes] I forget that" (Allen et al., 2002, p. 315). Ms. Thomas noted that children had many responsibilities and accomplished many chores at home—more than they did at school. Ms. Thomas also learned that one at-risk student's mother didn't know how to help her son succeed at school: "I've learned that when parents ask, 'What can I do to help my child at school?' I need to have specific instructions and materials" (Allen et al., 2002, p. 318). Over time, lines of communica-tion were opened that resulted in a more positive academic experience for the child, the mother, and Ms. Thomas.

Sharing the Photo Essays

Children and their families came together at school for a photo- and story-sharing picnic. Families, many of whom had not actively partici-pated in school functions before, brought favorite foods, read each oth-er's albums, and shared personal stories. Kindergarten children, many of whom had been disenfranchised and friendless at school, found new identities as friends with other students. For example, one child who was a loner in class found connections and began relationships with other students who noticed that he had a bedspread with a popular cartoon character design. Other families took photographs and dis-cussed religious faith and practices. A few children took photographs of video gaming devices, televisions, CD players, and computers. Narra-tives explained how older siblings, aunts, or parents introduced young kindergarten-age children to technology and the role the technology played in their lives. Ms. Thomas noted that many children were com-puter literate and had funds of knowledge that needed to be acknowl-edged and nurtured in the classroom.

As Ms. Thomas delved more closely into and across the photo albums of her students' families, she noticed the various languages and dialects that were spoken at home. Music or religion frequently formed a basis for meaning making. Prayer times were family rituals in some families. Gathering around favored shows televised from Mexico were favorite events in other families. In all cases, families gathered and knit together experience stories that were uniquely expressed through digi-tal photos and text. Ms. Thomas transferred the photos to digital slide shows, accompanied by selected poems and narratives that captured the essence of family values and beliefs. Community and neighborhood strengths were filters between home and school. For example, a community center provided access to computers for one family—a space for writing e-mails and conducting Internet searches. Through these hands-on explorations and digital reflections, Ms. Thomas and her students were able to find semiotic traversals that celebrated and encouraged the types of literacies that occurred at home and at school.

FINAL THOUGHTS

Now that we are firmly moving through the 21st century, the time is ripe for delving into the complexities of young children's literacy development in electronic formats. At no other time in educational history have young children had access to communicative tools that are also used in the home and the workplace. The time has come for children's e-literacies to be recognized as e-funds of knowledge. By doing so, teachers who are interested in building on students' home cultural knowledge may be more open to inviting traversals between e-literacies at home and e-literacies at school. Unfortunately, when it comes to integrating computer technologies with literacy instruction, Cuban's (2001) observation about the use of new technologies in schools, and especially in the early grades, reflects a harsh reality:

> Where favorable conditions exist, teacher use will increase. . . . Where unfavorable conditions exist . . . schoolwide use will be spotty . . . I predict no great breakthrough in teacher use patterns [of computers] at either level of schooling. The new technology, like its predecessors, will be tailored to fit the teacher's perspective and the tight contours of school and classroom settings. (p. 9)

Researchers, educators, parents, policymakers, and other stakeholders who are interested in developmentally appropriate uses of computers in the early grades can overcome the tight contours of school and classroom settings and gain valuable insights by taking a semiotic perspective on the potential benefits of electronic symbol making. By doing so, they can support young children's development of traditional and conventional literacies and foster their ability to traverse the complexities of the current and future literacy landscape.

REFERENCES

Allen, J. (2007). *Creating welcoming schools: A practical guide to home–school partner-ships with diverse families.* New York: Teachers College Press.

Allen, J., Fabergas, V., Hankins, K., Hull, G., Labbo, L., Lawson, H., et al. (2002). PhOLKS lore: Learning from photographs, families, and children. *Language Arts, 79*(4), 312–322.

Bangert-Drowns, R. L. (1989). *Research on word processing and writing instruction.* Paper presented at the meeting of the American Educational Research Association, San Francisco.

Calkins, L. (1983). *Lessons from a child.* Portsmouth, NH: Heinemann.

Clarke, L. (1988). Encouraging invented spelling in first graders' writing: Effects of learning to spell and read. *Research in the Teaching of English, 22,* 281–309.

Clements, D. H. (1994). The uniqueness of the computer as a learning tool: Insights from research and practice. In J. L. Wright & D. D. Shade (Eds.), *Young children: Active learners in a technological age* (pp. 31–49). Washington, DC: National Association for the Education of Young Children.

Cochran-Smith, M. (1991). Word processing and writing in elementary class-rooms: A critical review of related literature. *Review of Educational Research, 61,* 107–155.

Crenshaw, S. R. (1985). *A semiotic look at kindergarten writing* (Tech. Rep. No. 143). Urbana: University of Illinois (ERIC Document Reproduction Service NO. ED 269 765).

Cuban, L. (2001). *Oversold and underused: Computers in the classroom.* Cambridge, MA: Harvard University Press.

Dyson, A. H. (1988). Learning to write/learning to do school: Emergent writers' interpretations of school literacy tasks. *Research in the Teaching of English, 18,* 233–264.

Dyson, A. H. (1991). Viewpoints: The word and the world—Reconceptualizing written language development or, do rainbows mean a lot to little girls? *Research in the Teaching of English, 25*(1), 97–123.

Eco, U. (1976). *A theory of semiotics.* Bloomington: Indiana University Press.

Eco, U. (1990). *The limits of interpretation.* Bloomington: Indiana University Press.

Gillan, G. (1982). *From sign to symbol.* Atlantic Highlands, NJ: Humanities Press.

Goldberg, K., & Sherwood, R. D. (1983). *Microcomputers: A parent's guide.* New York: Wiley.

Goodman, N. (1976). *Languages of art.* Indianapolis: Hackett.

Graves, D. (1983). *Writing: Teachers and children at work.* Portsmouth, NH: Heinemann.

Halliday, M. A. K. (1978). *Language as a social semiotic.* Baltimore: University Park Press.

Harste, J., Woodward, V. A., & Burke, C. L. (1984). *Language stories and literacy Lessons.* Portsmouth, NH: Heinemann.

Haughland, S. W. (1992). Effects of computer software on preschool children's developmental gains. *Journal of Computing in Childhood Education, 3,* 15–30.

Healy, J. (2000). Five commentaries: Looking to the future (Commentary 2). *Children and Computer Technology, 10,* 171–173. Retrieved July 15, 2005, from *www.futureofchildren.org.*

International Reading Association and National Association for the Education of Young Children. (1998). *Literacy development in the preschool years: A position statement of the international reading association.* Retrieved June 25, 2005, from *www.reading.org/resources/issues/positions_preschool.html.*

Jones, I., & Pelligrini, A. D. (1996). The effects of social relationships, writing media, and microgentic development on first-grade students' written narratives. *American Educational Research Journal, 33*(3), 691–718.

Kahn, J. (1997). Scaffolding in the classroom: Using CD-ROM storybooks at a computer reading center. *Learning and Leading with Technology, 25,* 17–19.

Kaiser Family Foundation. (2003, October). *Zero to six: Electronic media in the lives of infants, toddlers, and preschoolers.* Retrieved November, 8, 2006, from *www.kff.org/entmedia/3378.cfm.*

Labbo, L. D. (1996). A semiotic analysis of young children's symbol making in a classroom computer center. *Reading Research Quarterly, 27*(3), 185–201.

Labbo, L. D., Eakle, A. J., & Montero, K. M. (2002). Digital language experience approach (D-LEA): Using digital photographs and creativity software as LEA innovation. *Reading Online, Electronic Journal of the International Reading Association.* Retrieved July 15, 2009, from *www.readingonline.org/default.asp.*

Labbo, L. D., & Kuhn, M. (1998). Electronic symbol making: Young children's computer-related emerging concepts about literacy. In D. Reinking, M. C. McKenna, L. D. Labbo, & R. D. Kieffer (Eds.), *Handbook of literacy and technology: Transformations in a post-typographic world* (pp. 79–91). Mahwah, NJ: Erlbaum.

Labbo, L. D., Love, M. S., & Ryan, T. (2007). A vocabulary flood: Making words "sticky" with computer response activities. *The Reading Teacher, 60*(6), 582–588.

Lehr, R., Levin, B., Dehart, P., & Comeaux, M. (1987). Voice feedback as a scaffold for writing: A comparative study. *Journal of Educational Computing Research, 3,* 335–353.

Lemke, J. (1993, December). *Multiplying meaning: Literacy in a multimodal world.* Paper presented at the 43rd Annual Meeting of the National Reading Conference, Charleston, SC.

Lemke, J. (2004). Multiplying intelligences: Hypermedia and social semiotics. In J. L. Kincheloe (Ed.), *Multiple intelligences reconsidered* (pp. 177–200). New York: Peter Lang.

Leu D. J., Jr., & Kinzer, C. K. (2000). The convergence of literacy instruction with networked technologies for information, communication, and education. *Reading Research Quarterly, 35,* 108–127.

Leu D. J., Jr., & Kinzer, C. K. (2003). *Effective literacy instruction: Implementing best practice K–8* (5th ed.). Upper Saddle River, NJ: Merrill/Prentice Hall.

Lomangio, A. G., Nicholson, J., & Sulzby, E. (1999). *The nature of children's interactions while composing together on the computer* (CIERA Report NO. 2-005). Ann Arbor: Center for the Improvement of Early Reading Achievement, University of Michigan.

Moll, L., Amanti, D., Neff, D., & Gonzales, N. (1992). Funds of knowledge for teaching. *Theory into Practice, 31*(2), 132–141.

Neuman, S. B., & Celano, D. (2006, April/May/June). The knowledge gap: Implications of leveling the playing field for low-income and middle-income children. *Reading Research Quarterly, 41*(2), 176–201.

Office of Social and Economic Data Analysis. (2003, January). *Analysis of 2002 MAP results for eMINTS students.* Retrieved May 27, 2003, from *emints.more. net/evaluation/reports/map2002.pdf.*

Piaget, J. (1962). *Play, dreams, and imitation in childhood.* New York: Norton.

Reinking, D., McKenna, M. C., Labbo, L. D., & Kieffer, R. D. (Ed.). (1998). *Handbook of literacy and technology: Transformations in a post-typographic world.* Mahwah, NJ: Erlbaum.

Rosengrant, T. J. (1988). Talking word processors for the early grades. In J. L. Hoot & S. B. Silvern (Eds.), *Writing with computers in the early grades* (pp. 143–159). New York: Teachers College Press.

Rowe, D. W. (1994). *Preschoolers as authors: Literacy learning in the social world of the classroom.* Cresskill, NJ: Hampton Press.

Salomon, G. (1970). What does it do to Johnny? *Viewpoints: Bulletin of the School of Education, 46*(5), 33–62.

Salomon, G., Perkins, D. N., & Globerson, T. (1991). Partners in cognition: Extending human intelligence with intelligent technologies. *Educational Researcher, 20,* 2–9.

Schaar, J. (n.d.). Quotes by John Schaar. Retrieved June 15, 2008, from *quotes. zaadz.com/John_Schaar.*

Sedris Technologies. (2007). *Traversals.* Retrieved August 15, 2008, from *www. sedris.org/glossary.htm.*

Stauffer, R. G. (1970). *The language experience approach to the teaching of reading.* New York: Harper & Row.

Suhor, C. (1992). Semiotics and the English language arts. *Language Arts, 69,* 228–230.

Sulzby, E. (1989). Assessment of writing and children's language while writing. In L. M. Morrow & J. Smith (Eds.), *The role of assessment and measurement in early literacy instruction* (pp. 83–109). Englewood Cliffs, NJ: Prentice Hall.

Teale, W. H., & Sulzby, E. (1989). Emergent literacy: New perspectives. In D. S.

Strickland & L. M. Morrow (Eds.), *Emerging literacy: Young children learn to read and write* (pp. 1–15). Newark, DE: International Reading Association.

Turbill, J. (2003). Exploring the potential of digital language experience approach in Australian classrooms. *Reading Online, Electronic Journal of the International Reading Association, 6*(7). Retrieved June 6, 2009, from *www.readingonline.org/default.asp.*

U.S. Department of Education. (2003). *Young children's access to computers in the home and at school in 1999–2000* (NCES 2003-036). Washington, DC: National Center for Education Statistics.

U.S. Department of Education. (2004). *Computer and Internet Use by Children and Adolescents in 2001* (NCES 2004-014). Washington, DC: National Center for Education Statistics.

Vygotsky, L. (1978). *Mind in society: The development of higher psychological processes.* Cambridge, MA: Harvard University Press.

Wells, G. (1993). *The meaning makers: Children learning language and using language to mean.* Portsmouth, NH: Heinemann.

Wright, J. L., & Shade, D. D. (1994). *Young children: Active learners in a technological age.* Washington, DC: National Association for the Education of Young Children.

CHILDREN'S LITERATURE

Angelou, M. (1994). *My painted house, my friendly chicken, and me.* New York: Crown.

Moutoussamy-Ashe, J. (1993). *Daddy and me: A photo story of Arthur Ashe and his daughter.* New York: Knopf Books for Young Readers.

SOFTWARE

Hickman, C. (1994). *KidPix Studio Deluxe.* Novato, CA: Broderbund Software.

Microsoft PowerPoint [Computer software]. (2003). Redmond, WA: Microsoft Corporation.

Microsoft Word [Computer software]. (2003). Redmond, WA: Microsoft Corporation.

CHAPTER 6

Cognitive Processing Perspectives on the New Literacies

DIANE H. TRACEY
ALEX W. STORER
SOHROB KAZEROUNIAN

How do we perform complex mental tasks, such as reading the newspaper or browsing for information online? Specifically, how are words on a page or screen effortlessly transformed into rich internal representations? One approach to address such questions is to build theories and models of the various internal mental processes that are thought to be undertaken, and evaluate their ability to shine light on empirical data. These theories and models are known as cognitive processing frameworks, or perspectives, and are common in the fields of psychology and cognitive science to describe how mental tasks take place.

The present chapter examines how cognitive processing perspectives can inform our understanding of new literacies. We begin by clarifying our definition of new literacies and then articulate four categories of cognitive processing perspectives that can be used to deepen our understanding of them: narrative theories, box-and-pointer models, computational models, and cognitive neuroscience. In addition to reflecting on how each framework can be used to consider new literacies, we discuss their implications for research, instruction, and policy-making.

DEFINITION OF NEW LITERACIES

In attempting to elucidate the term *new literacies* scholars reflect on issues such as "What do we mean by *literacy?*" and "What do we mean by *new?*" (Coiro, Knobel, Lankshear, & Leu, 2008). In answering these questions we examine topics such as the nature of texts, technology, communication, comprehension, social practices, and culture. Writers in the area of new literacies agree that our schema for "literacy" must now be expanded beyond paper-and-pencil conceptualizations (Anstey, 2002; Asselin, 2004; Cervetti, Damica, & Pearson, 2006; Kist, 2000; Luke, 2000). Expansion of the definition is needed due to the nature of the new texts that individuals must navigate to function in the modern digital world, the new skills that are needed to negotiate and comprehend these texts, the social practices that accompany the use of new technologies, and the understanding that being literate is now a changing rather than a static state of being. We discuss each of these further below.

Expansion of our literacy schema is required due to the new texts that individuals must navigate to function in the modern world (McKenna, Reinking, Labbo, & Kieffer, 1999). In the 1970s and 1980s an understanding of literacy was expanded to include media and cultural texts (Brodsky, 2009). More recently, texts are electronic, digital, interactive, and changing (i.e., interactive websites can change moment by moment as information is added, deleted, responded to, and modified). New texts are heavily Internet based and include e-mail, instant messages, chatrooms, threaded discussions, and message boards. They are also image based and include digital photography, video, movies, social networking, and animated, virtual worlds. Thus to be literate in the modern digital world, one must develop familiarity with the scope, depth, structure, and organization of these new texts.

With new texts come the new skills that are needed to negotiate them (Castek, Bevans-Mangelson, & Goldstone, 2006). Navigation of the Internet is a prime example of such a skill set. Henry (2006) reported that effective users of the Internet must set a focused purpose for Internet searches, employ efficient search strategies, synthesize search-engine results, cite sources, and ethically use findings. In addition to Internet navigational skills, skills required for processing new texts include keyboarding, word processing, electronic image creation, electronic image manipulation, and animation capabilities. Thus the new skills needed to negotiate electronic and digital texts become part of our expanded schema of literacy.

Our schema for literacy is further extended when one considers the social practices in which individuals engage when they use the new technologies (Anstey, 2002). Just one generation ago there were no social practices of cell phone use, e-mailing, texting, Listserv participation, Facebook, Twittering, Skypeing, or global positioning systems. New technologies now allow individuals to track the location of, and have almost unlimited visual and auditory contact with, others throughout most parts of the world and many parts of the solar system. Furthermore, through the Internet, users also have almost instantaneous access to endless bases of knowledge. In addition to changing personal social practices, new technologies have changed the social practices inherent in business, politics, media, and interactions of the global community. These new social practices all include new ways of communicating and therefore new ways of being literate, further stretching our past notions of what being literate means.

Finally, expansion of our literacy schema is required to integrate the understanding that new literacies evolve as new technologies evolve (Leu, Kinzer, Coiro, & Cammack, 2004). For hundreds of years the definition of what it has meant to be literate has not significantly changed: if one could read and write paper-based text one was considered literate. From this point forward, however, what it means to be literate may be a rapidly changing phenomenon, as individuals will have to master new and ever-changing technologies in order to stay literate. In the future it may be that individuals are schooled and evaluated both in terms of their capabilities in traditional paper-and-pencil literacies as well as in their capabilities in the constantly evolving world of new literacies. It is even possible to conceive of a future in which all paper-and-pencil literacies are replaced by digital literacies.

Integrating the thoughts of those above, our conclusion of the definition of new literacies is consistent with that succinctly put forth by Leu et al. (2004):

> New literacies of the Internet and other ICT's [information and communication technologies] include the skills, strategies, and dispositions necessary to successfully use and adapt to the rapidly changing information

and communication technologies and contexts that continuously emerge in our world and influence all areas of our personal and professional lives. These new literacies allow us to use the Internet and other ICTs to identify important questions, locate information, critically evaluate the usefulness of that information, synthesize information to answer those questions, and then communicate the answers to others. (p. 1572)

WHAT ARE COGNITIVE PROCESSING PERSPECTIVES?

As stated above, cognitive processing frameworks attempt to explain the internal workings of the mind as individuals engage in complex mental activities. Models of cognition are often general enough to be applied across domains, so that the same frameworks which help explain how we find information in a book or remember a phone number can be adapted to how we find information on a website or remember a URL. While cognitive scientists often focus their attention on how to explain a specific complex process, such as reading, the true goal of the field is to understand how complex tasks in general are learned and mastered, using the same underlying mechanisms. However, no theory or model of cognitive processing is complex enough to account for all of the subtleties of a cognitive process. Moreover, theorizing and modeling of cognitive processes may take place at many levels of detail in order to address varied aspects of the process at hand (Unrau & Ruddell, 2004).

Because new literacies are not as well defined or well established as traditional cognitive tasks, there are very few cognitive theories developed specifically to explain them. Regardless of the scope of models or the generality of the new cognitive tasks that are constantly being developed, cognitive processing frameworks provide a general tool for understanding the mental components of new literacies. By studying this aspect of higher-order cognitive tasks, we can gain insight into what general cognitive skills are needed for new literacies, what deficits might be expected, and how they may be addressed through educational, research, and policy initiatives.

Narrative Descriptions of Cognitive Processing

The simplest cognitive processing frameworks are *narrative descriptions*. These theories hypothesize about cognitive processes in a narrative form but do not attempt to create graphic depictions, computer simulations, or models of neural correlates of cognition. Historically, the earliest and most predominant theories of traditional literacy have been narrative in nature (Tracey & Morrow, 2006). The foremost reason for the historic popularity of narrative models is that only in the past few decades have researchers had the technological capabilities to begin to consider the process of reading from computational and neuroimaging perspectives. In addition, narrative models are popular because there is no expectation that theorists will create computer simulations or neuroimaging data to support their hypotheses. The absence of the constraints to produce computational simulations or neural evidence to support hypotheses frees theorists to contemplate the cognitive processing of literacy in an almost unbounded manner, a highly appealing position from which to work.

Examples of narrative cognitive processing theories of traditional literacy are the classic viewpoints of reading as either a *top-down* or *bottom-up* process. As is likely well known to our anticipated audience, top-down theorists (Goodman, 1967; Smith, 1971) argued that the reading experience is largely driven by readers' internal knowledge bases of language and content, while bottom-up theorists (Gough, 1972) perceived the reading experience as largely print driven. In accordance with these positions, top-down theorists argued that better readers were less reliant than poorer readers on print input and more reliant on context clues based on background knowledge because of their superior, top-down processing. However, in a series of brilliantly designed studies (e.g., West & Stanovich, 1978), it was determined that poorer, rather than better, readers made greater use of context cues during reading (Stanovich, 2000). This finding led to Stanovich's (1980) interactive–compensatory model of individual differences, another extremely valuable narrative cognitive processing theory that explained that poorer readers compensate for their weak decoding skills through an unusually heavy reliance on background and contextual knowledge. Thus, through their narrative descriptions, the researchers above contributed testable theories regarding cognition during reading.

The work of Zhang (1997), Dragsted (2006), and Liu and Bera (2005) represent cognitive researchers who have offered narrative theoretical concepts that can be useful in understanding the processing of new literacies. Zhang (1997) was instrumental in providing a framework for considering the relationships between external events and the workings of the internal mind. Liu and Bera (2005, p. 7) write, "According to Zhang (1997), external representations are the knowledge and structure in the environment, while internal representations are the knowledge and structure in memory." Together, the external information provided to the student and the student's internal representation of a problem create a distributed cognitive task (Zhang & Norman, 1994). Therefore Zhang (1997, p. 180) concluded, "External representations are not simply inputs and stimuli to the internal mind; rather they are so intrinsic to many cognitive tasks that they guide, constrain, and even determine cognitive behavior" (as cited in Dragsted, 2006).

Building on the belief of the critical importance of the external environment to shape the internal workings of the mind, Lajoie (1993) theorized that design features of instructional software could actually be considered *cognitive tools* (Jonassen, 1996; Kommers, Jonassen, & Mayes, 1992), scaffolds that support and/or enhance learners' abilities to think, learn, and problem solve (Liu & Bera, 2005). Lajoie identified four types of cognitive tools available through hypermedia: (1) those that support cognitive and metacognitive function in a general way; (2) those that carry a portion of the cognitive load (e.g., supplementing short-term or long-term memory); (3) those that allow learners to access types of thinking, reasoning, or problem solving that would otherwise be beyond their capabilities; and (4) those that assist learners in generating and testing hypotheses (Liu & Bera, 2005).

Liu and Bera (2005) applied Lajoie's categories in an investigation of how cognitive tools provided in hypermedia application were used by sixth graders for problem solving. They also sought to determine whether the tools were differentially used by high- and low-performing students. In their work, 110 sixth graders of varying abilities participated in a 3-week study during which the hypermedia application Alien Rescue (Liu, Williams, & Pederson, 2002) was used as the science curriculum. Designed to build students' problem-solving abilities, Alien Rescue presents six alien species that have arrived on Earth due to explosions on their planets. Each of the species has different requirements to sustain life and, using a set of 13 "cognitive tools" built into the software, the students' task is to locate optimal housing for each of the species. The cognitive tools are grouped according to Lajoie's four categories. For example, databases were available as tools that share a cognitive overload, video clips of expert scientists explaining how they would solve aspects of the problem were available to support general cognitive functioning, tools to virtually create scientific equipment were available to support "otherwise out-of-reach cognitive activities," and resources for compiling and analyzing data were available to support hypothesis testing. Features of the software allowed the researchers to track which cognitive tool each student used as he/she moved through the five stages of problem solving (exploration, research, hypothesis generation, hypothesis testing, and solution generation). The software also tracked how much time each student spent using a specific cognitive tool during the problem-solving stages. Data were analyzed in three ways. First, descriptive analyses captured the frequency and duration of cognitive tool use. Second, cluster analysis allowed for a determination of which cognitive tools were associated with varying stages of problem solving. Third, multivariate analysis of variance permitted the researchers to compare the cognitive use of high- and low-performing students.

Results of the Liu and Bera investigation revealed that the use of tools associated with supporting and sharing the load of cognitive functioning were typically seen earlier in the problem-solving activities while tools associated with "otherwise-out-of-reach cognitive activities" and hypothesis testing were associated with the latter stages of problem solving. The researchers were also able to illustrate that the higher-ability students were able to use the cognitive tools more effectively and efficiently than the lower-ability students.

By investigating the cognitive tasks underlying problem solving in a hypermedia environment, Liu and Bera were able to empirically shine light on not only the specific problem of Alien Rescue, but on effective problem-solving strategies in general. Like the contributions of the classic "bottom-up" and "top-down" theorists, this work exemplifies a narrative perspective of the cognitive processing because testable hypotheses were created based on narrative descriptions of presumed cognitive behaviors; in this case the cognitive behaviors were those of students engaged in new literacies. For similar reasons, the work of Hartman, Morsink, and Zheng, presented in Chapter 7 of this text, also provides valuable contributions to a narrative perspective of the cognitive processing of new literacies.

Box-and-Pointer Models of Cognitive Processing

In contrast to narrative descriptions of cognition processing, *box-and-pointer models* present diagrams or flowcharts designed to differentiate between types of processing and/or processors within the brain and are therefore valuable for visualizing cognitive processing. Like narrative descriptions, box-and-pointer models share the unbounded advantage of not requiring computer architecture or neuroimaging data to support their positions, and are further strengthened by the addition of a graphic organizer. Also like narrative theories, these perspectives can yield inferential explanations for biological phenomena.

The dual-route theory (Coltheart, Rastle, Perry, Langdon, & Ziegler, 2001) is an example of a box-and-pointer model of traditional reading (see Figure 6.1). It is also important to note that this model has been fully developed into a computational model (see next subheading below). The theory's intuitive appeal and ability to explain a variety of data have made it one of the more popular box-and-pointer models of reading. The primary feature of the dual-route theory is that there exist two primary routes to word identification. The first mechanism, known as the *lexical* route, involves a look-up procedure wherein readers presented with familiar words simply access a mental lexicon in which each entry has an associated speech sound representation. The second mechanism, known as the *nonlexical* (or grapheme-to-phoneme correspondence) route, involves a process by which graphemes are converted to phonemes on an individual basis. In the absence of an entry in the mental lexicon (e.g., in the case of novel words or pseudowords), a

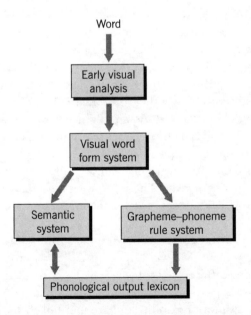

FIGURE 6.1. Box-and-pointer model of the dual-route cascaded theory. From Jobard, Crivello, and Tzourio-Mazoyer (2003). Copyright 2003 by Elsevier. Reprinted by permission.

reader can rely on this second route in order to correctly identify unfamiliar words.

Given the broad range of tasks and goals inherent in new literacies, box-and-pointer models of cognitive processing provide an adequate level of description from which more detailed computational models (described below) may later emerge. There are, however, fundamental differences between the challenges facing models of new literacies versus traditional characterization of reading. Models that explain new literacies must be created that strive to explain particular tasks in sufficiently well-constrained environments. Wilson's (1997) model of information-seeking behavior is one such example that has a simple and natural extension to new literacies (see Figure 6.2).

The model of information-seeking behavior shown here was used by Ford, Miller, and Moss (2005) to explore individual differences in Web search strategies. As mentioned earlier, the ability to efficiently employ search strategies, as well as filter and synthesize the wealth of results any given search may produce, is intricately linked with how we define new literacies. Acknowledging the myriad techniques used in Web search, Ford et al.'s study attempted to determine whether there were any consistent relationships between underlying cognitive variables vis-à-vis Wilson's model and particular Internet search strategies.

The various cognitive variables measured individuals as "wholist/ analytic" and "verbalizer/imager," as well as preferences for cognitive complexity. Citing Riding and Cheema (1991), the wholist/analytic dimension distinguished whether an individual tends to process information in wholes or parts, and the verbal/imagery dimension measured whether an individual is inclined to represent information verbally or in images. The cognitive complexity variable attempted to determine subjects' preference for thinking of problems to solutions as being "black or white" versus "shades of gray." These variables were then correlated with the degree to which subjects used Boolean versus best-match search strategies.

Using a series of regression analyses, the authors were able to obtain statistically significant evidence supporting the notion that Web-based search strategies differed for subjects on the basis of their individual cognitive styles. In particular, they found that subjects rated as wholists, who tend to show more flexibility and are more likely to readily change their minds, adapted their search strategies as the complexity of the search task varied. Specifically, on low-complexity tasks wholists tended to use both Boolean as well as best-match searches, shifting toward

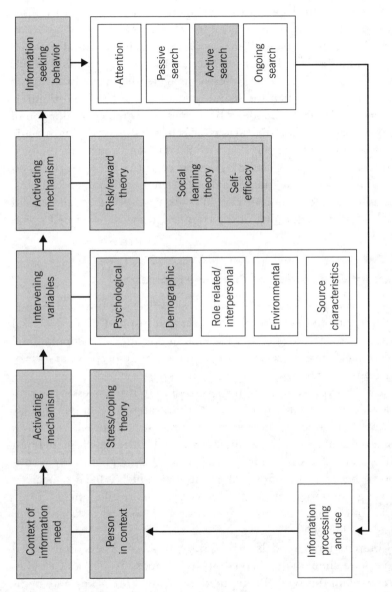

FIGURE 6.2. Wilson's model of information seeking behavior. From Wilson (1997). Copyright 1997 by Elsevier. Reprinted by permission.

Boolean search as the task complexity increased. Analytics on the other hand, who tend to be better at providing their own structure in intellectual activity and display a greater degree of rigidity than wholists, more consistently relied on Boolean search across all levels of task complexity. Along the verbalizer/imager dimension, it was found that verbalizers (who display a higher degree of verbal fluency) tended to rely more on best-match searches, whereas imagers were more likely to use Boolean search, in which the search structure is less reliant on purely verbal means. While the model is by no means a complete evaluation of all the factors that underlie various search styles, formulating specific hypotheses about the various stages involved in search behavior enabled researchers to begin to identify relevant cognitive variables. Furthermore, while this model is not formal in any computational sense, it illustrates how box-and-pointer models of cognitive processing can be used increase our understanding of the cognitive dimensions of new literacies.

Computational Models of Cognitive Processing

Computational models strive to quantitatively reflect cognitive processing. Details of computational frameworks may be inspired by, or designed to mimic, actual biological systems. The importance of computational models of cognitive processing is that they begin to specify what sorts of predictions can be made regarding human performance on any particular task. A correct computational model of cognitive processes can provide a wide array of quantitative predictions ranging from how quickly letters are perceived to when word meanings are identified. Variations of computational models are often compared to see which model best predicts and reflects actual human behavior. Using quantitative results to choose between alternative computational models is likely to become increasingly important as we attempt to create more and more accurate theories of cognitive processes associated with specific tasks and skills such as new literacies.

Computational models of cognitive processing are often based on computer simulations. Berersdorf, Narayanan, Hillier, and Hughes (2007) explain this type of computational framework. They state many researchers

> attempt to model neural and cognitive functioning, typically by running
> computer simulations of groups of neurons, synaptic connections, and

changes in synaptic strength due to learning (Cohen, 1994; Rumelhart & McClelland, 1986). Artificial groups of neurons (or nodes) are typically organized in interconnecting layers, commonly three types (input layer, interconnecting layers, output layer), and each interconnection between layers has an associated "weight" which can be adjusted to produce the desired output. The network is "trained" through numerous presentations of the data with feedback resulting in adjustments to weights until it computes the desired output at its output layer. (p. 1041)

One class of computational models used to describe traditional reading comes under the parallel distributed processing (PDP) framework. Unlike the dual-route theory described earlier, PDP models of reading propose a single word-identification route through which reading occurs. Although there are a number of PDP models of reading (Plaut, McClelland, Seidenberg, & Patterson, 1996; Seidenberg & McClellend, 1989; Sejnowski & Rosenberg, 1986) we briefly consider the basic computer architecture of the model presented by Seidenberg and McClelland (for a detailed critique of and computational alternative to the PDP models of word reading, see Grossberg [1984]).

In general, PDP models are structured in three layers: the first layer contains orthographic representations (the input), and the third layer contains phonological representations (the output). The layer between the two is composed of what are known as *hidden units*, which have been shown to be necessary in these types of models in order to "learn" complex relationships between input and output. Furthermore, it has been suggested that additional modules can help (or at least alter) processing in a variety of ways; for example, a syntactic or semantic module might affect the speed and ability of a model to convert a visual input (e.g., words or letter strings) into a phonological output.

Also referred to as *connectionist models* designed to reflect human neural networks, PDP models attempt to simulate how complex behavior can emerge from a network of interconnected computer-based processing units. One of the distinguishing features that make the PDP models popular is the "learning" rule (Rumelhart, Hinton, & Williams, 1986; Werbos, 1974), which enables multilayer networks of computer architecture to "learn" and generalize from past experience while simultaneously minimizing future errors. This is accomplished by allowing a model to begin with randomly selected connection weights. When presented with an input, the model will subsequently make a "prediction" about the output (i.e., given that connection weights are random at first, the model simply predicts a random output in response to any given input). The model is then given the actual output that should have been predicted, from which it goes back and changes the connection strengths between nodes such that the next time it is presented with a similar input, it will be more likely to predict the correct output.

The PDP models differ from the dual-route theories in that they show that the complex mappings between visual input and phonological output need not require two word-identification routes. The three-layer architecture coupled with the learning law allows these models to "learn" the nonlinear relationship between written and spoken word forms and can explain how familiar words can be spoken more quickly and more reliably than unfamiliar words. That is, by virtue of repeated presentations of familiar words, the connection strengths between nodes in the model are increased such that processing time is decreased, and the reliability of the output is increased. (The common saying in the neuroscience community regarding this type of learning comes to mind: "Neurons that fire together, wire together.") It is in these ways that computational models strive to replicate cognitive functioning during a variety of tasks.

While it is difficult to propose specific computational models of cognitive processes in domains as varied as new literacies, one framework that has gained a popular following is known as the "adaptive character of thought" (ACT). Initially proposed by Anderson (1976) following his work on human memory, much of the popularity of this framework stems from the fact that it has been implemented in various computer languages, with modularity and ease of use in mind.

The underlying structure for the representation of knowledge in ACT relies on a distinction between declarative and procedural knowledge. As described by Anderson and Lebiere (1998),

> Declarative knowledge corresponds to things we are aware we know and can usually describe to others. Examples of declarative knowledge include "George Washington was the first president of the United States" and "Three plus four is seven." Procedural knowledge is knowledge that we display in our behavior but we are not conscious of. Procedural knowledge basically specifies how to bring declarative knowledge to bear in solving problems. (p. 5)

In computational implementations of ACT, declarative knowledge is represented in structures known as "chunks" and procedural knowledge in production rules, which together constitute the building blocks of any computer model built within the ACT framework. In addition to the modules that make ACT capable of representing knowledge, there exist perceptual and motor modules that allow an ACT model to interact with its (virtual) environment. These interacting components allow the ACT framework to simulate a large variety of data regarding psychological, behavioral, and cognitive human performance.

Moreover, the ACT framework has been used to simulate various models of the skills required by new literacies. One interesting example was presented by Pirolli and Card (1999). Known as information foraging theory (ACT-IF), the model used the ACT framework to simulate information gathering and sense making as cognitive processes analogous to models of food-foraging strategies drawn from an evolutionary ecological perspective. While such a model may initially seem far-fetched, both information gathering and food gathering can be analyzed according to the "resource currency" returned (e.g., the salience of a website or the calories in newly discovered food), and costs incurred. The latter can be further broken down into resource costs (e.g., expenditure of calories, or money) and opportunity costs (e.g., the benefits that could be gained by engaging in other activities). Framed in this manner, the similarities between electronic information searching and food foraging become clearer.

In the computer simulation itself, the ACT-IF model was presented with a large collection of full-text documents stored in a system called scatter–gather (see Figure 6.3). This system clustered documents according to category tags, upon which selection (gathering) of any cluster would create a new subcollection that could itself then be clustered into a new set of categories.

This organizational scheme of the scatter–gather system is itself highly conducive to comparison with food-foraging strategies. Pirolli and Card offered the example of a bird foraging for berries found in patches of berry bushes. Some amount of time is spent between patches during the search process. Upon selection of any patch, as the bird forages within this patch the amount of food diminishes. There is a point at which the expected future gains from the current patch decrease to a value less than the expected future gains of leaving the patch in search of a new one. Similarly, in the scatter–gather system shown above, there is time spent moving between patches (or categories), while foraging within any particular patch results in diminishing returns as the information in the selected patch is "used up."

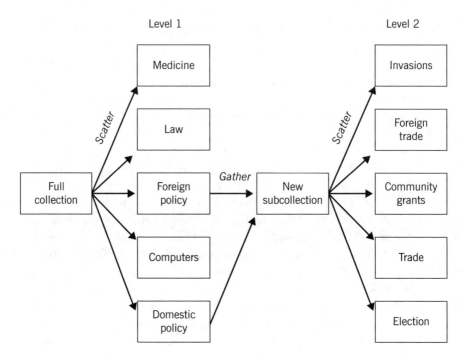

FIGURE 6.3. Scatter–gather interaction process. From Pirolli and Card (1999). Copyright 1999 by the American Psychological Association.

The organizational structure of the document database used in the search task in this study was itself quite similar to many emerging aspects of informational organization on the Internet. For example, on many news sites and blogs, information is increasingly tagged with relevant category labels. Furthermore, on sites like Wikipedia entries are often organized not only with links to relevant articles, but also with links leading to superset or subset categories. The computational model presented in the Pirolli and Card paper attempted to describe how a subject traverses these hierarchically linked resources, and how much time is spent within each cluster before deciding to move on. By showing that the ACT-IF computer simulation's cluster choices were significantly correlated with students performing the same search task, the authors argued that information-seeking behavior is similar to other evolutionary cognitive tasks associated with searching, such as searching for food. Aside from being an interesting finding in its own right, the link between information-foraging and food-foraging strategies can begin to inform optimal design strategies for informational organization, and to diagnose inefficient or suboptimal strategies of searching for information on the Internet. It is important to note that such a link could only be shown through computational simulation of information foraging. Whereas other models (narrative, box-and-pointer, etc.) may have suggested such a link, only computer simulations could rigorously show that not only is a model's behavior similar to human performance, but that the model itself is structurally and functionally equivalent to models of foraging behavior in other domains.

Neuroscience Perspectives of Cognitive Processing

While cognitive scientists create narrative descriptions, box-and-pointer models, computational algorithms, and computer simulations regarding how they believe cognitive processing occurs, neuroscientists are concerned with understanding the biological function of the brain and the nervous system. *Cognitive neuroscience* refers to the intersection of these fields, in which the study of the brain is utilized to understand specific cognitive functions, such as reading. Cognitive neuroscientists strive to draw connections between the brain processes that underlie certain cognitive processes, and build models that account for this diversity of brain function. Many cognitive neuroscientists study how brain areas are utilized during certain tasks, how they interact with each other, and how deficits in these areas can affect cognitive function. The primary tool in the hands of cognitive neuroscientists is neuroimaging, which enables a view into the structure and function of the brain. Although there are many diverse neuroimaging modalities, none are so detailed as to enable the study of single neurons, or even groups of neurons. Neuroimaging can, however, capture brain activation during complex cognitive functioning and is therefore a useful tool in the study of many cognitive processes.

Magnetic resonance imaging (MRI) is an increasingly common technique to obtain full three-dimensional images of biological structures, such as the brain. By placing a person in a very strong magnetic field, the spin of atomic particles aligns with the magnetic field and it is possible to apply a second magnetic field and measure the perturbations of the different atoms as they return to rest. Because different tissues contain different ratios of these atomic structures, it is further possible to generate an image of this tissue content. After brain injury, MRI is a common technique used to identify where the brain is damaged.

Functional MRI (fMRI) refers to picking the magnetic field parameters and perturbations such that instead of observing tissue differences, it is possible to image the amount of oxygen in the blood. This blood-oxygen-level-dependent (BOLD) signal is thought to be associated with neural activity, although the details of this association comprise an area of active research. While fMRI allows a three-dimensional picture of brain function in a noninvasive manner, it is very expensive, very loud, requires subjects to be very still, and cannot be used with any metal parts (due to the magnetic field). Furthermore, it cannot address changes in brain function that occur faster than 1 or 2 seconds.

Other neuroimaging techniques may be used to obtain more precise timing of neural activation. For example, electroencephalography (EEG) uses electrodes on the scalp to measure changes in electrical activity in the brain. Similarly, magnetoencephalography (MEG) uses coils arranged to cover the head surface to measure magnetic field changes associated with neural activity. Neither EEG nor MEG has excellent spatial resolution, but both can be combined with MRI to better infer the location of neural signals.

Cognitive neuroscientists who study reading often use fMRI or other neuroimaging techniques to look for the neural correlates of each aspect of the models of reading to assess and refine our picture of how reading takes place. Hundreds of studies have been published that examine the neural correlates of traditional reading (for reviews see Goswami, 2004; Schlaggar & McCandliss, 2007; Shaywitz, Morris, & Shaywitz, 2008; Wolf, 2007). Goswami (2004) summarized many studies that describe brain activity during literacy activities, such as the bias toward the left hemisphere during reading, and Pugh et al. (2001) summarized the general brain regions responsible for print processing. Furthermore, connecting the psychological models of cognition with their neural correlates is necessary for a deep understanding of how reading ability develops in both normal and struggling readers (Schlaggar & McCandliss, 2007). While neuroimaging is a powerful tool, present methods are unable to distinguish between brain regions that are very close to each other. Thus while it is easy to determine, generally, which brain regions are active during reading, it is much more challenging to find the distinct neural correlates that underlie specific reading skills.

Many neuroscience studies have been undertaken to determine the neural correlates of dyslexia, which can not only help illuminate this disorder, but can also inform models of reading (Wolf, 2007). For example, Simos et al. (2002) studied the neural correlates of dyslexia and the neural effects of an instructional intervention. Simos and colleagues identified eight children with dyslexia, as defined by extensive phonological and decoding problems. These children were asked to identify whether visually presented sets of two pseudowords rhymed, while undergoing MEG to measure brain activity. During the pretest of this task, dyslexic subjects showed reduced activation in the left superior temporal gyrus, an area associated with the conversion of print to speech, as compared with nonimpaired control subjects. After 2 months of intensive phonological reading intervention, however, dyslexic subjects displayed not only dramatically increased reading ability, but also increased activity in the left superior temporal gyrus. This research demonstrates that neuroimaging can be used to identify both the neural correlates of deficits in reading and the degree to which intervention may have succeeded. Furthermore, it demonstrates that intervention generally may yield changes in brain circuitry that underlie reading performance. It also provides insights into the localization of specific cognitive processes and evidence that these changes in brain circuitry can be realized in a short period of time. Although the effects of instructional interventions can be measured in many ways, only neuroimaging allows researchers to directly view biological changes within the brain that are associated with or result from (depending on the research design of the project) specific instructional interventions.

As suggested above, neuroimaging and cognitive neuroscience can provide a state-of-the-art approach to studying new literacies. One such investigation was undertaken by Small, Moody, Siddarth, and Bookheimer (2009) to identify the neural correlates of Internet use in both Web-experienced and Web-naïve geriatric populations. The researchers used fMRI to obtain measurements of brain activity during either a simulated book reading task or a simulated Internet search task. One challenge facing Small and his colleagues was finding a way to represent the experience of reading a book or viewing the Web inside a MRI scanner. As mentioned previously, MRI scanners are very loud and require that a subject be perfectly still while lying inside a small tube. Furthermore, no metal may be present within the scanner, so visual information must be presented through a projector and a series of mirrors, and communication with experimenters is achieved through use of a series of plastic buttons. In the Small et al. study, simulated books were presented by displaying a table of contents, sections of which could be presented by pressing a plastic button. The selected section was displayed as text within a schematic of a page within a book.

Simulated Internet sites were presented by displaying a Web search in a Web browser, and allowing subjects to press a button to "click" on one of three pages. Following this, the selected page was displayed as a website. In both conditions, identical content (text and images) was presented; the only difference was the "book" formatting versus the "Web" formatting.

Small et al. (2009) discovered that experienced Internet users had different patterns of brain activation while viewing the simulated Web pages as compared to the simulated book pages; when viewing the Web pages increased activity in multiple brain regions was observed. In contrast, Web-naïve subjects had similar patterns of activation in both conditions. The researchers use this difference to suggest that naïve Web users treated the Internet as though it were merely a traditional text, while experienced Web users used their prior knowledge of Internet searching to modify their reading behaviors, resulting in visible differences in cortical activity. The additional brain areas activated by the experienced Web users during the reading of simulated Web pages included prefrontal networks commonly associated with decision making, temporal areas associated with visual processing, and hippocampal areas associated with memory. These results indicate that hypermedia, and in particular Internet searches, may elicit many more cognitive processes than reading traditional text, even when identical content is presented.

COGNITIVE PROCESSING PERSPECTIVES ON NEW LITERACIES: IMPLICATIONS FOR RESEARCH, INSTRUCTION, AND POLICYMAKING

Thus far, we have discussed four categories of cognitive processing perspectives that can be used to consider new literacies: narrative descriptions, box-and-pointer models, computational models (often presented through computer simulations), and neuroscience. Each of these categories contains multiple specific theories, of which we have shared representative examples. More specifically, within the category of narrative descriptions we presented the cognitive processing frameworks of bottom-up (Gough, 1972), top-down (Goodman, 1967; Smith, 1971), compensatory-interactive (Stanovich, 1980), and distributed cognition (Zhang, 1997). As examples of box-and-pointer models we discussed the dual-route theory (Coltheart et al., 2001) and Wilson's model of information seeking behavior (Wilson, 1997). Within the context of computational models we articulated the PDP model (Plaut et al., 1996; Seidenberg & McClellend, 1989; Sejnowski & Rosenberg, 1986), the ACT model (Anderson & Lebiere, 1998) and its derivation, the ACT-IF model (Pirolli & Card, 1999). Within neuroscience we shared several imaging techniques that are used to capture cognitive activities, and examples of how such data can be studied to test research hypotheses and evaluate the impact of instructional interventions (Schlaggar & McCardliss, 2007).

By definition, all theories and models, including cognitive processing frameworks, are explanations that attempt to predict and explain phenomena. As stated at the beginning of this chapter, the more accurately cognitive processing theories and models can predict and explain human behavior, as determined by the relationship between a model's predictions and actual collected data, the more accurate the theory or model is judged to be. Thus, ideally, there is a dynamic relationship between the building of theories and models and the research through which they are created, tested, supported, refuted, and/or modified. Furthermore, ideally, theories and models for which there is strong empirical support are used to shape instructional interventions and educational policy. Therefore, as is the case in all fields of academic inquiry, research within new literacies should be first and foremost designed to test theories and models. *More specifically, the primary goal of cognitive processing research in new literacies should be to determine which theories and models within each of the four presented categories most accurately represent human cognition when engaged with new literacies.* As articulated earlier, because new literacies encompass multiple forms of texts, multiple skills, multiple social practices, and are constantly evolving, determining which cognitive processing theories most accurately represent cognition in these areas is a major undertaking. Researchers who strive to make meaningful contributions to the development of cognitive processing perspectives related to new literacies are urged to systematically address the topic in one of two ways. Either the predictive and explanatory value of a single cognitive processing framework (e.g., a PDP model) should be examined in relation to a wide variety of new literacies such as different types of texts, skills, and social practices, *or* a single new literacy (e.g., navigation of the Internet) should be examined from multiple cognitive processing theories to see the relative predictive and explanatory value of each. It is only through thoughtful, well-informed, and systematic research that recognizes the dynamic relationship between research and theory that accurate depictions of cognitive processing during new literacies can be constructed.

Cognitive processing perspectives hold much potential for the instruction of new literacies. A few examples of the ways in which cognitive processing perspectives have informed traditional reading instruction help clarify this position (for additional information on this see Tracey & Morrow, 2006). The historically early cognitive processing perspective of schema theory (Anderson & Pearson, 1984; Bartlett, 1932) led to the effective instructional practice of building background knowledge through activities such as brainstorming and semantic mapping. LaBerge and Samuel's (1974) automatic information-processing model articulated the concept of limited cognitive attention, which then led to the understanding that if readers have to allocate too much internal attention to decoding there will not be adequate remaining cognitive resources for comprehension. This led to the effective instructional practice of providing readers with texts that are on their correct instructional levels so as to increase the level of comprehension. PDP models (Plaut et al., 1996; Rumelhart & McClelland, 1986; Seidenberg & McClellend, 1989) yielded knowledge regarding the relationships between letters within words (Adams, 1990), and the subsequent effective instructional practices of teaching word families.

Similarly, cognitive processing frameworks are beginning to inform the instruction of new literacies. For example, the cognitive processing concept of distributed cognition (Zhang, 1997) helps educators consider the relationship between the external stimuli inherent in electronic texts and the internal resources needed to process such texts. Examination of the ACT-IF model suggests ways in which instruction of Internet navigation can be optimally structured. Data collected from neuroimaging are promising for a future in which the effects of instructional interventions can be evaluated by direct, observable measures of biological change. A comprehensive examination of how cognitive processing perspectives can inform educational initiatives in new literacies would require that every theory and model within the four presented categories (narrative, box and pointer, computational, and neuroscience) be considered in light of all new literacies—texts, skills, social practices, and evolving change.

We hope that policymakers become increasingly aware of the changing definition of what it means to be literate in the modern, digital world. Furthermore, we hope that policymakers use empirically supported findings from cognitive processing theories and models to craft and fund educational initiatives. In this regard, policymakers, like educational practitioners, depend on researchers to design studies that produce information truly needed to advance the facilitation of new literacies. Similarly, it is incumbent on researchers to disseminate empirically supported findings to policymakers and practitioners. When researchers fully implement high-quality investigations designed to test theories of cognitive processing and effectively distribute their findings to educational practitioners and policymakers, facilitation of new literacies can be maximized throughout our global community.

CONCLUDING THOUGHTS

The field of new literacies is an emerging one and, as a result, consensus with regard to which cognitive processing frameworks most accurately depict human cognition when engaged in new literacies is similarly emerging. In this manuscript we have presented our understanding of the definition of new literacies and four categories of cognitive processing perspectives from which they can be considered. We have also highlighted ways in which cognitive processing perspectives can inform educational research, practice, and policymaking. In short, cognitive processing perspectives are ways of understanding how the mind works during various complex tasks. Surely, there is much to be gained from these perspectives of new literacies.

REFERENCES

Adams, M. J. (1990). *Beginning to read.* Cambridge, MA: MIT Press.

Anderson, J. R. (1976). *Language, memory, and thought.* Hillsdale, NJ: Erlbaum.

Anderson, J. R., & Lebiere, C. (1998). *The atomic components of thought.* Mahwah, NJ: Erlbaum.

Anderson, R. C., & Pearson, P. D. (1984). A schema-theoretic view of basic processes in reading. In P. D. Pearson (Ed.), *Handbook of reading research* (Vol. 1, pp. 185–224). New York: Longman.

Anstey, A. (2002). "It's not all black and white": Postmodern picture books and new literacies. *Journal of Adolescent and Adult Literacy, 45*(6), 444–457.

Asselin, M. (2004). New literacies: Toward a renewed role of school libraries. *Teacher Librarian, 31*(5), 52–53.

Bartlett, F. C. (1932). *Remembering: A study in experimental and social psychology.* Cambridge, UK: Cambridge University Press.

Berersdorf, D. Q., Narayanan, A., Hillier, A., & Hughes, J. D. (2007). Network model of decreased context utilization in autism spectrum disorder. *Journal of Autism Developmental Disorders, 37,* 1040–1048.

Brodsky, S. (2009). *New literacies: A single-subject experiment.* Unpublished master's thesis, Kean University: Union, NJ.

Castek, J., Bevans-Mangelson, J., & Goldstone, B. (2006). Reading adventures online: Five ways to introduce the new literacies of the Internet through children's literature. *The Reading Teacher, 59,* 714–728.

Cervetti, G., Damico, J., & Pearson, D. P. (2006). Multiple literacies, new literacies, and teacher education. *Theory into Practice, 45*(4), 378–386.

Cohen, I. L. (1994). An artificial neural network analogue of learning in autism. *Biological Psychiatry, 36,* 5–20.

Coiro, J., Knobel, M., Lankshear, C., & Leu, D. (Eds.). (2008). *Handbook of research on new literacies.* New York: Routledge.

Coltheart, M., Rastle, K., Perry, C., Langdon, R., & Ziegler, J. (2001). DRC: A dual route cascaded model of visual word recognition and reading aloud. *Psychological Review, 108*(1), 204–256.

Dragsted, B. (2006). Computer-aided translation as a distributed cognitive task. *Pragmatics and Cognition, 14*(2), 443–464.

Ford, N., Miller, D., & Moss, N. (2005). Web search strategies and human individual differences: Cognitive and demographic factors, Internet attitudes, and approaches. *Journal of the American Society for Information Science and Technology, 56*(7), 741–756.

Goodman, K. S. (1967). Reading: A psycholinguistic guessing game. *Journal of the Reading Specialist, 6,* 126–135.

Goswami, U. (2004). Neuroscience and education. *British Journal of Educational Psychology, 74,* 1–14.

Gough, P. B. (1972). One second of reading. In J. F. Kavanough & I. G. Mattingly (Eds.), *Language by ear and eye.* Cambridge, MA: MIT Press.

Grossberg, S. (1984). Unitization, automaticity, temporal order, and word recognition. *Cognition and Brain Theory, 7,* 263–283.

Henry, L. (2006). SEARCHing for an answer: The critical role of new literacies while reading on the Internet. *The Reading Teacher, 59*(7), 614–627.

Jobard, G., Crivello, F., & Tzourio-Mazoyer, N. (2003). Evaluation of the dual route theory of reading: A meta-analysis of 35 neuroimaging studies. *NeuroImage, 20*(2), 693–712.

Jonassen, D. H. (1996). *Computers in the classroom: Mind tools for critical thinking.* Columbus, OH: Merrill/Prentice Hall.

Kist, W. (2000). Beginning to create the new literacy classroom: What does the new literacy look like? *Journal of Adolescent and Adult Literacy, 43*(8), 710–718.

Kommers, P., Jonassen, D. H., & Mayes, T. (Eds.). (1992). *Cognitive tools for learning*. Heidelberg, Springer-Verlag.

LaBerge, D., & Samuels, S. J. (1974). Toward a theory of automatic information processing in reading. *Cognitive Psychology, 6*, 293–323.

Lajoie, S. P. (1993). Computer environments as cognitive tools for enhancing learning. In S. P. Lajoie & S. J. Derry (Eds.), *Computers as cognitive tools* (pp. 261–288). Hillsdale, NJ: Erlbaum.

Leu, D. J., Jr., Kinzer, C. K., Coiro, J., & Cammack, D. W. (2004). Toward a theory of new literacies emerging from the Internet and other communication technologies. In R. Ruddell & N. Unrau (Eds.), *Theoretical models and processes of reading* (5th ed., pp. 1570–1613). Newark, DE: International Reading Association.

Liu, M., & Bera, S. (2005). An analysis of cognitive tool use patterns in a hypermedia learning environment. *Educational Technology Research Development, 53*(1), 5–21.

Liu, M., Williams, D., & Pedersen, S. (2002). Alien rescue: A problem-based hypermedia learning environment for middle school science. *Journal of Educational Technology Systems, 30*(3), 255–270.

Luke, C. (2000). New literacies in teacher education. *Journal of Adolescent and Adult Literacy, 43*(5), 424–435.

McKenna, M. C., Reinking, D., Labbo, L. D., & Kieffer, R. (1999). The electronic transformation of literacy and its implications for the struggling reader. *Reading and Writing Quarterly, 15*(2), 111–126.

Pirolli, P., & Card, S. K. (1999). Information foraging. *Psychological Review, 106*, 643–675.

Plaut, D. C., McClelland, J. L., Seidenberg, M. S., & Patterson, K. (1996). Understanding normal and impaired word reading: Computational principles in quasi-regular domains. *Psychological Review, 103*, 56–115.

Pugh, K. R., Mencl, W. E., Jenner, A. R., Katz, L., Frost, S. J., Lee, J. R., et al. (2001). Neurobiological studies of reading and reading disability. *Journal of Communication Disorders, 34*(6), 479–492.

Riding, R., & Cheema, I. (1991). Cognitive styles—an overview and integration. *Educational Psychology, 11*(3), 193–215.

Rumelhart, D. E., Hinton, G. E., & Williams, R. J. (1986). Learning representations by back-propagating errors. *Nature, 323*, 533–536.

Rumelhart, D. E., & McClelland, J. L. (1986). *Parallel distributed processing: Explorations in the microstructure of cognition* (Vols. 1 & 2). Cambridge, MA: MIT Press.

Schlaggar, B. L., & McCandliss, B. D. (2007) Development of neural systems for reading. *Annual Reviews of Neuroscience, 30*, 475–503.

Seidenberg, M. S., & McClelland, J. L. (1989). A distributed, developmental model of word recognition and naming. *Psychological Review, 96*, 523–568.

Sejnowski, T. J., & Rosenberg, C. R. (1986). Parallel networks that learn to pronounce English text. *Complex Systems, 1*(1), 145–168.

Shaywitz, S. E., Morris, R., & Shaywitz, B. A. (2008). The education of dyslexic children from childhood to young adulthood. *Annual Review of Psychology, 59,* 451–475.

Simos, P., Fletcher, J., Bergman, E., Breier, J., Foorman, B., Castillo, E., et al. (2002). Dyslexia-specific brain activation profile becomes normal following successful remedial training. *Neurology, 58*(8), 1203–1213.

Small, G. W., Moody, T. D., Siddarth, P., & Bookheimer, S. Y. (2009). Your brain on Google: Patterns of cerebral activation during Internet searching. *The American Journal of Geriatric Psychiatry: Official Journal of the American Association for Geriatric Psychiatry, 17*(2), 116–126.

Smith, F. (1971). *Understanding reading: A psycholinguistic analysis of reading and learning to read.* New York: Holt, Rinehart, & Winston.

Stanovich, K. E. (1980). Toward an interactive compensatory model of individual differences in the development of reading fluency. *Reading Research Quarterly, 16,* 32–71.

Stanovich, K. E. (Ed.). (2000). *Progress in understanding reading: Scientific foundations and new frontiers.* New York: Guilford Press.

Tracey, D. H., & Morrow, L. M. (2006). *Lenses on reading: An introduction to theories and models.* New York: Guilford Press.

Unrau, N. J., & Ruddell, R. B. (Eds.). (2004). *Theoretical models and processes of reading.* Newark, DE: International Reading Association.

Werbos, P. J. (1974). *Beyond regression: New tools for prediction and analysis in the behavioral sciences.* Cambridge, MA: Harvard University Press.

West, R. F., & Stanovich, K. E. (1978). Automatic contextual facilitation in readers of three ages. *Child Development, 49,* 717–727.

Wilson, T. (1997). Information behavior: An interdisciplinary perspective. *Information Processing and Management, 33*(4), 551–572.

Wolf, M. (2007) *Proust and the squid: The story and science of the reading brain.* New York: Harper Perennial.

Zhang, J. (1997). The nature of external representations in problem solving. *Cognitive Science, 21*(2), 179–217.

Zhang, J., & Norman, D. A. (1994). Representations in distributed cognitive tasks. *Cognitive Science, 18,* 87–122.

CHAPTER 7

From Print to Pixels
The Evolution of Cognitive Conceptions of Reading Comprehension

DOUGLAS K. HARTMAN
PAUL MARK MORSINK
JINJIE ZHENG

> The Internet forces us to expand our understanding of each of these elements [text, task, reader, author, context] by considering new aspects of comprehension that are clearly related to traditional comprehension areas (e.g., locating main ideas, summarizing, inferencing, and evaluating) but also requires fundamentally new thought processes.
> —Coiro (2003, p. 459)

From a cognitive perspective, comprehending print on a page is not isomorphic with comprehending pixels online. Online comprehension is more complicated. It places many more processing demands on a reader. To be sure, many lower-level reading processes look much the same as readers shift from print to pixels. Decoding, word recognition, and comprehension of isolated sentences look very similar whether reading on- or offline. But the similarities are fewer with higher-level processes. Interpage, intersite, and intertextual comprehension, for instance, share some, but fewer, processing properties. The nature of each medium shapes the details of comprehension processing down garden paths of different sorts. The International Reading Association's (2002) position statement on literacy and technology anticipated the shape of these diverging paths when it stated that traditional conceptions of "reading, writing, and viewing, and traditional [conceptions] of best-practice instruction—derived from a long tradition of book and other print media—will be insufficient [in the future]" (p. 2).

Today, we see a slowly emerging consensus among researchers, educators, and the public at large that new conceptions of reading comprehension are needed (Coiro, 2005; Hartman, 2000). This consensus has been slow to emerge because so many of the differences between on- and offline reading appear to be differences of degree or frequency rather than qualitative differences. Isn't clicking on a website's hyperlinks a pretty close parallel to flipping through the pages of a print encyclopedia, quickly consulting the encyclopedia's index volume, and then jumping back to a particular section of a long encyclopedia article? Isn't the challenge of evaluating the provenance and credibility of online information a heightened version of a challenge print readers have always faced as they sift through political fliers and other literature stuffed in their mailbox? Our view is that the accumulation of many small and large differences of frequency, degree, and speed has indeed produced a qualitative change and a new kind of cognitive challenge for comprehending online. We concur with, among others, Burbules and Callister (2000), who argued that, while parallels between on- and offline reading certainly exist, hypertext makes possible "something different, and indeed virtually unprecedented" (p. 47), as well as with Coiro (2003), who asserted that online comprehension requires "fundamentally new thought processes" (p. 459). To be sure, a reader may still report that he learned more or less the same things from reading a textbook as he did from browsing a website. But researchers are now in a position to describe where and how the processes of constructing meaning in these two contexts diverge, where the processes of constructing meaning from a social studies textbook chapter on Jacksonian "manifest destiny" in fact cease to overlap with the processes orchestrated to construct meaning from information on the same topic that is dispersed over several hyperlinked and hypermedia-rich websites. These distinctive processes motivate research in online reading comprehension and shape the structure of this chapter.

EVOLVING CONCEPTIONS AND MODELS OF READING COMPREHENSION

The path toward a cognitive conception of online reading comprehension has been marked by a series of expanding "interaction frames"

(Tannen, 1979; Tannen & Wallat, 1987). These conceptual frames initially focused on the two most immediate and concrete elements of reading comprehension: the reader and the text. These initial frames were also rooted in the culture and technology of print on the page. In time, the framing of these interactions expanded, reflecting a parallel expansion in the type of questions asked, texts read, tasks prompted, methods used, theories formed, and technologies available. The path of this expansion is sketched below and organized around two major shifts in our conception of reading comprehension: (1) from offline print text toward online pixelized texts, and (2) from two interacting elements toward many complex elements interacting dynamically.

Offline Conceptions

The research on print-based comprehension has framed the elements of reading by using a range of conceptual pairings. Beginning with the most immediate and concrete level of interaction, the elements of reading comprehension were initially framed by means of a dyadic conception: reader–text interaction.

Dyadic Conceptions

The act of reading comprehension has largely been framed as a reader–text interaction. This dyadic conception of comprehension has been articulated in a number of empirical studies, research syntheses, dictionary entries, and policy reports during the last 100 years (e.g., Anderson & Pearson, 1984; Golden, 1986; Gray, 1925; Harris, 1940; Harris & Hodges, 1981; Huey 1900, 1901). As one of the first research-based policy reports to include a focus on comprehension, the 1985 National Academy of Education report *Becoming a Nation of Readers* framed comprehension as a dyadic concept, where the reader engages in "the process of constructing meaning from written texts" (Anderson, Hiebert, Scott, & Wilkinson, 1985, p. 7). The same two elements have been used to frame the interaction of comprehension in research-based methods textbooks. For example, Durkin (1993) defined comprehension as the act where "meaning is constructed through interactions between text and reader" (p. 10).

The intricacies of this dyadic interaction have been articulated by several dynamic reader–text conceptions of comprehension processes. One conception, the construction–integration model, has been developed by Kintsch and colleagues (Kintsch, 1988, 1998; Kintsch & Kintsch, 2005; Kintsch & van Dijk, 1978; van Dijk & Kintsch, 1983). This body of work envisions the text as an element composed of several overlapping levels. The micro level is composed of parsed t- or idea-units. The meso level is composed of organizational structures that provide cohesion and order for the micro-level units. And the macro level represents the conventions and regularities of genre that give overall shape to the prose. The reader element of the dyadic interaction involves the construction of a textbase (a hierarchical mental representation of information from the text) and a situation model (a representation of the text that integrates information from the reader's prior knowledge). Many elements from the textbase and situation model contribute to reading comprehension, but prior knowledge and coherence have been found to contribute the most. Thus the Kintschian construction–integration model starts from a dyadic conception of what reading involves but ultimately provides a rich picture of a complex, many-layered comprehension process.

Another dyadic conception of comprehension, dynamic text comprehension, has been developed by van den Broek and colleagues (Rapp & van den Broek, 2005; van den Broek, Rapp, & Kendeou, 2005; van den Broek, Young, Tzeng, & Linderholm, 1999). The text is envisioned as possessing properties similar to those described in the Kintschian model. What is new is the dynamic text comprehension model's focus on fluctuations in the mental activation of concepts as the reader proceeds through the text, resulting in an understanding of the text's information that emerges gradually over time. Features of the text and characteristics of the reader "jointly and interactively affect these fluctuations, influencing and being influenced by the reader's understanding and memory of what is read" (Rapp & van den Broek, 2005, p. 276).

Triadic Conceptions

Building on these dyadic conceptions of comprehension, scholars over the years have expanded the conceptual frame of reading to include a third element. This new slot—typically added in order to focus attention on a particular hitherto neglected aspect of a reader's interactions with a text—has usually been filled by one of the following: author, task, or context. With the addition of this new element to a now-enlarged interaction frame, the focus shifts from the immediate and concrete elements of reading comprehension (i.e., reader and text) to more distant and abstract elements (i.e., author, task, or context). In each triadic conception, the reader and text are conceived in terms similar to those of the dyadic explanations outlined in the previous section. But the inclusion of a new third element both expands the frame and complicates the interactions among the elements. Three triadic conceptions of reading comprehension are found in the research literature.

A reader–text–author conception has been articulated by a number of scholars (Beck, McKeown, Worthy, Sandora, & Kucan, 1996; Harker, 1988; Nystrand & Himley, 1984; Pearson & Tierney, 1984; Shanahan, 1992). This triadic conception of reading comprehension is based on two simple questions: What would happen if the author of a text were visible to a reader? If made visible and personable, would the author view the reader as a potential ally in comprehending the text? Such questions indicate that this triadic conception is a social conception of reading comprehension, where conversations with an imagined author about his or her craft, intentions, and knowledge constitute the act of comprehension. More precisely, it is a social-perspective-taking conception of reading, where readers invoke an author and strive to think as this writer did while he or she wrote the text. Evidence indicates that by thinking beyond the words on the page and considering the author's purpose and viewpoint, along with recognizing gaps in the text, readers wrestle more vigorously with comprehending a text's meaning (Sandora, Beck, & McKeown, 1999).

A reader–text–task conception looks at the role that task plays in the interaction between reader and text (Chang, 1983; Linderholm & van den Broek, 2002; Narvaez, van den Broek, & Ruiz, 1999; van den Broek, Lorch, Linderholm, & Gustafson, 2001). Two aspects of task have been explored in the context of a triadic conception. One is how task influences readers' comprehension. Mills (1995) and Narvaez et al. (1999), for example, found that the task demands of a reader–text situation had profound effects on what was comprehended from a text. The other is how readers intentionally adjust comprehension processes to the task demands stated or implied by a range of reading activities (Linderholm & van den Broek, 2002). In both cases, the comprehension product and process of reader–text interaction is shaped by or toward stated or implied task demands.

A reader–text–context conception has been articulated in the work of several scholars (e.g., Carey & Harste, 1987; Mosenthal, 1983; Nystrand, 1987; Smagorinsky & Coppock, 1994; Smolkin & Donovan, 2001). The meaning of the context element varies widely in the research on comprehension. It can refer to the particular setting in which a reading event occurs (e.g., a classroom), the cultural values and practices that influence a particular reader's choices and thoughts while reading, or the larger sociocultural framework within which meaning-making behavior exists. The shared feature of these varied meanings of context is the idea that sociocultural factors impinge on how the reader–text interaction proceeds. Put another way, context has been variously envisioned as a local, regional, or global variable that needs to be controlled, measured, or taken into account so that the more immediate and concrete elements of reading comprehension can be accurately understood.

Tetradic Conceptions

The broadest interaction frames for print-based conceptions of comprehension have included four interacting elements. These interaction frames still include the immediate and concrete elements of reading comprehension (i.e., reader and text), but also include two or more of the more distant and abstract elements (i.e., author, task, and context). In each tetradic conception, the reader and text are conceived in ways similar to the previously discussed dyadic interaction frames, but the inclusion of two new elements expands and complexifies the interactions among elements even more. Two tetradic conceptions of reading comprehension are found in the research literature.

A number of reports and conceptual frameworks articulate a reader–text–task–context conception (e.g., Gaskins, 2002; Organisation for Economic Co-operation and Development, 2003). The most widely circulated articulation appeared in the RAND Reading Study Group's (RRSG) report on reading for understanding (RRSG, 2002), which abstracted from the research literature a tetradic conception of reading comprehension that emphasized the dynamic interchange among the elements of reader–text–activity–context. Substituting the term *activity* for *task,* the report defined reading comprehension as "the process of simultaneously extracting and constructing meaning through interaction and involvement with written language . . . within a larger sociocultural context that shapes and is shaped by the reader and that interacts with [all the other elements] iteratively throughout the process of reading" (p. xiii).

In this conception of the comprehension act, the reader brings capacities, skills, knowledge, and experiences to the act. The text is broadly construed as any form of "written language." (Interestingly, the 2002 RRSG report acknowledged that the idea of text comprises "any printed text or electronic text" [p. 11] and further recognized that "we live in a society that is experiencing an explosion of alternative texts" [p. xiv], yet the report ended up focusing almost exclusively on printed text.) And the activity includes the purposes, processes, and consequences associated with a particular act. The interaction of these three elements, however, occurs within the milieu of a fourth element, the larger sociocultural context that shapes and is shaped by the reader and other elements. "The identities and capacities of readers, the texts that are available and valued, and the activities in which readers are engaged with those texts are all influenced by, and in some cases determined by, the sociocultural context. The sociocultural context mediates students' experiences, just as students' experiences influence the context" (p. 12).

Another set of studies articulates a reader–text–author–context conception by drawing from work conducted at the intersection of cognitive psychology, social psychology, philosophy, and literary theory (Hartman, 1992a, 1992b, 2004). Based in research that conceives of comprehension as a fundamentally intertextual enterprise—as always shaped by and drawing on the meaning and form of other texts—this tetradic conception adds a new layer of complexity by seeing texts as irreducibly plural. According to this model, no text stands alone, sui generis. Like letters of the alphabet or paintings in a museum, texts generate meaning from within a web of similarities and differences, references and allusions. Even when the reader is consciously focusing on just one text at a time, her act of comprehension assumes and implicitly responds to a larger set of texts (Hartman & Hartman, 1993). Nor is the text the only unit of analysis that becomes plural. Because a reader often comprehends texts from a variety of stances (locating a piece of information in one text to corroborate an opinion derived from other texts, appreciating the way an author has broken with traditional genre expectations, and so forth), the notion of the singular and single-minded reader also falls apart, to be replaced by a conception of the plural, protean reader. The reader is plural in a social constructivist sense as well: meaning making is seen as an inherently social and collaborative undertaking.

As such, the text is not a single element in the interaction, but a plural one. It is one of many texts in the act of comprehending. Because texts are often comprehended in relation to other texts (e.g., an auto mechanic clarifies a set of procedures in a technical manual before reading descriptions of parts in a distributor's catalog, after which he reads the directions on a new part requisition form), the unit of analysis is not a single print text but sets of print-based texts (i.e., "text sets") (Hartman & Hartman, 1993). Similarly, the reader is not one, but one of many in the interaction frame of comprehension. Because a reader often comprehends texts by taking on various stances (e.g., to locate a piece of information in several texts, to evaluate the veracity of information across magazine articles, to appreciate the evocative language and imagery in an author's oeuvre), or by collaborating with others (e.g., reading a news article of interest with a family member, asking a colleague to read a memo you've just received to ensure you are not misunderstanding its tone, second-grade book buddies comprehending several books together during the language arts time block), the unit of analysis for reading is not the single reader but the reader who flexibly approaches texts from various stances (e.g., Many, 1991) or who partners with other readers to comprehend a set of texts (e.g., Short, 2004).

Also from this intertextual view of comprehension, author and context are pluralized. Authors are plural in the sense that they often write with others (as co-authors, with feedback from editors, by drawing on the writing of other authors, etc.) or intend that a set of texts be read as a unit belonging to a larger text-set conversation (e.g., Sendak wrote *Where the Wild Things Are* [1963], *In the Night Kitchen* [1970], and *Outside Over There* [1981] as a trilogy that represents and re-represents a set of basic storylines, ideas, and themes that interact with other children's texts of the time [Cott, 1983]). For its part, context is pluralized because the setting-context of comprehension often changes (i.e., from home to school to work to church) and the situation-context within each setting-context is dynamic (e.g., readers comprehending a set of primary source texts in first-period history class is a situational school context potentially different than another set of peers comprehending a set of informational physics articles in fourth period or a packet of study-guide worksheets used in sixth period English as students read Shakespeare). As a whole, this tetradic conception of reading comprehension represents the reader, text, author, and context as nested and networked entities, independent of each other in an everyday sense, but interdependent in the not-so-obvious ways in which they actually function across many locations and times. Understanding where the boundary within and across elements begins and ends is a less straightforward process, but one that strives to capture the ecology in which the act of comprehension occurs.

The preceding review presents research on print-based reading comprehension as representing three overlapping conceptions of reading: dyadic, triadic, and tetradic. Each of these conceptions is composed of a frame, the elements within the frame, and the interactions among elements in the frame. Over time, the frames have broadened to include a greater number of interacting elements, although the evolution of these conceptions has not been strictly linear. As the review makes clear, research on print-based comprehension represents theoretical and material choices about the size of frame, number of elements, and type of interactions to be examined. The theoretical and material choices for online conceptions of comprehension are exponentially more complex, which we take up in the next section.

Online Conceptions

As discussed previously, the conceptual elements, interactions, and frames for online reading comprehension share "family resemblances" with offline comprehension (Prien, 2004; Wittgenstein, 1953), especially (1) when lower-level processes are compared and (2) when particular processes are considered in isolation from one another. But the resemblances between online and offline comprehension fade when higher-level processes are compared. When several elements of online comprehension are considered in relation to one another, and when reading is seen as a dynamic interaction among an increasing number of elements, a point is reached where differences of degree turn into a qualitative change.

This qualitative turn of elements, interactions, and frames for online comprehension marks a substantive change in the features commonly invoked for offline reading. Put another way, the features of offline comprehension have been refeatured as they have migrated online. Because this migration is of the first magnitude, a discussion of how the elements, interactions, and frames of online reading comprehension are being reconceived follows.

Elements

The conceptual elements of online reading comprehension share a family resemblance to those of offline comprehension in one respect: studies have used various combinations of the reader, text, author, task, and context. But as an emerging body of work, online comprehension is conceived of as a hexadic ($n = 6$) set of elements: reader–text–author–task–context–technology. For example, Zhang and Duke (2008) conceived of online comprehension as: 12 readers with various tasks in mind reading across a number of online texts composed by different authors to form relevant contexts through the technologies at hand. Thus the elements of online comprehension are more numerous. As such, the conceptual adicity of online reading comprehension is greater than that of offline reading comprehension; more elements are present in the interaction frames of online reading comprehension, suggesting either the need for or reality of a more complex conception of reading comprehension (Falk, 2007; Ludlow, 1996).

The conceptual elements of online reading comprehension are multiplied in another sense, too. Online, it quickly becomes impossible to ignore that each individual element is already by itself plural. Indeed, in a typical session of online reading, as the reader clicks hyperlinks to pursue a line of inquiry from one website to another, enters terms in a search engine, types a comment in a comment box at the end of an article she just read, and adjusts her purpose for reading on the basis of other readers' comments, the very notion of a unified "individual" element quickly breaks down.

As we saw earlier, offline conceptions of reading comprehension have largely conceived of the reader, text, author, task, and context as singulare tantum (i.e., as an element singular in nature). But online comprehension has conceived of these elements as plurale tantum (i.e., as plural elements that are constituted by singular aspects) (Little, Brown, & Trumble, 2002). More to the matter, online comprehension has conceived of the elements as multiple plurals, that is, plural in several ways at once. For example, the element of text is plural online in at least two ways: plural in number and in constitution. Online text is plural in number because any "lexia text" (i.e., a segment of print and other signs on a single screen) is linked to myriad other texts that make up the meta-text being read (Landow, 1997; Rosenberg, 1999). Online text is also plural because its "textual constitution" is "made up" of textual substance drawn from other texts (Giese, 1998; Landow, 2006). To comprehend online is neither conceived of nor experienced as reading a unitary text, but instead as reading across an evolving range of texts to construct meaning that meets goals or answers questions. The online interaction frame, then, is populated by texts that are made of other texts and that in turn make up the network of other texts that readers comprehend. As Delany and Landow (1991) described, "the text [in a

Web-based hypertext] appears to break down, to fragment and atomize into constituent elements (the lexia or blocks of text), and these reading units take on a life of their own as they become more self-contained and less dependent on what comes before or after in a linear succession" (p. 10).

The reader is also plural in number and constitution. For example, online reading is conceived of as highly collaborative in practice. Students gather around a single computer in their classroom to read online texts together as they search for answers about the origins of a particular dog breed. Or students use their personal wireless laptops in a civics class to collaboratively search for texts that explain the finer points in a court battle over the teaching of intelligent design and evolution. Still yet, students in Dublin, Sydney, Wellington, Pretoria, Washington, DC, London, and Edinburgh collaboratively read a series of online texts that explain how cities and communities around the globe are designing carbon-neutral economies and lives. Traces of this collaborative reading are everywhere online. Blogs and wikis provide ample evidence that readers are jointly constructing meaning of common texts that are "intensively" read and reread (Hall, 1996). As the work of Jacobs and Gallo (2002) has illustrated, even a reader sitting at home in front of her computer screen is "reading alone together" when it comes to comprehending online.

Readers comprehending online are also plural in their constitution. They perform different "comprehending selves" when they read across online texts (Goffman, 1959; Sternberg, 2003; Tierney, 2006). These selves, which have variously been called identities, stances, and approaches, represent the plural nature that reading online affords and demands (Wiszniewski & Coyne, 2002). Flexibly and purposively marshaling the comprehension strategies that accompany the stances of these various reading selves, readers become critics of the veracity of information online, aesthetes of sudden fiction and online poetry slams, searchers for the minutiae of media star trivia, and synthesizers and linkers of disparate people, information, and events. Drawing on the metaphors of Calinescu (1996) and Goffman (1959), readers online must wear many faces and perform many selves—that is, be plural—as they comprehend their way in pursuit of texts that together make sense of a question, goal, or purpose. The online interaction frame, then, is populated by readers whose singular "I's" have become plural "we's" (Hartman, 2004)—comprehending together as they perform various reading selves.

The author is also plural. Online, authorship has been conceived of as a highly collaborative practice (Lowry, Curtis, & Lowry, 2004). A number of examples illustrate the numerically plural conception of the author in the online interaction frame. Students gather around a single computer in their classroom to compose an online text that represents their collective understanding of how a bill becomes law. A group of five students use their personal wireless laptops in a Spanish III class to collaboratively author an online text in real time using online authoring software that permits real-time coediting with peers in Madrid and Santiago (e.g., Writeboard, Google Docs); the software tracks all changes in real time, keeps all versions, stores marginal comments made by authors, and notifies authors of changes made throughout the process via RSS or e-mail alerts. Colleagues from around the globe negotiate round upon round of authoring and re-authoring a Wikipedia entry on the definition of online reading comprehension (Emigh & Herring, 2005). And writers add links to other authors' texts online, thereby implicating the many-authored nature of the texts that readers read online. In all these cases, authoring online has been conceived of as a form of "hyperauthorship," where dozens if not hundreds of authors make their mark on an ever-evolving corpus of online texts that are read by others (Cronin, 2001, p. 560). As such, authoring online has been conceived of as a distributed practice—"bowling alone together" (Cronin, 2004, p. 557)—that involves writing with "a cast of thousands" (Cronin, Shaw, & La Barre, 2003, p. 855).

Writers composing for online readers are also plural in their constitution. They borrow, adapt, appropriate, and transform texts that come to them secondhand, already imbued with the texts of other authors (Hartman, 2004). They perform different "authoring selves" when they compose from off- and online texts (Holland, Lachiotte, Skinner, & Cain, 1998; Jacucci, Jacucci, Wagner, & Psik, 2005). These authorly selves represent the plural nature that writing online affords and demands (Wallace, 2001). Flexibly and purposively marshaling the composition strategies that accompany the stances of these various writing selves, authors shape the veracity of information online by vetting it and recirculating it, borrow and recombine aesthetic features, search for and report the minutiae of media star trivia, and synthesize and link disparate people, information, and events through blogs, wikis, and MOOs. Drawing on the metaphors of Sussman (2000) and Goffman (1959), authors online must wear many faces and perform many selves—that is, be plural—as they compose texts from many other texts to make sense of a desire, goal, or purpose. The online interaction frame, then, is populated by authors who write together as various authoring selves. As such, online authoring highlights the social derivation of writing. The name on the byline or About link indexes an authoring status that differs from the one we have associated with authorship of print on the page.

The task of comprehending online has been viewed as plural in both number and constitution. For instance, online reading has been conceived of as involving many sets of tasks and subtasks (Gebauer & Shaw, 2002). A middle school reader sitting in front of a search engine page in a browser has very little text to process initially, but after typing in a few keywords and pressing return he is reading pages of complex search results to make decisions about websites' relevance to his goals, the veracity of the information provided, and how information on a particular website compares with what he just read on other websites (Henry, 2006, 2007a). These online reading tasks are not carried out in a strictly linear fashion, but as rapid, recursive, iterative comprehension cycles where multiple self-regulated decisions and understandings drive high-level sense-making strategies (Coiro & Dobler, 2007).

The context of online reading comprehension has been conceived of as plural in two complementary ways. One is the plural-in-number concept that Cole (1996) called "context as that which surrounds" (p. 132). This conception often represents comprehension as a set of concentric circles with the reader and text interaction at the center, such as the diagram used by the RAND Reading Study Group (2002) to depict the key elements of reading comprehension research. As such, the reader–text interaction of online reading is "surrounded" by the other plural elements—texts, readers, authors, and tasks—plus a number of other contextual strands, such as socially organizing structures (e.g., classroom rules and graduation requirements) and socially interactive collaborators (e.g., peers, teachers, parents, neighbors). This host of "surrounding" elements creates contexts of various sorts. For example, the element of online texts can be thought of as surrounded by the context—which literally means "accompanying text"—of other texts to form the textual context of online reading (Hartman, 2004). There is the lexia text that the reader is currently interacting with on the screen, but this text resides in a network of accompanying texts to which it is explicitly linked and those that the reader finds and acknowledges are significant in some respect to each other (e.g., by topic, theme, genre, concept). The image of an online lexia text surrounded by the context of other texts is probably best imagined in connection with Bronfenbrenner's (1979) instantiation of the ecology of human development as a set of embedded systems. Starting with the microsystem at the center and proceeding outward through the mesosystem and exosystem to the macrosystem, the context of any online text can be imagined as surrounded by similar tiers of texts. But a numerical sense of context need not be framed by one element in the action frame. Many other combinations of elements have been imagined for the nested-contexts approach to conceiving of online reading comprehension (Volet, 2001).

The context of online reading comprehension has also been conceived of as "that which weaves together" (Cole, 1996, p. 135). This conception, plural in constitution, represents the context of online comprehension as a threaded or woven system. Following from the Latin root of context (*contexere*), which means "to weave together" (Oxford English Dictionary, *www.oed.com/*), the context of online comprehension has been conceived as a "qualitative relation" between at least two elements (i.e., threads) (p. 135). As such, the reader, text, author, task, event, and physical environment are the context because of how they interact (i.e., weave together) as multiple elements in a single momentary process.

This conception of online comprehension requires a relational interpretation of context, one that includes the many elements of a comprehending act as part of a woven system "whenever they are relevant" (Bateson, 1972, p. 458). Imagine for a moment that an adolescent girl is sitting in front of an open Web browser at home reading pages online. She goes click, click, click with the mouse on textual links while reading. What is the relational context of her reading? It includes her, her purposes, the mouse, monitor, Web links, websites, authors of those websites, the immediate physical environment, and other elements as they work together to form the comprehending act during this moment in time. She lifts her hand from the mouse and grasps an open book lying next to the monitor; she begins reading it. By moving her hand from mouse to book the relational context has changed. The elements and relations among them have changed. Her hand now links to a new element and purpose, although many elements of her immediate physical environment remain the same. It is now the book and the purposes associated with it that become relevant for conceiving what is the new context. And if she places the book back on the table and reaches to pick up the spoon in her soup bowl on the same table to eat lunch, the relevant context changes again. In each case, the mouse, book, and spoon in her hand change the relations as to what constitutes the context. Because our minds work through elements (sometimes called artifacts or tools), comprehension has been seen as distributed throughout the elements of reading that "are woven together and which weave together individual human action in concert" to form the relevant context (Cole, 1996, pp. 136–137). Thus the context of online comprehension is contingent upon the goals that afford and constrain the particular set of elements that interact when comprehending in a given moment. So when our adolescent reader clicks from a *Seventeen.com* column about facial skin care to an *Acne.org* text on "How to Pop a Pimple" to a blog about "Tween and Teen Acne Skin Care" to an instant messaging application to share with a friend what she is learning about the best way to care for a pimple on her face, she is changing the context for comprehending with each move of the hand, screen, text, site, and application.

And finally, the technology element for comprehending online is plural in number and constitution. Historically, technology has been a "shadow" element in the offline print environment, given that book binding, page sizing, ink choice, and so forth have always shaped and constrained a typical reader's experience and cognitive performance. But online, the prominence of digital technology as a factor increases dramatically. The reader's browser version, screen size, screen resolution, plug-ins (for rendering images, animations, etc.), Internet connection speed—all these things impinge very directly and explicitly on what the reader is able to do. Even more so, these technologies are interactive and malleable like never before. The online reader adjusts font size, screen brightness, and scroll speed to suit her needs; she also makes use of desktop and Web-based tools to support her reading experience, bookmarking websites, tagging Web content, clipping snippets of text, and so on. There are multiple platforms on which reading can occur (e.g., Windows, Vista, OSX, Linux), multiple software applications (e.g., Web browsers, PDF readers, blogs, e-mail, word processors, wikis), multiple brands of applications (e.g., Firefox, Safari, Explorer), and multiple versions of a single software application brand (e.g., Firefox 1.0, 2.0, 3.0). The effect is that the technologies that transmit pixels to display information to be comprehended online count as a crucial element of cognitive processing, more so than offline where the book's technology is less interactive and malleable. Technology, then, is as much a part of the pattern of pluralization and increasing complexity as are the other elements of online comprehension (e.g., for the reader, author, text). The online interaction frame is populated by technologies that are more prominent and protean, both in number and constitution.

Interactions

How is an online reader to manage and direct the interplay of comprehension elements outlined in the previous section? With more elements at play, the pluralization of these elements, and the resulting exponential multiplication of possible interactions among these pluralized elements, the ability to think about one's own thinking—the ability to be metacognitive—becomes paramount.

Two important dimensions of metacognition—knowledge and regulation—emerge from the culture of comprehending print offline. To know and regulate one's own thinking while reading a newspaper, for example, a reader needed three kinds of knowledge: declarative (knowledge of what), procedural (knowledge of how), and conditional (knowledge of when) (Paris, Wasik, & Turner, 1991). Equipped with facts, concepts, and vocabulary, the reader orchestrates skills like previewing, predicting, summarizing, rereading, inferencing, and questioning (to name a few) in a timely manner to make sense of a newspaper article. If the reader became aware that she was not understanding a part of the article, she could check memory to see if she had any facts, concepts, or vocabulary that would help her comprehend that portion of text better or else employ a different skill to make sense of the print on the page. Thus by drawing on her knowledge of what, how, and when, a reader could orchestrate her cognitive resources to optimize her comprehension of the printed text.

When comprehending online, are these three familiar types of knowledge sufficient for being metacognitive? The evidence to date indicates that three additional kinds of metacognitive knowledge are now elevated to positions of decisive importance—knowledge of identity, location, and goal. While not entirely new, these three forms of metacognition may be counted as "additional" in the sense that, whereas in the world of print they appeared useful in a subset of reading situations, now they appear generally indispensable.

Identity knowledge (knowing who) is now a crucial part of the metacognitive picture because the online medium affords vast numbers of authors the opportunity to invent and broadcast identities of various sorts—some blandly institutional and some ironic, some borrowed and some outright fraudulent—through online texts. In light of this new reality, readers need to know at least the basic facts about how authors construct, represent, and project online identities. For example, online readers need to know about user-authored content, and about the differences between the text in a blog entry or blog reply and the text displayed in a multiauthored and editorially vetted wiki such as Wikipedia (Zhang, 2007). Online readers also need to know about different levels of credibility that can be assigned to an online text in accordance with its origin. For example, medical advice on a personal website created by a patient needs to be interpreted differently than information on a website sponsored by a pharmaceutical company or than information published online by an independent medical research agency such as the National Institutes of Health. To be sure, knowing who wrote something has always been important. Now, however, for better and for worse, the powers and possibilities of identity creation are hugely multiplied, and rapidly evolving technologies are bringing new forms of online identity into existence every few months. (One example: feed aggregators and online text summarization tools now make it possible to generate text whose authorship is part human, part machine.) Consequently, online readers face many more choices and challenges than before, and there is a premium on being both more creative and more critical.

Locational knowledge (knowing where) is also integral to comprehending metacognitively online. At the most basic level, knowing how to use and adapt the locational features in a Web browser's interface is a prerequisite skill for online readers. Traditional offline texts are printed on numbered paper pages of a consistent size, which serves as a constant metacognitive reminder to readers about the length of the text and their position in the text. Page numbers, together with the sensation of the physical weight of the text being read, connect the typical print reader to a very definite sense of where she is, how much reading lies ahead, and where to turn for particular kinds of guidance (e.g., where to find the table of contents or the index). Online reading is different and requires more specialized locational metacognition. To start, in an Internet browser with up-and-down and left-to-right scroll bars, the previously prevailing conception of page length and page number disappears. Faced with websites of varying length and without page breaks, online readers are challenged to locate information with the aid of new tools, such as the scroll bar or the mouse cursor. This means that, already for basic navigation purposes, online readers need to know about the conventional structure and layout of websites, such as where the tabs are, how to return to a site's homepage or find a "site map" page (if one exists), and how websites and their elements are linked and nested. This locational knowledge allows readers to see the full range of choices they have and navigate efficiently to the most relevant information.

At the same time, these skills are about more than just finding information; they enable the online reader to orient herself and form the kinds of expectations and plans that the print reader was able to form based on her sense of being in the middle or near the end of the text she was reading. Having oriented herself in relation to a particular website's architecture, as well as in relation to "surrounding" websites, the online reader is in a position to set goals, to choose to read long pages in their entirety or to jump from one page to another for the sake of comparison or contrast, to drill down to less-trafficked pages or focus on top-level pages, and so on. At a more advanced level, locational metacognition is crucial as online readers move beyond orienting themselves along already well-trodden Web pathways (such as the interlinked pages of an existing website) and engage in trailblazing more idiosyncratic pathways of their own. This blazing of new pathways is in fact what happens every time an online reader uses a search engine. As the online reader scans the search results, and then fine-tunes her search terms and clicks "search" again, she creates a new map to a new information landscape. Thus the online reader's locational knowledge is, and has to be, both retrospective (focused on already existing or already visited locations) and prospective (focused on locations and itineraries yet to be created). This locational knowledge is what saves online readers from the type of textual vertigo that can easily strike as one wades waist deep—figuratively speaking—through the torrent of textual resources available through the Web. Thus locational knowledge is essential not only for knowing where particular features and information are located, it is essential for orienting oneself in a website, or more generally, in cyberspace (Lawless & Schrader, 2008; Leander & McKim, 2003).

Goal knowledge (knowing why) provides sustained purposes for comprehending online. One of the primary metacognitive challenges in online reading is that of openness. As Burbules and Callister (2000) explained, "this [online] environment provides much greater freedom in making determinations as a reader of a text about what relates to what, or what ideas should follow or precede others" (p. 45). This "freedom" is at the same time a metacognitive challenge. It represents a significant change from the cognitive activity profile of a typical print reader. Without explicit reading goals and focus, online readers may easily become lost and overwhelmed in the boundless online environment. As Delany and Landow (1991) explained, "Hypertext has no center . . . [which]

means that anyone who uses hypertext makes his or her own interests the de facto organizing principle (or center) for the investigation at the moment. One experiences hypertext as an infinitely decenterable and recenterable system" (p. 18). Seductive details, images, ads, titles, videos, and the sort can reshape the focus or redirect the goal at any click along the way. As Coiro (2003) noted, "Hypertext and interactive features can offer too many choices and too many animations that may distract and disorient otherwise strong readers" (p. 462). Consequently, the ability to set and manage clear reading goals becomes absolutely essential. This metacognitive ability enables an online reader to formulate relevant and realistic goals, categorize and evaluate Web content in relation to these goals, adjust goals in response to what the reader finds is available and relevant, monitor progress, and determine when the goal has been attained (Zhang & Duke, 2008). Goal knowledge helps the online reader stay focused and not waste his time on eye-catching but ultimately irrelevant information. It allows an online reader to make efficient and situation-appropriate decisions regarding information or knowledge "saturation": whether he has satisfied his initial goals for reading, whether he needs to form a new reading goal, and what connections exist between original reading goals and emerging ones.

These three additional types of metacognitive knowledge (identity knowledge, locational knowledge, and goal knowledge) do not supplant earlier forms of declarative, procedural, and conditional knowledge. Rather, they extend and enrich them in startling ways. They are complementary forms of knowledge that provide a fuller set of metacognitive resources that readers can draw upon to comprehend in a more complex and open textual environment. What is it about comprehending online that creates these additional forms of knowledge? Simply put, the metacognitive challenge/burden is increased when comprehending online. Reading online places significantly greater metacognitive demands than offline print reading on readers' knowledge and control (Coiro & Dobler, 2007; DeStefano & Le Fevre, 2007). This is so not just because readers are learning about the affordances of new technologies and tools (which keep evolving) and daily encountering new kinds of texts, but because online there are so many more choices, more pathways, and more juxtapositions, that for most readers there's a dramatically bigger need for metacognitive oversight and strategizing. The nature of the relationship between heightened metacognitive activity and comprehension may be highly variable (Kiili, Laurinen, & Marttunen, 2008, 2009; Zhang & Duke, 2008).

Frames

How are these newly constituted elements and newly enriched meta-cognitive interactions framed when a reader comprehends pixel texts online? The answer lies in an emerging contrast between the conceptual frames for off- and online reading. The frame for comprehending print on the page has largely been a static frame, with dyadic, triadic, or tetradic interactions among elements at play. As conceived, multiple vectors of influence occur between different elements (reader, text, task, author, context) within the offline reading frame, but the elements, interactions, and frame exist—or at least give the appearance of existing—in a relatively stable, enduring system.

In contrast, the frame for comprehending pixels on the screen has emerged as a dynamic frame, with n-adic interactions among exponentially multiplied elements and interactions. As conceived, a dynamic frame highlights the fact that these vastly multiplied elements directly influence each other, with the result that reader, text, task, author, context, and technology actually and visibly co-evolve, not just gradually, but in the course of a typical act of comprehending online. Put another way, when reading online a reader is faced with much more than simply a multitude of elements. In very explicit ways (unlike in the offline print environment, where these things are implicit and not directly experienced by most readers), a reader online interacts with elements that actually mutate as she reads. Thus, for example, a reader's initial purpose/question and the first search she runs in a search engine together define the contours of a provisional, projected/anticipated text. But this "definition" of the text being read is almost immediately adjusted. As she clicks to a page and scans the headings, clicks on an audio clip or backtracks to her search results to select a different website, the contours and substance of the text change. In the print world, the reader would typically consult a stable index and then flip backward and forward to scan pages within the confines of a single book; online, the reader is, in effect, creating an index, and then culling and discarding pages from a vast archive of texts to construct a "text of the moment" or a "text fitted for her present purpose." The nature of the online reader's reading activity mutates as well. For example, coming to a website where links to further information take the form of animated, mouse-activated buttons on an image, the reader must switch reading modes and become, for a minute, a reader of images and diagrams.

In summary, the new frame for online reading is impossible to represent in a two-dimensional diagram with labeled elements arranged on the page in a more or less intricate pattern, with a certain number of arrows indicating interactions. The new frame for online reading must be conceived in three-dimensional or *n*-dimensional terms and, metaphorically, as the traversal of a system. This system is dynamic and evolving and simply cannot be mapped in advance, since the elements and interactions made while comprehending from point A to point B actually change the potential frames, elements, and interactions between and among points B, C, D, and so on.

IMPLICATIONS

In this chapter we have described the evolution of cognitive conceptions of reading comprehension from offline to online by tracing three trajectories. One trajectory is the expansion of elements at play in the act of comprehension, in terms of both number and constitution. A second is the shift from simple interactions among the elements of comprehension to more complex interactions. And a final trajectory is the shift from a relatively fixed frame of interaction for comprehension's elements to more dynamic frames for these interactions. The implications of these trajectories for how we practice, assess, study, and conceive of comprehension follow.

First, the evolution from print on the page to pixels on the screen suggests that a "simple view of reading" (Hoover & Gough, 1990, p. 127) is no longer tenable for skilled online comprehension. While evidence at one point in time could have permitted the assertion that reading is reducible to two interacting elements (such as readers' decoding skills and language comprehension, in the simple view of reading), the evidence and argument put forth in this chapter suggest otherwise. Today, understanding the elements, interactions, and frames that are at play when a reader comprehends online is at least as complex conceptually as so-called rocket science (cf. Moats, 1999). We say "at least" because the idea of rocket science may not sufficiently capture the truly Gordian character of the model we have sketched, whose intricacies resemble the interdisciplinary strands of nanotechnology, quantum mechanics, social network analysis, computational neuroscience, design semiotics, and cognitive flexibility theory. Indeed, the evidence from such synthe-

ses as Coiro, Knobel, Lankshear, and Leu (2008) and the New Literacies
Research Team (2007) suggests that to develop a more fully conceptualized contemporary cognitive view of online reading comprehension
will require more than a description of the "most intricate workings
of the human mind" (Huey, 1908, p. 6), since the mind of a reader is
only one of the interacting elements in the deictic frame (Leu, 2000) of
online comprehension that includes other readers, as well as texts, tasks,
authors, contexts, and technologies. Thus the pattern of research data
from the first decade of the 21st century suggests a cognitive conception
of online comprehension that is more complex, iterative, and protean
than Huey (1908) could have ever imagined a century earlier.

Second, the evolution from print to pixels suggests that the spectrum of texts, tasks, contexts, and technologies populating curricula
needs to be more inclusive. With everyone—from children to retir-
ees—doing more and more of their daily reading online, restricting
the range of text genres and formats taught in our schools risks leaving rising generations of readers ill prepared for the reading challenges
and opportunities they will face in their personal and professional lives
(Duke, Schmar-Dobler, & Zhang, 2006). From the earliest grades, students need to start building the knowledge and strategies they will need
to access and interpret digital information. Indeed, as Malloy and Gambrell (2006) pointed out, the future is already here:

> Many elementary students are already adept at searching and surfing,
> using reading and spelling in ways not explicitly taught. Reading online is
> not only something that many students do in their leisure time but is also a
> skill they will need to develop as they learn to research and create in their
> middle school years and beyond. (p. 482)

At the same time, new texts and technologies require new lesson plans;
most students will benefit very little from simply being turned loose on
the Web without guidance or training (even if school "net safety" policies were to permit this). Today, then, sustained attention is urgently
needed on how K–12 education can best equip all students with the
strategies and skills they need to be resourceful and effective compre-
henders of online information, as well as discerning and critical evaluators of online sources. Furthermore, not making online navigation and
reading comprehension a priority for *all* students—regardless of how
they score on traditional measures of reading proficiency with print
texts—will only exacerbate existing achievement gaps and create new

ones (Henry, 2007b; Leu et al., 2009). Fortunately, much good work is already happening in these areas (e.g., Afflerbach & Cho, 2009; Castek, 2008; Coiro, 2007, 2009a; Coiro & Dobler, 2007; Eagleton & Dobler, 2007; Eagleton, Guinee, & Langlais, 2003; Henry, 2007a, 2007b; Salmon, 2003), and we hope to see this work spread and accelerate in the years ahead.

A third, and related, suggestion is that comprehension pedagogy needs to redouble its efforts to equip readers to learn for themselves and to make self-regulation and improvement of reading comprehension strategies an expected and familiar aspect of reading for all readers. This suggestion emerges from our earlier discussion of the increased prominence of metacognitive knowledge and strategies in online reading. Given that online readers are required to orchestrate more different processes and strategies than print readers and face many more choices (regarding which Web tools to use, which hyperlinks to follow, how to delimit the contours of the text at hand, etc.), it seems appropriate for teachers at all levels of education to devote more time than before to instruction and practice in metacognitive knowledge and strategies. The results from studies with print-based reading and instruction strongly suggest the effectiveness of teaching reading comprehension strategies (Pressley & Harris, 2006). Similar studies with online texts are still few and far between (cf. Leu et al., 2005; Castek, 2008; Coiro, 2009a; Stadtler & Bromme, 2007; Zhang, 2007). However, it seems reasonable to expect that instruction in metacognitive strategies tailored to online reading will be similarly beneficial to younger and older readers. As new technologies for presenting and processing text continue to be developed at a breathtaking pace (consider free Web tools such as *www.wordle.net, www.diigo, com, delicious.com, www.ibreadcrumbs.com,* and *ultimate-research-assistant.com,* and extrapolate from there), students also need to be adept at applying their metacognitive knowledge and strategies to making choices about how to encounter and interact with text for different purposes, using the interfaces and the tools that are most beneficial for them. Looking ahead, we anticipate that the practice of comprehension will become ever more deictic, shifting in form, function, and purpose as the underlying technologies for representing textual information continue to evolve in ways we cannot anticipate.

A fourth suggestion, building on the previous two, is that we need new instruments to assess online reading comprehension. These instruments may incorporate traditional reading comprehension questions from existing instruments but will also assess the skills and strategies

that, for online readers, are now essential ingredients of successful reading activity: efficient searching for information, evaluation of sources,
synthesizing information from two or more sources, accessing information in different media, and so forth. The need for these instruments
is urgent for at least three reasons: to provide reliable data about what
online readers can and can't do; to show which curricula, teaching
methods, and technologies are associated with the best learning outcomes; and to prod the research and assessment communities to keep
sharpening their focus on the key underlying constructs of online reading comprehension. In 2009 the fourth international PISA assessment
was administered in 22 of the 67 main survey countries, and for the
first time included a 30-minute section assessing the reading literacy
of 15-year-olds with electronic texts (Searle, Lumley, & Mendelovits,
2009). In the near future, we can expect to see other assessments and
standardized tests begin to move in the same direction (Coiro, 2009b;
Leu et al., 2008, 2009; Searle et al., 2009). All these assessments face the
challenge of not overemphasizing narrowly defined skills (such as using
Boolean search operators) or particular tools and technologies (such
as e-mail programs) but instead probing key underlying cognitive abilities (formulating questions, breaking a problem into component parts,
synthesizing and communicating results, etc.).

Fifth, the evolution of conceptions of reading comprehension suggests two related conclusions: that research on online comprehension
is in its infancy, and that the maturing of scholarship on the cognitive
aspects of online comprehension will require the highest forms of imagi-
native rigor that reading research has yet seen in the scholarly literature.
Thanks to research by Leu (2000), Coiro and Dobler (2007), Zhang and
Duke (2008), Coiro et al. (2008), Muller-Kalthoff & Moller (2006), and
others, we have taken important first steps toward describing and understanding the skills and strategies required for successful online reading.
But there is much we don't know, and much that is extremely difficult
to study using traditional study designs and methods. As we have seen,
one obvious example of this difficulty pertains to the way online readers choose what to read and how much to read; given that no two online
readers follow exactly the same reading itinerary, and given the virtual
disappearance of the idea of a stable, unitary text, researchers face formidable challenges in terms of (1) disentangling and then controlling
a large number of variables and (2) establishing a basis for generalizations. These difficulties are further complicated by the fact that the technologies of online reading continue to evolve at a rapid pace. Can results

obtained from subjects using version 1.8 of a particular Web browser be compared with results from an earlier study where subjects used version 1.2? Possibly, but not without a burdensome set of caveats, limitations, stipulations, and provisos. At the same time, today new possibilities exist for observing and tracking reader behavior. For example in digital environments, tools abound for tracking the search keywords readers use, the websites they visit, the time they spend on each page, the hyperlinks they click, and so forth. As researchers get better at harnessing these data-harvesting features, we can expect to learn a great deal about the behaviors of large numbers of readers. The reading comprehension research of the future will need to triangulate these kinds of data with nano-grained observations of individual online readers.

Finally, the evolution suggests that we will need to conceive, execute, and disseminate research about online comprehension at breakneck speed. Although the underlying cognitive processes evolve more slowly, new technologies and new tools for reading are evolving so rapidly that findings based on a particular tool or a particular aspect of online reading (such as sorting and evaluating search engine results) may have a very short shelf life. By the same token, the "goodness of fit" for any working model of online reading comprehension will become increasingly time sensitive; data collected to understand the forms of comprehension made possible by new tools, texts, and tasks will likely not fit the model constructed from data just a few years ago (e.g., Small, Moody, Sidarth, & Bookheimer, 2009). At the same time, while nothing we say about reading can today be carved in stone (if it ever could be), it seems particularly important at present to articulate a working model of what online reading comprehension looks like. The practical relevance and usefulness of such a model has never been greater. Clearly, the transition from print to online reading is fraught with tensions and frustrations, as well as tremendous opportunities for an enhanced cognitive conception of reading comprehension. An evolving and cohering cognitive model of comprehension will help everyone—classroom teachers and researchers, policy makers and nonspecialist commentators—steer clear of hyperbolic claims for and against online reading (as though online reading were an "issue" one could be for or against [see, for e.g., Bauerlein, 2008]) and instead focus on addressing problems and frustrations and taking full advantage of benefits and opportunities (Leu, O'Byrne, Zawilinski, McVerry, & Everett-Cacopardo, 2009). Our aim in this chapter has been to survey past developments and provide context for the articulation of such a working model.

ACKNOWLEDGMENTS

Preparation of this chapter was made possible in part by a grant from Carnegie Corporation of New York's *Advancing Literacy Initiative*. The statements made and views expressed are solely the responsibility of the authors.

REFERENCES

Afflerbach, P., & Cho, B. U. (2009). Determining and describing reading strategies: Internet and traditional forms of reading. In H. S. Waters & W. Schneider (Eds.), *Metacognition, strategy use, and instruction* (pp. 201–225). New York: Guilford Press.

Anderson, R. C., Hiebert, E. H., Scott, J. A., & Wilkinson, I. A. G. (1985). *Becoming a nation of readers: The report of the Commission on Reading.* Washington, DC: U.S. Department of Education.

Anderson, R. C., & Pearson, P. D. (1984). A schema-theoretic view of basic processes in reading comprehension. In P. D.Pearson, R. Barr, M. L. Kamil, & P. Mosenthal (Eds.), *Handbook of reading research* (pp. 255–291). New York: Longman.

Bateson, G. (1972). *Steps to an ecology of mind.* New York: Ballantine.

Bauerlein, M. (2008). *The dumbest generation: How the digital age stupefies young Americans and jeopardizes our future.* New York: Penguin.

Beck, I. L., McKeown, M. G., Worthy, J., Sandora, C. A., & Kucan, L. (1996). Questioning the author: A year-long classroom implementation to engage students with text. *Elementary School Journal, 4,* 385–414.

Bronfenbrenner, U. (1979). *The ecology of human development: Experiments by nature and design.* Cambridge, MA: Harvard University Press.

Burbules, N. C., & Callister, T. A. (2000). *Watch IT: The risks and promises of information technologies for education.* Boulder, CO: Westview.

Calinescu, M. (1996). Faces of rereading. *Poetics Today, 17*(2), 253–261.

Carey, R. F., & Harste, J. C. (1987). Comprehension as context: Toward reconsideration of a transactional theory of reading. In R. J. Tierney & P. L. Anders (Eds.), *Understanding readers' understanding: Theory and practice* (pp. 189–204). Hillsdale, NJ: Erlbaum.

Castek, J. M. (2008). *How do 4th and 5th grade students acquire the new literacies of online reading comprehension?: Exploring the contexts that facilitate learning.* Unpublished doctoral dissertation, University of Connecticut, Storrs.

Chang, F. R. (1983). Mental processes in reading: A methodological review. *Reading Research Quarterly, 18*(2), 216–230.

Coiro, J. (2003). Reading comprehension on the Internet: Expanding our understanding of reading comprehension to encompass new literacies. *Reading Teacher, 56*(5), 458–465.

Coiro, J. (2005). Making sense of online text. *Educational Leadership, 63*(2), 30–35.

Coiro, J. (2007). *Exploring changes to reading comprehension on the Internet: Paradoxes and possibilities for diverse adolescent readers.* Unpublished doctoral dissertation, University of Connecticut, Storrs.

Coiro, J. (2009a). Promising practices for supporting adolescents' online literacy development. In K. D. Wood & W. E. Blanton (Eds.), *Promoting literacy with adolescent learners: Research-based instruction* (pp. 442–471). New York: Guilford Press.

Coiro, J. (2009b). Rethinking reading assessment in a digital age: How is reading comprehension different and where do we turn now? *Educational Leadership, 66*(6), 59–63.

Coiro, J., & Dobler, E. (2007). Exploring the comprehension strategies used by sixth-grade skilled readers as they search for and locate information on the Internet. *Reading Research Quarterly, 42*(2), 214–257.

Coiro, J., Knobel, M., Lankshear, C., & Leu, D. J. (Eds.). (2008). *Handbook of research on new literacies.* New York: Routledge.

Cole, M. (1996). *Cultural psychology: A once and future discipline.* Cambridge, MA: Harvard University Press.

Cott, J. (1983). *Pipers at the gates of dawn: The wisdom of children's literature.* New York: Random House.

Cronin, B. (2001). Hyperauthorship: A postmodern perversion or evidence of a structural shift in scholarly communication practices? *Journal of the American Society for Information Science and Technology, 52*(7), 558–569.

Cronin, B. (2004). Bowling alone together: Academic writing as distributed cognition. *Journal of the American Society for Information Science and Technology, 55*(6), 557–560.

Cronin, B., Shaw, S., & La Barre, K. (2003). A cast of thousands: Coauthorship and subauthorship collaboration in the 20th century as manifested in the scholarly journal literature of psychology and philosophy. *Journal of the American Society for Information Science and Technology, 54*(9), 855–871.

Delany, P., & Landow, G. P. (1991). *Hypermedia and literary studies.* Cambridge, MA: MIT Press.

DeStefano, D., & LeFevre, J.-A. (2007). Cognitive load in hypertext reading: A review. *Computers in Human Behavior, 23*(3), 1616–1641.

Duke, N. K., Schmar-Dobler, E., & Zhang, S. (2006). Comprehension and technology. In M. C. McKenna, L. D. Labbo, R. D. Kieffer, & D. Reinking (Eds.), *International handbook of literacy and technology* (Vol. 2, pp. 317–326). Mahwah, NJ: Erlbaum.

Durkin, D. (1993). *Teaching them to read* (6th ed.). Boston: Allyn & Bacon.

Eagleton, M. B., & Dobler, E. (2007). *Reading the Web: Strategies for Internet inquiry.* New York: Guilford Press.

Eagleton, M. B., Guinee, K., & Langlais, K. (2003). Teaching Internet literacy strategies: The hero inquiry project. *Voices from the Middle, 10,* 28–35.

Emigh, W., & Herring, S. C. (2005). *Collaborative authoring on the Web: A genre analysis of online encyclopedias.* Proceedings of the 38th Annual Hawaii International Conference on System Sciences (HICSS'05) (Track 4, 99a). Retrieved January 24, 2007, from *csdl2.computer.org/persagen/DLAbsToc.jsp?resourcePath=/dl/proceedings/&toc=comp/proceedings/hicss/2005/2268/04/2268toc.xml&DOI=10.1109/HICSS.2005.149.*

Falk, A. E. (2007). D. Pep talk: Then the adicity of propositional attitudes and their contents. *Desire and Belief.* Retrieved January 24, 2007, from *homepages.wmich.edu/~afalk/db2nd_d_R.pdf.*

Gaskins, I. W. (2002). Taking charge of reader, text, activity, and context variables. In A. P. Sweet & C. E. Snow (Eds.), *Rethinking reading comprehension* (pp. 141–165). New York: Guilford Press.

Gebauer, J., & Shaw, M. J. (2002, September). *A theory of task/technology fit for mobile applications to support organizational processes.* Paper presented at Web 2002: The First Workshop on e-Business, SIGeBiz of the Association for Information Systems, Barcelona, Spain. Retrieved January 24, 2007, from *citebm.business.uiuc.edu/B2Bresearch/TTF-theory.pdf.*

Geise, M. (1998). Self without body: Textual self-representation in an electronic community. *First Monday, 3*(4). Retrieved January 27, 2007, from *www.firstmonday.org/issues/issue3_4/giese/index.html.*

Goffman, E. (1959). *The presentation of self in everyday life.* Edinburgh, Scotland: University of Edinburgh Social Sciences Research Centre.

Golden, J. M. (1986). Reader–text interaction. *Theory into Practice, 25*(2), 91–96.

Gray, W. S. (1925). *Summary of investigations related to reading.* Chicago: University of Chicago Press.

Hall, D. D. (1996). *Cultures of print: Essays in the history of the book.* Amherst: University of Massachusetts Press.

Harker, W. J. (1988). Literary communication: The author, the reader, the text. *Journal of Aesthetic Education, 22*(2), 5–14.

Harris, A. J. (1940). *How to increase reading ability: A guide to diagnostic and remedial methods.* New York: Longman.

Harris, T. L., & Hodges, R. E. (Eds.). (1981). *A dictionary of reading and related terms.* Newark, DE: International Reading Association.

Hartman, D. K. (1992a). Eight readers reading: The intertextual links of able readers using multiple passages [Outstanding Dissertation Award summary]. *Reading Research Quarterly, 27*(2), 122–123.

Hartman, D. K. (1992b). Intertextuality and reading: Reconceptualizing the reader, the text, the author, and the context. *Linguistics and Education, 4*(3&4), 295–311.

Hartman, D. K. (2000). What will be the influences of media on literacy in the next millennium. *Reading Research Quarterly, 35*(2), 280–282.

Hartman, D. K. (2004). Deconstructing the reader, the text, and the context: Intertextuality and reading from a "cognitive" perspective. In N. Shuart-Faris & D. Bloome (Eds.), *Uses of intertextuality in classroom and educational research* (pp. 353–372). Greenwich, CT: Information Age.

Hartman, D. K., & Hartman, J. A. (1993). Reading across texts: Expanding the role of the reader. *Reading Teacher, 47*(3), 202–211.

Henry, L. A. (2006). SEARCHing for an Answer: The critical role of new literacies while reading on the Internet. *Reading Teacher, 59*(7), 614–627.

Henry, L. A. (2007a). *Investigation of literacy skills and strategies used while searching for information on the Internet: A comprehensive review and synthesis of research.* Final report submitted to the Nila Banton Smith Research Dissemination Support Grant, International Reading Association, Newark, Delaware.

Henry, L. A. (2007b). *Exploring new literacies pedagogy and online reading comprehension among middle school students and teachers: Issues of social equity or social exclusion?* Unpublished doctoral dissertation, University of Connecticut, Storrs.

Holland, D., Lachiotte, W., Skinner, D., & Cain, C. (1998). Authoring selves. In D. Holland, W. Lachiotte, D. Skinner, & C. Cain (Eds.), *Identity and agency in cultural worlds* (pp. 169–191). Cambridge, MA: Harvard University Press.

Hoover, W. A., & Gough, P. B. (1990). The simple view of reading. *Reading and Writing: An Interdisciplinary Journal, 2*, 127–160.

Huey, E. B. (1900). On the psychology and physiology of reading, I. *American Journal of Psychology, 11*(3), 283–302.

Huey, E. B. (1901). On the psychology and physiology of reading, II. *American Journal of Psychology, 12*(3), 292–312.

Huey, E. B. (1908). *The psychology and pedagogy of reading: With a review of the history of reading and writing and of methods, texts, and hygiene in reading.* New York: Macmillan.

International Reading Association. (2002). *Integrating literacy and technology in the curriculum.* Newark, DE: International Reading Association.

Jacobs, G., & Gallo, P. (2002). Reading alone together: Enhancing extensivReadie reading via student–student cooperation in second-language instruction. *Reading Online, 5*(6). Retrieved on January 27, 2007, from *www.readingonline.org/articles/art_index.asp?HREF=jacobs/index.html.*

Jacucci, C., Jacucci, G., Wagner, I., & Psik, T. (2005). A manifesto for the performative development of ubiquitous media. In *Proceedings of the 4th Decennial Conference on Critical Computing: Between Sense and Sensibility Table of Contents* (pp. 19–28). Aarhus, Denmark: Critical Computing.

Kiili, C., Laurinen, L., & Marttunen, M. (2008). Students evaluating Internet sources: From versatile evaluators to uncritical readers. *Journal of Educational Computing Research, 39*(1), 75–95.

Kiili, C., Laurinen, L., & Marttunen, M. (2009). Skilful Internet reader is metacognitively competent. In L. T. Wee Hin & R. Subramaniam (Eds.), *Handbook of research on new media literacy at the K–12 level: Issues and challenges* (Vol. 2, pp. 654–668), Hershey, PA: Information Science Reference.

Kintsch, W. (1988). The use of knowledge in discourse processing: A construction integration model. *Psychological Review, 95,* 163–182.

Kintsch, W. (1998). *Comprehension: A paradigm for cognition.* New York: Cambridge University Press.

Kintsch, W., & Kintsch, E. (2005). Comprehension. In S. G. Paris & S. A. Stahl (Eds.), *Current issues on reading comprehension and assessment* (pp. 71–92). Mahwah, NJ: Erlbaum.

Kintsch, W., & van Dijk, T. A. (1978). Toward a model of text comprehension and production. *Psychological Review, 85*(5), 363–394.

Landow, G. P. (1997). *Hypertext 2.0: The convergence of contemporary critical theory and technology.* Baltimore: Johns Hopkins University Press.

Landow, G. P. (2006). *Hypertext 3.0: Critical theory and new media in an era of globalization.* Baltimore: Johns Hopkins University Press.

Lawless, K., & Schrader, P. G. (2008). Where do we go now? Understanding research on navigation in complex digital environments. In J. Coiro, M. Knobel, C. Lankshear, & D. J. Leu (Eds.), *Handbook of research on new literacies* (pp. 267–296). New York: Routledge.

Leander, K. M., & McKim, K. K. (2003). Tracing the everyday "sitings" of adolescents on the Internet: A strategic adaptation of ethnography across online and offline spaces. *Education, Communication, and Information, 3*(2), 211–239.

Leu, D. J. (2000). Literacy and technology: Deictic consequences for literary education in an information age. In M. L. Kamil, R. Barr, P. B. Mosenthal, & P. D. Pearson (Eds.), *Handbook of reading research* (Vol. 3, pp. 743–770). Mahwah, NJ: Erlbaum.

Leu, D. J., Castek, J., Hartman, D. K., Coiro, J., Henry, L. A., Kulikowich, J. M., et al. (2005). *Evaluating the development of scientific knowledge and new forms of reading comprehension during online learning. Final Research Report.* Naperville, IL: North Central Regional Educational Laboratory/Learning Point Associates.

Leu, D. J., Coiro, J., Castek, J., Hartman, D. K., Henry, L. A., & Reinking, D. (2008). Research on instruction and assessment in the new literacies of online reading comprehension. In C. C. Block & S. Parris (Eds.), *Comprehension instruction: Research-based best practices* (pp. 321–345). New York: Guilford Press.

Leu, D. J., McVerry, G., O'Byrne, I. Zawilinski, L., Castek, J., & Hartman, D. K. (2009). The new literacies of online reading comprehension and the irony of

No Child Left Behind: Students who require our assistance the most actually receive it the least. In L. M. Morrow, R. Rueda, & D. Lapp (Eds.), *Handbook of research on literacy and diversity* (pp. 173–194). New York: Guilford Press.

Leu, D. J., O'Byrne, W. I., Zawilinski, L., McVerry, J. G., & Everett-Cacopardo, H. (2009). Comments on Greenhow, Robelia, and Hughes: Expanding the new literacies conversation. *Educational Researcher, 38*(4), 264–269.

Linderholm, T., & van den Broek, P. (2002). The effects of reading purpose and working memory capacity on the processing of expository text. *Journal of Educational Psychology, 94*, 778–784.

Little, W., Brown, L., & Trumble, W. (2002). *Shorter Oxford English dictionary* (5th ed.). Oxford, UK: Oxford University Press.

Lowry, P. B., Curtis, A., & Lowry, M. R. (2004). Building a taxonomy and nomenclature of collaborative writing to improve interdisciplinary research and practice. *Journal of Business Communication, 41*(1), 66–99.

Ludlow, P. (1996). The adicity of "believes" and the hidden indexical theory. *Analysis, 56*(2), 97–101.

Malloy, J., & Gambrell, L. B. (2006). Approaching the unavoidable: Literacy instruction and the Internet. *Reading Teacher, 59*(5), 482–484.

Many, J. E. (1991). The effects of stance and age level on children's literary responses. *Journal of Reading Behavior, 23*(1), 61–85.

Mills, C. B. (1995). Reading procedural texts: Effects of purpose for reading and predictions of reading comprehension models. *Discourse Processes, 21*(1), 79–107.

Moats, L. C. (1999). *Teaching reading is rocket science: What expert teachers of reading should know and be able to do.* Washington, DC: American Federation of Teachers.

Mosenthal, P. (1983). The influence of social situation on children's classroom comprehension of text. *Elementary School Journal, 83*(5), 537–547.

Muller-Kalthoff, T., & Moller, J. (2006). Browsing while reading: Effects of instructional design and learners' prior knowledge. *ALT-J: Research in Learning Technology, 14*(2), 183–198.

Narvaez, D., van den Broek, P., & Ruiz, A. B. (1999). The influence of reading purpose on inference generation and comprehension in reading. *Journal of Educational Psychology, 91*, 488–496.

New Literacies Research Team (Castek, J., Coiro, J., Hartman, D. K., Henry, L. A., Leu, D. J., & Zawilinski, L.). (2007). New literacies, new challenges, and new opportunities. In M. B. Sampson, P. E. Linder, F. Falk-Ross, M. M. Foote, & S. Szabo (Eds.), *Multiple Literacies in the 21st century: Twenty-eighth yearbook of the College Reading Association* (pp. 31–50). Logan, UT: College Reading Association.

Nystrand, M. (1987). The role of context in written communication. In R. Horowitz & S. J. Samuels (Eds.), *Comprehending oral and written language* (pp. 197–215). New York: Academic Press.

Nystrand, M., & Himley, M. (1984). Written text as social interaction. *Theory into Practice, 23*(3), 198–207.

Organisation for Economic Co-operation and Development. (2003). *The PISA 2003 assessment framework: Mathematics, reading, science and problem solving knowledge and skills.* Paris: OECD Publications.

Paris, S. G., Wasik, B. A., & Turner, J. C. (1991). The development of strategic readers. In R. Barr, M. L. Kamil, P. Mosenthal, & P. D. Pearson (Eds.), *Handbook of reading research, Vol. 2* (pp. 609–640). New York: Longman.

Pearson, P. D., & Tierney, R. J. (1984). On becoming a thoughtful reader: Learning to read like a writer. In A. C. Purves & O. Niles (Eds.), *Becoming readers in a complex society: Eighty-third yearbook of the National Society of the Study of Education* (pp. 144–173). Chicago: National Society for the Study of Education.

Pressley, M., & Harris, K. R. (2006). Cognitive strategies instruction: From basic research to classroom instruction. In P. A. Alexander & P. H. Winne (Eds.), *Handbook of educational psychology* (2nd ed., pp. 265–286). Mahwah, NJ: Erlbaum.

Prien, B. (2004). Family resemblances: A thesis about the change of meaning over time. *Kriterion, 18*, 15–24.

RAND Reading Study Group. (2002). *Reading for understanding: Toward an R&D Program in Reading Comprehension.* Santa Monica, CA: RAND.

Rapp, D. N., & van den Broek, P. (2005). Dynamic text comprehension: An integrative view of reading. *Current Directions in Psychological Science, 14*(5), 276–279.

Rosenberg, J. E. (1999, February). *A hypertextuality of arbitrary structure: A writer's point of view.* Paper presented at the ACM Conference on Hypertext and Hypermedia: First Structural Computing Workshop, Hypertext 99, Darmstadt, Germany. Retrieved January 22, 2007, from *www.well.com/user/jer/HAS.html.*

Salmon, G. (2003). *E-moderating: The key to teaching and learning online.* New York: Routledge.

Sandora, C., Beck, I., & McKeown, M. (1999). A comparison of two discussion strategies on students' comprehension and interpretation of complex literature. *Journal of Reading Psychology, 20*, 177–212.

Searle, D., Lumley, T., & Mendelovits, J. (2009, September). *Reading for the new ERA: Assessing reading in a digital environment.* Paper presented at the meeting of the International Association for Educational Assessment, Brisbane, Australia. Retrieved October 30, 2009, from *www.iaea2009.com/papers/506.doc.*

Shanahan, T. (1992). Reading comprehension as a conversation with an author. In M. Pressley, K. Harris, & J. Guthrie (Eds.), *Promoting academic competence and literacy in schools* (pp. 129–148). San Diego: Academic Press.

Short, K. (2004). Researching intertextuality within collaborative classroom learning environments. In N. Shuart-Faris & D. Bloome (Eds.), *Uses of intertextualtiy in classroom and educational research* (pp. 373–393). Charlotte, NC: Information Age.

Smagorinsky, P., & Coppock, J. (1994, April). *The reader, the text, the context: An exploration of a choreographed response to literature.* Paper presented at the annual meeting of the American Educational Research Association, New Orleans, LA.

Small, G. W., Moody, T. D., Sidarth, P., & Bookheimer, S. Y. (2009). Your brain on Google: Patterns of cerebral activation during Internet searching. *American Journal of Geriatric Psychiatry, 17*(2), 116–126.

Smolkin, L. B., & Donovan, C. A. (2001). The contexts of comprehension: The information book read aloud, comprehension acquisition, and comprehension instruction in a first-grade classroom. *Elementary School Journal, 102*(2), 97–122.

Stadtler, M., & Bromme, R. (2007). Dealing with multiple documents on the WWW: The role of metacognition in the formation of documents models. *International Journal of Computer-Supported Collaborative Learning, 2*(2–3), 191–210.

Sternberg, M. (2003). Universals of narrative and their cognitivist fortunes (I). *Poetics Today, 24*(2), 297–395.

Sussman, H. (2000). Deterritorializing the text: Flow-theory and deconstruction. *MLN, 115*(5), 974–996.

Tannen, D. (1979). What's in a frame?: Surface evidence for underlying expectations. In R. Freedle (Ed.), *New directions in discourse processing* (pp. 137–181). Norwood, NJ: Ablex.

Tannen, D., & Wallat, C. (1987). Interaction frames and knowledge schemas in interaction: Examples from a medical examination/interview. *Social Psychology Quarterly, 50*, 205–217.

Tierney, R. J. (2006). Global/cultural teachers creating possibilities: Reading worlds, reading selves, and learning to teach. *Pedagogies, 1*(1), 77–86.

van den Broek, P., Lorch, R. F., Jr., Linderholm, T., & Gustafson, M. (2001). The effects of readers' goals on the generation of inferences. *Memory and Cognition, 29*, 1081–1087.

van den Broek, P., Rapp, D. N., & Kendeou, P. (2005). Integrating memory-based and constructionist processes in accounts of reading comprehension. *Discourse Processes, 39*, 299–316.

van den Broek, P., Young, M., Tzeng, Y., & Linderholm, T. (1999). The landscape model of reading: Inferences and the online construction of a memory representation. In H. van Oostendorp & S. R. Goldman (Eds.), *The construction of mental representations during reading* (pp. 71–98). Mahwah, NJ: Erlbaum.

van Dijk, T. A., & Kintsch, W. (1983). *Strategies of discourse comprehension*. New York: Academic Press.

Volet, S. (2001). Emerging trends in recent research on motivation in learning contexts. In S. Volet & S. Järvelä (Eds.), *Motivation in learning contexts: Theoretical and methodological implications* (pp. 319–334). Oxford, UK: Elsevier.

Wallace, P. M. (2001). *The psychology of the Internet*. Cambridge, UK: Cambridge University Press.

Wiszniewski, D., & Coyne, R. (2002). Mask and identity: The hermeneutics of self-construction in the information age. In K. A. Renninger & W. Shumar (Eds.), *Building virtual communities: Learning and change in cyberspace* (pp. 191–214). New York: Cambridge University Press.

Wittgenstein, L. (1953). *Philosophical investigations*. New York: Blackwell.

Zhang, S. (2007). *Instruction in the WWWDOT approach to improving students' evaluation of websites*. Unpublished doctoral dissertation, Michigan State University, East Lansing.

Zhang, S., & Duke, N. K. (2008). Strategies for Internet reading with different reading purposes: A descriptive study of twelve good Internet readers. *Journal of Literacy Research, 40*(1), 128–162.

CHAPTER 8

A Situated–Sociocultural Approach to Literacy and Technology

JAMES PAUL GEE

In this chapter I first sketch out the background to the approach I take to literacy and technology—an approach I would call "situated–sociocultural." By this term I mean a blend of themes from work on situated cognition dealing with mind and learning and work on sociocultural approaches to language, literacy, and technology. I sketch out this background by overviewing several interdisciplinary intellectual movements that have arisen over the last few decades. I start with the new literacy studies and move on to situated cognition studies, the new literacies studies, and the new media literacy studies.

After my background sketch, I turn to one specific application of the ideas in this sketch to the interactions between literacy and technology in and out of schools. This application starts with reading and ends with a discussion of video games.

THE NEW LITERACY STUDIES

In my book *Sociolinguistics and Literacies* (Gee, 2007b) I attempted to name what I saw as an emerging field of study. I called this field "the new literacy studies." Today it is sometimes just referred to as "the NLS" (Brandt & Clinton, 2002; Gee, 2000; Hull & Schultz, 2001; Pahl & Rowsel, 2005, 2006; Prinsloo & Mignonne, 1996; Street, 1984, 1993, 1995, 1997, 2005). And, of course, it is no longer new.

The scholars I saw as composing the emerging field of the new literacy studies were people from linguistics, history, anthropology, rhetoric and composition studies, cultural psychology, education, and other areas (e.g., Bazerman, 1989; Cazden, 1988; Cook-Gumperz, 1986; Gee, 1987; Graff, 1979; Heath, 1983; Sribner & Cole, 1981; Scollon & Scollon, 1981; Street, 1984; Wertsch, 1985). These scholars all came from different disciplines and wrote in different theoretical languages. Nonetheless, it seemed to me that they were converging on a coherent and shared view about literacy, although they never did come to share a common language out of which they wrote.

The NLS opposed a traditional psychological approach to literacy. Such an approach viewed literacy as a "cognitive phenomenon" and defined it in terms of mental states and mental processing. The "ability to read" and "the ability to write" were treated as things people did inside their heads.

The NLS saw literacy as something people did not just do inside their heads but inside society. It argued that literacy was not primarily a mental phenomenon, but, rather, a sociocultural one. Literacy was a social and cultural achievement—it was about ways of participating in social and cultural groups—not just a mental achievement. Thus literacy needed to be understood and studied in its full range of contexts—not just cognitive, but also social, cultural, historical, and institutional.

Traditional psychology saw readers and writers as engaged in mental processes like decoding, retrieving information, comprehension, inferencing, and so forth. The NLS saw readers and writers as engaged in social or cultural *practices*. Written language is used differently in different practices by different social and cultural groups. And in these practices, written language never sits all by itself, cut off from oral language and action. Rather, within different practices it is integrated with different ways of using oral language; different ways of acting and interacting; different ways of knowing, valuing, and believing; and often different ways of using various tools and technologies.

For example, people read and write religious texts differently than legal ones and differently again than biology texts or texts in popular culture like video game strategy guides or fan fiction. And people can read the same text in different ways for different purposes; for example, they can read the Bible as theology, literature, history, or as a self-help guide. They can read a comic book as entertainment, as insider details for expert fans, as cultural critique, or as heroic mythology.

People don't just read and write these texts. They do things with these texts, things that often involve more than just reading and writing. They do them with other people—people like fundamentalists, lawyers, biologists, manga otaku, gamers, or whatever—who sometimes (often) make judgments about who are "insiders" and who are not. So what determines how one reads or writes in a given case? Not just what is in one's head, but, rather, the conventions, norms, values, and practices of different social and cultural groups: lawyers, gamers, historians, religious groups, and schools, for instance, or larger cultural groups like (certain types of) Native Americans, African Americans, or "middle-class" people.

For example, Ron and Suzanne Scollon (Scollon & Scollon, 1981) argued that some Native American and Canadian groups viewed essays (a prototypical literacy form in school) quite differently than do many Anglo-Americans and Canadians. Athabaskians—the group the Scollons studied in the United States and Canada—have a cultural norm in which they prefer to communicate only in familiar circumstances with people who are already known. Essays require the writer to communicate to a "fictional" audience—the assumed general "rational reader," not someone already known—and thus violate a cultural communicational norm for Athabaskians. To write an essay, for Athabaskians, is to engage in a form of cross-cultural conflict. Essays are not "neutral"; they are socially, historically, and culturally value-laden. Indeed, how, when, and why they arose in history is a well-studied phenomenon.

People learn a given way of reading or writing by participating in (or, at least, coming to understand) the distinctive practices of different social and cultural groups. When these groups teach or "apprentice" people to read and write in certain ways, they never stop there. They teach readers to act, interact, talk, know, believe, and value in certain ways as well, ways that "go with" how they write and read (Gee, 2007b).

So, for example, knowing how to write a "game FAQ" (a strategy guide for a video game)—or how to read one—requires that you know how game FAQs are used in the social practices of gamers, practices that involve a lot more than just reading and writing. You need to know how gamers talk about, debate over, and act in regard to such things as "spoilers" and "cheats" and "cheating," all defined as gamers define them, not just in general terms (Consalvo, 2007).

The same is true of knowing how to write or read a legal document, a piece of literary criticism, a religious tract, or a memo from the boss. You can come to appreciate some texts without actually participating in the group whose texts they are, but you still have to know how the "texts" fit into those practices. And you can only be a "central participant" if you have actually participated and undergone an "apprenticeship" with the group (Lave, 1996; Lave & Wenger, 1991).

So *literacy* becomes plural: *literacies.* There are many different social and cultural practices that incorporate literacy; so, too, do many different "literacies" (legal literacy, gamer literacy, country music literacy, academic literacy of many different types). People don't just read and write in general, they read and write specific sorts of "texts" in specific ways determined by the values and practices of different social and cultural groups.

That is why the NLS often tended to study not literacy itself directly, but such things as "activity systems" (Engeström, 1987); "discourses" (Gee, 2007b); "discourse communities" (Bizzell, 1992); "cultures" (Street, 1995); "communities of practices" (Lave & Wenger, 1991; Wenger, 1998); "actor–actant networks" (Latour, 2005); "collectives" (Latour, 2004); "affinity groups" or "affinity spaces" (Gee, 2004)—the names differ and there are others, but they are all names for ways in which people socioculturally organize themselves to engage in activities. The moral was: follow the social, cultural, institutional, and historical organizations of people (whatever you call them) first and then see how literacy is taken up and used in these organizations, along with action, interaction, values, and tools and technologies.

The NLS, thanks to its opposition to traditional cognitive psychology (not to mention its hostility to earlier forms of psychology like behaviorism), tended to have little or nothing to say about the mind or cognition. It paid attention only to the social, cultural, historical, and institutional contexts of literacy. It had little to say about the individual apart from the individual's "membership" in various social and cultural groups. Thus it, too, had little to say about learning as an individual phenomenon. Learning was largely treated—if it was treated at all—as changing patterns of participation in "communities of practice" (Lave & Wenger, 1991).

SITUATED COGNITION STUDIES

The NLS talked little about learning at the level of the individual, largely due to its hostility to psychology. However, in the 1980s psychology itself changed. New movements in "cognitive science" and "the learning sciences" began to argue that the mind is furnished not primarily by abstract concepts, but by records of actual experience (e.g., Barsalou, 1999a, 1999b; P. S. Churchland & Sejnowski, 1992; Clark, 1989, 1993, 1997; Damasio, 1994; Gee, 1992; Glenberg, 1997; Kolodner, 1993, 2006).

Earlier work in cognitive psychology—often based on a metaphor that saw the human mind as like a digital computer—argued that memory was severely limited, as it is in a digital computer (Newell & Simon 1972). This newer work argued that human memory is nearly limitless and that we can and do store almost all our actual experiences in our heads and use these experiences to reason about similar experiences or new ones in the future (P. M. Churchland, 1989; P. S. Churchland, 1986; P. S. Churchland & Sejnowski, 1992; Gee, 2004).

This newer work comes in many different varieties and constitutes a "family" of related but not identical viewpoints. For want of a better name, we might call the family "situated cognition studies" (see also Brown, Collins, & Dugid, 1989; Hawkins, 2005; Hutchins, 1995; Lave & Wenger, 1991). These viewpoints all hold that thinking is connected to, and changes across, actual situations and is not usually a process of applying abstract generalizations, definitions, or rules.

Situated cognition studies argues that thinking is tied to *people's experiences of goal-oriented action in the material and social world.* Furthermore, these experiences are stored in the mind/brain not in terms of abstract concepts, but in something like dynamic images tied to perception both of the world and of our own bodies, internal states, and feelings (P. S. Churchland, 1986; Damasio, 1994; Gee, 1992). Thus consider the following quotes, which give the flavor of what it means to say that cognition is situated in embodied experience:

> . . . comprehension is grounded in perceptual simulations that prepare agents for situated action. (Barsalou, 1999a, p. 77)

> . . . to a particular person, the meaning of an object, event, or sentence is what that person can do with the object, event, or sentence. (Glenberg, 1997, p. 3)

. . . increasing evidence suggests that perceptual simulation is indeed central to comprehension. (Barsalou, 1999a, p. 74)

. . . higher intelligence is not a different kind of process from perceptual intelligence. (Hawkins, 2005, p. 96)

Human understanding, then, is not primarily a matter of storing general concepts in the head or applying abstract rules to experience. Rather, humans think, understand, and learn best when they use their prior experiences (so they must have had some) as a guide to prepare themselves for action. I discuss about how they do below.

Work on situated cognition does not take a digital computer as a model of the human mind. Rather, it often uses as a model so-called connectionist or parallel distributed computers (P. M. Churchland, 1989; P. S. Churchland, 1986; P. S. Churchland & Sejnowski, 1992; Gee, 1992; Rumelhart, McClelland, & the PDP Research Group, 1986). Such computers look for and store patterns (networks of associations) among elements of input from the world. The argument is that humans—like connectionist computers—look for patterns in the elements of their experiences in the world and, as they have more and more experiences, find deeper and more subtle patterns that help predict what might happen in the future when they act to accomplish goals (this is, of course, a dynamic version of schema theory; see Gee, 1992).

For example, say I ask you to think of a typical bedroom (Gee, 1992; Rumelhart, McClelland, & the PDP Research Group, 1986). Thanks to your experiences in the world, what you think of may be a room of moderate size with things like a bed, side tables, a dresser, drapes, lamps, pictures, a clock, a carpet, and other things. These have all been elements in your experiences that you have come to see as a pattern (or network of elements). But, say, I tell you there is a small refrigerator in the bedroom. Now you may envision something like a student's bedroom in a dorm (e.g., a smaller room, a bed, a desk, a lamp on the desk, and maybe a mess on the floor). You have formed a different pattern out of the elements of your experience. Such associations and how you use them change as you gain more experiences.

You can see the same thing happening if I say "The coffee spilled, go get a mop" (where you bring in an association with coffee as a liquid) versus "The coffee spilled, go get a broom" (where you bring in an association with coffee as grains). Compare also: "The coffee spilled, stack it again" (Clark, 1993).

Despite the fact that the NLS had little interest in the mind, there is a natural affinity between situated cognition studies and the NLS. This affinity has, for the most part, not been much built on from either side. Situated cognition studies argues that we think through paying attention to elements of our experiences. While this is a claim about the mind, we can ask "What determines what experiences a person has and how they pay attention to those experiences (i.e., how they find patterns in their experiences or what patterns they pay attention to)?"

The answer to this question is this: Participation in the practices of various social and cultural groups determines what experiences people have and how they pay attention to the elements of these experiences. These practices are mediated by various tools and technologies whether these be print or digital media or other tools.

And, of course, this was just what the NLS wanted to study. For example, bird-watching clubs and expert bird watchers shape how new bird-watchers pay attention to their experience of birds and environments in the field (Gee, 1992). And these experiences are mediated in important ways by various tools and technologies such as bird books, scopes, and binoculars. Obviously one experiences a wood duck in a vastly different way when looking at it through a powerful scope than with unaided vision. Furthermore, such technologies allow distinctive social practices to arise that could not otherwise exist (e.g., debating the details of tiny aspects of feathers on hard-to-tell-apart gulls).

Thus a situated view of the mind leads us to social and cultural groups and their tools and technologies. Both situated cognition studies and the NLS point not to the "private mind" but to the world of experience—experience that is almost always shared in social and cultural groups—as the core of human learning, thinking, problem solving, and literacy (where literacy is defined as getting and giving meanings using written language). This was the argument I made in my book, *The Social Mind* (Gee, 1992) at a time when I was trying to integrate learning into the NLS and to link situated cognition studies and the NLS.

THE NEW LITERACIES STUDIES

The NLS argued that written language was a technology for giving and getting meaning. In turn, what written language meant was determined by the social, cultural, historical, and institutional practices of different groups of people.

The new literacies studies simply carries over the NLS argument about written language to new digital technologies. By the way, "the new literacies studies" is parsed grammatically differently than "the new literacy studies." The NLS was about studying literacy in a new way. "The new literacies studies" is about studying new types of literacy beyond print literacy, especially digital literacies and literacy practices embedded in popular culture.

The new literacies studies views different digital tools as technologies for giving and getting meaning, just like language (Coiro, Knobel, Lankshear, & Leu, 2008; Gee 2004, 2007a; Kist, 2004; Kress, 2003; Lankshear, 1997; Lankshear & Knobel, 2006, 2007). Like the NLS, the new literacies studies also argues that the meanings to which these technologies give rise are determined by the social, cultural, historical, and institutional practices of different groups of people. And, as with the NLS, these practices almost always involve more than just using a digital tool—they also involve ways of acting, interacting, valuing, believing, and knowing, as well as often using other sorts of tools and technologies, often including oral and written language.

Just as the NLS wanted to talk about different literacies in the plural—that is, different ways of using written language within different sorts of sociocultural practices—so, too, the New Literacies Studies wants to talk about different "digital literacies," that is, different ways of using digital tools within different sorts of sociocultural practices. In this sense, the new literacies studies is a natural offshoot of the NLS, although the two fields do not contain just the same people by any means.

The new literacies studies has had an important historical relationship with the NLS, from which it partly stems. At the same time as the new literacies studies has been emerging as a field, there has emerged, as well, another area, what we can call the new media literacy studies, for short, "the NMLS." The NMLS has not had a significant historical relationship with the NLS, at least not until recently.

THE NEW MEDIA LITERACY STUDIES

The NMLS is an offshoot of a movement that has been around for some time, namely "media literacy" (on NMLS and its relation to traditional media literacy see, e.g., Beach, 2006; Brunner & Tally, 1999; Buckingham, 2003, 2007; Hobbs, 1997, 2007; Jenkins, 2006; Warschauer, 1998).

Both the NMLS and the earlier media literacy are connected in large part to people in the field of communications or related fields, though interest in both has spread well beyond communications.

Media literacy as a field was concerned with how people give meaning to and get meaning from media, that is, things like advertisements, newspapers, television, and film. Of course, giving and getting meaning from media sometimes involves giving and getting meaning from oral and written language, but in cases where this language is used in media contexts. Giving and getting meaning from media can, of course, involve giving and getting meaning from images, sounds, and "multimodal texts" (texts that mix images and/or sounds with words) as well.

Media literacy did not aim to study just how people give meaning to and get meaning from media, but also to intervene in such matters by studying how people can be made more "critical" or "reflective" about the sorts of meanings they give and get from media (see Vasquez, Harste, & Albers, Chapter 12, this volume). People can be "manipulated" by media and can "manipulate" others with media. It is often relevant to ask whose (vested) interest is served by a given media message and to wonder whether people mistake whose interest such messages really serve, for example, an ad whose message really serves the profit motives of a company but which a consumer can mistakenly take to be in his or her best interest.

Such an approach also raised issues about the extent to which consumers of media are "dupes" or "savvy." Some approaches to media literacy tended to stress the ways in which consumers can and sometimes do use media and media messages for their own interests and desires, even in ways that the producers of those messages did not intend (Alvermann, Moon, & Hagood, 1999; Fiske, 1989; Lankshear & Knobel, 2006). Whether such proactive use of media is or is not a politically effective counter to consumerism and the power of profit-seeking businesses is a matter of debate.

The NMLS inherited a good deal of the concerns and issues of media literacy. However, today it is not just media professionals and corporations that can produce and manipulate people with media. Everyday people—former "consumers"—can now produce their own media and compete with professionals and corporations. Thus the NMLS stresses the ways in which digital tools and media built from them are transforming society and, in particular, popular culture.

Digital tools are giving rise to major transformations in society. These transformations are crucial to the NMLS. First, digital tools are changing the balance of production and consumption in media. It is easier today for people not just to consume media but to produce it themselves. Everyday people—not just experts and elites—can produce professional-looking movies, newscasts, video games (thanks to "modding"), and many other such products.

Second, digital tools are changing the balance of participation and spectatorship. More and more today, people do not have to play just the role of the spectator. Because they can now produce their own music, news, games, and films, for example, they can participate in what used to be practices reserved for professional or elite musicians, filmmakers, game designers, and newspeople (Shirky, 2008).

Third, digital tools are changing the nature of groups, social formations, and power. Prior to our current digital tools, it was hard to start and sustain a group. It usually required an institution, with all its attendant bureaucracy and top-down power. Today, with things like Flickr, MySpace, Facebook, and digital devices like mobile phones, it is easier than ever to form and join groups, even for quite short-term purposes. Often no formal institution is required, and groups can organize themselves bottom up through constant communication and feedback. These quickly formed groups can engage in social, cultural, and political action in a fast, pervasive, and efficient manner. Such groups can readily form and re-form, transforming themselves as circumstances change. In fact, it can sometimes be hard for more traditional groups and institutions to keep up with such flexible group formation.

Fourth, all the above trends are leading to the phenomenon known as "pro-ams." Today young people are using the Internet and other digital tools outside of school to learn and even become experts in a variety of domains. We live in the age of "pro-ams": amateurs who have become experts at whatever they have developed a passion for (Anderson, 2006; Gee, 2008; Leadbeater & Miller, 2004).

Many of these are young people who use the Internet, communication media, digital tools, and membership in often virtual, sometimes real, communities of practice to develop technical expertise in a plethora of different areas. Some of these areas are digital video, video games, digital storytelling, machinima, fan fiction, history and civilization simulations, music, graphic art, political commentary, robotics, anime, and fashion design (e.g., for Sims in *The Sims*). In fact, there are now pro-ams in nearly every endeavor the human mind can think of.

These pro-ams have passion and go deep rather than wide. At the same time, pro-ams are often adept at pooling their skills and knowledge with other pro-ams to bring off bigger tasks or to solve larger problems. These are people who don't necessarily know what everyone else knows, but do know how to collaborate with other pro-ams to put knowledge to work to fulfill their intellectual and social passions.

The NMLS, thus, engages with a new sense of "media literacy." The emphasis is not just on how people respond to media messages, but also on how they engage proactively in a media world where production, participation, social group formation, and high levels of nonprofessional expertise are prevalent. Issues of being critical and reflective are still paramount, of course, but so are issues of how digital media are and are not changing the balance of power and status in society.

POPULAR CULTURE, VIDEO GAMES, AND LEARNING

Now I want to turn to a specific application of the ideas I have just sketched out. Through this discussion, I will show one way—but only one among many—to relate in an integrated way NLS, situated cognition studies, the New Literacies Studies, and NMLS to education.

Consider the situation of a child learning to read. What should our goal for this child be? On the face of it, the goal would seem to be that the child learn to decode print and assign basic or literal meanings to that print. But the situation is not that simple. We know from the now well-studied phenomenon of the "fourth-grade slump" (the phenomenon whereby many children, especially poorer children, pass early reading tests, but cannot read well enough to learn academic content later on in school) that the goal of early reading instruction has to be more forward looking than simple decoding and literal comprehension (*American Educator*, 2003; Chall, Jacobs, & Baldwin, 1990; Gee, 2008; Snow, Burns, & Griffin, 1998).

The goal has to be that children learn to read early on in such a way that this learning creates a successful trajectory throughout the school years and beyond. Such a trajectory is based, more than anything else, on the child's being able to handle increasingly complex language, especially in the content areas (e.g., science and math), as school progresses. Children need to get ready for these increasing language demands as early as possible. It is as if school were more and more conducted in Greek as the grades increased: surely it would be better to be exposed to Greek as early as possible and not wait until school becomes the equivalent of advanced Greek.

Let's call this a "trajectory approach" to early reading. Such an approach has to look not only forward, but backward, as well. Early phonemic awareness and early home-based practice with literacy are the most important correlates with success in first grade, especially in learning to read in the "decode and literally comprehend" sense (Dickinson & Neuman, 2006). However, the child's early home-based oral vocabulary and early skills with complex oral language are the most important correlates for school success—not just in reading, but in the content areas—past the first grade, essentially for the rest of schooling (Dickinson & Neuman, 2006; Gee, 2004; Senechal, Ouellette, & Rodney, 2006). Thus a child's oral language development is key to a successful trajectory approach to reading, that is, an approach that seeks to make a long-term school-based reader of academic content (and that's what's in the high school biology textbook, for example). It is the key to avoiding, even eradicating, the fourth-grade slump.

I must pause because we are on the brink of what could be a major misunderstanding. Decades of research in linguistics has shown that every normal child's early language and language development are just fine (Chomsky, 1986; Labov, 1979; Pinker, 1994). Every child, under normal conditions, develops a perfectly complex and adequate oral language, the child's "native language" (and, of course, sometimes children develop more than one native language). It never happens, under normal conditions—and normal here covers a very wide variation—that, in acquiring English, say, little Janie develops relative clauses, but little Johnnie just can't master them. That, is, of course, in a way, a surprising fact, showing that the acquisition of one's native language is not particularly a matter of ability or skill.

But when I say that children's early oral language—vocabulary and skills with complex language—is a crucial correlate of success in school, a correlate that shows up especially after the child has learned to decode in first grade (one hopes), I am not talking about children's everyday language, the sort of language that is equal for everyone. I am talking about their early preparation for language that is not "everyday," for language that is "technical" or "specialist" or "academic" (Gee, 2004; Schleppegrell, 2004). I refer to people's everyday language—the way they speak when they are not speaking technically or as specialists of some sort—as their "vernacular style." I refer to their language when they are speaking technically or as a specialist as a "specialist style" (people eventually can have a number of different specialist styles, connected to different technical, specialist, or academic concerns).

AN EXAMPLE

Let me give an example of what I am talking about, both in terms of specialist language and in terms of getting ready for later complex specialist language demands early in life. Kevin Crowley has talked insightfully about quite young children developing what he calls "islands of expertise." Crowley and Jacobs (2002, p. 333) define an island of expertise as "any topic in which children happen to become interested and in which they develop relatively deep and rich knowledge." They provide several examples of such islands, including a boy who develops relatively deep content knowledge and a "sophisticated conversational space" (p. 335) about trains and related topics after he is given a Thomas the Tank Engine book.

Now consider a mother talking to her 4-year-old son, who has an island of expertise around dinosaurs (the transcript below is adapted from Crowley & Jacobs 2002, pp. 343–344). The mother and child are looking at replica fossil dinosaur and a replica fossil dinosaur egg. The mother has a little card in front of that says:

- Replica of a dinosaur egg
- From the oviraptor
- Cretaceous period
- Approximately 65 to 135 million years ago
- The actual fossil, of which this is a replica, was found in the Gobi desert of Mongolia

CHILD: This looks like this is a egg.

MOTHER: OK well this . . . That's exactly what it is! How did you know?

CHILD: Because it looks like it.

MOTHER: That's what it says, see look egg, *egg* . . . Replica of a dinosaur egg. From the oviraptor.

MOTHER: Do you have a . . . You have an oviraptor on your game! You know the egg game on your computer? That's what it is, an oviraptor.

MOTHER: And that's from the Cretaceous period. And that was a really, really long time ago.

. . .

MOTHER: And this is . . . the hind claw. What's a hind claw? (*pause*)
A claw from the back leg from a velociraptor. And you know
what . . .

CHILD: Hey! Hey! A velociraptor!! I had that one my [*inaudible*]
dinosaur.

MOTHER: I know, I know and that was the little one. And remember they have those, remember in your book, it said something
about the claws . . .

CHILD: No, I know, they, they . . .

MOTHER: Your dinosaur book, what they use them . . .

CHILD: Have so great claws so they can eat and kill . . .

MOTHER: They use their claws to cut open their prey, right.

CHILD: Yeah.

This is a language lesson, not primarily a lesson on vernacular language,
although, of course, it thoroughly mixes vernacular and specialist language. It is a lesson on specialist language. It is early preparation for the
sorts of academic (school-based) language children see increasingly in
talk and in texts as they progress in school. It is also replete with "moves"
that are successful language teaching strategies, although the mother is
no expert on language development.

Let's look at some of the features this interaction has as an informal
language lesson. First, it contains elements of nonvernacular, specialist
language, for example: "*replica* of a dinosaur egg"; "from the *oviraptor*";
"from the *Cretaceous period*"; "the *hind claw*"; "their *prey*." The specialist
elements here are largely vocabulary, although such interactions soon
come to involve elements of syntax and discourse associated with specialist ways with words as well.

Second, the mother asks the child the basis of his knowledge—
Mother: "How did you know?" Child: "Because it looks like it." Specialist domains are almost always "expert" domains that involve claims to
know and evidence for such claims. They are in Shaffer's (2007) sense
"epistemic games."

Third, the mother publicly displays reading of the technical text,
even though the child cannot yet read: "That's what it says, see look *egg*,
egg . . . Replica of a dinosaur *egg*. From the oviraptor." This reading also
uses print to confirm the child's claim to know, showing one way this

type of print (descriptive information on the card) can be used in an epistemic game of confirmation.

Fourth, the mother relates the current talk and text to other texts the child is familiar with: "You have an oviraptor on your game! You know the egg game on your computer? That's what it is, an oviraptor"; "And remember they have those, remember in your book, it said something about the claws." This sort of intertextulaity creates a network of texts and modalities (books, games, and computers), situating the child's new knowledge not just in a known background, but in a system the child is building in his head.

Fifth, the mother offers a technical-like definition: "And this is . . . the hind claw. What's a hind claw? (*pause*) A claw from the back leg from a velociraptor." This demonstrates a common language move in specialist domains, that is, giving relatively formal and explicit definitions (not just examples of use).

Sixth, the mother points to and explicates hard concepts: "And that's from the Cretaceous period. And that was a really, really long time ago." This signals to the child that "Cretaceous period" is a technical term and displays how to explicate such terms in the vernacular (this is a different move than offering a more formal definition).

Seventh, she offers technical vocabulary for a slot the child has left open—Child: "Have so great claws so they can eat and kill . . . " Mother: "They use their claws to cut open their *prey*, right." This slot and filler move co-constructs language with the child, allowing the child to use language "above his head" in ways in line with Vygotsky's concept of a "zone of proximal development" (Vygotsky, 1978).

INFORMAL SPECIALIST-LANGUAGE LESSONS

So, let's be clear about two things. This is an informal language lesson, and such lessons involve more than language and language learning. They involve teaching and learning cognitive (knowledge) and interactional moves in specialist domains. Finally, they involve teaching and learning identities, the identity of being the sort of person who is comfortable with specialist technical knowing, learning, and language. Of course, even formal language lessons—in learning a second language in school, for instance—should involve language, knowledge, interaction, and identity. But this is not formal teaching, it is informal teaching, the teaching equivalent of informal learning. Let's call such informal language lessons, with the sorts of features I have just discussed, "informal specialist-language lessons" (ironically, they are informal formal-language lessons!).

Along with all we know about "emergent literacy" at home (Dickinson & Neuman, 2006; Gee, 2004), informal specialist language lessons are crucial if one wants to take a trajectory view of reading development. They are preschool prereading activities that lead to the early reading instruction that prevents the fourth-grade slump. Of course, the reading instruction the child receives at school must continue these language lessons, informally and formally. It must place reading from the get-go in the context of learning specialist styles of language, just as this mother has done. This, however, raises the issue of what happens for children who come to school without such informal specialist-language teaching, and, often, without other important aspects of emergent literacy. My view is that this cannot be ignored. We cannot just move on to reading instruction of the "decode and literally comprehend" sort as if it just doesn't matter that these children have missed out on early specialist-language learning. For these children, language teaching needs to start with a vengeance, and be sustained throughout the course of reading instruction. And, again, remember, this claim has nothing to do with teaching "standard" English or ESL, per se: it is a claim that even native speakers of vernacular standard English need language learning to prepare for specialist varieties of language.

SPECIALIST LANGUAGE IN POPULAR CULTURE

There are other things, beyond such informal specialist-language lessons that can prepare children for the increasing language demands of school in the content areas. And we can see one of these if we look, oddly enough, at young people's popular culture today. Something very interesting has happened in children's popular culture. It has gotten very complex and it contains a great many practices that involve highly specialist styles of language (Gee, 2004, 2007a). Young children often engage with these practices socially in informal peer learning groups. Some parents recruit these practices to accelerate their children's specialist language skills (with their concomitant thinking and interactional skills).

For example, consider the text below, which appears on a *Yu-Gi-Oh!* card. *Yu-Gi-Oh!* is a card game involving quite complex rules. It is often played face to face with one or more other players, sometimes in formal competitions, more often informally, although it can be played as a video game, as well.

Armed Ninja

Card-Type: Effect Monster

Attribute: Earth | **Level:** 1

Type: Warrior

ATK: 300 | **DEF:** 300

Description: FLIP: Destroys 1 Magic Card on the field. If this card's target is face-down, flip it face-up. If the card is a Magic Card, it is destroyed. If not, it is returned to its face-down position. The flipped card is not activated.

Rarity: Rare

The "description" is really a rule. It states what moves in the game the card allows. This text has little specialist vocabulary (though it has some, e.g., "activated"), unlike the interaction we saw between mother and child above, but it contains complex specialist syntax. It contains, for instance, three straight conditional clauses (the "if" clauses). Note how complex this meaning is: First, if the target is face down, flip it over. Now check to see if it is a magic card. If it is, destroy it. If it isn't, return it to its face-down position. Finally, you are told that even though you flipped over your opponent's card, which in some circumstances would activate its powers, in this case, the card's powers are not activated. This is "logic talk," a matter, really, of multiple related "either–or", "if–then" propositions.

Note, too, that the card contains a bunch of classificatory information (e.g., type, attack power, defense power, rarity). All of these linguistic indicators lead the child to place the card in the whole network or system of *Yu-Gi-Oh!* cards—and there are more than 10,000 of them—and the rule system of the game itself. This is complex system thinking with a vengeance.

Consider, also, the *Yu-Gi-Oh!* card below:

Cyber Raider

Card-Type: Effect Monster

Attribute: Dark | **Level:** 4

Type: Machine

ATK: 1400 | **DEF:** 1000

Description: "When this card is Normal Summoned, Flip Summoned, or Special Summoned successfully, select and activate 1 of the following effects: Select 1 equipped Equip Spell Card and destroy it. Select 1 equipped Equip Spell Card and equip it to this card."

Rarity: Common

This card—and remember it is one of 10,000—contains nearly nothing but words and phrases that are technical, specialist terms in *Yu-Gi-Oh!* Few texts children see in school will be this saturated with such technical language.

I have watched 7-year-old children play *Yu-Gi-Oh!* with great expertise. They must read each of the cards. They endlessly debate the powers of each card by constant contrast and comparison with other cards when they are trading them. They discuss and argue over the rules and, in doing so, use lots of specialist vocabulary, syntactic structures, and discourse features. They can go to websites to learn more or to settle their disputes. If and when they do so, here is the sort of thing they will see:

8-CLAWS SCORPION Even if "8-Claws Scorpion" is equipped with an Equip Spell Card, its ATK is 2400 when it attacks a face-down Defense Position monster. The effect of "8-Claws Scorpion" is a Trigger Effect that is applied if the condition is correct on activation ("8-Claws Scorpion" declared an attack against a face-down Defense Position monster.) The target monster does not have to be in face-down Defense Position when the effect of "8-Claws Scorpion" is resolved. So if "Final Attack Orders" is active, or "Ceasefire" flips the monster face-up, "8-Claws Scorpion" still gets its 2400 ATK.

The ATK of "8-Claws Scorpion" becomes 2400 during damage calculation. You cannot chain "Rush Recklessly" or "Blast with Chain" to this effect. If these cards were activated before damage calculation, then the ATK of "8-Claws Scorpion" becomes 2400 during damage calculation so those cards have no effect on its ATK. (*www.upperdeckentertainment.com/ yugioh/en/FAQ_card_rulings.aspx?first=A&last=C*)

I don't really think I have to say much about this text. It is, in every way, a specialist text. In fact, in complexity, it is far above the language many young children will see in their school books, until they get to middle school at best and perhaps even high school. But 7-year-old children deal and deal well with this language (although *Yu-Gi-Oh!* cards—and, thus, their language—are often banned at school).

Let's consider a moment what *Yu-Gi-Oh!* involves. First and foremost it involves what I will call "lucidly functional language." What do I mean by this? The language on *Yu-Gi-Oh!* cards, websites, and in children's discussions and debates is quite complex, as we have seen, but it relates piece by piece to the rules of the game, to the specific moves or actions one takes in the domain. Here language—complex specialist language—is married closely to specific and connected actions. The relationship between language and meaning (where meaning here is the rules and the actions connected to them) is clear and lucid. The *Yu-Gi-Oh!* company has designed such lucid functionality because it allows them to sell 10,000 cards connected to a fully esoteric language and practice. It directly banks on children's love of mastery and expertise. Would that schools did the same. Would that the language of science in the early years of school was taught in this lucidly functional way. It rarely is.

So we can add "lucidly functional language" to our informal specialist-language lessons as another foundation for specialist-language learning, one currently better represented in popular culture than in school. And note here, too, that such lucidly functional language is practiced socially in groups of kids as they discuss, debate, and trade cards with each other, including more advanced peers. They learn to relate oral and written language of a specialist sort, a key skill for specialist domains, including academic ones at school. At the same time, many parents (usually, but not always, more privileged parents) have come to know how to use such lucidly functional language practices—like *Yu-Gi-Oh!* or *Pokemon* and, as well as we will see below, digital technologies like video games—to engage their children in informal specialist-language lessons.

My 13-year-old son, Sam, recently told me recently that he felt he had learned to read by playing *Pokemon*, another card and video game. He was referring to the games on the Nintendo Game Boy, games he played before he could read, when he was 5. His mother or I sat with him and read for him—the game requires a lot of reading. In a real sense, Sam did learn to read by playing *Pokemon*. But he learned to read, then, in a context that was also early preparation for dealing with complex specialist language, a type of language he would see later in school, although, for the most part, only after the first couple of grades. Of course, he learned other sorts of reading in other activities, as well. I am not arguing for early literacy that is focused on only specialist languages.

Of course, the sorts of lucidly functional language practices and informal specialist-language lessons that exist around *Yu-Gi-Oh!* or *Pokemon* could exist in school—even as early as first grade—to teach school valued content. But they don't. Here the creativity of capitalists has far outrun that of educators.

SITUATED MEANING AND VIDEO GAMES

So far we have talked about two underpinnings of a trajectory view of reading: informal (and later formal) specialized-language lessons and practices built around lucidly functional language. Why are these underpinnings for reading, in a trajectory sense? Because they place reading development in the context of specialized language development, which is the basis for being able to keep up with the ever-increasing demands for learning content in school via complex technical and academic varieties of language (and, indeed, other sorts of technical representations used in areas like science and math).

Now we move to a third underpinning of a trajectory view of reading development. Lots of research has shown for years now that in areas like science, many students with good grades and passing test scores cannot actually use their knowledge to solve problems (Gardner, 1991). For example, many students who can write down for a test Newton's Laws of Motion cannot correctly say how many forces are acting on a coin when it is tossed into the air and at the top of its trajectory—and, ironically, this is something that can be deduced from Newton's Laws (Chi, Feltovich, & Glaser, 1981). They cannot apply their knowledge, because they don't see how it applies—they don't see the physical world and the language of physics (which includes mathematics) in a way that makes it clear to them how that language applies to that world.

There are two ways to understand words. I will call one way "verbal" and the other way "situated" (Gee, 2004, 2007a). A situated understanding of a concept or word implies the ability to use the word or understand the concept in ways that are customizable to different specific situations of use (Brown et al., 1989; Clark, 1997; Gee, 2004, 2007a). A general or verbal understanding implies an ability to explicate one's understanding in terms of other words or general principles, but not necessarily an ability to apply this knowledge to actual situations. Thus while verbal or general understandings may facilitate passing certain sorts of information-focused tests, they do not necessarily facilitate actual problem solving.

Let me quickly point out that, in fact, all human understandings are situated. What I am calling verbal understandings are, of course, situated in terms of other words and, in a larger sense, the total linguistic, cultural, and domain knowledge a person has. But they are not necessarily situated in terms of ways of applying these words to actual situations of use and varying their applications across different contexts of use. Thus I will continue to contrast verbal understandings to situated ones, where the latter implies the ability to do and not just say.

Situated understandings are, of course, the norm in everyday life and in vernacular language. Even the most mundane words take on different meanings in different contexts of use. Indeed, people must be able to build these meanings on the spot in real time as they construe the contexts around them. For instance, people construct different meanings for a word like "coffee" when they hear something like "The coffee spilled, get the mop," versus "The coffee spilled, get a broom," versus "The coffee spilled, stack it again." Indeed, such examples have been a staple of connectionist work on human understanding (Clark, 1993).

Verbal and general understandings are top down. They start with the general, that is, with a definition-like understanding of a word or a general principle associated with a concept. Less abstract meanings follow as special cases of the definition or principle. Situated understandings generally work in the other direction—understanding starts with a relatively concrete case and gradually rises to higher levels of abstraction through the consideration of additional cases.

The perspective I am developing here, one that stresses knowledge as tied to activity and experiences in the world before knowledge as facts and information, and knowledge as situated as opposed to verbal understandings, has many implications for the nature of learning and teaching, as well as for the assessment of learning and teaching (Gee, 2003). Recently, researchers in several different areas have raised the possibility that what we might call "game-like" learning through digital technologies can facilitate situated understandings in the context of activity and experience grounded in perception (Games-to-Teach, 2003; Gee, 2005, 2007c; McFarlane, Sparrowhawk, & Heald, 2002; Squire, 2006).

Consider a phenomenon that all gamers are well aware of. This phenomenon gets to the heart and soul of what situated meanings are and why they are important: Written texts associated with video games are not very meaningful, certainly not very lucid, unless and until one has played the game.

Let me take the small booklet that comes with the innovative shooter game *Deus Ex* to use as an example of what I mean by saying this. In the 20 pages of this booklet, there are 199 bolded references that represent headings and subheadings (to take one small randomly chosen stretch of headings and subheadings that appears at the end of page 5 and the beginning of page 6: **Passive Readouts**, **Damage Monitor**, **Active Augmentation & Device Icons**, **Items-at-Hand**, **Information Screens**, **Note**, **Inventory**, **Inventory Management**, **Stacks**, **Nanokey ring**, **Ammunition**). Each of these 199 headings and subheadings is followed by text that gives information relevant to the topic and relates it to other information throughout the booklet. In addition, the booklet gives 53 keys on the computer keyboard an assignment to some function in the game, and these 53 keys are mentioned 82 times in the booklet in relation to the information contained in the 199 headings and subheadings. So although the booklet is small, it is just packed with concise and relatively technical information.

Here is a typical piece of language from this booklet:

> Your internal nano-processors keep a very detailed record of your condition, equipment and recent history. You can access this data at any time during play by hitting F1 to get to the Inventory screen or F2 to get to the Goals/Notes screen. Once you have accessed your information screens, you can move between the screens by clicking on the tabs at the top of the screen. You can map other information screens to hotkeys using Settings, Keyboard/Mouse. (p. 5)

This makes perfect sense at a literal level, but that just goes to show how worthless the literal level is. When you understand this sort of passage at only a literal level, you have only an illusion of understanding, one that quickly disappears as you try to relate the information in this passage to the hundreds of other important details in the booklet. Such literal understandings are precisely what children who feel the fourth-grade slump have. First of all, this passage means nothing real to you if you have no situated idea about what "nano-processors," "condition," "equipment," "history," "F1," "Inventory screen," "F2," "Goals/Notes screen" (and, of course, "Goals" and "Notes"), "information screens," "clicking," "tabs," "map," "hotkeys," and "Settings, Keyboard/Mouse" mean in and for playing games like *Deus Ex*.

Second, although you know literally what each sentence means, they raise a plethora of questions if you have no situated understandings of this game or games like it. For instance, are the same data (condition, equipment, and history) on both the Inventory screen and the Goals/Notes screen? If so, why is it on two different screens? If not, which type of information is on which screen and why? The fact that I can move between the screens by clicking on the tabs (but what do these tabs look like, will I recognize them?) suggests that some of this information is on one screen and some on the other. But then is my "condition" part of my Inventory or my Goals/Notes—doesn't seem to be either, but what is my "condition" anyway? If I can map other information screens (and what are these?) to hotkeys using "Setting, Keyboard/Mouse," does this mean there is no other way to access them? How will I access them in the first place to assign them to my own chosen hotkeys? Can I click between them and the Inventory screen and the Goals/Notes screens by pressing on "tabs"? And so on and so forth—20 pages is beginning to seem like a lot—remember there are 199 different headings under which information like this is given a brisk pace throughout the booklet.

Of course, all these terms and questions can be defined and answered if you closely check and cross-check information over and over again in the little booklet. You can constantly turn the pages backward and forward. But once you have one set of links relating various items and actions in mind, another drops out just as you need it and you're back to turning pages. Is the booklet poorly written? Not at all. It is written just as well or poorly, just like, in fact, any number of school-based texts in the content areas. It is, outside the practices in the domain from which it comes, just as meaningless, although one could, of course, garner literal meanings from it with which to verbally repeat things or pass tests, as one often does with texts in school.

And, of course, you can utter something like "Oh, yeah, you click on F1 (function key 1) to get to the Inventory screen and F2 to get to the Goals/Notes screen" and sound like you know something. The trouble is this: in the actual game, you can click on F2 and meditate on the screen you see at your leisure. Nothing bad will happen to you. However, you very often have to click on F1 and do something quickly in the midst of a heated battle. There's no "at your leisure" here. The two commands really don't function the same way in the game—they actually mean different things in terms of embodied and situated action—and they never really *just* mean "click F1, get screen." That's their general meaning, the one with which you can't really do anything useful until you know how to spell it out further in situation-specific terms in the game.

When you can spell out such information in situation-specific terms in the game, then the relationship of this information to the other hundreds of pieces of information in the booklet becomes clear and meaningful. And, of course, these relationships are what really count if you are to understand the game as a system and, thus, play it at all well. *Now* you can read the book if you need to piece in missing bits of information, check on your understandings, or solve a particular problem or answer a particular question you have.

When I first read this booklet before playing *Deus Ex* (and at that time I had played only one other shooter game before, a very different one)—yes, I, an overly academic baby boomer, made the mistake of trying to read the book first, despite my own theories about reading—I was sorely tempted to put the game on a shelf and forget about it. I was simply overwhelmed with details, questions, and confusions. When I started the game I kept trying to look up stuff in the booklet. But none of it was well-enough understood to be found easily without continually researching for the same information. In the end, you have to just actively play the game and explore and try everything. Then, at last, the booklet makes good sense, but then you don't need it all that much any more.

So now I would make just the same claim about any school content domain as I have just said about the video game *Deus Ex*: Specialist language in any domain—games or science—has no situated meaning and thus no lucid or applicable meaning unless and until one has "played the game," in this case the game of science, or, better put, a specific game connected to a specific science. Such "games" ("science games") involve seeing the language and representations associated with some part of science in terms of activities I have done, experiences I have had, images I have formed from these, and interactional dialogue I have heard from and had with peers and mentors outside and inside the science activities. School is too often about reading the manual before you get to play the game, if you ever do. This is not harmful for kids who have already played the game at home, but is disastrous for those who have not.

Good video games don't just support situated meanings for the written materials associated with them in manuals and on fan websites—and these are copious—but also for all language within the game. The meaning of such language is always associated with actions, experiences, images, and dialogue. Furthermore, players get verbal information "just in time," when they can apply it or see it applied, or "on demand," when they feel the need for it and are ready for it—and then, in some cases, games will give the player walls of print (e.g., in *Civilization IV*).

So my claim: "Game-like" learning can lead to situated and not just verbal meanings. In turn, situated meanings make specialist language lucid, easy, and useful. Of course, video games are only one digital medium among many that can be used to support learning and literacy. The key to all of them, though, is that they situate meaning in worlds of experience—the stuff out of which the human mind is made—that is ultimately shared, collaborative, social, and cultural.

REFERENCES

American Educator. (2003). The fourth-grade plunge: The cause. The cure. Special issue, Spring.

Alvermann, D. E., Moon, J. S., & Hagood, M. C. (1999). *Popular culture in the classroom: Teaching and researching critical media literacy.* Mahwah, NJ: Erlbaum.

Anderson, C. (2006). *The long tail: Why the future of business is selling less of more.* New York: Hyperion.

Barsalou, L. W. (1999a). Language comprehension: Archival memory or preparation for situated action. *Discourse Processes, 28,* 61–80.

Barsalou, L. W. (1999b). Perceptual symbol systems. *Behavioral and Brain Sciences, 22,* 577–660.

Bazerman, C. (1989). *Shaping written knowledge.* Madison: University of Wisconsin Press.

Beach, R. (2006). *Teachingmedialiteracy.com: A web-linked guide to resources and activities.* New York: Teachers College Press.

Bizzell, P. (1992). *Academic discourse and critical consciousness.* Pittsburgh: University of Pittsburgh Press.

Brandt, D., & Clinton, K. (2002). Limits of the local: Expanding perspectives on literacy as a social practice. *Journal of Literacy Research 34,* 337–356.

Brown, J. S., Collins, A., & Dugid, P. (1989). Situated cognition and the culture of learning. *Educational Researcher, 18,* 32–42.

Brunner, C., & Tally, W. (1999). *The new media literacy handbook: An educator's guide to bringing new media into the classroom.* New York: Anchor.

Buckingham, D. (2003). *Media education: Literacy, learning and contemporary culture.* Cambridge, UK: Polity Press.

Buckingham, D. (Ed.). (2007). *Youth, identity, and digital media* (John D. and Catherine T. MacArthur Foundation Series on Digital Media and Learning). Cambridge, MA: MIT Press.

Cazden, C. (1988). *Classroom discourse: The language of teaching and learning.* Portsmouth, NH: Heinemann.

Chall, J. S., Jacobs, V., & Baldwin, L. (1990). *The reading crisis: Why poor children fall behind.* Cambridge, MA: Harvard University Press.

Chi, M., Feltovich, P., & Glaser, R. (1981). Categorization and representation of physics problems by experts and novices. *Cognitive Science, 5,* 121–152.

Chomsky, N. (1986). *Knowledge of language.* New York: Praeger.

Churchland, P. M. (1989). *A neurocomputational perspective: The nature of mind and the structure of science.* Cambridge, MA: MIT Press.

Churchland, P. S. (1986). *Neurophilosophy: Toward a unified science of the mind/brain.* Cambridge, MA: MIT Press.

Churchland, P. S., & Sejnowski, T. J. (1992). *The computational brain.* Cambridge, MA: Bradford/MIT Press.

Clark, A. (1989). *Microcognition: Philosophy, cognitive science, and parallel distributed processing.* Cambridge, MA: MIT Press.

Clark, A. (1993). *Associative engines: Connectionism, concepts, and representational change.* Cambridge, UK: Cambridge University Press.

Clark, A. (1997). *Being there: Putting brain, body, and world together again.* Cambridge, MA: MIT Press.

Coiro, J., Knobel, M., Lankshear, C., & Leu, D. J. (Eds.). (2008). *Handbook of research on new literacies.* Philadelphia: Erlbaum.

Consalvo, M. (2007). *Cheating: Gaining advantage in videogames.* Cambridge, MA: MIT Press.

Cook-Gumperz, J. (Ed.). (1986). *The social construction of literacy.* Cambridge, UK: Cambridge University Press.

Crowley, K., & Jacobs, M. (2002). Islands of expertise and the development of family scientific literacy. In G. Leinhardt, K. Crowley, & K. Knutson (Eds.), *Learning conversations in museums* (pp. 333–356). Mahwah, NJ: Erlbaum.

Damasio, A. R. (1994). *Descartes' error: Emotion, reason, and the human brain.* New York: Avon.

Dickinson, D. K., & Neuman, S. B. (Eds.). (2006). *Handbook of early literacy research, Vol. 2.* New York: Guilford Press.

Engeström, Y. (1987). *Learning by expanding: An activity theoretical approach to developmental research.* Helsinki: Orienta Konsultit.

Fiske, J. (1989). *Understanding popular culture.* London: Routledge.

Games-to-Teach Team. (2003). Design principles of next-generation digital gaming for education. *Educational Technology, 43,* 17–33.

Gardner, H. (1991). *The unschooled mind: How children think and how schools should teach.* New York: Basic Books.

Gee, J. P. (1987). What is literacy? *Teaching and Learning, 2,* 3–11.

Gee, J. P. (1992). *The social mind: Language, ideology, and social practice.* New York: Bergin & Garvey.

Gee, J. P. (2000). The new literacy studies: From "socially situated" to the work of the social. In D. Barton, M. Hamilton, & R. Ivanic (Eds.), *Situated literacies: Reading and writing in context* (pp. 180–196). London: Routledge.

Gee, J. P. (2003). Opportunity to learn: A language-based perspective on assessment. *Assessment in Education, 10,* 25–44.

Gee, J. P. (2004). *Situated language and learning: A critique of traditional schooling.* London: Routledge.

Gee, J. P. (2005). *Why video games are good for your soul: Pleasure and learning.* Melbourne: Common Ground.

Gee, J. P. (2007a). *Good video games and good learning: Collected essays on video games, learning, and literacy.* New York: Lang.

Gee, J. P. (2007b) *Social linguistics and literacies: Ideology in discourses* (3rd ed.). London: Taylor & Francis.

Gee, J. P. (2007c). *What video games have to teach us about learning and literacy* (2nd ed.). New York: Palgrave/Macmillan.

Gee, J. P. (2008). *Getting over the slump: Innovation strategies to promote children's learning.* New York: The Joan Ganz Cooney Center at Sesame Workshop.

Glenberg, A. M. (1997). What is memory for? *Behavioral and Brain Sciences, 20,* 1–55.

Graff, H. J. (1979). *The literacy myth: Literacy and social structure in the 19th-century city.* New York: Academic Press.

Hawkins, J. (2005). *On intelligence.* New York: Holt.

Heath, S. B. (1983). *Ways with words: Language, life, and work in communities and classrooms.* Cambridge, UK: Cambridge University Press.

Hobbs, R. (1997). Expanding the concept of literacy. In R. Kuby (Ed.), *Media literacy in the information age: Current perspectives* (pp. 163–183). New Brunswick, NJ: Transaction.

Hobbs, R. (2007). *Reading the media: Media literacy in high school English.* New York: Teachers College Press.

Hull, G. A., & Schultz, K. (2001). *School's out: Bridging out-of-school literacies with classroom practice.* New York: Teachers College Press.

Hutchins, E. (1995). *Cognition in the wild.* Cambridge, MA: MIT Press.

Jenkins, H. (2006). *Confronting the challenges of participatory culture: Media education for the 21st century.* Chicago: MacArthur Foundation.

Kist, W. (2004). *New literacies in action: Teaching and learning in multiple media.* New York: Teachers College Press.

Kolodner, J. L. (1993). *Case-based reasoning.* San Mateo, CA: Kaufman.

Kolodner, J. L. (2006). Case-based reasoning. In R. K. Sawyer (Ed.), *The Cambridge handbook of the learning sciences* (pp. 225–242). Cambridge, UK: Cambridge University Press.

Kress, G. (2003). *Literacy in the new media age.* London: Routledge.

Labov, W. (1979). The logic of nonstandard English. In P. Giglioli (Ed.), *Language and social context* (pp. 179–215). Middlesex, UK: Penguin Books.

Lankshear, C. (1997). *Changing literacies.* Berkshire, UK: Open University Press.

Lankshear, C., & Knobel, M. (2006). *New literacies* (2nd ed.). Berkshire, UK: Open University Press.

Lankshear, C., & Knobel, M. (Eds.). (2007). *A new literacies sampler.* New York: Lang.

Latour, B. (2004). *Politics of nature: How to bring the sciences into democracy.* Cambridge, MA: Harvard University Press.

Latour, B. (2005). *Reassembling the social: An introduction to actor–network–theory.* Oxford, UK: Oxford University Press.

Lave, J. (1996). Teaching, as learning, in practice. *Mind, Culture, and Activity, 3,* 149–164.

Lave, J., & Wenger, E. (1991). *Situated learning: Legitimate peripheral participation.* New York: Cambridge University Press.

Leadbeater, C., & Miller, P. (2004). *The pro-am revolution: How enthusiasts are changing our society and economy.* London: Demos.

McFarlane, A., Sparrowhawk, A., & Heald, Y. (2002). *Report on the educational use of games: An exploration by TEEM of the contribution which games can make to the education process.* Cambridge, UK: Teem Ltd.

Newell, A., & Simon, H. A. (1972). *Human problem solving.* Englewood Cliffs, NJ: Prentice Hall.

Pahl, K., & Rowsel, J. (2005). *Literacy and education: Understanding the new literacy studies in the classroom.* London: Chapman.

Pahl, K., & Rowsel, J. (Eds.). (2006). *Travel notes from the new literacy studies: Instances of practice.* Clevedon, UK: Multilingual Matters.

Pinker, S. (1994). *The language instinct: How the mind creates language.* New York: Morrow.

Prinsloo, M., & Mignonne, B. (Eds.). (1996). *The social uses of literacy: Theory and practice in contemporary South Africa.* Philadelphia: Benjamins.

Rumelhart, D. E., McClelland, J. L., & the PDP Research Group. (1986). *Parallel distributed processing: Explorations in the microstructure of cognition: Vol. 1. Foundations.* Cambridge, MA: MIT Press.

Schleppegrell, M. (2004). *Language of schooling: A functional linguistics perspective.* Mahwah, NJ: Erlbaum.

Scollon, R., & Scollon, S. B. K. (1981). *Narrative, literacy, and face in interethnic communication.* Norwood, NJ: Ablex.

Scribner, S., & Cole, M. (1981). *The psychology of literacy.* Cambridge, MA: Harvard University Press.

Senechal, M., Ouellette, G., & Rodney, D. (2006). The misunderstood giant: Predictive role of early vocabulary to future reading. In D. K. Dickinson &

S. B. Neuman (Eds.), *Handbook of early literacy research* (Vol. 2, pp. 173–182). New York: Guilford Press.

Shaffer, D. W. (2007). *How computer games help children learn.* New York: Palgrave/Macmillan.

Shirky, C. (2008). *Here comes everybody: The power of organizing without organizations.* New York: Penguin.

Snow, C. E., Burns, M. S., & Griffin, P. (Eds.). (1998). *Preventing reading difficulties in young children.* Washington, DC: National Academy Press.

Squire, K. D. (2006). From content to context: Video games as designed experience. *Educational Researcher, 35*, 19–29.

Street, B. (1984). *Literacy in theory and practice.* Cambridge, UK: Cambridge University Press.

Street, B. (1993). Introduction: The new literacy studies. In B. Street (Ed.), *Cross-cultural approaches to literacy* (pp. 1–21). New York: Cambridge University Press.

Street, B. (1995). *Social literacies: Critical approaches to Literacy in development, ethnography, and education.* London: Longman.

Street, B. (1997). The implications of the "new literacy studies" for literacy education. *English in Education, 31*, 45–59.

Street, B. (2005). At last: Recent applications of new literacy studies in educational contexts. *Research in the Teaching of English, 39*, 417–423.

Vygotsky, L. S. (1978). *Mind in society: The development of higher psychological processes.* Cambridge, MA: Harvard University Press.

Warschauer, M. (1998). *Electronic literacies: Language, culture, and power in online education.* Mahwah, NJ: Erlbaum.

Wenger, E. (1998). *Communities of practice: Learning, meaning, and identity.* Cambridge, UK: Cambridge University Press.

Wertsch, J. V. (1985). *Vygotsky and the social formation of mind.* Cambridge, MA: Harvard University Press.

CHAPTER 9

Screens and Scrapbooking
Sociocultural Perspectives on New Literacies

KELLY CHANDLER-OLCOTT
ELIZABETH LEWIS

I think that everyone has a different way of keeping their memories whether it's just photographs in a box or a photo album. Scrapbooking is my favorite way of keeping memories because it's something that I can do with my mom and my sister, and it's my way of being creative with something.
—Laura (e-mail correspondence, July 14, 2008)

Laura is a 13-year-old eighth grader from Prince William County, Virginia, who is a member of Elizabeth's extended family. Laura represents a growing population of adolescents who preserve their memories with scrapbooks of various kinds, including print and digital formats. As is the case with many adolescents, her scrapbooking is deeply embedded in social relationships with friends and family members, and she shares her special satisfaction with the visual elements of the process—the selection of pictures, color schemes, backgrounds, and embellishments such as stickers—to complement print text. (See Figure 9.1 for an example.) The practices she reports clearly reflect the "multiple forms of representation" that Kist (2005) argues are one hallmark of new literacies (p. 16).

The two of us, both former secondary English teachers, came to our exchanges with Laura about her scrapbooking with a deep and

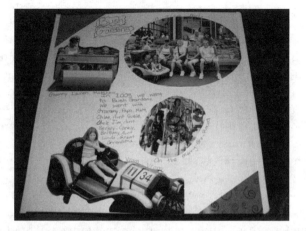

FIGURE 9.1. Laura's scrapbook page representing her family's trip to Busch Gardens.

abiding interest in new literacies, particularly in how youth use multiple modes and popular media to construct and express meaning. We
have previously conducted research on middle school girls' use of digital technologies to pursue their interest in anime (Chandler-Olcott &
Mahar, 2003) as well as on practicing teachers' perspectives on integrating new literacies into their English language arts instruction (Lewis &
Chandler-Olcott, 2007; Lewis, 2008). In these studies, we began with
a broad definition of new literacies, one influenced by Lankshear and
Knobel's (2003) argument that some of these literacies involve the use
of new technological tools, while others simply use existing tools in new
or unsanctioned ways. As the studies progressed, however, we found
ourselves placing disproportionate emphasis on digital literacies such
as instant messaging and the use of social networking sites. Our teacher
informants appeared to make the same assumptions, often shifting in
their talk from a broad conception of new literacies to a narrower discussion of how they integrated various technologies into instruction. As
we discussed this tendency in ourselves and others, we realized that one
new literacy practice we found most fascinating—scrapbooking—had
clearly been influenced by emerging information and communication
technologies, but it was not solely dependent on them. That is to say,
there were plenty of scrapbookers whose work still appeared to qualify
as a new literacy on several counts but who employed digital technologies sparingly, if at all (we discuss this more in a subsequent section).

Consequently, we decided to use scrapbooking in this chapter as a case to help us examine how sociocultural perspectives—the theoretical orientation we review here and the one we have used most often in our own research—can illuminate the dimensions of new literacies, including those that aren't strictly technologically mediated, in provocative ways. In doing so, we hope to offer fresh insights about both new literacies and sociocultural theory, as well as—secondarily—scrapbooking, while at the same time grounding our discussion in everyday practices with which many people, both adolescents and adults, are familiar.

In the pages that follow, we provide an overview of scrapbooking and its history and explain why we think it should be seen as a new literacy. We then lay out key tenets of sociocultural theory that we see as useful when inquiring into new literacies including, but not limited, to scrapbooking. Next, we analyze scrapbooking as a community of practice (Lave & Wenger, 1991; Wenger, 1998, n.d.), using a construct that has been widely taken up by scholars drawing on sociocultural theory. We consider some limitations of these sociocultural perspectives in illuminating new literacies such as scrapbooking and, finally, close with some implications of these ideas for further research and practice.

A BRIEF HISTORY OF SCRAPBOOKING

Some people might be surprised at our designation of scrapbooking as a new literacy practice because scrapbooks have been around, in one form or another, since the 17th century. Known as "commonplace books," they first appeared as journals in which quotations and observations were recorded—an important tool in an era when handwriting was the only method of replicating text for most people. Philosopher John Locke, an early proponent, wrote an instructional guide on the process entitled *New Method of Making Common-place Books* that suggested that individuals use subject headings, space for references, and an index to help keep their texts organized (Ott, Tucker, & Buckler, 2006).

By the late 18th century, the concept for such books expanded considerably, and the name "scrapbook" came into vogue, taken from the colorful pieces of printed paper images called "scrap" that were used to create the albums (Taylor, 2003). In addition to recording text, albums featured objects such as illustrations, clippings, greeting cards, diary entries, poetry, autographs, and pressed flowers. Some scrapbook keepers even included wallpaper and knitting in their albums. Others created "friendship albums," volumes dedicated to memorializing relationships, which included written notes and even locks of hair from friends (Taylor, 2003). Print text was still involved in scrapbook keeping, but it was no longer at the center as it had been in the commonplace book era.

A peak in scrapbook keeping occurred in the 1880s, when manufacturers began creating sheets of scrap designed to appeal specifically to women and children (Taylor, 2003). Magazines of the time included articles heralding the value of scrapbook keeping for entertaining and educating the family. In addition, manufacturers of mass-produced scrapbooks peddled the albums as necessities for documenting the maturity of family members and keeping legal records of births, deaths, and marriages (Siegel, 2006). Consequently, scrapbooks became linked to discourses circulating in the culture about families, history, and domesticity.

Around this same time, the appearance of scrapbooks changed again. Before the advent of the Kodak camera in the late 1880s, scrapbooks did not contain photographs. Once the Kodak camera and roll film went on sale for the general population, photographs became an integral staple of scrapbook pages, one that remains central to the current practice. By the 1930s, photo albums were the most common form of scrapbook (Rothamel, 2005).

Scrapbook keeping waned in the mid-20th century, but the 1970s and 1980s brought a resurgence due to the influence of Alex Haley's historical saga *Roots*, which sparked interest in family history for many people (Taylor, 2003). In 1987 Creative Memories, a direct-sales company, capitalized on such interest by marketing tools and techniques to scrapbookers through interactions with independent consultants that some compare to the traditional Tupperware party (Ott et al., 2006). A more recent surge in the number of scrapbookers took place at the beginning of the 21st century, which some attribute to the terrorist attacks of September 11, 2001, and the resulting emphasis by many Americans on family traditions and domestic life (*Washington Times*, 2004). In this same time period, faithbooking—a term coined to describe scrapbooking with an explicit focus on spiritual commitments, most often by Christians—became popular as well. As we write, the Craft and Hobby Association (2008) estimates that nearly 20% of all American households include a scrapbooker, and it reports that Americans spent $2.6 billion on scrapbooking supplies and products last year.

WHAT'S "NEW" ABOUT SCRAPBOOKING?

As we hope is clear from this brief history, scrapbooks themselves aren't new. They have existed for many years, although their forms and purposes have evolved as new technologies have been developed and new social practices have emerged. We think it's fair to say, however, that scrapbook*ing*—the distinctive social relationships, communication strategies, and tools associated with this activity in contemporary times—has a number of features that qualify it as a new literacy practice.

It's not clear to us whether Knobel and Lankshear (2007), scholars who have greatly influenced our thinking about the term, would argue that scrapbooking meets the first of their two criteria for new literacies—an emphasis on "technical stuff" associated with digital technologies (p. 7). The past decade has indeed seen a proliferation of scrapbooking blogs (one Australian site links to 50 of them alone) and other kinds of websites where scrapbook keepers across the globe can access information, post their work, and communicate with others who share their interest. A bit less directly, the look and feel of many contemporary scrapbook layouts—including some made with hands-on strategies out of physically tangible materials—have been influenced by the increasing presence of digital scrapbooks within the scrapbooking community (Rothamel, 2005). Nonetheless, many individuals like Elizabeth's relative Laura report that they do not use digital technologies to inform or pursue their scrapbooking, even when they use those online tools for other purposes.

Although the extent of the influence of new technologies is debatable, we are sure that scrapbooking in the early 21st century exemplifies what Knobel and Lankshear (2007) call new "ethos stuff," phenomena characterized by more collaborative, fluid, and distributed ways of using literacy than those "typically associated with established literacies" (p. 9). First of all, scrapbooking, in contrast to print-driven, established literacies, involves participants in combining what Albers and Harste (2007), another team of scholars with a keen interest in new literacies (see also Vasquez, Harste, & Albers, Chapter 12, this volume), call *modes*, or "forms within various sign systems that carry the meanings that a social collective recognizes and understands" (p. 9), to create powerful new meanings. A scrapbook page requires its creator to make decisions about what images and personal mementos to use, what colors to highlight, what textures to feature, what embellishments to add, what types of text to craft, and how all of these elements will be sized and organized in space. This multimodal and recursive process has little in common with the largely linear way that many young people appear to approach print-driven school writing tasks (Lewis & Fabos, 2005).

In addition, scrapbooking represents a new "ethos" because its expertise is distributed across a range of people whose voices would likely not be seen as authoritative within traditional institutions, including stay-at-home mothers, teens, seniors, and so forth. To have credibility within the scrapbooking community, one need not have a degree in graphic design or a background in creative writing. Scrapbookers of various ages and experience levels provide tips, models, and feedback to each other using a variety of loosely organized channels, including books, magazines, blogs, at-home parties, community-based workshops, and commercially sponsored retreats. Scrapbookers are encouraged, both explicitly and implicitly, to borrow ideas from all these social spaces and the texts that circulate within them; hybridity, the recombination of existing genres, discourses, and meanings into new designs (New London Group, 1996), is the typical result. When these hybrid products are shared publicly, whether on the Web or in a private gathering, they contribute new representations on which others are invited—even expected—to innovate. In this way, new literacies continue to be made anew.

WHY SOCIOCULTURAL THEORIES?

The past decade has seen many linkages between sociocultural theories and the idea of new literacies. Some scholars have even argued that what is most new about these literacies is neither the tools they employ nor the products they create but rather how they foreground "the very notion of literacy as a social process" (Kist, 2005, p. 5). We, too, believe that our field has experienced a fundamental shift from a paradigm largely dominated by behaviorism and cognitive psychology (see Hasselbring, Chapter 2; McKenna & Conradi, Chapter 3; Tracey, Storer, & Kazerounian, Chapter 6; and Hartman, Morsink, & Zheng, Chapter 7, this volume) to one concerned with what Gee (2000) calls the "social turn" (p. 180) and that this shift has been hastened by scholars exploring emerging forms of literacy (Alvermann, 2002; Lankshear & Knobel, 2003; Lewis & Fabos, 2005). That said, we recognize that literacy researchers were drawing on sociocultural perspectives long before the term "new literacies" was coined, and we acknowledge that other theo-

retical lenses can fruitfully be applied to the construct—hence the rationale for the multiple perspectives offered in this volume.

For the sake of clarity and precision, then, we offer in this section
an overview of the key tenets of sociocultural theory as we see them,
with a particular emphasis on those that appear to be the most relevant
to illuminating new literacies. The limits of space and our determination to consider these tenets in light of the concrete case of scrapbooking requires our treatment to be brief and, inevitably, incomplete. For
more detail, we refer you to the sources we cite here.

We see sociocultural theory as a broad cover term for a number of
perspectives with different names that have been articulated by scholars
working across disciplines such as sociology, psychology, linguistics, and
education. These perspectives include cultural psychology (Bakhtin,
1986; Cole, 1996; Wertsch, 1991); situated cognition (Lave & Wenger,
1991; Wenger, 1998), discourse theory (Gee, 2001, 2008), and activity
theory (Engestrom, Miettinen, & Punamaki, 1999; Smagorinsky, 2002).
Although they may differ on such dimensions as how they frame units
of analysis and the terminology they use to describe the components of
their frameworks, we agree with Lewis, Enciso, and Moje (2007) that
they "share a view of human action as mediated by language and other
symbol systems within particular cultural contexts" (p. 5). In this view,
meaning in language, written or otherwise, is "not some abstract propositional representation" but rather "is tied to people's experiences of
situated action in the material and social world" (Gee, 2001, p. 715). In
summary, sociocultural theory is the understanding that individuals'
development in particular areas (e.g., literacy) is influenced by social
and cultural factors that extend beyond their psychological development such as interactions with other people as well as their society's
particular values, beliefs, and ways of thinking.

Barton and Hamilton (2000) laid out a useful summary of what we
think most sociocultural theories have to say about literacy:

1) Literacy is best understood as a set of social practices; these can be
   inferred from events which are mediated by written texts;
2) There are different literacies associated with different domains of life;
3) Literacy practices are patterned by social institutions and power relationships, and some literacies are more dominant, visible, and influential than others;
4) Literacy practices are purposeful and embedded in broader social goals
   and cultural practices;

5) Literacy is historically situated; and

6) Literacy practices change and new ones are frequently acquired through processes of informal learning and sense making. (p. 8)

Barton and Hamilton's first premise drew on early work in the sociocultural tradition that distinguished between literacy events and literacy practices, and this distinction is still helpful for scholars who study new literacies. Heath (1982) defined the former as "any occasion in which a piece of writing is integral to the nature of the participants' interaction and their interpretive processes" (p. 93). Expanding upon this notion, Street (1995) argued that literacy events can only be understood within the context of literacy practices, his term for the "behaviour and the social and cultural conceptualizations that give meaning to the uses of reading and/or writing" (p. 2). For Street and others, framing literacy as a social practice acknowledged that it is not autonomous, isolated, or neutral; instead, it is connected to social hierarchies, relations of power, and institutional norms. As Brandt and Clinton (2002) observed a number of years later, the two concepts in conjunction with each other "provide important analytical leverage in making literacy understood principally as a form of social participation and literacy learning principally as a form of socialization" (p. 342).

Because sociocultural theory posits that individuals develop through social interactions with other people as well as their society's values, beliefs, and ways of thinking, identity construction may then be considered closely tied to literacy practices within particular communities. Gee (2001, 2008) defines *Discourses* as "identity kits." He expands on this definition by explaining that Discourses are identities that individuals enact and through which they engage in specific activities associated with that identity. These identity-related activities include but are not exclusively one's actions, words, interactions, attitudes, values, beliefs, and choice and use of objects (e.g., images, clothing, technologies). The detectable manifestations of identity as revealed through social languages and social activities are termed Discourse, or identity, markers. According to Gee, Discourses are ways of "being and doing."

The concept of environment is an important aspect of Gee's theory. Certain Discourses can be enacted in certain environments, and individuals who identify as these Discourses engage in certain social languages and social activities that are associated with them. Each Discourse includes social perspectives and is value-laden according to the individual's and communities' everyday theories about what is typical, normal, or natural in contrast to what is deviant or inappropriate. These everyday theories make up *cultural models* that are accepted or rejected by Discourse communities (social groups).

Gee's conception of Discourses has a good deal in common with the situated learning perspective offered by Lave and Wenger (1991). At the heart of their theory is the community of practice, their term for "groups of people who share a concern or a passion for something they do and learn how to do it better as they interact regularly" (Wenger, n.d., n.p.). The learning in these contexts depends, among other elements, on legitimate peripheral participation, a term these researchers use to describe how novices are apprenticed into the community by performing less complicated tasks that are still central to its mission.

In addition, Vygotsky (1978) and other sociocultural theorists suggest that mental processes are mediated by tools and signs to which members in a community, whether one calls it a Discourse, an activity system, or a community of practice, have collectively ascribed meaning. Akin to Gee's notion of identity kits but calling himself an activity theorist, Smagorinsky (2002) has asserted that individuals have cultural tool kits. The tools in cultural tool kits are the ways of thinking, being, and doing that individuals enact in order to make sense of and take part in activities within the communities of which they are members. Beach (2000) states, "Tools are therefore used within an activity to function as extensions of certain ways of thinking in an activity" (pp. 5–6). The use of particular tools mediates individuals' pursuit of particular outcomes of the activities as well as construction of various identities. Simply put, using a tool to perform an activity changes the nature of the activity, and participating in the changed activity always changes members of the community.

Many sociocultural theorists also call for expanded notions of text and investigate literacy events and practices that involve a range of multimodal communication. From this perspective, anything that communicates may be considered a *text* (Kist, 2005), and the application of modes beyond the linguistic—the spatial and visual, for instance—to communicate in various contexts becomes increasingly important to study (New London Group, 1996). One example of work in this tradition comes from Hamilton (2000), who conducted research centered on visual texts that explored the actions, or inactions, captured in a photograph. She generated four categories of literacy representations found in 1,790 sample photographs from a number of national newspapers in the United Kingdom. These categories were (1) "interactions between people and written texts, (2) literacy in the environment, (3) writing on the body, and (4) [the] reproduction of documents" (p. 27). One of Hamilton's main implications was that individuals are confronted with a range of literacy representations in their everyday lives and, in turn, create representations of themselves from which others interpret who they are and/or what is stated. How individuals interpret representations reveals the sociocultural literacy practices that they have adopted and in which they engage—practices that are integrally tied to the various communities with which they identify.

SCRAPBOOKING AS A COMMUNITY OF PRACTICE

In this section, we take a finer-grained look at scrapbooking as a new literacy from a sociocultural lens. We focus on the idea of scrapbooking as a community of practice, a construct articulated by Jean Lave and Etienne Wenger (Lave & Wenger, 1991; Wenger, 1998, n.d.), two of the most widely cited sociocultural theorists writing about learning, because we think it offers a good deal of explanatory power for the close ties that scrapbookers feel to each other and the considerable amounts of new learning required to participate in their community. Like Gee (2000) and Lewis et al. (2007), we see this construct as compatible, although perhaps not identical, with premises about the social nature of learning associated with theories of Discourse and activity theory.

As Wenger (2006) articulates it, "Communities of practice are formed by people who engage in a process of collective learning in a shared domain of human endeavor" (p. 1). They differ from other kinds of organizational structures such as businesses or teams because they emphasize "the learning that people have done together rather than the unit they report to, the project they are working on, or the people they know" (Wenger, 1998, p. 4). More specifically, they have three characteristics in common: the domain, the community, and the practice, each of which we discuss below with reference to scrapbooking.

The Domain

Members of a community of practice have competence associated with a shared interest. They do not belong simply on the basis of shared affiliation with a formal organization, but neither are they just a club of friends. According to Wenger (n.d.), two people could belong to the

same community of practice, depending on its size and how it is organized, "and never know it" (n.p.). What links members together, then,
is a common set of skills and knowledge associated with their common
interest—what Wenger and others call the domain or, in some instances,
the joint enterprise.

The joint enterprise for contemporary scrapbook keepers revolves
around preserving memories by creating aesthetically pleasing multimodal texts that are often shared with others. The knowledge and skills
associated with this enterprise range widely, including the items in this
representative—but not exhaustive—list:

- How to choose a unifying theme for a project.
- How to select materials (e.g., albums, borders, embellishments,
  photo paper) with archival integrity.
- How to search an online archive (e.g., *www.scrapbook.com*) for
  design ideas.
- How to create a visual focal point for a layout.
- How to crop a photograph by hand or with editing software.
- How to use a die-cut machine to create uniform shapes.
- How to apply an adhesive.
- How to write a concise but powerful title or caption.
- How to secure multiple items on a page with paper fasteners (e.g.,
  grommets, brads, eyelets).
- How to edit journaling (extended written text) for grammatical
  and spelling errors.

Some of these skills—for instance, writing a caption or editing a text for
errors—do parallel those emphasized in what Lankshear and Knobel
(2003) call "established literacies." Far more of them, however, relate
to content that would only be taught in the art or graphic design classroom, *if at all*, in school. Within the traditional paradigm, they would
rarely be considered literacies. A sociocultural perspective on new literacies, however, makes them visible.

Scrapbooking as a community of practice, however, does not
require that members master all of these skills and possess all of this
knowledge right away (13-year-old Laura is not thus required to have
the same proficiency that her mother, an older and more experienced
scrapper, would have). The community is organized in such a way that
scrapbook keepers can participate at various levels, both because of the

direct support provided by other members (e.g., a demonstration provided by an expert at a scrapbooking event) and because of the built-in
scaffolding provided by many scrapbooking materials and supplies. A
good example of the latter can be found in the ready-made scrapbooking kits available in many craft stores: those who purchase them are
typically provided with an album, background papers, fasteners, and an
assortment of embellishments, but they still provide their own pictures;
write their own accompanying text; and make their own design choices
about which of the provided items to use, and in what ways. This, to us,
is a vivid example of what Lave and Wenger (1991) termed "legitimate
peripheral participation," the process by which less experienced members are socialized into a community of practice by taking on manage-
able tasks.

According to Wenger (n.d.), the skills and knowledge possessed by
the members of a particular community of practice are not necessarily
recognized or valued by people outside of the group, and scrapbooking certainly fits this pattern. Some of the best evidence of this comes
from scrapbooking parodies on YouTube or other websites, such as this
excerpt from "Scrapbooking Popular among Iraqi Insurgents," an article posted on *www.unconfirmedsources.com*:

> Scrapbooking experts are surprised by the sophistication of the work
> being done by the Iraqi insurgents in the field. "These guys aren't messing
> around," says scrapbook expert Stan Julian of Scrapbooking Magazine.
> "They are using great locally made papers, very intricate die cuts and are
> making very daring cropping choices. They prefer the small albums rather
> than the large size Americans prefer, but under the circumstances I think
> the small size is a good choice." (El-Din, 2005, n.p.)

In this case, the author certainly recognizes some of the tools and skills
associated with scrapbooking, and the irony of the piece depends on its
readership—which may include scrapbookers but is clearly not limited
to them—having some working familiarity with the domain as well. But
the juxtaposition of these tools and skills with a politically weighty subject such as the Iraq war also serves them to trivialize them. The article's
punch depends on the reader agreeing that scrappers' concerns about
album size or cropping choices matter very little in the larger world
(although, in fairness, it pokes fun at the Central Intelligence Agency's
failure to gather genuine intelligence on terrorists as much as it does
the minutiae of scrapbooking).

More seriously, the domain of scrapbooking has been underexamined by scholars in general (see Ott et al., 2006, for a notable exception) and virtually ignored by literacy researchers, even those interested in such topics as popular culture and multimodality, despite recent analysis of new literacies such as instant messaging (Lewis & Fabos, 2005), fan-related online mailing lists (Chandler-Olcott & Mahar, 2003), and 'zines (Guzzetti & Gamboa, 2004). Other researchers have investigated visual thinking and its ties to literacy (cf. Frey & Fisher, 2008), but the texts under consideration—anime, graphic novels, picture books, and so forth—have tended to represent more traditional narrative structure than scrapbooks typically do. Such patterns suggest that the domain of scrapbooking has not yet intersected with the domain of expertise recognized and valued by most literacy scholars.

The Community

A second key component of a community of practice, according to Wenger, is the community itself. As he explains, "In pursuing their interest in their domain, members engage in joint activities and discussions, help each other, and share information. They build relationships that enable them to learn from each other" (n.d., n.p.). With scrapbooking, sometimes the relationships precede the practice, as was the case when Laura learned to construct pages from her mother, a scrapbooking consultant; in other cases, the connections are first forged in the context of the common interest. Either way, when viewed from a sociocultural perspective, the relationships are not the by-product of learning; they are what allows the learning to take place.

One of the best examples of a joint activity meant to disseminate expertise as well as interest in scrapbooking is the *crop*, the name used to describe opportunities for scrapbookers to work on their individual pages in a group setting (the term is, interestingly enough, also used by scrapbookers to describe another central activity in page construction: trimming the edges of an image to improve its composition). Some crops are informal and loosely organized (e.g., many teachers at the elementary school where Kelly's mother is a principal meet once a month to scrapbook together), while others are more institutionalized (e.g., a particular retailer might convene a crop to introduce new products to the market). In either case, scrapbookers report that they convene for the social interaction as well as to work on ongoing projects. The central nature of this activity to scrapbooking as a community is demonstrated by the plethora of online and print articles offering tips about how to organize one. In addition to these local efforts, members of the scrapbooking community participate in regional and national gatherings (Michelle McVaney, the scrapbooking editor at Bella Online: The Voice of Women, lists more than 20 scrapbooking retreats and conventions in locations across the United States, ranging from weekend conferences in West Virginia to a spa for scrapbookers on Lake Michigan).

One notable trend related to adolescents and scrapbooking is the increasing number of public libraries sponsoring crops as a way to entice youth into the buildings. For instance, the Tompkins County Public Library located about an hour south of Kelly sponsored a series of free scrapbooking workshops in 2007–2008 aimed at teens ages 12 to 17 with, according to the promotional material, "a penchant for paper or a collection of phenomenal photographs." While contemporary libraries have always offered services beyond the borrowing of print texts, the timing of this particular series—the first event was held during the Teen Reads Week annually sponsored by the American Library Association—suggests that organizers saw it as a way to link scrapbooking to literacy.

Scrapbookers have other ways to apprentice members into increasing sophistication or variety in their work that do not necessarily involve face-to-face interaction, and a community-of-practice lens insists that these be acknowledged. Scrapbooking blogs and websites have an instructional overtone as they provide spaces for scrapbookers to post questions about procedure or technique, provide tips and shortcuts, and share advice and praise for others' creations. In these spaces, individuals can upload examples of their work to illustrate their directions and suggestions as well as display their final album pages.

Last but not least, the conventions for many scrapbooking publications, especially books and magazines, involve explicit sharing about what scrapbook keepers call "credits and supplies." For example, *Totally Teen Scrapbook Pages* (Memory Makers, 2006), a nonfiction book available in the young adult section of Kelly's local library, includes "Friends Forever," a page by 13-year-old Emma Laffoley from New Brunswick, Canada, about her relationship with a close friend and fellow equestrienne, Shelby. Not only is the layout itself pictured, but most of the materials used to create it and their sources are also listed. This transparency about the design choices made by the creator enables other scrapbookers, including less experienced ones, to recreate the design with their own content or to innovate on it using different visual elements.

The Practice

In addition to the domain and community, communities of practice are characterized by what Wenger (n.d.) calls "a shared repertoire of resources: experiences, stories, tools, [and] ways of addressing recurring problems" (n.p.) that are developed over time. According to him, this shared practice may be more or less self-conscious (members may or may not realize that they are developing a shared repertoire), but it always takes time and sustained interaction to develop.

From a sociocultural perspective, the concept of tools as part of a shared repertoire is an interesting one to apply to the scrapbooking community because some of the tools used by members are material, employing specialized technologies (both digital and otherwise), while others are mental tools, shared ways of thinking and communicating about the tasks associated with scrapbooking. The material tools used by scrapbookers include those that look like traditional arts and crafts supplies—paint, dye, pinking shears, ribbon, and so forth—all of which are used to create specific visual effects, but they also include those associated with writing, including various kinds of paper, pre-cut words and letters, and stickers with phrases and sayings on them. The mental tools include shared vocabulary (e.g., crops, die-cuts, borders) and procedures (e.g., strategies for avoiding color bleeding when stamping an image on a page).

One case of tool development that spans both categories is the Arccivo portfolio invented by three scrapbookers, all working mothers from North Carolina, who were frustrated with challenges associated with the need to move unfinished layouts at the end of a scrapbooking session. According to the website for *Everyday Edisons*, a public television show that featured them and their product, the Arccivo is a "must-have tool for scrapbooking wizards and novices alike" for these reasons:

> Removable magnetic sheets cover and protect unfinished pages, locking loose paper, photos and embellishments in place. Zipping the case shut protects the layout and makes it easy to transport in-progress pages safely and securely. Their invention is an elegant and fashionable solution to both problems that countless scrapbookers all face. (n.d., n.p.)

For us, their invention represents a terrific example of how ordinary members can transform a community of practice by introducing a new tool for their own and others' use.

From a print literacy standpoint, one of the most compelling practices associated with scrapbooking is journaling, the community's term for the writing that accompanies photographs and other visual elements on a scrapbook page. Some pages feature very limited writing—titles for the page itself (e.g., "Going to Kindergarten") or captions for pictures (e.g., "Lucy and Quinn riding the merry-go-round"). Others include extensive handwritten or typed text about the events or experiences captured on the page, some of which appears on the page as part of the design and some of which may be hidden in pockets, under flaps, or behind pictures. Regardless of how the scrapbooker approaches the task of journaling, both print-based and online instructional materials emphasize its importance in the overall impact of the album, with comments like these serving as typical: "An album without journaling may be charming and even fun to look at now, but it will lose much of its meaning when the families who inherit the albums do not even know the names of the people, much less the places and events they represent" (Rothamel, 2005, p. 141).

Also of interest to literacy educators is the scrapbook keepers' practice of making pages for other people, not just themselves. Many pages that are featured online and in print-based instructional resources are by mothers for their children, but gifts grounded in other relationships are also common. For example, *Totally Teen Scrapbook Pages* (Memory Makers, 2006) features a layout by Jennifer Eschak that was designed for her niece, Sheryl. Jennifer was 15 when Sheryl was born. When Sheryl herself turned 15, Jennifer created a page that featured a dictionary definition of "niece," multiple pictures of the two of them together, captions with dates and ages noted, and a 150-word handwritten note to Sheryl hidden behind a flap to lift. When individuals are apprenticed into the scrapbooking community, models like Jennifer's point out numerous potential recipients for their work, creating a clear audience and sense of purpose for those texts. Such a practice stands in contrast to school writing, which remains in most cases aimed at the teacher as sole audience and has demonstrating competence, not genuine communication, as a primary purpose (Strong, 2006).

Considering scrapbooking across Wenger's three dimensions—the domain, the community, and the practice—makes it clear how complex the community of practice actually is. Far from the fussy pastime of bored housewives as it has sometimes been caricatured in the media, scrapbooking practices draw on nearly all of the modes of communica-

tion included in the New London Group's (1996) conception of multiliteracies, and the scrapbooking community involves members who demonstrate significant commitment to each other and to their common
interest. A sociocultural perspective helps us to position these members
and these new literacies in a more complex, and often more favorable,
light than a perspective grounded in what Gallego and Hollingsworth
(2000) call "school literacies" would do.

LIMITATIONS OF SOCIOCULTURAL PERSPECTIVES

Although sociocultural perspectives like Lave and Wenger's (1991) community of practice are helpful in illuminating numerous aspects of new
literacies, these perspectives do have their limitations. A significant critique of socioculturally-oriented literacy research was recently offered
by Lewis et al. (2007), who argued that many studies in this tradition
have not attended enough to what they call "issues of power, identity,
and agency" (p. 2). Applying this argument to scrapbooking helps to
make their critique even more compelling and concrete.

One obvious issue to interrogate is the overrepresentation of white
women and girls in the scrapbooking community. While some scholars
who situate themselves within the sociocultural tradition might explore
the gender and race issues associated with this demographic pattern,
those who draw explicitly on feminist theory (see Guzzetti, Chapter 11,
this volume) and critical race theory (Ladson-Billings & Tate, 1995)
would likely foreground these issues even more explicitly. Of interest in
this regard is not just who feels welcome to join the scrapbooking community but also what representations of daily life are offered by instructional materials and scrapbooks themselves. For instance, *Mastering
Scrapbook Page Design* (2004) by Michele Gerbrandt, a founding editor of
the popular scrapbooking magazine *Memory Makers*, pictures 150 page
layouts in her guide. By our count, only three of them—2%—feature an
identifiable person of color. The daily life, issues, and concerns of African American, Native American, Latino, and Asian American families
are thus rendered less visible to all who use such as a text as a model,
and narrow, traditionally European American conceptions of beauty
are reified, creating and reinforcing an unrepresentative and unrealistic portrait of contemporary life.

Scholars drawing on feminist theory or gender studies would also
be sure to interrogate the traditionally gendered language that perme-

ates many scrapbooking publications, both print and online, and many layouts themselves. For example, *Totally Teen Scrapbook Pages* (Memory Makers, 2006), a how-to guide we cited before, describes both products and layouts in language that constructs stereotypical differences between the sexes as natural, dichotomous, and inevitable, as these text snippets show:

> **Pretty 'n' Trendy:** Discover products that will adorn pictures of your prettiest girly girl. Patterned papers in soft pastels, sparkly beads and feminine clips will make your pages simmer with fashionista flair! (p. 8)

> **It's a Guy Thing:** Boys will be boys and there's no better way to feature their masculine personalities than with urban-style papers, border stickers and rubber tire tracks that speak true macho charm. (p. 9)

While some researchers using sociocultural perspectives would undoubtedly point out these patterns and the way they limit who can be a scrapbooker as well as what can be included in a scrapbook, Enciso (2007) argues convincingly that inequities related to gender have often been homogenized or omitted in the narratives told by those working within this tradition. Invoking gender studies explicitly in concert with more generally focused sociocultural schemas such as Lave and Wenger's (1991) community of practice may reduce such omissions and elisions.

In addition, the emergence of scrapbooking as big business calls out for the application of a theoretical lens such as Marxism (e.g., Shannon, 2001) that will interrogate how scrapbooking materials, tools, and instruction are produced and marketed. Such an analysis would likely yield different kinds of insight than one that primarily examined how those items are taken up and used by scrapbookers themselves. In this view, companies like Creative Memories that recruit and train consultants to work with individuals interested in scrapbooking their memories and retailers like Target that offer whole aisles of scrapbooking supplies in their superstores *create* tastes and styles as much as they offer products that reflect existing tastes.

And the patterns they create stand to benefit some groups more than others. For instance, while some might argue that the sale of scrapbooking services and materials by stay-at-home mothers benefits them by providing an additional source of income while allowing them to care full time for their children, others might argue that the mothers' labor is exploited, as the loose nature of many of these agreements allows for little negotiation about the value of what they do and little opportunity for collective bargaining among those who do similar kinds of work. A class-based economic analysis might yield insight into how the beliefs and practices of scrapbookers intersect or contrast with those of other communities of practice (e.g., manufacturers, retailers). New literacies such as scrapbooking are often not fully integrated into typical workplace patterns and practices; as they become more established, they are of more interest to those who control the means of production and thus may require more attention from theoretical perspectives that foreground those issues.

CONCLUDING THOUGHTS

To our way of thinking, scrapbooking represents an aspect of new literacies that Luke (2000) has written about: that they often have clear roots in so-called "old" literacies that have evolved in new and interesting ways. We doubt that John Locke, if transported to the 21st century, would immediately recognize a digital scrapbook posted on *www.shutterfly.com* as the inheritor of his commonplace book from three centuries ago. The look and feel of those creations is dramatically different, and a strictly text-based analysis would likely yield few commonalities. At the same time, a socioculturally oriented analysis of that same digital scrapbook—one that locates it in a social, cultural, and historical context—reveals traces of Locke's book at the same time it reveals representations of ideas and identities, tools, and techniques of which he could not conceive.

That very little attention has been paid by literacy researchers to scrapbooking to date may be linked to patterns and structures that originated in the context of so-called old literacies. The professional organizations, publications, and academic appointments associated with literacy research as a community of practice have tended to reinforce specialization by age group. Literacy scholars identify themselves as working in early literacy, the middle grades, adult literacy, and so forth. Thus far, the work on new literacies has been dominated by scholars with a simultaneous interest in adolescent literacy (indeed, our own previous inquiries into new literacies were not sparked by an interest in new technologies or even new practices but rather by a deep curiosity about what our own teenage students were doing outside of school as readers and writers). Such a starting point would likely not have led us to the rich world of scrapbooking, however, as scrapbookers are not so neatly classified by age. Although middle-aged women tend to be the most common members, the community is truly intergenerational, involving children, adolescents, and seniors as well. Those interested in capturing the wide range and complexity of new literacies beyond the obvious text messaging and blogging done by teens and reported so prominently in the media would do well to use community-oriented research designs like those of Shirley Brice Heath (1982), whose work spanned generations as well as communities.

Although scrapbooking has received little attention from literacy scholars, we've seen some small hints that it may be on teachers' radar screens. For example, ReadWriteThink, a website of peer-reviewed literacy lesson plans sponsored by the International Reading Association and the National Council of Teachers of English, includes a lesson entitled "Literary Scrapbooks Online" (Annan, n. d.) that we believe would not have been posted previous to the rise of scrapbooking among hobbyists. The task for students is to create a multimedia scrapbook on some aspect of the novel *The Adventures of Huckleberry Finn* or Mark Twain's life, using PowerPoint. On one hand, the inclusion of such an assignment in school is encouraging to us, as it is likely to be more engaging to students than, say, a traditional essay analyzing a theme in the text, and it allows them to employ multiple modes of communication, as most new literacies do. At the same time, examination of the task from a sociocultural perspective—one informed by an analysis of scrapbooking in the world outside school—suggests that it misses some of the most powerful practices associated with both new literacies and that community of practice. Students will not use many of the characteristic tools, both material and otherwise, associated with scrapping, nor does it appear that they will access any of the instructionally focused texts, online or in print, that mediate and inform multimodal page design. The assignment has merit because it seeks to revalue and harness the sophistication of literacies such as scrapbooking and incorporate them in the classroom, but if scrapbooking is a practice through which community members construct and express their identities to others with whom they have personal, not hierarchical, relationships, then this type of academic activity will probably fail to capture its ethos.

After all, if there is anything clear from our analysis of scrapbooking as a new literacy, it is that members of this community of practice compose their pages to represent themselves and their experiences as much as they do to communicate to others. As Laura explains it, "I like to think of what I like and what I want my page to look like for me" (e-mail correspondence, July 12, 2008), even as she constructs a page of pictures from her mother's childhood, while scrapbooking alongside a same-age peer. This complex balance of the individual with the social, the traditional with the innovative, and the visual with the linguistic seems to us to be the best of what many new literacies, not just scrapbooking, offer to adolescents today.

REFERENCES

Albers, P., & Harste, J. C. (2007). The arts, new literacies, and multimodality. *English Education, 40*(1), 6–20.

Alvermann, D. (2002). *Adolescents and literacies in a digital world.* New York: Lang.

Annan, J. (n.d.). Literary scrapbooks online: An electronic reader-response project. *ReadWriteThink.* Retrieved June 26, 2008, from *www.readwritethink. org/lessons/lesson_view.asp?id=787.*

Bakhtin, M. (1986). *Speech genres and other late essays.* Austin: University of Texas Press.

Barton, D., & Hamilton, M. (2000). Literacy practices. In D. Barton, M. Hamilton, & R. Ivaniéc (Eds.), *Situated literacies: Reading and writing in context* (pp. 7–15). New York: Routledge.

Beach, R. (2000). Using media ethnographies to study response to media as activity. In A. Watts Paillotet & P. Mosenthal (Eds.), *Reconceptualizing literacy in the media age* (pp. 3–39). Stamford, CT: JAI Press.

Brandt, D., & Clinton, K. (2002). The limits of the local: Expanding perspectives on literacy as a social practice. *Journal of Literacy Research, 34*(3), 337–356.

Chandler-Olcott, K., & Mahar, D. (2003). Tech-savviness meets multiliteracies: An exploration of adolescent girls' technology-mediated literacy practices. *Reading Research Quarterly, 38*(1), 356–385.

Cole, M. (1996). *Cultural psychology.* Cambridge, MA: Belknap.

Craft and Hobby Association. (2008). National Scrapbooking Day media alert. Retrieved September 1, 2008, from *www.craftandhobby.org/cgi-bin/pressrelease.cgi?func=ShowRelease&releaseid=264.*

El-Din, K. (2005). Scrapbooking popular among Iraqi insurgents. Retrieved August 28, 2008, from *www.unconfirmedsources.com/index.php?itemid=1011.*

Enciso, P. (2007). Reframing history in sociocultural theories: Toward an expansive vision. In C. Lewis, P. Enciso, & E. B. Moje (Eds.), *Reframing sociocultural research on literacy: Identity, agency, and power* (pp. 49–74). Mahwah, NJ: Erlbaum.

Engestrom, Y., Miettinen, R., & Punamaki, R. (1999). *Perspectives on activity theory.* New York: Cambridge University Press.

Everyday Edisons. (n. d.). The Arccivo scrapbooking portfolio. Retrieved September 5, 2008, from *www.everydayedisons.com/deborahPamMary.html.*

Frey, N., & Fisher, D. (2008). *Teaching visual literacy: Comic books, graphic novels, anime, cartoons, and more to develop comprehension and thinking skills.* Thousand Oaks, CA: Corwin.

Gallego, M., & Hollingsworth, S. (2000). *What counts as literacy? Challenging the school standard.* New York: Teachers College Press.

Gee, J. P. (2000). The new literacy studies: From socially situated to the work of the social. In D. Barton, M. Hamilton, & R. Ivaniéc (Eds.), *Situated literacies: Reading and writing in context* (pp. 177–194). New York: Routledge.

Gee, J. P. (2001). Reading as situated language: A sociocognitive perspective. *Journal of Adolescent and Adult Literacy, 44*(8), 714–725.

Gee, J. P. (2008). *Social linguistics and literacies: Ideology in discourses* (3rd ed.). New York: Routledge.

Gerbrandt, M. (2004). *Mastering scrapbook design.* Denver, CO: Memory Makers.

Guzzetti, B. J., & Gamboa, M. (2004). Zines for social justice: Adolescent girls writing on their own. *Reading Research Quarterly, 39*(4), 408–436.

Hamilton, M. (2000). Expanding the new literacy studies: Using photographs to explore literacy as social practice. In D. Barton, M. Hamilton, & R. Ivaniéc (Eds.), *Situated literacies: Reading and writing in context* (pp. 16–34). London: Routledge.

Heath, S. B. (1982). Protean shapes in literacy events: Ever-shifting oral and literate traditions. In D. Tannen (Ed.), *Spoken and written language: Exploring orality and literacy* (pp. 91–117). Norwood, NJ: Ablex.

Kist, W. (2005). *New literacies in action: Teaching and learning in multiple media.* New York: Teachers College Press.

Knobel, M., & Lankshear, C. (2007). *A new literacies sampler.* New York: Lang.

Ladson-Billings, G., & Tate, W. (1995). Toward a critical race theory of education. *Teachers College Record, 97,* 47–68.

Lankshear, C., & Knobel, M. (2003). *New literacies: Changing knowledge and classroom learning.* Philadelphia: Open University Press.

Lave, J., & Wenger, E. (1991). *Situated learning: Legitimate peripheral participation.* Cambridge, UK: Cambridge University Press.

Lewis, C., Enciso, P., & Moje, E. (2007). *Reframing sociocultural research on literacy: Identity, agency, and power.* Mahwah, NJ: Erlbaum.

Lewis, C., & Fabos, B. (2005). Instant messaging, literacies, and social identities. *Reading Research Quarterly, 40*(4), 470–501.

Lewis, E. (2008). *Secondary English teachers' perspectives on the incorporation of new literacies in their pedagogy.* Unpublished dissertation, Syracuse University, Syracuse, New York.

Lewis, E., & Chandler-Olcott, K. (2007, December). *Secondary English teachers' perspectives on incorporating new literacies into their pedagogy.* Paper presented at the annual meeting of the National Reading Conference, Austin, TX.

Luke, C. (2000). Cyber-schooling and technological change: Multiliteracies for new times. In B. Cope & M. Kalantzis (Eds.), *Multiliteracies: Literacy learning and the design of social futures* (pp. 69–91). New York: Routledge.

Memory Makers. (2006). *Totally teen scrapbook pages: Scrapbooking the almost grown-up years.* Denver, CO: Memory Makers.

New London Group. (1996). A pedagogy of multiliteracies: Designing social futures. *Harvard Educational Review, 66*(1), 60–92.

Ott, K., Tucker, S., & Buckler, P. (2006). An introduction to the history of scrapbooks. In S. Tucker, K. Ott, & P. Buckler (Eds.), *The scrapbook in American life* (pp. 1–28). Philadelphia: Temple University Press.

Rothamel, S. P. (2005). *The encyclopedia of scrapbooking tools and techniques.* New York: Sterling.

Shannon, P. (2001). A Marxist reading of literacy education. *Cultural Logic, 4*(1). Retrieved September 1, 2008, from *clogic.eserver.org/4–1/shannon.html.*

Siegel, E. E. (2006). "Miss Domestic" and "Miss Enterprise": Or, how to keep a photograph album. In S. Tucker, K. Ott, & P. Buckler (Eds.), *The scrapbook in American life* (pp. 251–267). Philadelphia: Temple University Press.

Smagorinsky, P. (2002). Activity theory. In B. J. Guzzetti, (Ed.), *Literacy in America: An encyclopedia of history, theory, and practice* (pp. 10–13). Santa Barbara, CA: ABC-CLIO, Inc.

Street, B. V. (1995). *Social literacies: Critical approaches to literacy in development, ethnography, and education.* London: Longman.

Strong, W. (2006). *Write for insight: Empowering content area learning, grades 6–12.* New York: Pearson.

Taylor, M. (2003). *The history of scrapbooking.* Retrieved July 20, 2008, from *www.thesavvyscrapper.com/historyof.htm.*

Vygotsky, L. (1978). *Mind in society: The development of higher psychological processes.* Cambridge, MA: Harvard University Press.

Washington Times. (2004). *Scrapbooking evolves into art and archiving.* Retrieved July 19, 2008, from *www/washingtontimes.com/news/2004/feb/18/20040218-110705-5613r/?page=6.*

Wenger, E. (1998). Communities of practice: Learning as a social system. *The Systems Thinker, 9*(5). Retrieved August 23, 2008, from *www.ewenger.com/pub/index.htm.*

Wenger, E. (2006). *Communities of practice: A brief introduction.* Retrieved October 28, 2009, from *www.ewenger.com/theory/index.htm.*

Wenger, E. (n.d.). *Communities of practice: A brief introduction.* Retrieved June 27, 2008, from *www.ewenger.com/theory/index.htm.*

Wertsch, J. (1991). *Voices of the mind: A sociocultural approach to mediated action.* Cambridge, MA: Harvard University Press.

CHAPTER 10

An Examination of Workplace Literacy Research from New Literacies and Sociocultural Perspectives

LARRY MIKULECKY

Successful literacy use in the workplace to complete tasks regularly involves using multiple sequences of communication forms (e.g., reading, writing, speaking, and listening) and several displays of information (e.g., print, handwriting, computer display, visual representations) in order to accomplish social functions. By 2003, the Department of Labor had reported that 77 million Americans, or 55% of employees, were using computers as part of their jobs (Bureau of Labor Statistics, 2005). It is logical and sensible to examine workplace literacy through the lenses associated with the multiliteracies, new literacies, and sociocultural language use. During the last decade, several new definitions of literacy have been put forth. Among the most useful for examination of literacy in the workplace are:

> Literacy is the flexible and sustainable mastery of a repertoire of practices with the texts of traditional and new communications technologies via spoken, print, and multimedia. (Luke & Freebody, 2000, p. 8)

> socially recognized ways of generating, communicating, and negotiating meaningful content through the medium of encoded texts within contexts

of participation in Discourses (or, as members of Discourses). (Lankshear
& Knobel, 2006, p. 64)

These definitions incorporate the roles that values, group membership,
identity, and power play in communications and transactions.

Gee, Hull, and Lankshear (1996), in *The New Work Order*, noted
that it is impossible to simply discuss reading and writing or even just
language when examining the meaning of literacy related to the workplace. One must understand the social practices and functions in which
text is immersed because individuals "not only read texts of this type in
this way but also talk about such texts in certain ways, hold certain attitudes and values about them, and socially interact over them in certain
ways" (p. 3).

This broad statement is most certainly true, but it does tend to skim
over several challenging complexities of doing sociocultural research
focused on workplace literacy and, in particular, research that can be of
specific and immediate value to educators. Among the complexities to
be negotiated are:

1. The array of theoretical frameworks available to analyze the
   various aspects of workplace literacy.
2. The rapidly changing nature of workplace literacy (i.e., both
   types of text used and social practices), given the powerful and
   rapidly transforming influences of technology, economics, and
   political decisions in restructuring how work is performed.
3. The multitude of levels of analysis and foci for workplace literacy
   research (i.e., political/social discussion of workplace literacy
   policy, actual literacy use as part of workplace practice in millions of workplaces, and educational practice related to workplace literacy).
4. The specialized language as well as cognitive, social, and political practices of thousands of different occupations and millions
   of different workplaces.
5. The "What should I teach?" challenge faced by educators
   charged with preparing potential employees to succeed with
   tasks involving workplace literacy *before* students are immersed
   in a particular workplace culture and often before the educator
   knows *exactly* which literacy texts, tasks, and social practices the
   students will encounter.

DEALING WITH THE COMPLEXITIES

Sociocultural examinations and discussions of workplace literacy have been present for a good long time and have increased in number over the past two decades. What follows is a discussion of how scholars and researchers have addressed (or sometimes sidestepped) the complexities listed above.

Theoretical Frameworks for Sociocultural and Sociolinguistic Examinations

Space limitations preclude an exhaustive discussion of all the various ways scholars and researchers have examined workplace literacy through sociocultural lenses. A selected sampling, however, can provide a sense of approaches employed in the past and potentially useful in the future. These studies range from early studies that borrowed theoretical frameworks from sociology, anthropology, psychology, linguistics, and economics to more recent studies that employ frameworks specifically designed for the sociocultural examination of literacy.

Scribner and Cole (1981) examined the use of literacy by the Vai in Africa, noting that the type of literacy and indeed the language of the literacy used by the Vai were directly related to social function. An entirely separate form of literacy was used for buying, selling, and transacting business while a different form was used for other communications. These findings grew from a multi-year ethnographic study using theoretical frameworks directly borrowed from anthropology and social/cognitive psychology. This work extended identifications of the functions of literacy and sociocultural considerations beyond earlier work that had categorized workplace literacy into simpler functions such as reading to do, learn, and assess (Mikulecky, 1982; Sticht, 1976). Scribner, in a later case study of dairy workers published in the *Anthropology and Education Quarterly*, drew on both anthropological frameworks and activity theory to document how culturally organized actions guided dairy workers as they acquired and organized their work knowledge when involved with literacy and other tasks. Scribner documented how individuals needed to creatively synthesize knowledge from several domains, including social and cultural, to organize their actions (Scribner, 1985). The research of Scribner and her colleagues on workplace literacy was anchored in several theoretical frameworks, including Vygotsky's socially mediated learning as well as situated cognition. This work brought early sociocultural perspectives to workplace literacy research.

In the mid-1980s, a few other qualitative researchers began to use the theoretical frameworks of ethnography and critical literacy to examine literacy practices in communities and workplaces from sociocultural perspectives. Shirley Brice Heath's groundbreaking *Ways with Words* (1983) examined the functions and uses of literacy in two Piedmont communities. Although workplace literacy use received only slight attention in this broad study of two communities, the ethnographic focus on the functions and roles played by literacy in larger contexts set the stage for dozens of other studies. About the same time, Hannah (Arlene) Fingeret began publishing research documenting how power relationships and value differences influenced workplace literacy and workplace education. An early case study documents the destruction of a collaborative workplace literacy program intended to train power plant technicians in safety procedures. Fingeret's research attributes the program's demise to differences between the values and practices of university educators and workplace administrators (Fingeret, 1984). In Fingeret's work, a clear intent and foundation for analyzing the impact of power relationships and value differences on workplace literacy programs had been established using Frierian learner-centered sociocultural theory as a basis.

During the late 1980s and into the 1990s workplace literacy studies continued to borrow theoretical frameworks from other academic areas. These studies incorporated social and cultural perspectives to differing degrees, often employed multiple theoretical frameworks, and began to note requirements for new technological skills associated with literacy. Some simply recognized social aspects of workplace literacy at superficial levels by adding a few social practices, such as working with teams or negotiating differences, to existing competency frameworks (e.g., SCANS report, U.S. Department of Labor, 1992). Others drew on cognitive/sociocultural approaches from situated learning and situated cognition (Lave & Wenger, 1991; Taylor & Blunt, 2001). Still others (e.g., Gowen, 1992; Hull, 1993) drew upon frameworks borrowed from anthropology and critical pedagogy. Several of these studies are discussed in more detail in later sections of this chapter. Each broadened our sociocultural understanding of workplace literacy beyond simply teaching reading and writing skills for use in the workplace and began to present complex, integrated examples of how social functioning in the workplace required a wide range of literate communications that embraced new technologies.

In the fields of linguistic and literacy scholarship, James Gee was introducing his sociocultural concepts of Discourses/discourses (Gee, 1989, 1991; see also Chapter 8, this volume), which were developed to focus specifically on socioculturally relevant ways to understand language and literacy. Gee presented Discourses as socially recognized ways of using language (reading, writing, speaking, listening), gestures, and other semiotics (images, sounds, graphics, signs, codes). In addition to the broadly defined forms of language, he indicated that we must take into account broader aspects of context such as ways of thinking, believing, feeling, valuing, acting/doing, and interacting in relation to people and things. Through Discourse, thus broadly defined, one communicates these things so that one can be identified and recognized as playing a role or being a member of a socially meaningful group (e.g., parent, member of a social group, member of an ethnic group, or member of occupational group). Language, according to Gee, is only one dimension (along with how one dresses, acts, etc) of this larger Discourse, and he uses *discourse* with a small *d* to distinguish how language fits into the larger Discourse. He also distinguished between one's primary Discourse and secondary Discourses, which one learns and acquires in order to be a member of or play roles in new social groups. According to Gee, literacy or literacies involve mastering and developing competent performance in a variety of secondary Discourses, which include Discourses of occupations and levels within occupations and can involve learning the literacies of different technologies.

Gee et al.'s book *The New Work Order* (1996) examined public workplace rhetoric and two workplaces. The scholarship employed several theoretical approaches and drew upon the research and previous scholarship of each of its three authors. The book begins with a sociocultural linguistic analysis of the ideologically loaded Discourse of "fast capitalism," noting and documenting the misrepresentation of the workplace in this Discourse. It also highlights how this Discourse attempts to displace existing cultural roles and functions of community and church by redefining for mercantile purposes the meaning of several important concepts such as empowerment, democracy, collaboration, and learning. The book then goes on to focus on case studies of specific workplaces (e.g., a Silicon Valley electronic assembly plant and a Nicaraguan village light manufacturer) in order to examine the Discourse of fast capitalism compared with actual functions and practices of literacy empirically revealed in the case studies. New forms and organization of literacy and technological communication are documented, especially in the Silicon Valley case. The sociocultural analyses reveal, however, that practice of these new literacies is more complex than what is portrayed in the rhetoric of fast capitalism and is heavily influenced by preexisting and new issues of power and identity. It is not a case of simply learning new skills.

By the beginning of the 21st century, workplace literacy scholarship was drawing on an even wider variety of sociocultural frameworks, many designed specifically with language and literacy education in mind. Baynham and Prinsloo (2001), for example, synthesize elements growing out of the work of dozens of scholars who characterize their work as "new literacy studies." They summarize elements of new literacy studies as follows:

- Literacy is best understood as a set of social practices; these are observable in events which are mediated by written texts.
- There are different literacies associated with different domains of life.
- Literacy practices are patterned by social institutions and power relations and some literacies are more dominant, visible, and influential than others.
- Literacy practices are purposeful and embedded in broader social goals and cultural practices.
- Literacy is historically situated.
- Literacy practices change and new ones are frequently acquired through processes of informal learning and sense making as well as formal education and training. (p. 84)

By the midpoint in the first decade of the 21st century, workplace literacy researchers were framing their sociocultural analyses by examining dozens of theoretical frameworks. For example, in 2005 Kleifgen published in the *Reading Research Quarterly* a study comparing the "official literacies" of an international quality assurance program (ISO 9002) to the localized literacies employed by workers in a circuit board manufacturing plant. In presenting the theoretical and conceptual frameworks she used for analysis, Kleifgen cited the work of Gee, Barton, Street, and new literacy studies as general frameworks for understanding multiple literacies. She also drew upon the theoretical and conceptual ideas of Bourdieu (linguistic capital; 1977, 1991) and Foucault (power/knowledge; 1977) as her basis for examining power relationships with particular emphasis on the ideas of a more neglected theorist, linguist Valentin

N. Volosinov (1929/1973) of the Bakhtin Circle, whose work focused on the social life of the verbal sign. More specifically, Kleifgen indicated, her study built on the workplace literacy studies of a half-dozen workplace literacy researchers (many previously mentioned in this section). During the analysis portion of her study, Kleifgen added several more theoretical frameworks to inform her analysis, mentioning early research of Goody and Watt (1963), Olson (1977), Ong (1982), and their understandings of what it means to be literate (Kleifgen, 2005). Still more frameworks were mentioned later in the analysis portion of the study. Kliefgen documents new technological forms of workplace literacy used to monitor quality of production and communicate among workers, but focuses on how actual use of these new literacies is influenced by power relationships.

It is clear here that researchers examining workplace literacy from sociocultural perspectives now draw on the wealth of sociocultural theory stretching back nearly a century. The conceptual frameworks proliferate well beyond the dozen or so Kleifgen cited. Several researchers (e.g., Jolliffe, 1997; Malcolm & Field, 2005; Searle, 2002; Wojecki, 2007) have studied workplace literacy in relation to worker identities and roles (sense of self) and as well as agency (control over one's life), drawing on an array of models for identity and agency. Other researchers and educators look at the linguistic/social concepts of genre of social use to more systematically categorize and characterize the functions of language used in different settings (Friedman, Adam, & Smart, 1994). In Australia, the Sydney School of genre analysis has combined linguistic and critical literacy analyses of power relations to present pedagogical choices that include the explicit teaching of power relations in language and literacy instruction (Christie & Martin, 2000; Johns, 2002). In Canada, the United States, and several other countries, Purcell-Gates and colleagues have collected and analyzed uses of literacy in many different social contexts and done studies to examine the impact of more socially authentic literacy instruction on learning (Purcell-Gates, Duke, & Martineau, 2007, and Cultural Practices of Literacy Studies website *cpls. educ.ubc.ca*). Although the cultural practices genre studies have not yet directly addressed workplace literacy, this theoretical framework could easily lend itself to workplace literacy research. Choosing which of these many theoretical frameworks to use and which aspects of sociocultural language and literacy to focus on is becoming more complex for workplace literacy researchers. Furthermore, the focus of these frameworks does not specifically highlight newer technological literacy practices, but rather how these and other literacy practices fit within larger socio-cultural understandings of the workplace.

Complexities of Changing Workplace Literacy Tasks and Settings

The very richness in possibilities inherent in studying workplace literacy from sociocultural perspectives makes the endeavor daunting. Simply deciding on the levels and foci of analysis can be a challenge because there are so many different venues and types of literacy in the work-place. Sheryl Greenwood Gowen's (1992) book *The Politics of Workplace Literacy: A Case Study* is a good example of how to choose wisely and do an exemplary job of sociocultural analysis.

The book, based on her multiyear dissertation study, focused on low-paid hospital workers and the workplace literacy associated with their jobs, their aspirations, and the classes they were encouraged and sometimes required to take at the hospital. Gowen invested hundreds and perhaps thousands of hours observing classes and work, doing interviews with employees, supervisors, and teachers, examining class-room and workplace documents, reinterviewing individuals about the meaning of the documents and literacy tasks, and extensively analyzing her data from several different perspectives using several different theo-retical frameworks.

The choices of occupation and workplace were good choices that warranted the extensive research effort. Low-paid health care workers are a growing demographic, and they qualified as obvious targets of the prevailing 1980s–1990s rhetoric about workplace literacy (i.e., unless workers with low literacy improved their abilities to handle new liter-acy demands, negative consequences for all would be the result). Even though qualitative research is cautious about limiting what can be gen-eralized, nearly every major hospital in developed nations has some sort of education effort targeted to low-skilled, low-paid employees. Insights from Gowen's study were more likely to be of broad use than a study of more exotic and rare occupations.

Gowen's multichapter, multitheoretical approach allowed her to reveal the complexities of the hospital situation in ways that captured the voices and perspectives of participants and revealed important insights about the dangerous fallout that can stem from embracing simplistic understandings of workplace literacy. Federally funded work-place programs of the time were built, in part, on research that showed limited transfer from one type of literacy learning to performance of other types (Mikulecky, Albers, & Peers, 1994; Sticht, 1988), a finding not too different from later theoretical arguments for multiple literacies. In an attempt to mandate authenticity, federal policy guidelines that grew out of this research required that workplace literacy instruction in federally funded programs be linked to literacy tasks employees actually performed in the workplace. Sticht (1988) had labeled this approach "functional context education." Gowen's sociocultural analyses revealed that many workers didn't particularly want to learn about their existing jobs, they wanted to learn how to get *different, better* jobs or how to accomplish nonwork-related goals for themselves and their families. Furthermore, Gowen documented the inadequacy of educator attempts to construct authentic instructional materials linked to official job descriptions of workplace tasks and official guidelines for how entry-level hospital workers were to do their jobs. Gowen's observations of how job tasks were actually performed indicated that such observations were needed. Gowen presents one example that indicates janitors' lives might have been endangered by following official guidelines for retrieving used needles from waste cans. In actual practice (as Gowen learned from interviews and observations), doctors and nurses sometimes discarded used needles in careless manners, which made following specified retrieval techniques life threatening to the janitors. Other evidence suggested that racism and social class differences as well as conflicting values played much larger roles than literacy skills in determining what workers did on the job. Gowen's insights about problems that can arise from simply teaching how to perform new literacy tasks as isolated skills remains relevant as the list of new workplace literacy skills increases in length and technological complexity.

Gowen's (1992) work helped inform later discussion of who should pay for workplace literacy programs and what their structure should be. Employers were reluctant to fund programs that focused broadly on general skills due to the fear that other employers would "steal" higher-trained employees and the original employer's investment when newly educated employees departed. This was a realistic fear, and indeed Gowen's research revealed that many employees wanted to be "stolen" away to better jobs. In many cases, employer-determined priorities meant narrower program foci. Taxpayer- and union-funded workplace literacy programs, on the other hand, could argue for placing higher priority on the development of the individual and some (but less) emphasis on the bottom line for the individual employer. A later survey of 121 workplace literacy programs revealed that slightly fewer than half focused completely on workplace skills (i.e., totally functional context), with 45% using a combination of workplace- and learner-centered approaches and only 10% emphasizing just general skills (Mikulecky, Lloyd, Horowitz, Masker, & Siemantel, 1996). A later examination of this transfer question (Mikulecky & Lloyd, 1997) found that although *some* connection to authentic workplace literacy materials and tasks was needed for transfer to occur, having as little as 20% of program time and activities directly linked to workplace tasks (e.g., monitoring and reporting quality control data from computer screens) was a break point for demonstrating improvement in performance of workplace literacy tasks. Some, but not complete, attention to new workplace literacy uses was required for improvement to occur. This provided evidence in support of balanced programs.

While some clear connection to occupational literacy tasks is still a part of most workplace literacy programs (Imel, 2003), the emphasis has shifted from mandating a total "functional context" approach to a balance of emphasis that includes worker goals as well as preparing program participants for higher levels of certification and formal education such as community college enrollment, commercial driver's license certification, international mover's certification, and so forth (Mikulecky, 2007). The use and preparation of workers for new technological literacies is considered within these broader sociocultural frameworks.

There is continuing debate about what the proper balance should be between learner-centered and business-centered workplace program emphases and the degree to which programs take worker voices, purposes, and needs into account along with those of other stakeholders (Castleton, 2002). As someone who has participated in policy discussions and debates on workplace literacy at the national level in the United States, it seems to this author that the complexities of the workplace and workplace literacy revealed by sociocultural literacy researchers have increasingly become very useful parts of these discussions and debates. This rarely means that all the views of these researchers predominate, but does indicate that the research has had influence.

Another example of how to negotiate the complexities of doing workplace literacy research can be seen in the work of Glynda Hull. In her early work (Hull, 1991, 1993), she performed extensive examination of the rhetoric of workplace literacy/illiteracy present in the press and public documents during the late 1980s identifying what she termed "uncontested beliefs." These uncontested beliefs were about "low-skilled" workers, the nature of mistakes they were charged with making, the types of education being called for, and the matches/mismatches between actual workplace literacy use and the sort of workplace literacy education provided. In *Hearing Other Voices*, Hull (1991) systematically challenged the assumptions she found in public rhetoric and much existing scholarship as providing "a smokescreen, covering up certain key societal problems by drawing our attention to other issues that, while important, are only symptomatic of a larger ill" (p. 9). Increased demand for literacy related to new technologies was one of the smokescreen issues identified by Hull. In making her case, she introduced sociocultural research of several other researchers whose work (at the time) was not easily located or was not part of the public debate (e.g., the dairy study work of Scribner and colleagues; the then dissertation of Gowen; technical reports by Fields and colleagues; early work by Hart-Landsberg and Reder; and several unpublished manuscripts from Darrah). This sociocultural workplace literacy research was not yet widely known or in some cases even accessible without considerable effort. Hull was able to use it to demonstrate the important complexities that simplified assumptions about workplace literacy did not take into account. A second ethnography of her own (Hull, 1993) on the relationship between banking industry literacy practice and vocational training produced data to further document some of the arguments she had made in *Hearing Other Voices*.

While Hull continued to be active as a scholar, her next workplace literacy scholarship based on a multiyear study of a Silicon Valley circuit board manufacturer took another 3 years to make its appearance in technical reports (Hull, Jury, Ziv, Oren, & Katz, 1996) and also as part of the Gee et al. (1996) book previously discussed. The study was worth the wait. In addition to reinforcing some of the arguments of her earlier work, the study provided detailed examples of how workers actually used literacy to perform tasks as individuals and as parts of teams. It developed and modified several useful techniques for gathering and organizing information on literacy use in the workplace, including classifications (e.g., literate activities, functions, and documents) and several meta-categories of literacy. *These meta-categories and listings were described as intended for use as heuristics for analyzing and understanding literate activity.* This is an important point that identifies a tension for sociocultural scholars of workplace literacy and which I discuss in more detail later.

Scholars like Hull very much want their research to influence how educators teach, but at the same time are concerned that their insights and tools might become one more oversimplification.

Literacy uses identified by Hull included such basic functions as "copying," "keyboarding," "proofreading," and "labeling," but also went on incorporate such social functions as "gaining consensus," "gauging reactions," and "requesting action." New literacies and new technologies are recognized, but not given any special focus within the sociocultural frameworks and analyses. Among the overarching category labels were "Performing Basic Literate Functions," "Using Literacy to Explain," "Participating in the Flow of Information," and "Using Literacy to Exercise, Acknowledge or Resist Authority" (Hull et al., 1996, p. 175). Similar taxonomies were developed to describe and categorize literacy use in workplace classrooms. Developing the meta-categories was, in part, an attempt to create sociocultural tools that could extend and possibly generalize beyond the particular workplace and occupations of the study. In addition, the project experimented with using compact discs to present video examples of different sorts of workplace literacy use. The study technical report did much more than this and provided a foundation for other publications over the next several years (e.g., Hull, 1999, 2000).

Even though there are many ways to do workplace literacy research from sociocultural perspectives, much of this research has been of four types: (1) examination of the rhetoric surrounding workplace literacy and who is in charge (e.g., Castleton, 2002; Gee et al., 1996; Jackson, 2000); (2) in-depth examination of a particular workplace or type of occupation (e.g., Hull et al., 1996; Searle, 2002; Tannock, 2001); (3) examination of how workplace literacy interacts with the construction of workplace identities and exercise of agency (Billett & Somerville, 2004; Hunter, 2007; Jolliffe, 1997); and (4) capturing the voices of workplace participants and the impact of programs on individuals (e.g., Gowen, 1992; Hart-Landsberg & Reder, 1995; Hull, 1999). Individual studies may engage in more than one of these types of analysis and many include new and technological literacies among literacies analyzed, but not as a key focus.

As discussed earlier, doing in-depth sociocultural literacy research in workplaces can be very expensive in terms of time and resources. When workplace educators are also competing for limited resources with those seeking resources for instruction, pressure develops for researchers to find ways to generalize information beyond the intense focus on individual participants and workplaces. Dealing with this tension is the topic of the next section of this chapter.

What to Teach When There Are Thousands of Occupations and Millions of Workplaces

Like practitioners of critical pedagogy, sociocultural researchers of workplace literacy face the question from classroom educators of: "Beyond contesting unchallenged beliefs and documenting complexities, what can you do to help us teach?" In a sense, this is an unfair question, because documenting complexities and challenging uncontested beliefs is doing a great deal.

Even though sociocultural researchers and scholars of workplace literacy are constrained by expense and the vast number of occupations and workplaces to be studied, they are able to make some suggestions for classroom educators and program developers. One educational recommendation from sociocultural workplace scholars is to make programs more participatory and oriented to critical inquiry (Nash, 2001). A second is for educators to help workers reflect more on their own knowledge of how authentic workplace materials are used (Castleton, 2000, 2002). Castleton is also particularly concerned at how much existing workplace literacy instruction looks like traditional, teacher-directed schooling, which perpetuates existing power structures and passive roles for learners (Castleton, 2002, p. 561). Computer-lab classes on how to use new workplace technologies fit within this concern. Castleton calls for instructors and scholars to be more creative and assertive in finding ways for education to "give workers an authentic and authoritative say in their own destinies" (p. 564) and fulfill real purposes for all stakeholders. Hull (1999) supports a similar approach when she suggests a stronger focus on the connection between learning and doing, with the doing including the incorporation of social networks and relationships into what is taught.

Purcell-Gates, Degener, Jacobson, and Soler (2002) developed a taxonomy for rating the use of authentic materials and authentic literacy tasks in adult literacy programs. They have used this taxonomy to demonstrate that learner gains in adult literacy programs can be explained, in part, by the degree to which programs are rated highly authentic versus highly school-like. This taxonomy might be used by workplace literacy instructors for a rough determination of the authenticity, from a sociocultural practices perspective, of their own instructional approaches. The study employed four ratings that ranged from highly authentic to highly school-like. The description for receiving a highly authentic rating was:

> Classes that use only realia, or texts that occur naturally in the lives of people outside of a classroom (e.g., newspapers, journals, authentic novels, work manuals, driver's license materials). Further, the reading/writing activities that occur with these texts are the same as those that would occur with the texts outside of a learning situation. It is the confluence of these two factors that make programs highly authentic. (p. 80)

Full descriptions of other ratings will not be provided here other than to note that school-like ratings involve a heavy emphasis on skills, usually using prepublished materials and rarely (if ever) focusing on the use of skills for communicative purposes.

Shaffer et al. (2005) suggest we might employ technology to capture the sociocultural nuances of occupational learning by developing games "that simultaneously build situated understandings, effective social practices, powerful identities, shared values, and ways of thinking" (p. 108), but they also note that this is clearly no small task. They do describe an already existing game, Madison 2200, as being based on the practices of urban planning that takes the game player through many of the realistic stages and tasks of an urban planner. This vision does suggest some interesting possibilities for partially acquiring workplace literacy through games when access to a workplace is not possible. It also suggests means by which we might be able to incorporate the complexities of cultural values, communities of practice, and developing new identities. While such games are being and may be developed in the foreseeable future for some jobs (currently in the military and a handful of other "high-stakes" occupations), it is likely to be quite some time before this approach could be used for a wider range of occupations and in a way that takes into account cultural differences such as how an occupation might be practiced in the urban northeastern United States as compared to other countries or even the rural southwestern United States. It may also be a very, very long time (if ever) before game developers or others holding purse strings decide to invest the considerable resources needed to develop such games for less exciting occupations such as those accessible to adults in most workplace literacy programs.

Involving all stakeholders (especially workers and learners) in the development of workplace literacy programs and their implementation

is a desirable goal endorsed by sociocultural workplace literacy scholars that has been increasingly within reach. Imel (2003), in her review
of more recent workplace literacy programs, mentions several programs (often union sponsored) that have been built upon participatory
approaches. School-to-work transition programs have also employed the
use of job shadowing and mentors as means to more realistically capture
some of the sociocultural aspects of workplace learning (e.g., communities of practice, observing authentic functions of language and literacy
use, developing identity, situated cognition).

Workplace learning research, however, has also begun to reveal some
of the limitations of these job-shadowing and mentoring approaches.
For example, Bailey, Hughes, and Barr (2000) found that many companies didn't want to participate in mentoring programs unless a positive impact on their bottom lines could be demonstrated, and Evanciew
and Rojewski (1999) found several examples of negative, failed mentor
relationships and employer concerns about bringing into workplaces
immature adolescents or individuals whose values conflicted with those
of the workplace.

What to Teach When the Exact Jobs or Settings Are Not Yet Known

Often literacy educators are asked to prepare learners for the workplace
when the exact job and social setting are not known. In fact, this situation is more often the case than when such things are known. This makes
it difficult for adult and adolescent literacy educators to use results from
sociocultural workplace literacy research.

Government agencies and collaborative groups generally concerned with preparing adolescents and adults for changing workplace
demands have attempted to provide educators with guidelines that, to
some extent, respond to influences from sociocultural workplace literacy research. In the late 1980s, and early 1990s the U.S. Departments
of Labor and Education reviewed existing workplace studies and con-
vened panels of representatives from business, labor, and education to
try to determine what "skills" or competencies were necessary for 21st-
century workplace success. The competency listings developed as part
of the Secretary's Commission on Achieving Necessary Skills (SCANS,
U.S. Department of Labor, 1992) included a variety of cognitive, technological, and social skills and competencies, including literacy. The
SCANS competencies went beyond the teaching of isolated skills, call-

ing for skills to be integrated with job tasks and using written and oral language as well as computation in the following areas:

1. *Resources:* allocating time, money, materials, space, staff.
2. *Interpersonal skills:* working on teams, teaching others, serving customers, leading, negotiating, and working well with people from culturally diverse backgrounds.
3. *Information:* acquiring and evaluating data; organizing and maintaining files, interpreting information, and using computers to process information.
4. *Systems:* understanding social, organizational, and technological systems; monitoring and correcting performance; and designing or improving systems.
5. *Technology:* selecting equipment and tools, applying technology to specific tasks, and maintaining and troubleshooting technologies.

In the two decades since the SCANS competency list was released, it has been justifiably criticized from many directions and particularly by sociocultural literacy scholars. One criticism is that the list was composed without direct, in-depth observation of how literacy operates in actual jobs. A second was that insufficient provision was made for how literacy use in the workplace fit into larger sociocultural value and power frameworks.

While both these statements are indeed true, they do tend to obfuscate some important points. First, in the late 1980s and early 1990s only a few in-depth observational studies of workplace use existed, and those had usually been built upon the cognitive frameworks available at the time. Second, it is unclear how many direct, in-depth observational studies of actual workplace literacy with the incorporation of sociocultural perspectives would be sufficient to begin generalizing (five studies? 50? 500?). Third, it is also not clear what would be a useful form of information compiled from of a *sufficient* number of sociocultural workplace literacy studies in a sufficient number of occupations.

The need and demand for guidance about how to prepare adolescents and adults for the literacy challenges of workplaces clearly continues. In the public schools during the first decade of the 21st century, the academic standards movement was and continues to be in full sway. Academic standards for technology and communication in the new workplace are often part of those standards. Projects like the 21st Century

Skills project (*www.21stcenturyskills.org*) have been producing updated lists of skills and competencies that incorporate new technologies and perceived knowledge demands for employment. Other standards and skills documents for the new century and workplace have been developed by the Metiri Group working with the North Central Regional Education Laboratory (*www.metiri.com/features.html*) and still more by other regional educational partnerships like the Southern Regional Educational Board (*www.sreb.org/states/SREBStates.asp*).

Arguably the most thorough government attempt to address this need for guidance in terms of new literacies for the workplace comes from Human Resources and Skills Development Canada, as part of its Essential Skills and Workplace Literacy Initiative (*srv108.services.gc.ca/english/general/home_e.shtml*). This project has produced nearly 250 worker's task profiles based on more than 3,000 interviews. For each occupation, the profiles describe several dozen job tasks and functions (often related to literacy and computer use). Occupational descriptions tend to be lengthy (e.g., 10–13 pages long), and nearly 60 occupational descriptions include examples of actual documents used for job tasks along with detailed descriptions of how they are used. Complexity of tasks and functions is also rated on a scale from 1 to 5.

A representative example of the 250 occupations addressed by the project is automotive service technician. I use this occupation to describe and demonstrate what sort of information the project collects on occupations and how it is made available to educators. Automotive service technicians inspect, diagnose, repair, and service mechanical, electrical, and electronic systems/components of cars, buses, and light/commercial trucks. This job pays about 5% below the Canadian national average, according to the Essential Skills and Workplace Literacy Initiative.

For automotive service technicians, most tasks for which information was gathered were daily tasks rated 1 or 2 on the 5-point scale for complexity. The most difficult (and often less frequent) tasks were rated at level 3. A few of the examples provided for literacy and computer use with complexity level in parentheses include:

- Give instructions and guidance to shop helpers (1).
- Order parts and supplies from parts department, automotive suppliers and "jobbers." They also call parts department staff and service support representatives to gain more information about the use and installation of parts (2).

- Use word processing to write professional letters to organizations such as police and insurance brokers to present results of mechanical inspections (2).
- Use databases. For example, they may log in to the company database to access job assignments, input information on new jobs, retrieve and review past service information, and complete work orders (2).
- Use other computer and software applications. For example, they may use engine analyzers to display operational data, diagnostic scanners to access data from vehicles' onboard sensors, and computerized machinery such as wheel alignment machines (2).
- Participate in discussion groups and learning seminars with coworkers and supervisors to share experiences, discuss problems, and learn new methods of increasing productivity and providing customer service (3).

These examples do not include the important nuances and detailed descriptions of actual practice found in ethnographic workplace studies, but they do provide a stronger sense of functions than earlier lists of skills such as the SCANS list from 1988. Several dozen of these functions and tasks are listed under more than 15 categories such as reading text, document use, writing, oral communication, working with others, computer use, and continuous learning.

An indication of the depth of information gathered can be seen in a sampling of the text and document reading tasks (along with complexity ratings) gathered from interviews and visits to workplaces where this occupation is performed. The reading/writing tasks include:

- Read e-mail, notes from other colleagues, and short descriptors on parts (1).
- Read comments from service representatives and customers on work orders to get subjective accounts of problems and understand work scheduled for customers' vehicles (2).
- Read repair manuals (often online) to find technical information for each model so that they can diagnose and repair mechanical faults (3).
- Enter repair and service data onto work orders or into electronic billing and database systems. They enter the time spent, parts used, and steps taken to repair each car. They may add comments to explain unusual repairs or additional parts used (3).

- Take information from diagnostic graphs on analysis scanners that display operational data for automotive systems. The displays indicate the location of the faults. The technicians then integrate this with information from other sources such as their own observations (3).

Interactions between types of print or modes of communication and purposes for reading and writing are presented through summary charts for each occupation in each category area. Automotive service technicians read print and online forms, labels, notes, letters, memos, manuals, specifications, regulations, books, reports, and journals. Summaries of writing tasks are organized in terms of length (e.g., less than a paragraph to longer texts) and include such writing purposes as to organize, document, inform/request, persuade/justify, analyze, evaluate/critique, and entertain.

Purposes for oral communication range from such basic functions as "greet" and "take messages" to more complex functions like "to persuade" and "to negotiate, resolve conflict." In addition to asking about work tasks, job incumbents were asked about future trends likely to influence the job. Interviews indicated automotive service technicians thought they will increasingly rely on computer skills in both diagnosis and repair as the trend toward more sophisticated electronic vehicle systems continues. As vehicles become more complex and as diagnosis and repair information is increasingly accessed through technological sources, the essential skills of continuous learning, reading, and thinking skills (finding information) will play an even more important role in the occupation.

The website also provides downloadable examples of authentic workplace literacy materials for automotive service technician and 60 of the 250 other occupations. Along with detailed descriptions of how the materials are used on the job, user tips provide suggestions for how educators can use the descriptions and downloaded materials (*srv108. services.gc.ca/awm/main/writeups/078d_e.shtml*).

Extensive descriptions of the other 250 occupations parallel that of automotive service technician. Although these 13-page descriptions are less detailed than new literacy studies scholars might wish and don't address issues of power and values, they are extensive and provide a more detailed picture of what people do on their jobs than has been previously available. Some of the categories and functions used to describe workplace literacy tasks resemble Hull's (Hull et al., 1996) metacategories of "performing basic literate functions," "using literacy to explain," and "participating in the flow of information." Hull's "using literacy to resist authority" meta-category is noticeably missing from the Canadian work (except possibly as negotiating and resolving conflict), but then this is a major government-funded project, and expecting a "resisting authority" category to be included may be expecting too much.

The full job profiles are lengthy, and these descriptions go a long way past the SCANS listing in attempting to at least recognize and provide detail about the settings and functions involved with literacy tasks of particular jobs. As indicated earlier, this is far from enough to satisfy a sociocultural researcher concerned about values, power relations, and more detailed information about the impact of literacy performance on individuals. These descriptions also do not document the nuances of social networks, communities of practice, how new workplace identities are developed, and capture authentic motivations for learning how to become an accomplished member of a workplace group.

Although there are limitations to the nuances of sociocultural literacy captured by the Canadian project, comparison of the SCANS initiative of two decades ago and the ongoing (as of 2007–2008) Canadian government effort does, however, reveal the positive impact and influence of sociocultural workplace literacy research. Calls have been heeded for going beyond simple "skills lists" to more detailed descriptions of literacy functions and social settings in the workplace. Unless or until sociocultural researchers engage with finding better ways to fulfill the persistent need for generalizable guidelines for educators, this sort of influence at a distance may be the most that can be expected.

CONCLUSION

Scholars of workplace literacy taking sociocultural perspectives have taught us to be highly suspicious of the rhetoric surrounding discussions of literacy and work—especially if the rhetoric focuses solely on blaming the "low skills" or "absent technological literacy skills" of workers for a host of other difficulties and challenges related to the global economy. Scholarly analysis of "uncontested beliefs" as well as empirical documentation from detailed case studies have contrasted rhetoric about the workplace and workplace literacy programs with actual practice in ways that help mediate this rhetoric and suggest important new considerations for research and instruction.

Sociocultural scholars of workplace literacy do not focus merely on skills or new technological literacy demands but, rather, document and highlight the complexities involved in workplace literacy practice with special emphasis upon literacy functions, social networks, power relations, identity development, and agency. These scholars have alerted us to the dangers of overly simple approaches to instruction and program development. This work has influenced (sometimes in ways the scholars would not endorse) the modification of guidelines for government-supported workplace literacy programs, the complexity of how others view the workplace, and the kinds of information they gather to inform educators about workplace literacy practices and demands. The scholarship has also underscored the importance of including workers among the stakeholders directly involved in designing programs and instruction, developed more detailed guidelines for what "authentic" means, and made strong cases for more participatory forms of education that challenge rather than perpetuate existing hierarchies.

Doing this type of research in workplaces is very expensive and time consuming. Exhaustive, in-depth sociocultural workplace literacy studies will most likely never exist for more than a minority of occupations and workplaces. In the decades ahead, workplace literacy researchers taking a sociocultural perspective will need to decide how they believe their work generalizes (if at all) to settings beyond the workplace studied. They will also need to determine whether their work can provide guidance to educators preparing students for the workplace beyond warnings about avoiding simple skills teaching. This guidance will need to take into account that educators often may not know for which workplaces and perhaps not even which exact occupations their students are preparing.

To date, workplace literacy research hasn't addressed one of the key contentions of new literacy scholars like Leu and colleagues (Leu et al., 2008), which is that there are new online literacy skills such as using effective search strategies and being able to critically select from masses of online information. The extent to which these new skills need to be directly taught and to which they are simply acquired in the workplace is not yet clear.

Perhaps the most intriguing vision for the future is that of workplace literacy scholars collaborating with video game developers to create workplace simulations that are socioculturally accurate, provide truly helpful mentors, and can address the new understandings of literacies in the workplace. To succeed at such endeavors, however, we may need to turn a critical sociocultural eye on our *own* academic workplace practices compared to those of the game developers with whom we might collaborate. Twenty-five years ago, Fingeret (1984) found that value differences can destroy collaborative programs. In the workplace, the people with whom one must collaborate quite often have values that differ from one's own.

REFERENCES

Bailey, T., Hughes, K., & Barr, T. (2000). Achieving scale and quality in school-to-work internships: Findings from two employer surveys. *Educational Evaluation and Policy Analysis, 22*(1), 41–64.

Baynham, M., & Prinsloo, M. (2001). New directions in literacy research. *Language and Education, 15*(1), 83–91.

Billett, S., & Somerville, M. (2004). Transformations at work: Identity and learning. *Studies in Continuing Education, 26*(2), 309–326.

Bourdieu, P. (1977). The economics of linguistic exchanges. *Social Science Information, 16*(6), 645–668.

Bourdieu, P. (1991). *Language and symbolic power* (G. Raymond & M. Adamson, Trans.). Cambridge, MA: Harvard University Press.

Bureau of Labor Statistics. (2005, August 3). Computer use at work in 2003. *Monthly Labor Review Editor's Desk*. Retrieved October 1, 2006, from *www.bls.gov/opub/ted/2005/aug/wk1/art03.htm*.

Castleton, G. (2000). Workplace literacy: Examining the virtual and virtuous realities in (e)merging discourses on work. *Discourse: Studies in the Cultural Politics of Education, 21*(1), 91–104.

Castleton, G. (2002). Workplace literacy as a contested site of educational activity. *Journal of Adolescent and Adult Literacy, 45*(7), 556–566.

Christie, F., & Martin, J. R. (2000). *Genre and institutions: Social processes in the workplace and school*. London: Continuum International Publishing Group.

Evanciew, C., & Rojewski, J. (1999). Skill and knowledge acquisition in the workplace: A case study of mentor–apprentice relationships in youth apprenticeship programs. *Journal of Industrial Teacher Education, 36*(2). Retrieved November 2, 2009, from *scholar.lib.vt.edu/ejournals/JITE/v36n2/*.

Fingeret, A. (1984). Who's in control? A case study of university–industry collaboration. *New Directions for Continuing Education, 23*, 39–63.

Foucault, M. (1977). *Discipline and punish* (A. Sheridan, Trans.). New York: Pantheon.

Freedman, A., Adam, C., & Smart, G. (1994). Wearing suits to class: Simulating genres and simulation as a genre. *Written Communication, 11*(2), 193–226.

Gee, J. P. (1989). Literacy, discourse, and linguistics. *Journal of Education, 171*(1), 5–17.

Gee, J. P. (1991). What is literacy? In C. Mitchell & K. Weiler (Eds.), *Rewriting literacy: Culture and the discourse of the other* (pp. 1–11). New York: Bergin and Garvey.

Gee, J. P., Hull, G., & Lankshear, C. (1996). *The new work order: Behind the language of new capitalism*. Boulder, CO: Westview Press.

Goody, J., & Watt, I. (1963). The consequences of literacy. *Comparative Studies in Society and History, 5,* 304–345.

Gowen, S. G. (1992). *The politics of workplace literacy.* New York: Teachers College Press.

Hart-Landsberg, S., & Reder, S. (1995). Teamwork and literacy: Teaching and learning at Hardy industries. *Reading Research Quarterly, 30,* 1016–1052.

Heath, S. B. (1983). *Ways with words: Language, life, and work in communities and classrooms.* New York: Cambridge University Press.

Hull, G. A. (1991). *Hearing other voices: A critical assessment of popular views on literacy and work* (Technical Report). Berkeley: National Center for Research in Vocational Education, University of California at Berkeley.

Hull, G. A. (1993). Critical literacy and beyond: Lessons learned from students and workers in a vocational program and on the job. *Anthropology and Education Quarterly, 24,* 373–396.

Hull, G. A. (1999). What's in a label? *Written Communication, 16*(4), 379–411.

Hull, G. A. (2000). Critical literacy at work. *Journal of Adolescent and Adult Literacy, 43*(7), 648–652.

Hull, G., Jury, M., Ziv, O., & Katz, M. (1996). *Changing work, changing literacy? A study of skill requirements and development in a traditional and restructured workplace.* Berkeley, CA: National Center for the Study of Writing and Literacy.

Hunter, J. (2007). Language, literacy, and performance: Working identities in the back of the house. *Discourse: Studies in the Cultural Politics of Education, 28*(2) 243–257.

Imel, S. (2003). Whatever happened to workplace literacy? In *Myths and Realities No. 30* (pp. 1–2). Columbus, OH: Center on Education and Training for Employment.

Jackson, N. (2000). *Writing up people at work: Investigations of workplace literacy* (Working Paper 34). Sydney, Australia: University of Technology Sydney Research Centre Vocational Education & Training.

Johns, A. (Ed.). (2002). *Genre in the classroom: Multiple perspectives.* Mahway, NJ: Erlbaum.

Jolliffe, D. (1997). Finding yourself in the text: Identity formation in the discourse of workplace documents. In G. Hull (Ed.), *Changing work, changing workers* (pp. 335–349). New York: State University of New York Press.

Kleifgen, J. A. (2005). ISO 9002 as literacy practice: Coping with quality-control documents in a high-tech company. *Reading Research Quarterly, 40*(4), 450–468.

Lankshear, C., & Knobel, M. (2006). *New literacies: Changing knowledge in the classroom*. Berkshire, UK: Open University Press.

Lave, J., & Wenger, E. (1991). *Situated learning: Legitimate peripheral participation*. New York: Cambridge University Press.

Leu, D., Coiro, J., Casstek, J., Hartman, D., Henry, L., & Reinking, D. (2008). Research on instruction and assessment in the new literacies of online comprehension. In C. Block, S. Parris, & P. Afflerback (Eds.), *Comprehension instruction: Research-based best practices* (2nd ed.). New York: Guilford Press.

Luke, A., & Freebody, P. (2000). *Literate futures: Report of the Literacy Review for Queensland State Schools*. Brisbane, Queensland Government Printer.

Malcolm, I., & Field, J. (2005, July). Researching learning/working lives: Issues of identity, agency, and changing experiences of work. Paper presented at the 35th Annual SCUTREA Conference, University of Sussex. Retrieved August 15, 2008, from *www.leeds.ac.uk/educol/documents/141982.htm*.

Mikulecky, L. (1982). Job literacy: The relationship between school preparation and workplace actuality. *Reading Research Quarterly, 17*(3), 400–419.

Mikulecky, L. (2007). Workplace literacy. In B. Guzzetti (Ed.), *Literacy for the new millennium: Adult literacy* (pp. 137–155). Westport, CT: Praeger.

Mikulecky, L., Albers, P., & Peers. M. (1994). *Literacy transfer: A review of the literature* (Technical Report TR 94-05). Philadelphia: National Center on Adult Literacy.

Mikulecky, L., & Lloyd, P. (1997). Evaluation of workplace literacy programs: A profile of effective instructional practices. *Journal of Literacy Research, 29*(4), 555–585.

Mikulecky, L., Lloyd, P., Horowitz. L., Masker, S., & Siemantel, P. (1996). *A review of recent workplace literacy programs and a projection for future changes* (Technical Report TR 96-4). Philadelphia: National Center for Adult Literacy.

Nash, A. (2001). Participatory workplace education: Resisting fear-driven models. In P. Campbell & B. Burnaby (Eds.), *Participatory practices in adult education* (pp. 185–196). Mahwah, NJ: Erlbaum.

Olson, D. R. (1977). From utterance to text: The bias of language in speech and writing. *Harvard Educational Review, 47*, 257–281.

Ong, W. J. (1982). *Orality and literacy: The technologizing of the word*. New York: Methuen.

Purcell-Gates, V., Degener, S., Jacobson, E., & Soler, M. (2002). Impact of authentic literacy instruction on adult literacy practices. *Reading Research Quarterly, 37*(1), 70–92.

Purcell-Gates, V., Duke, N., & Martineau, J. (2007). Learning to read and write genre specific text: Roles of authentic experience and explicit teaching. *Reading Research Quarterly, 42*(1), 8–45.

Scribner, S. (1985). Knowledge at work. *Anthropology and Education Quarterly, 16*(3), 199–206.

Scribner, S., & Cole, M. (1981). *The psychology of literacy*. Cambridge, MA: Harvard University Press.

Searle, J. (2002). Situated literacies at work. *International Journal of Educational Research, 37*(1), 17–29.

Shaffer, D. W., Squire, K., Halverson, R., & Gee, J. P. (2005). Video games and the future of learning. *Phi Delta Kappan, 87*(2), 104–111.

Sticht, T. G. (1976). Comprehending reading at work. In M. Just & P. Carpenter (Eds.), *Cognitive processes in comprehension* (pp. 221–246). Hillsdale, NJ: Erlbaum.

Sticht, T. G. (1988). *Functional context education: Workshop resource notebook*. San Diego: Applied Behavioral and Cognitive Sciences.

Tannock, S. (2001). The literacies of youth and the youth workplace. *Journal of Adult and Adolescent Literacy, 45*(2), 40–43.

Taylor, M., & Blunt, A. (2001). A situated cognition perspective on literacy discourses: Seeing more clearly through a new lens. *The Canadian Journal for the Study of Adult Education, 15*(2), 79–103.

U.S. Department of Labor. (1992). *Learning a living: A blueprint for high performance*. Washington, DC: Secretary's Commission on Achieving Necessary Skills.

Volosinov, V. N. (1973). *Marxism and the philosophy of language* (L. Matejka & I. R. Tutnik, Trans.). Cambridge, MA: Harvard University Press. (Original work published 1929)

Wojecki, A. (2007). What's identity got to do with it, anyway?: Constructing adult learner identities in the workplace. *Studies in the Education of Adults, 39*(2), 168–182.

CHAPTER 11

Feminist Perspectives on the New Literacies
Practices and Research

BARBARA J. GUZZETTI

Young people across the globe are leading the way in exploring new forms of literate practice by using both print-based and digital texts and textual forums to communicate, investigate, and represent themselves. In doing so, these millennial youth are becoming increasingly savvy in using innovative and creative forms of literate expression. By engaging in such new literacies as 'zining (creating alternative, self-published magazines), e-zining (producing 'zines on the Internet), instant messaging, text messaging, online journaling, blogging, moblogging (making online journal entries through texting), and video gaming, young people demonstrate their abilities as competent consumers and producers of novel forms of communication that are referred to as the new literacies. These new literacies include digital texts, hybrid or multimodal texts, and new media forms that involve "new and changing ways of producing, distributing, exchanging and receiving texts" (Lankshear & Knobel, 2003, p. 16). These new forms of literate practice are relatively new in a chronological sense and reflect both the social nature of literacy and a shift to a global society in such areas as communications, manufacturing, and finance (Lankshear & Knobel, 2003).

Both the media and commercial industry have recognized young people's explorations with the tools of these new literate practices. For example, television commercials depict adolescents advising their parents on how to use cell phones and Bluetooth technology to text message and communicate with them; children, parents, and grandparents talk aloud using Internet slang and the language of instant messaging. Clothing manufacturers accommodate adolescents' penchant for "being wired" by including special pockets and flaps on jackets, belts, and pants to store cell phones, digital cameras, and iPods. MIT has displayed their technologically experimental fashion and interactive garments in which electronic devices are essential parts of clothing and accessories by producing an annual fashion show, Seamless Computation Couture (Wright, 2005). Fashion is infused with technology in jackets that display LED designs and texts and use radio waves to illuminate stripes according to Wi-Fi signal strength.

Researchers in literacy have joined in celebrating and publicizing these new literacies and the tools and technologies that enable these practices. These investigators have described the benefits of instant messaging and chatting online that keep adolescents in the know socially (Lewis & Fabos, 2005). Researchers have described how young people use online journaling to maintain social contacts and make connections to academic literacies (Guzzetti & Gamboa, 2005). Others documented how 'zines and e-zines have been vehicles for stimulating youths' creative subversion and for staking and negotiating identities (Guzzetti & Gamboa, 2004a, 2004b; Knobel & Lankshear, 2001). Lam (2000) described how e-mailing and chatting helped a teenage English language learner learn English by social networking with his peers online.

Amid the plethora of praise for the benefits of these new literacies, some researchers have examined issues of social justice associated with these new forms of literate practice. Investigators have documented differential access to these new literacies based on individuals' socioeconomic status (Andrews, 2008) and geographical location (Beaudoin, 2008). Those from the working poor or lower socioeconomic classes and those located in isolated areas often have less access than their more affluent and centrally located peers (Andrews, 2008). Students of color are also less likely to be engaged with the new digital literacies (Ono & Tsai, 2008; DeBell & Chapman, 2006), and girls of color in particular are less inclined than their white peers to engage with computers (Varma, 2002) and less apt to study or choose careers in fields that demand the use of new digital literacies (American Association of University Women, 2000; Goode, Estrella, & Margolis, 2006).

Although race, socioeconomic status, geography, and culture influence access to these new literacies, gender also influences whether and how individuals engage with these new textual forms and forums (Subrahmanyam & Greenfield, 1998). Together, these "subjectivities" or multiple layers intertwine to position individuals and shape their literacy practices. Hence, issues of gender justice informed by gender and feminist theories are also important when examining young people's interactions with these new literate practices. Language and literacy are especially powerful forces in constructing gender, and gender is also a powerful force in constructing language and literacy practices (Commeyras, Faulstich-Orellana, Bruce, & Neilsen, 1996).

Therefore it is necessary to examine the new literacies in light of gender and feminist issues. In this chapter, I first provide a brief overview of one popular theory of gender and three feminist theories that are germane to the new literacies. Although gender theory is not a feminist theory, I include it here due to its applicability to the new literacies. Because there is no single view of feminism, I have selected those feminist theories that are most relevant to the new literacies. In doing so, I provide examples of how particular principles of these theories have been applied in or apply to studies of both traditional and new literacy practices. Second, I examine specific practices of the new literacies in light of feminist and gender theories through a critical characterization of key studies of students' engagement with various types of new literacies. Finally, I consider implications from feminist frameworks for supporting and teaching the new literacies.

GENDER AND FEMINIST THEORIES

This section describes one popular theory of gender and three relevant feminist theories that have been used in studies of new print-based or digital literacies. These four theories include gender schema theory, a feminist sociology, feminist poststructuralism, and cyberfeminist theory. Each of these perspectives is pertinent in examining the new literacies and each of these theories is germane to advancing educators' understandings of who engages in these new literate practices and how they are enabled or marginalized in their participation.

Gender Schema Theory

Gender schema theory refers to the idea that children learn what it means to be male and female from the culture in which they live (Bem, 1981). Children internalize this knowledge from a very early age as gender schema and adjust their behaviors to fit within the gender norms and expectations of their culture (Bem, 1993). Their gender schema is then used to organize their subsequent experiences.

Gender roles are formed by observing and learning how others act and by accomplishing social and cognitive tasks specific to the culture's role expectations for men and women. Young people's concepts of maleness and femaleness influence their perceptions and behaviors. Children's gender schemas guide their information processing and problem solving, regulate their personal interactions, and influence their self-concepts (Brannon, 2002). Individuals examine the gender appropriateness of particular behaviors, acting as gender conformists by rejecting behaviors that do not match their views of gender roles (schematic) or becoming gender nonconformists (aschematic) by rejecting traditional gender roles (Lemons & Parzinger, 2007).

Gender schema theory combines both social learning theory and cognitive theory. Individuals incorporate their own self-images into their gender schema and assume the traits and behaviors that they believe are suitable for their gender (Bem, 1993). Young people's perceptions of men and women are, therefore, an interaction between their cognitive schema and their social experiences. Children internalize a lens of gender polarization and thereby become gender polarizing or gender schematic themselves (Bem, 1993).

Children perform in more gender-typical ways than not and tend to better remember gender-consistent information. Individuals begin to evaluate all actions in terms of their gender schema. Any behavior that does not match their established schemas is rejected (Bem, 1993). Children's gender schema may bias their memories to a point where they misremember or distort information to make it fit within their existing schemas. An example of this occurred in a study in which Davies (1991) read a story aloud to preschoolers that told the tale of a princess who saved a prince from a dragon. She then asked those children to draw a picture of what happened in the story. Most of the children drew the prince saving the princess, demonstrating that even 3- and 4-year-olds have definite ideas of gender roles and relations firmly entrenched in their schemas and will change their memories of events and experiences accordingly. In another study, children in elementary school were shown two Caldecott Award–winning picture books and they were asked to retell the stories and answer questions that were related to both gender-consistent and -inconsistent information contained in each story (Frawley, 2008). The children tended to misremember gender-inconsistent story information that did not fit within their gender schema. Their retellings included stereotyped and misrepresentative interpretations of the main characters' behaviors and emotions, and the children gave gendered responses to questions about the books that were consistent with their gender schemas.

As these examples illustrate, establishing a gender schema may lead to forming stereotypical or gendered views and dichotomous representations of gender, known as essentializing. Essentializing is attributing natural or essential traits or characteristics to members of specific (gender, age, cultural, racial) groups (Armstrong, 2003). In essential-ing others, people assume that individual differences can be explained by inherent biological or natural characteristics shared by members of that group. Essentializing occurs whenever a person thinks, speaks, or acts in ways that advance stereotypical interpretations of differences between individuals. Feminists note that people essentialize women when they assume that girls and women have natural characteristics, such as being emotional, docile, weak, and dependent (Armstrong, 2003).

Children are typically led to think in dichotomies or dualistic categories by believing that women should think and behave in one way and men in another. Often, men are portrayed as macho, detached, and aggressive, whereas women are characterized in opposite ways as submissive, emotional, and passive (Armstrong, 2003; Bem, 1993). These stereotypical notions of gender guide how children predict others' actions, make sense of the world, and manage their relationships. These gendered beliefs often result in young people's inaccurate perceptions and their failure to accept information that does not fit within their gender stereotypes.

Gender schema theory has been used in studies of both print-based and post-typographic texts in several ways. For example, gender schema has been used as a framework for investigating adolescent girls' preferences for website design and content (Agosto, 2004). In this research, gender schema theory served as a perspective on understanding why women continue to engage less than men in digital literacies and to explain why so few females major in computer science. Researchers also have used gender schema theory to explain why boy-friendly books are important to some boys' reading development, but not important to others (Sokal et al., 2005). Gender schema theory has also helped to elucidate how people use stereotypes and gender-based identification in encoding, retrieving, and making inferences from texts and to explain differences in males' and females' responses to texts (Day, 1994).

Although useful in examining children's views and behaviors in literacy studies like these, gender schema theory does not take into account other subjectivities, such as race, social class, culture, and ethnicity. Each of these multiple subjectivities interacts with gender in forming young people's notions of gender roles and behaviors (Stanley & Wise, 1993). In particular, race and ethnicity influence notions of gender and gender performance as evidenced by various feminist theories that do account for these subjectivities, such as black feminism (hooks, 1989) and Latina feminism (e.g., Anzaldua, 1990). These views of feminism examine the intersection of race, class, and gender in producing and perpetuating systems of domination and oppression. Despite these limitations, gender schema theory continues to serve as a framework for research from both literacy and technology.

Feminist Sociology

One feminist theory that I have used in my own research on both traditional literacies and new literacies is that of a feminist sociology (Stanley & Wise, 1993). This theory is closely aligned with literacy because of its high value on language as a medium of constructing and deconstructing gender. From this perspective, language and social context work together to construct and reproduce gendered behaviors.

Feminist sociologists view gender less as a category of difference and more as a process. Feminist sociologists such as Connell (1987) and Thorne (1993) do not focus on gender differences per se, but on "the social relations and practices that help to construct, establish, and maintain gender as difference and on variations in the degree of salience that such constructed differences assume in various contexts" (Commeyras et al., 1996, p. 461). In this view, literacy is a social practice in which gender is constructed and enacted through language and literacy practices. Enactments of gender may vary based on the contexts, tasks, and settings in which those practices are performed.

The perspective of a feminist sociology is particularly useful in studies of both traditional and new literacies because it is consistent with the

practice of offering students opportunities to explore gendered identities in and through reading, writing, and discussion. In classrooms,
young people may be provided with critical literacy activities or activities that use literacy to help oppressed groups challenge structures of
inequality (Lankshear & McLaren, 1993) and to deconstruct the categories of male and female. Discussions in both online and offline spaces
that critically examine the silences in texts, as well as the hidden messages that oppress and subordinate others, are consistent with critical
literacy activities promoted by a feminist sociology.

An example of a critical literacy activity appeared in a study in
which Fey (1998) investigated undergraduates' and high school students' language patterns during online discussions examining feminist
theory. These young men were prevented by their own language behaviors from learning their female peers' alternative views. Except for the
few females in the class with strong feminist views, the young women
were prevented from speaking their minds by males' discourse patterns,
particularly the language behaviors of one young man referred to as
"Big Guy," as he dominated the discussions and ridiculed females' views.
His language patterns of condescending and dominating prevented
these young women from using language to form and represent their
ideas, a necessary way of learning (Vygotsky, 1978). This study demonstrated how males are also disadvantaged as they marginalize females.
Although they did not realize it, men like Big Guy were themselves
oppressed. Through their patriarchal language of domination that
interrupted females' voices in online forums, these young men failed to
learn and practice active listening, a skill that would serve them well in
their future studies and careers.

Of all of the feminist theories, a feminist sociology is perhaps the
most inclusive. I base this statement on two other principles of feminist
sociology that illustrate how this theory is inclusive both in terms of
whom and what it encompasses. The first of these notions is the belief
that men and men's behaviors in their interactions with women are worthy of study (Stanley & Wise, 1993). This principle is useful in examining studies of instructional discussions in online spaces. For example in
Fey's (2008) study, online discussions on a message board replicated the
gendered language patterns commonly found in offline spaces (Tannen, 1990). Males' language patterns in cyberspace were analytical,
objective, and hierarchical. Conversely, women's language was typically
more caring, tentative, and open-ended, and referenced personal experience. This study illustrated that conversations are no more gender fair

or gender neutral in virtual spaces than they are in offline spaces. This investigation illustrates the value of studying males and their interactions with females, a basic tenet of a feminist sociology.

The second principle of a feminist sociology that demonstrates the inclusiveness of the theory is a nonessentialist view of gender. This perspective acknowledges multiple subjectivities, such as age, generation, race, socioeconomic status, and ethnicity. In this view, gender interacts with a confluence of these multiple layers of personhood in influencing and determining an individual's attitudes, beliefs, and behaviors. An example of this tenet was illustrated in a study in which adolescent girls produced three issues of a 'zine, a do-it-yourself publication created by young people as an alternative to commercial magazines (Guzzetti & Gamboa, 2004a). The young women in this study used 'zining to express themselves and to find their voices that went unrecognized in their classroom settings. They wrote about issues of social justice, such as feminism, classism, and racism that were important to them—topics that did not appear in the popular press, particularly not in magazines marketed to and written for adolescent females.

These girls were enabled by their upper socioeconomic class to write about these issues and collaborate with their classmates in creating their 'zine through the use of sophisticated forms of digital technologies, such as word-processing programs, e-mail, high-speed Internet access, and digital cameras. They deconstructed their own social class by examining how affluence promoted their female peers' superficial and materialistic views of the world and influenced their enactment of gendered behaviors. Ironically, these girls did not analyze how their same upper-middle social class enabled the new literate practices that allowed them to express themselves, and they failed to deconstruct their own literacy practices through their engagement with new literacies. Hence, this study demonstrates the importance of examining other subjectivities such as social class that interact with gender.

Feminist Poststructuralist Theory

Like those who subscribe to a feminist sociology, feminist poststructuralist theorists share a nonessentialist view of gender. In this theory, there are no essential properties that exist outside of culturally and socially constructed categories of gender. Rather, these differences only appear to be natural or essential because they are reproduced over time in interactions with others and with texts (Butler, 1990).

Critical and poststructuralist feminist theories of gendered subjectivity, agency, and power have emphasized how individuals seemingly unique and autonomous decisions and actions are actually shaped by language, culture, and institutions (Davies, 1993; Jones, 1993; St. Pierre & Pillow, 2000). Feminist poststructuralist theory focuses on "the way each person actively takes up the discourses through which they and others speak and write the world into existence as if they were their own" (Davies, 1993, p. 13). Individuals are often unaware of how their gender beliefs and behaviors are influenced and determined by the actions of others.

From a poststructuralist perspective, gender is not fixed in advance of social interaction, but is constructed in interactions and must be understood in light of the larger social structures and processes at work (Connell, 1995). In this view, there are multiple ways of being and creating or negotiating subjectivity. These multiple and diverse positions create possibilities of constituting subjectivities as multiple, fluid, and at times, competing and contradictory (Davies, 1993). Every individual accesses, performs, and transforms multiple versions of femininity and masculinity in various settings at various times.

Feminist poststructuralism recognizes that there are multiple ways to perform gender. Those ways that promote and reinforce hegemonic versions of masculinity and advance the dominant position of men and the subordination of women are most highly valued by society, however (Connell, 1995). Often, subordination of women is accomplished through patriarchal displays and discourses. This marginalizing behavior is typically displayed in whole-class discussions as documented by numerous researchers (e.g., Evans, Anders, & Alvermann, 1997; Fey, 1998; Guzzetti, 2001).

In the view of feminist poststructuralists, gender is a social construction that affects learning both inside classrooms and outside of school. Notions of appropriate ways to do gender dictate what is and what can be learned, and what is outside the realm of gendered boundaries. Girls' alienation from the computer game culture is one example of this gender exclusivity (Green & Adam, 2001). Sanford and Madill (2006) documented gender exclusivity in video gaming by describing how boys used video games to establish spaces for domination and resistance. Young men resisted notions of femininity by creating non-female alternative identities and avatars (graphical representations of self). These boys created their avatars as muscular, big, and dangerous-looking personas, thereby enacting gendered notions of masculinity and excluding any possibilities of enacting alternative representations of their gender.

Cyberfeminist Theory

Cyberfeminism is a theory representative of third-wave feminism that was introduced in the early 1990s as a reaction to past feminist theories that tended to assume a universal or essentialist female identity and overemphasized the experiences of upper-middle-class white women. Cyberfeminism extends other feminist theories described earlier in this chapter by examining representations and interactions in cyberspace. This perspective acknowledges that gender can influence literacy and life online in the socially mediated spaces of virtual worlds (Hall, 1996). Like the feminist poststructuralists, cyberfeminists view gender as a social construction enacted online in ways that recreate offline interactions (Valentine & Holloway, 2002). Cyberfeminists acknowledge that there are differences in power relations between women and men in digital discourse just as there are power differentials in language patterns outside of cyberspace (Hawthorne & Klein, 1999; Herring, 2001). It is the aim of cyberfeminism to change that situation.

In the past, liberal cyberfeminists insisted that virtual space promote equality, fluidity, and unity through body-free interactions that foster gender neutrality (e.g., Haraway, 1991b). Cyberfeminists now caution that these ideal and mythic constructions of cyberspace must be resisted (Wilding, 1998). Current theory supports the notion that it is not possible to leave the body behind in cyberspace and have interactions in virtual spaces that are gender neutral.

In describing the relationship between the body and technology, Haraway (1991a, 1991b), a pioneer in cyberfeminism, coined the term "cyborg" to represent her vision of the intersection of the body and machine. She claimed that distinctions between body and machine are false as we all now exist as cyborgs, or hybrids of machine and technology. In her view, the body and machinery become one as boundaries are blurred between where the individual begins and technology ends. Her classic "Cyborg Manifesto" (1991a) initiated a new wave of feminist thinking about embodiment and the portrayal of females in virtual spaces.

The debate about whether a netizen (a citizen of the Internet) can leave the body behind in cyberspace was taken up by feminists who posit that gender intelligibility is signaled through language, the connection between the body and online identity (Bury, 2005). Although the physical body may be absent in cyberspace, a new kind of body is self-produced through words and images within the social and discursive practices of cybercommunity. In this view, there is an intimate connection between the body and the mind, as the virtual community both originates in and must return to the physical (Stone, 1991).

Markers of identity, such as gender, race, ethnicity, and age are strongly evident in virtual worlds and have been referred to as "the semiotics of identity" (Thomas, 2007, p. 6). Haraway declared that there can be no common feminine identity, but that identity is fluid, "strategic, contradictory, and partial" (Haraway, 1991b, p. 155). As in offline spaces, language is used to represent and negotiate identity in virtual worlds.

One study to which cyberfeminist theory may be applied is an investigation of how adolescent girls used digital literacies to form identities through chatting online (Thomas, 2004). The young women in this study used words and images to self-create a virtual presence through discourses of sexuality and idealized beauty. Like the boys in the study of video gamers who designed avatars that represented exaggerated notions of masculinity (Sanford & Madill, 2006) these young women created avatars that represented gendered and exaggerated notions of femininity. The girls in this study used cyberspeak (Internet slang and emoticons, or symbols to represent emotions) to represent their fantasies and desires. This language empowered them to create new representations of self, but conversely also served to reproduce the same gendered notions of femininity in cyberspace that exist in offline places. These findings illustrate how language and graphics signal gender intelligibility in virtual worlds, a fundamental principle of cyberfeminist theory.

EXAMINING THE NEW LITERACIES
FROM FEMINIST PERSPECTIVES

In this section, I examine particular practices of the new literacies in light of the feminist and gender theories previously described. In doing so, I focus on four practices of the new literacies that represent digital and print-based or hybrid textual forms. These practices include posting online and chatting through instant messaging (IMing) in private spaces or public forums of chat rooms, message boards, and role-playing games; 'zining or e-zining; online journaling or blogging; and video gaming. Findings from relevant research on these new forms of textual practice are described below in light of insights from these theories.

Examining Computer-Mediated Communication from Feminist Frames

Several recent studies examined adolescents' chatting as computer-mediated communication (Cammack, 2002; Guzzetti, 2006a, 2006b; Jacobs, 2006; Kelly, Pomerantz & Currie, 2006; Lewis & Fabos, 2005; Subrahmanyam, Smahel, & Greenfield, 2006). These studies were conducted from various theoretical perspectives, including literacy as a social practice (Street, 1995). In this view, literacy serves as a powerful medium for creating and representing oneself. Young people engage in new literacies such as chatting to form, negotiate, and express their identities.

In examining the research on online conversations from a cyber-feminist perspective, it is noteworthy that young women were facilitated to express themselves only when participating in restricted cyberspaces or when their technological competencies and language styles disguised their gender by being more representative of men than women. For example, message boards on websites that were designed for females only allowed adolescent girls to feel comfortable in cyberculture and to share their definitions of feminism (Cammack, 2002). Chatting privately to selected individuals enabled one adolescent girl to serve as a constructor and transmitter of knowledge to her male peer (Jacobs, 2006). Assuming the language style of males by using expletives (Johnson & Finley, 1997) and gender-neutral representations and by displaying the sophisticated tactical competencies of the virtual class typically associated with men (Valentine & Holloway, 2002) enabled two adolescent girls to represent themselves as do-it-yourselfers and punk-rock fans on message boards.

Conversely, when adolescent girls participated in open forums online and revealed their gender identity they met with resistance and interference in staking their identities. Adolescent girls who engaged in emphasized femininity by accommodating the interests and desires of males were objectified (Kelly et al., 2006). Girls resorted to hiding their age and gender because offline power inequalities were reproduced in their online communications (Lewis & Fabos, 2005). When females did reveal their gender in online message boards they were sexually harassed and marginalized (Guzzetti, 2006b). Teens' participation in unmonitored chat rooms resulted in explicitly sexual and degrading remarks that scared girls away (Subrahmanyam et al., 2006).

Hence, when examining this extant research from a cyberfeminist framework, it is clear that online forms of communication of chatting and posting to message boards limited as well as empowered the young women in these studies. Females were only facilitated under restricted conditions to express their identities and capabilities in online forums. As a whole, these studies illustrate the current thinking of cyberfeminists that interactions in cyberspace are no more gender fair or gender neutral than interactions in offline spaces.

Deconstructing Blogging and Online Journaling from Feminist Perspectives

Several recent studies examined adolescents' online journaling, blogging, and website construction (Chandler-Olcott & Mahar, 2003; Guzzetti & Gamboa, 2005; Lam, 2000). These studies described the academic and social benefits that both young men and young women received through these forms of technology-mediated communications. Nevertheless, these studies also demonstrated the reproduction of gendered interactions found in offline places in virtual spaces. For example, one of these studies (Lam, 2000) focused on a Chinese immigrant boy, Almon, who learned and practiced English through creating a weblog centered on Japanese popular culture. His blogging allowed him to construct new social networks and communicate with online pen pals outside the limitations of his physical surroundings. It is interesting to note, however, that his dialogic exchanges with his online peers reconstructed gendered social roles, as he preferred to communicate with Asian females due to their language style of being nurturing and supportive. He formed closer relationships with his female pen pals due to their ability to encourage him and instill confidence in his capabilities through caring and motherly language, a gendered communication style.

Similar findings were noted in a study in which a teenage girl posted excessively in her LiveJournal her moment-by-moment emotions (Guzzetti & Gamboa, 2005). This young woman used her online journaling primarily to foster and maintain her social relationships, particularly with her boyfriend, who was most frequently the subject or recipient of her posts. In dong so, she maintained gendered boundaries in her online communications, illustrating feminist poststructuralist theory that gender is performative and communicable through language (Butler, 1990). Conversely, when another adolescent girl in this study used her online journaling as social commentary and wrote of feminist issues she was ridiculed and resisted by a young man for her language style that crossed gendered boundaries. This policing of gender boundaries in online spaces has been noted by cyberfeminists (e.g., O'Brien, 1999).

Yet another study demonstrated that adolescent girls are acutely aware of the dangers of crossing gendered boundaries of discourse (Chandler-Olcott & Mahar 2003). In this investigation, an adolescent girl felt the need to hide her expertise with technology from her peers for fear of being positioned negatively and being seen as less desirable as both a friend and a potential romantic partner for boys. Although she took satisfaction from being a female techie and being able to construct her own websites, she also feared being seen by her peers as a "geek," and she took note of the discourses that associate men with technology. Her fears were justified, as technological skills have come to be recognized as masculine, whereas "women lack technological competence to the extent that they want to appropriately perform femininity" (Jensen, De Castell, & Bryson, 2003, p. 562).

Hence, these studies illustrate that gendered roles and relations are perpetuated in online spaces and demonstrate the costs as well as the benefits of acquiring technological competencies. Although females may be able to manipulate technology and become sophisticated users of digital literacies, they often pay a social price for exhibiting those abilities. Young women appear to be valued more for their ability to be supportive of males in their online interactions than for their ability to demonstrate their expertise with creating digital texts in virtual forums. Hence, traditional gender roles are perpetuated in girls' online interactions.

Interrogating Video Gaming from Feminist Views

Four recent studies examined adolescents' interactions with video games and their gaming practices (Andrews, 2008; Olson, Kutner & Warner, 2008; Sanford & Blair, 2008; Sanford & Madill, 2006). These studies focused on the amount and types of video games that boys and girls engage with as recreational literacy practices. These investigations have been embedded in sociocultural views of literacy and the theory of the new literacies (Gee, 2003, 2004; see also Chapter 8, this volume).

Engaging in a wide variety of video games, such as sports, cards, and fantasy games, enabled boys to gain conceptual and technical knowledge to build, write, and compose in digital forums (Sanford & Blair, 2008; Sanford & Madill, 2006), but marginalized females. These games provided social interaction and individual challenges. Boys learned strategies from these games that were applicable to life offline, such as setting priorities, ensuring balances, and learning from their mistakes. Girls, however, did not receive these same benefits from video gaming. The violence in the video games that boys played that allow players to kill their enemies or random people is a feature that girls typically find repellent (Agosto, 2004). Although Sanford and Madill (2006) reported that video games provided a way for males to resist traditional hegemonic masculinities by interacting with nonessentialist or gender aschematic characters in a safe space, violent video games like these promoted essentialist notions of gender by appealing to boys' images of masculinity as aggressive, competitive, and powerful. Hence, males' gendered schemas were also reinforced through these action and fantasy video games.

The appealing features of action and violence for boys' gaming practices has been documented by other researchers, who discovered that girls are likely to eschew these games because they perceive them to be violent and created for boys (Andrews, 2008; Olson et al., 2008). Girls are gaming in growing numbers, but they tend not to play the more complex hard-core games, such as first-person shooter and fantasy games, but rather engage in more casual video games (Hayes, 2005). Hence, girls are not receiving the same academic benefits as boys do in learning and practicing the complex thinking skills and strategies that these types of video games require.

Researchers have discovered social benefits that males receive from playing video games that girls are not benefiting from at an equal rate. Young men are able to work through their angry feelings, relieve stress, and experience feelings of power from engaging with violent fantasy and action video games (Olson et al., 2008). However, these benefits are not equally distributed even among young men; survey research has shown that high socioeconomic males are more likely than other groups to play these games (Andrews, 2008). This is an issue of both social and gender justice, as access to and engagement with the concomitant skills and abilities fostered by video games is neither gender nor class equitable.

Examining 'zining from Feminist Frames

Five studies in the new millennium examined adolescents' writing and self-publishing 'zines (Guzzetti & Gamboa, 2004a, 2004b; Knobel & Lankshear, 2001; Schilt, 2003; Sinor, 2002). These studies were conducted by examining the content of 'zines and by interviewing those young people who created them. These 'zinesters authored their personal experiences—both the ordinary and the extraordinary—and wrote in opposition to mainstream culture in both form and content (Sinor, 2002).

Of all the practices that characterize the new literacies, 'zining is the most pronounced in terms of constructing and deconstructing gender and resisting gendered roles and relations while taking into account other subjectivities. Historically, 'zine making has been a way for girls to form support networks and create a safe space to examine and resist the cultural devaluation of women (Schilt, 2003). Young men also have used 'zining in similar ways, as evidenced by one young man who constructed a 'zine called *Testosterone* by writing in ways that rebelled against traditional notions of the performance of masculinity (Guzzetti & Gamboa, 2004b).

Young men and women engage in 'zining to represent their views of race and gender (Guzzetti & Gamboa, 2004a, 2004b). For example in one study, a female rewrote traditional conceptions of and roles for Asian American women (Knobel & Lankshear, 2001). In another study, adolescent girls used 'zining to help them articulate and formulate their views of feminism over time (Guzzetti & Gamboa, 2004a). Several studies showed how girls 'zined about issues that are important to women, such as rape, eating disorders, and sexual objectification (Guzzetti & Gamboa, 2004a; Sinor, 2002). Young women used 'zining to write against racism, sexism, and classism (Guzzetti & Gamboa, 2004a). In doing so, girls used 'zines as spaces for action and resistance by writing toward social transformation.

One issue of social justice that affects the practice of 'zining is social class, a subjectivity that interacts with gender in influencing who creates 'zines and how they are produced. Although 'zines may be written and distributed in hard copy they are typically created by using technology, such as word-processing programs, accessing graphics on the Web to illustrate and supplement the narratives, and reproducing the texts through copiers. 'Zines are commonly distributed through online distros, or distribution centers on the Internet. Although 'zines facilitate young men's and women's representations of self, they represent textual forms that are accessible only to those who have the resources (time, money, and technology) to produce them. Hence, students of middle and upper socioeconomic classes are more likely to engage in 'zining than their working-poor and low-socioeconomic-status peers who lack equitable access to these resources.

IMPLICATIONS FROM FEMINIST THEORIES FOR SUPPORTING THE NEW LITERACIES

Examining the extant research on the practices of new literacies from the frameworks of feminist and gender theories has revealed that the same issues of social and gender justice that are reflected in traditional forms of literacy also are evidenced in the practices of the new literacies. Online discussion forums for academic purposes on message boards or social connections through chatting and blogging can result in differential power relations just as offline discussions in classrooms do. The perpetuation of gendered notions of masculinity and femininity are evidenced in video and computer games through avatars and graphics. Although 'zining is a powerful outlet for both men and women to resist against essentialist notions of masculinity and femininity, this new literacy is accessible primarily to those who have access to the resources allowed by their privileged social class.

Educators will need to keep these caveats in mind when supporting and teaching the new literacies. Some students may have prior knowledge and a wide range of expertise in particular forms of new literacies such as blogging and gaming while others may have had no experience. Individuals with little or no prior proficiency with these new forms of literate practice will need instructional scaffolding and encouragement to build confidence to engage in such activities as a class blog or an online message board, particularly females who typically lack self-assurance with technologies (Varma, 2002). In addition, students' participation in online activities will need to be monitored to prevent power imbalances in online discussions or engagement with computer games that often marginalize females' participation.

These new literacies can serve as a springboard for critical literacy activities in which students are guided to critically examine these practices. Students may be taught through their teacher's modeling to question and deconstruct the gendered messages that are conveyed through

and with technologies. Young people may be taught to examine gendered representations in their in-school discussions online or in their
out-of-school engagement with video games that are marketed to males
through use of aggression and violence and targeted to females through
enacting gendered notions of femininity in such computer games as
Barbie, where girls shop, design clothes, and meet boys.

Hence, one of the most important implications of the new literacies
is to serve as a vehicle for raising young people's awareness of the ways
in which gender interacts with other subjectivities such as social class
and race to serve or disenfranchise particular groups. Students will be
unable to change their behaviors and make informed choices until they
are made aware of the issues of social justice that surround these new
literate practices. Gender justice must be a key component in advancing
the agenda of social justice through the practice and promotion of the
new literacies.

Administrators, teachers, and policymakers will need to keep in
mind the implications of the new literacies when infusing these practices into classroom curriculum and instruction. As others have noted
(e.g., Knobel & Lankshear, 2001) and as I have found in working with
young people who produce new media, some new literacies such as 'zining should not be co-opted as classroom assignments. 'Zines in particular, although they allow adolescents a voice to express their nongendered
and feminist views, are done for fun, for subversion, and for the sheer
pleasure of being creative and are not appropriate for grading. Many
'zines also contain controversial content and subjects that are not school
sanctioned, making them unsuitable for classroom use. Specific practices of new literacies like 'zining will need to be carefully and individually examined from both feminist perspectives and from the perspectives of those who consume and produce them before being embraced
as motivating means of keeping current with evolving notions of literacy
instruction.

Feminist researchers will continue to have fruitful ground for investigating the new literacies as they continue to emerge and develop. For
example, research has yet to be conducted from a feminist perspective
into how gender roles are resisted or enacted in virtual worlds, such as
The Sims, Second Life, and Teen Second Life. New projects that promote girls have begun in Teen Second Life, such as "Tech-Savvy Girls"
(Hayes, Johnson, King, & Lammers, 2008), a project designed to teach
adolescent girls digital literacy skills in the contexts of virtual worlds.
Hence, investigations of how these environments may empower young

women are needed. Such studies will assist in advancing the agenda of gender justice by examining new literacies from feminist frames and will provide additional insight into ways to promote new literacies as vehicles for advocating social justice.

REFERENCES

Agosto, D. E. (2004). Using gender schema theory to examine gender equity in computing: A preliminary study. *Journal of Women and Minorities in Science and Engineering, 10*(12), 37–53.

American Association of University Women. (2000). *Tech savvy: Educating girls in the new computer age.* Washington, DC: Author.

Andrews, G. (2008). Game play, gender, and socioeconomic status in two American high schools. *E-Learning, 3*(2), 199–213.

Anzaldua, G. (Ed.). (1990). *Making face, making soul/Haciendo caras: Creative and critical perspectives by feminists of color.* San Francisco: Aunt Lute Books.

Armstrong, J. (2003). *Power and prejudice: Some definitions for discussion and analysis* (Unpublished document). Albuquerque: University of New Mexico. Retrieved August 26, 2008, from *www.umn.edu/jka/courses/archives.power. html.*

Beaudoin, M. F. (2008). Dissecting the African digital divide: Diffusing e-learning in sub- Sajaram Africa. *E-Learning, 4*(4), 442–453.

Bem, S. L. (1981). Gender schema theory: A cognitive account of sex typing. *Psychological Review, 88,* 354–364.

Bem, S. L. (1993). *The lens of gender: Transforming the debate on sexual inequality.* New Haven, CT: Yale University Press.

Brannon, E. (2002). *Gender: Psychological perspectives* (3rd ed.). Upper Saddle River, NJ: Allyn & Bacon.

Bury, R. (2005). *Cyberspaces of their own: Female fandom online.* New York: Lang

Butler, J. (1990). *Gender trouble: Feminism and the subversion of identity.* London: Routledge.

Cammack, D. W. (2002). Literacy, technology, and a room of her own: Analyzing adolescent girls' online conversations from historical and technological literacy perspectives. In D. Schallert, C. Fairbanks, J. Worthy, B. Maloch, & J. Hoffman (Eds.), *Fifty-first yearbook of the National Reading Conference* (pp. 19–141). Chicago: The National Reading Conference.

Chandler-Olcott, K., & Mahar, D. (2003). "Tech-savviness" meets multiliteracies: Exploring adolescent girls' technology-mediated literacy practices. *Reading Research Quarterly, 38*(3), 356–385.

Commeyras, M., Faulstich-Orellana, M., Bruce, B. C., & Nielsen, L. (1996). Conversations: What do feminist theories have to offer to literacy, education, and research? *Reading Research Quarterly, 31*(4), 458–468.

Connell, B. W. (1987). *Gender and power.* Stanford, CA: Stanford University Press.

Connell, R. W. (1995). *Masculinities.* Berkeley: University of California Press.

Davies, B. (1991) *Frogs and snails and feminist tales: Preschool children and gender.* North Sydney, Australia: Allen & Unwin.

Davies, B. (1993). *Shards of glass: Children reading and writing beyond gendered identities.* Cresskill, NJ: Hampton.

Day, S. X. (1994). Gender schema and reading. *Reading Psychology, 15*(2), 91–107.

DeBell, M., & Chapman, C. (2006). *Computer and Internet use by students in 2003.* Washington, DC: U.S. Department of Education National Center for Education Statistics.

Evans, K., Anders, P., & Alvermann, D. E. (1997). Literature discussion groups: An examination of gender roles. *Reading Research and Instruction, 37,* 107–122.

Fey, M. (1998). Critical literacy in school college collaboration through computer networking: A feminist research project. *Journal of Literacy Research, 30*(1), 85–117.

Fey, M. (2008). The influence of gender on group interactions through post-typographical text. In R. Hammel & K. Sanford (Eds.), *Girls, boys and the myths of literacy and learning* (pp. 183–198). Toronto, ON: Canadian Scholars Press.

Frawley, T. J. (2008). Gender schema and prejudicial recall: How children misremember, fabricate, and distort gendered picture book information. *Journal of Research in Childhood Education, 22*(3), 291–303.

Gee, J. P. (2003). *What video games have to teach us about learning and literacy.* New York: Palgrave.

Gee, J. P. (2004). *Situated language and learning: A critique of traditional schooling.* London: Routledge.

Goode, J., Estrella, R., & Margolis, J. (2006). Lost in translation: Gender and school computer science. In J. M. Cohoon & W. Apray (Eds.), *Women and information technology: Research on under representation* (pp. 89–114). Cambridge, MA: MIT Press.

Green, E., & Adam, A. (2001). *Virtual gender: Technology, consumption, and identity.* London: Routledge.

Guzzetti, B. J. (2001). Texts and talk: The role of gender in learning physics. In E. B. Moje & D. O'Brien (Eds.), *Constructions of literacy: Studies of teaching and learning literacy in secondary classrooms* (pp. 125–146). Mahwah, NJ: Erlbaum.

Guzzetti, B. (2006a). Cybergirls: Negotiating social identities on cybersites. *E-Learning, 3*(2), 158–169.

Guzzetti, B. (2006b, December). Identities and technoliteracies: A young woman's critique of cybrersites and cyberspace. In E. Rubinstein-Avilla (Chair),

Exploring the socially embedded nature of youths' technoliteracies. Symposium conducted at the meeting of the National Reading Conference, Los Angeles, CA.

Guzzetti, B. J., & Gamboa, M. (2004a). Zining: The unsanctioned literacy practice of adolescents. In C. Fairbanks, J. Worthy, B. Maloch, J. Hoffman, & D. L. Schallert (Eds.), *Fifty-third Yearbook of the National Reading Conference* (pp. 206–217). Oak Creek, WI: The National Reading Conference.

Guzzetti, B. J., & Gamboa, M. (2004b). Zines for social justice: Adolescent girls writing on their own. *Reading Research Quarterly, 39*(4), 408–435.

Guzzetti, B. J., & Gamboa, M. (2005). Online journaling: The informal writings of two adolescent girls. *Research in the Teaching of English, 40*(2), 168–206.

Hall, K. (1996). Cyberfeminism. In S. C. Herring (Ed.), *Computer-mediated communication: Linguistic, social and cross-cultural perspectives* (pp. 148–170). Amsterdam/Philadelphia: J. Benjamins.

Haraway, D. (1991a). A cyborg manifesto: Science, technology and socialist feminism in the late twentieth century. In D. J. Haraway (Ed.), *Simions, cyborgs, and women: The reinvention of nature* (pp. 149–181). New York: Routledge.

Haraway, D. J. (1991b). *Simians, cyborgs, and women: The reinvention of nature.* New York: Routledge.

Hawthorne, S., & Klein, R. (Eds.). (1999). *Cyberfeminism: Connectivity, critique and creativity.* North Melbourne, Victoria, Australia: Spinifex Press.

Hayes, E. (2005). Women, video gaming, and learning: Beyond stereotypes. *Tech Trends: Linking Research and Practice to Improve Learning, 49*(5), 23–28.

Hayes, E., Johnson, B., King, E., & Lammers, J. (2008, July). *The Sims 2 and Teen Second Life: Insights from tech-savvy girls, year 2.* Paper presented at the meeting of the Games, Learning, and Society Conference, Madison, WI. Retrieved October 18, 2008, from *www.glsconference.org/2008/session.html?id=76.*

Herring, S. C. (2001). *Gender and power in online communication.* Retrieved April 14, 2008, from *rkesi.indiana.edu/archive/CSI/WP/WPO1–05B.html.*

hooks, b. (1989). *Talking back: Thinking feminist, thinking black.* Cambridge, MA: South End Press.

Jacobs, G. (2006). Fast times and digital literacy: Participation roles and portfolio construction within instant messaging. *Journal of Literacy Research, 38*(20), 171–196.

Jensen, J., De Castell, S., & Bryson, M. (2003). "Girl talk": Gender, equity and identity discourses in a school-based computer culture. *Women's Studies International Forum, 26*(6), 561–571.

Johnson, S., & Finley, F. (1997). The role of expletives in the construction of masculinity. In S. Johnson & U. H. Meinhof (Eds.), *Language and masculinity* (pp. 144–158). Oxford, UK: Blackwell.

Jones, A. (1993). Becoming a "girl": Poststructuralist suggestions for educational research. *Gender and Education, 5*(2), 157–166.

Kelly, D., Pomerantz, S., & Currie, D. H. (2006). "No boundaries"?: Girls' interactive online learning about femininities. *Youth and Society, 38*(1), 3–27.

Knobel, M., & Lankshear, C. (2001). Cut, paste, publish: The production and consumption of zines. In D. E. Alvermann (Ed.), *Adolescents and literacies in a digital world in a digital world* (pp. 162–185). New York: Lang.

Lam, E. (2000). Second language learning and the design of the self: A case study of a teenage English language learner writing on the Internet. *TESOL Quarterly, 34*(3), 457–483.

Lankshear, C., & Knobel, M. (2003). *New literacies: Changing knowledge and classroom learning.* Buckingham, UK: Open University Press.

Lankshear, C., & McLaren, P. (Eds.). (1993). *Critical literacy: Politics, praxis, and the postmodern.* Albany: State University of New York Press.

Lemons, M. A., & Parzinger, M. (2007). Gender schemas: A cognitive explanation of discrimination of women in technology. *Journal of Business and Psychology, 22*(1), 91–98.

Lewis, C., & Fabos, B. (2005). Instant messaging, literacies, and social identities. *Reading Research Quarterly, 40*(4), 470–501.

O'Brien, J. (1999). Writing in the body: Gender (re)production in online interaction. In M. A. Smith (Ed.), *Communities in cyberspace* (pp. 75–106). London: Routledge.

Olson, C. K., Kutner, L. A., & Warner, D. E. (2008). The role of violent video game content in adolescent development: Boys' perspectives. *Journal of Adolescent Research, 23*(1), 55–75.

Ono, H., & Tsai, H. (2008). Race, parental socioeconomic status, and computer use time outside of school among young American children, 1997 to 2003. *Journal of Family Issues, 29*(12), 1650–1672.

Sanford, H., & Blair, H. (2008). Game boys: Where is the literacy? In R. F. Hammett & K. J. Sanford (Eds.), *Girls, boys and the myths of literacies and learning* (pp. 199–215). Toronto, ON: Canadian Scholars Press.

Sanford, K., & Madill, L. (2006). Resistance through video game play: It's a boy thing. *Canadian Journal of Education, 21*(1), 287–306.

Schilt, K. (2003). "I'll resist with every inch and every breath": Girls and zine making as a form of resistance. *Youth and Society, 35*(1), 71–97.

Sinor, J. (2002, March). *Adolescent girls' zines: Uncommon pages and practices.* Paper presented at the meeting of the conference on College Composition and Communication, Chicago, IL.

Sokal, L., Katz, H., Adkins, M., Giadu, A., Jason-Davis, K., & Kussin, B. (2005). "Boys will be boys": Variability in boys' experiences of literacy. *Alberta Journal of Educational Research, 51*(3), 216–230.

Stanley, L., & Wise, S. (1993). *Breaking out again: Feminist ontology and epistemology.* New York: Routledge.

Stone, S. (1991). Will the real body please stand up? In M. Benedikt (Ed.), *Cyberspace: First steps* (pp. 81–118). Cambridge, MA: MIT Press.

St. Pierre, E. A., & Pillow. W. S. (Eds.). (2000). *Working the ruins: Feminist post-structural theory and methods in education.* New York: Routledge.

Street, B. V. (1995). *Social literacies.* London: Longman.

Subrahmanyam, K., & Greenfield, P. M. (1998). Computer games for girls: What makes them play? In J. Cassell & H. Jenkins (Eds.), *From Barbie to Mortal Kombat: Gender and computer games* (pp. 46–71). Boston: MIT Press.

Subrahmanyam, K., Smahel, D., & Greenfield, P. (2006). Connecting developmental constructions to the Internet: Identity presentation and sexual exploration in online teen chat rooms. *Developmental Psychology, 42*(3), 395–406.

Tannen, D. (1990). *You just don't understand: Women and men in conversation.* New York: Ballantine Books.

Thomas, A. (2004). Digital literacies of the cybergirl. *E-Learning, 1*(3), 358–382.

Thomas, A. (2007). *Youth online: Identity and literacy in the digital age.* New York: Lang.

Thorne, B. (1993). *Gender play: Girls and boys in school.* New Brunswick, NJ: Rutgers University Press.

Valentine, G., & Holloway, S. L. (2002). Cyberkids?: Exploring children's identities and social networks in online and offline worlds. *Journal of the Association of American Geographers, 92*(2), 302–319.

Varma, R. (2002). Women in information technology: A case study of undergraduate students in a minority serving institution. *Bulletin of Science, Technology and Society, 22,* 274–282.

Vygotsky, L. (1978). *Mind in society: Development of high psychological processes.* Cambridge, MA: Harvard University Press.

Wilding, F. (1998). *Where is feminism in cyberfeminism?* Retrieved May 1, 2008, from *www.obn.org/cfunderf/faith_def.html.*

Wright, S. H. (2005, May). Seamless show wired for success. *Tech Talk, 49*(28), 1–4.

CHAPTER 12

From the Personal to the Worldwide Web

Moving Teachers into Positions of Critical Interrogation

VIVIAN VASQUEZ
JEROME C. HARSTE
PEGGY ALBERS

As English language arts teachers, our goal has always been to create a literate citizenry. We wish to argue that, despite this lofty goal, for the 21st century, our aim must be higher. Our goals ought to be to create a critically literate citizenry. This means we are not abandoning universal literacy but rather framing it from a different theoretical perspective. In essence, we want universal literacy plus—the plus being critical literacy.

By critical literacy we mean a citizenry that can unpack the implicit and explicit messages being conveyed by text. We are using the word *text* broadly to include spoken, written, or depicted language, including that which is electronically transmitted. The contention we want students to understand is that no text is neutral and that all texts are created from particular ideological positions or perspectives. We also want them to understand that our response or reaction to text is never neutral and that as we encounter text we do so from particular ideological positions based on our past experiences and the discourses through which we have engaged. With this in mind, our goal is to position students as citizens who understand the ideological nature of texts, be able to read, respond, and produce texts from a critical perspective, and who are agents of texts rather than victims of text.

Instructionally, the focus should be on meaning making, language study, and inquiry, all done from a critical literacy perspective. Students must have opportunities to make meaning as well as to interrogate who is served by that meaning. Students must see how their own experiences (their own situatedness) have conditioned them to make certain meanings rather than other meanings. Students must understand how texts work to get things done in the world (Comber & Kamler, 1997). Lakoff (2008) argued that we need to help students understand what "frames" are being used and how these frames support certain interpretations. He contrasted a "strict father image" against a "nurturing father image" to make his point. How a text is written or read and understood depends on which of these "frames" are invoked. Gee (1999) suggested we help students interrogate what authors have said in terms of the "cultural model" they are using. Gee's "cultural models" are very much like Lakoff's "frames" in that they are mental frames that work to shape perception. He used the example of "welfare money" and how students at Wisconsin read welfare as something they associated with minority groups and the poor rather than as a social insurance policy for all workers more generally. In addition, we join Kress and van Leeuwen (1996) in also arguing for visual literacy and the need to support students in developing the ability to critically unpack visual images and to use new literacies as tools in our critical literacy work.

With the screen now overtaking the page as a vehicle that is being used more and more to convey information, students must be able to interrogate all kinds of texts, as well reflect on their conclusions about such texts. However, they also need to take responsibility for becoming informed about the issues these texts address; in short, to inquire, interrogate and then redesign such texts. Literacy in the 21st century should be focused on agency and taking action as opposed to passivity and going with the flow. Said more clearly, critical literacy is not a spectator's sport.

As critical literacy scholars and teacher educators, one of our aims is to engage teachers in critical readings and viewings of the world. The world is largely visual (Kalantzis, Cope, & Cloonan, Chapter 4, this volume; Kress, 2003; Labbo & Ryan, Chapter 5, this volume), and largely multimedia (Doering, Beach, & O'Brien, 2007), so it is essential that teachers become more aware of and be able, themselves, to read and analyze the multitude of messages that are sent, visually and linguistically, in order to help their own students become critical readers of the world. This means working within a framework that creates opportunities for teachers to:

- Become critically conscious of their own personal beliefs.
- Experience reading their communities.
- Study the messages within their own communities.
- Move them into social action in which their transformed beliefs are made accessible to worldwide audiences using new literacies and various tools of technology.

With students, we start with personal responses to what critical means to them. Following this we move into a study of their school and community as well as social issues they observe at play in this setting. We then work with them to create multimedia texts that could be accessed worldwide, in essence, as a way of taking cyber-based social action.

CREATING CRITICAL CLASSROOMS FOR THE 21ST CENTURY

While describing pedagogies of responsibility and place, Comber, Nixon, and Reid (2007) noted that in teaching literacy, our role as teachers includes extending the repertoires of literacy and communications practices available to our students. Comber and her colleagues further noted, "Literacy teaching cannot, and we believe it should not, be a content-free zone. We know that there is great potential for students to expand their literate repertoires when they become deeply engaged in acquiring new knowledge about things that matter" (p. 2). From experience we also know that the potential for expanding their literate repertoires is enhanced when we give them opportunities to do life work using these literacies, such as social action projects. Such projects aim to contribute to changing inequities in the community and beyond.

Regarding things that matter, there is a line in the movie *Cars* (Lasseter, 2006) where Sally, one of the main characters, reflects on a time when roads and roadways moved with the land rather than cutting through it. She lamented that back then, "Cars didn't drive on the

road to make great time. They drove on the road to have a great time."
In pedagogies of responsibility and place as described by Comber et al.
(2007), the journey matters. We live in a fast-paced sound-bite world, so
today more than ever we need to slow down, stop and look more closely,
revisit, reflect, rethink, and reimagine. In this chapter, we describe how
new literacies, multimodality, and the arts created space for 90 teachers
to use visual discourse analysis (Albers, 2007) and the grammar of visual
design (Kress & van Leeuwen, 1996) to better understand what it means
to read everyday texts critically. We asked teachers to try their hand at
working through various strategies such as critically interrogating advertisements, creating counter-advertisements, and using audio bites and
digital images from their community and school to create multimedia
projects such as public service announcements, and upload them to the
Internet. We had them do this kind of work to help them better imagine
the kinds of critical classrooms needed for the 21st century.

SETTING THE CONTEXT FOR LEARNING
THROUGH NEW LITERACIES

In July 2008, the three of us led a 5-day workshop for 90 teachers in Mis-
sissauga, Ontario, Canada. Many of the teachers were doing the workshop as part of their master's of education in literacy program. Some
were new to the classroom, although most were experienced teachers
who had been in the classroom for at least 7 years. Because many of the
teachers had also previously participated in other literacy workshops led
by Jerry and Vivian and were thus privy to their research agendas, they
expected that the summer program would involve critical literacy and
inquiry, two areas of study central to Jerry and Vivian's work.

   The week prior to our workshop, the teachers had worked with
Colin Lankshear, Michelle Knobel, Guy Merchant, and Julia Davis.
Their focus was on new literacies whereby these teachers learned about
and tried their hand at using various Web-based social networking
tools including Flickr and Facebook. They also explored various virtual
worlds such as Moshi Monsters (located at *www.moshimonsters.com* and
Webkinz (located at *www.webkinz.com/us*) and worked with technological tools such as iMovie and iDVD.

   During the second week, with us, the focus was on experiencing
and developing a curriculum with the arts, new literacies, and critical
literacy as central constructs. Teachers were asked to bring a digital

camera, digital voice recorder, MP3 player, sketchbook, and a laptop with audio/video editing capabilities. This required materials list immediately positioned them within the world of new technologies, as users or soon-to-be users of that technology. The workshop was set in a hotel conference room close to where many of the teachers lived, and we met daily for a week from 9:00 A.M. to 3:30 P.M.

Interrogating the everyday world and everyday beliefs and practices that surround us is essential in developing critical literacy plus. All three of us discussed at length how we wanted the curriculum for this summer workshop to evolve and what we hoped teachers in Toronto would learn by engaging in this new literacies and critical literacy curriculum. We knew this curriculum had to be interactive and engaging. We believed that we needed to start with the teachers' experiences and knowledge.

As Burke (2004) argued, we cannot teach someone something that they are not already involved in thinking about. That is, we knew we needed to locate this study of the arts, multimodality, and new literacies in spaces and places that the teachers cared about—their school and the community in which it is located. We also knew that we wanted these new literacies engagements to be multimodal because we felt the use of different modalities would create for teachers different ways into the curriculum that we were designing. We also wanted them to be able to use different modalities in representing their thinking and their understanding. The range of facility with technology would offer a challenge, but we believed this was a challenge that would offer teachers further opportunities to teach each other and learn together. In the end, we expected that the teachers would take on a new perspective toward new literacies and themselves as critically literate citizens.

Based on the line of thinking described previously, we designed and developed a range of engagements that would move teachers from personal reflection to worldwide cyber-based social action using their experiences with new literacies technologies. Before the workshop began, we asked teachers to look more closely at their school and the community in which their school is located. We asked them to take digital photographs; record sound bites of the street or school; interview students, parents, and staff at the school; and gather any other materials they thought would allow them to explore issues of social significance to children, parents, families, and the community at large, as well as the systems of meaning that underpin them. These multimedia texts would be central as they explored critical literacy from their own perspective, and identified social issues that they believe were significant.

FROM THE PERSONAL TO THE WORLDWIDE WEB

We will describe each of the engagements independently; however, it is important to note that these engagements were recursive. Teachers returned to previous learning to develop future projects. We started with the personal by having teachers identify a social issue such as race, class or gender, that may be of importance to their school and the community in which it resides. They were then asked to take social action by using various social networking tools such as Twitter, Utterz, and Blogger to spread the word about the issues with which they were dealing. Twitter (*twitter.com*), as noted on the website, is intended to allow people who use it to communicate and stay connected through the exchange of quick, frequent answers to one simple question: What are you doing? Posting quick updates about what they were doing in creating their videos provided the teachers with instant responses or "tweets" from other Twitter users. Utterz (*www.utterli.com*) allowed for similar kind of social networking as did Blogger (*www.blogger.com*). In spreading the word they were able to refine their critique of particular texts dealing with their social issue. This made it a little easier to then re-present those issues through the use of counternarratives. As a new tool for presenting ideas and representing thinking, the use of new technologies caused the teachers to slow down and look more closely at the texts with which they were working. They had to carefully determine what the technology would afford the work they were doing. In essence, they were using the technology to make accessible to others via the worldwide web their critique of dominant ideologies and their redesigns of texts (counternarratives) representing those ideologies. Following is a description of how we did this work.

READING IMAGES: CREATING COUNTER-ADS AS CRITICAL RESPONSES TO ADVERTISEMENTS

Based on Jerry and Peggy's earlier work with everyday texts (Albers, Harste, Vander Zanden, & Felderman, 2008; Harste, Albers, Felderman, & Vander Zanden, 2007), we asked teachers to read advertisements. In particular, we had them highlight the messages they believed were being conveyed by the designer of the advertisement. Scholars have argued that we have become a culture of consumerism in which corporations, with or without our consent, define and shape through their products the identities they believe children and youth want (Beach, 2007; Steinberg & Kincheloe, 2004). Unfortunately, there is little opportunity in schools for students to critique such media texts, largely because such critique is not considered academically rigorous (Marsh, 2006). However, researchers have argued (and we concur) that our visual world, with its range of multimedia texts such as advertisements, TV, films, websites, and billboards, must be interrogated by even the youngest of children, who are very capable of examining and identifying significant concepts, symbols, and systems of representation (Carr, 2000; Lewison, Leland, & Harste 2007; Vasquez, 2004).

Stemming from this line of thinking, we began our workshop with a study of advertisements in which we wanted the teachers to make visible for themselves to what extent they engaged with professionally generated texts like advertisements and the position from which they read such texts. We also wanted them to make sense of the ways in which texts work to position them in particular ways. To do this we had them respond to questions like:

- Was it a good text? What made it effective for you?
- Did you like it? Why or why not?
- What came to mind as you made meaning from the text?
- What do you think the text aims to do to you?
- What meaning did you make of the text?
- What stances/perspectives did you use to frame your reading(s) of the text?

Following a discussion of their ads, we presented Kress and van Leeuwen's (1996) grammar of visual design, a method of examining images more systematically, both for implicit and explicit messages. Teachers were then invited to read a range of advertisements, some aimed at young children and others at adults. This discussion allowed the group to interrogate the implicit and explicit messages that encourage the formation of particular identities. This led to the teachers' having an opportunity to talk back to text (Britzman, 1995) through their own creation of a counter-ad.

Counter-ads are parodies of existing ads (magazine, newspaper, billboards, etc.) in which the designer of the counter-ad alters the original in some way, such as adding graphic elements or drawing, and/or creates a new ad that talks back to the original. In a counter-ad, the message suggests a different truth than that told by companies. We invited teachers to study five ads in particular used by the U.S. Army, Ralph Lauren, Disney, Home Depot, and Wal-Mart. They were asked to choose one of these ads or another they found online or in a magazine, and create their own counter-ad using a large range of art materials that we provided, such as markers, crayons, paint, clay, pipe cleaners, and construction paper. Figure 12.1 is an example of a counter-ad created by a group of teachers. Although Disney presents itself as the perfect place for families, these teachers interrogated what they saw as the corporate intent of Disney. Their written text "It's not a perfect world after all" and the visual symbols of the American flag and the dollar sign contained inside Mickey Mouse's head represent Disney's corporate agenda. The symbols and text are confined within Mickey's head, a metaphor that clearly shows the power of this one company to influence worldwide consumerism. That the head of Mickey floats above the earth like a satellite, with the ability to communicate to and across the entire world, further demonstrates how these teachers interpret the pervasiveness of Disney's message. The bold use of colors (in the original counter-ad) and large symbols signifies the clarity and success that Disney has had with its marketing strategy, described in the ad as a "marketing ploy."

Counter-ads enable teachers to see how multimedia (written, visual) converge to persuade viewers to buy into their messages. By creating such ads, teachers study not only the messages, but also how these messages are constructed through art and language, and, we hope, leave them better able to critically interrogate such ads. Once they have these

FIGURE 12.1. Collaboratively generated counter-ad.

experiences they are then better able to use the strategy in their own settings.

A STREET CALLED HOME: MAKING THE INVISIBLE VISIBLE

In the next activity, we moved beyond the personal and focused on the community. We invited teachers to read *A Street Called Home* (1997), a picture book written by outsider artist, Aminah Brenda Lynn Robinson, about the everyday people she remembers as a child in her neighborhood. Using poetry, fabric, and found art, she makes visible people whose jobs might be considered by some as not worthy of visibility. In this beautifully illustrated book that accordions out like a street, we read the stories of such people as the Sock Man, the Chickenfoot Lady, and the Ice Man, who has "Children run behind the/Iceman truck, Reaching in/for chips of ice" Robinson (1997, n.p.). After a discussion of Robinson's text, teachers were informed that they would create their own *A Street Called Home* that featured the everyday people who lived in their own communities and who were virtually invisible to passersby. Like Robinson, they would use a range of media to create their individual pages.

We distributed sheets of foam board (4½" × 8") and index cards (3" × 5") to each teacher, who then used these two materials to create the structure for his or her page of this collective community book. Using Robinson's book as a guide, teachers taped an index card to the front of the foam board, illustrated the front of their board using a variety of media, and drew an image of the person whom they chose to make visible on the inside of the index card. They then wrote an accompanying poem. Figures 12.2 and 12.3 represent the work of one teacher. Her poem was entitled "The Watcher": "The watcher sits in her chair and watches who comes, who goes . . . ." We taped the pages together like an accordion, as in Robinson's book. Finally, teachers volunteered to read and share their stories.

This multimedia and multilanguage engagement offered teachers an opportunity to critically consider who and what they pay attention to in the community. For many, this engagement was eye-opening, a way for them to consider how their students could look at their own community in the same way, and offered suggestions as to how to make more visible those positioned as invisible. It also helped bring to conscious-

FIGURE 12.2. Outside of illustrated foam board (index card illustrated with flowers/sun).

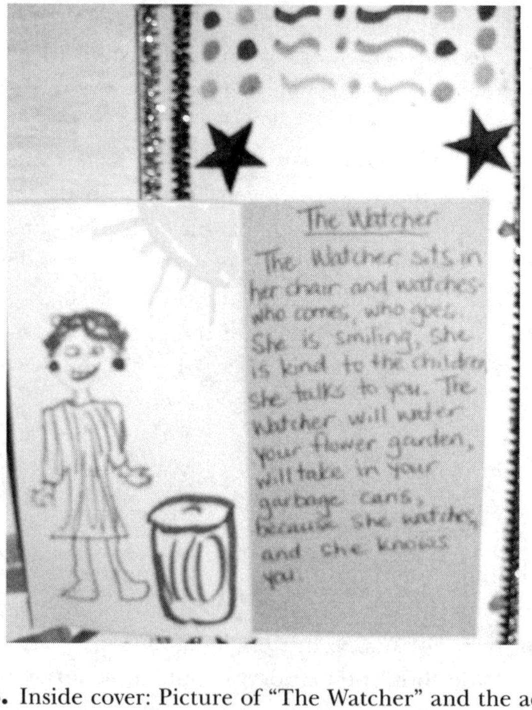

FIGURE 12.3. Inside cover: Picture of "The Watcher" and the accompanying poem.

ness some of their own ideologies as they pondered over whether they themselves had, in their lives, marginalized some of the very people they were now attempting to make visible. In other words, we were asking them to constantly reflect on their own complicity in maintaining the status quo. Making the invisible visible is part of what we have to do to be critically literate ourselves and to support students in taking on a critical stance themselves.

MURALS AS SOCIAL AND VISUAL PUBLIC STATEMENTS

Moving attention from the invisible or marginalized members of a community, we next focused attention on the issues that may contribute to the invisibility of some people and the visibility of others. We spent some time closely examining public displays of social statements, such as murals. We asked teachers to study the materials they had gathered before the workshop began, including photos, sound bites, and interviews, and identify the social issues at play in these materials. They considered such questions as, "Who is being privileged in the community and who is not? In what ways are these people privileged or disadvantaged? By whom? To serve what purpose? What are some of the issues that our students face daily and bring into the classroom? How can we take on the role of social agents to support students and families in the community?" With these questions in mind, we asked teachers who worked at the same school and in the same community to construct a panel for a larger mural that would become a public and collective statement about the range of issues that they felt were important and in need of interrogation and action in their communities.

Figure 12.4 is one group of teachers' representation of the social issues at play in their school and community. Although not shown in this image, this panel hung from a coat rack, symbolizing the tenuous interplay among alcoholism, drugs, violence, vandalism, and other issues that concerned these teachers. For them, these issues do not arise independently, but emerge from a combination of conditions. Teachers posted their panels on the walls of our room and then studied them collectively to identify some common and anomalous issues that were of concern to them as a group of educators. Developing panels for a larger mural reminded teachers of the connections between the underlying sociopolitical forces that contribute to and maintain the existence of these social issues.

FIGURE 12.4. Murals as visual and public statements.

PUBLIC SERVICE ANNOUNCEMENTS AND POSITIONING VIEWERS AS CHANGE AGENTS

Moving within community, but with a gesture toward a worldwide audience, we invited teachers to continue their multimedia exploration of social issues within their schools and communities through public service announcements (PSAs). We defined PSAs as short, 1-minute multimedia texts that present persuasive or informative messages about social issues. Engagement with PSAs was an opportunity for teachers to use digital media to communicate issues to a broader audience. Along with colleagues from their school, teachers studied the digital images that they had collected, sound bites of children, and other community members whom they interviewed, and other copyright-free images from sites like Flickr (*www.flickr.com*), one of the many online photo sharing tools available for free. They then created 1-minute PSAs on social issues that they wanted to examine. They used Windows MovieMaker, iMovie, or PowerPoint as platforms and integrated digital images, music, written text, and/or special effects·such as transitions. An important construct of PSAs is that they are self-running, are texts in and of themselves, and should be viewed without explanation. The entire message is meant to be carried by the various modes (visual, musical, spatial, etc.), and meaning both intended by the PSA text maker as well as interpreted by the viewer.

To contextualize this activity, we began with a discussion of both print-based materials like magazines, and non-print-based material on television or Internet sites. For example, a classic print-based PSA addresses drug use and is aimed at a teen audience. The top frame of the PSA is an image of a human brain with the written text "This is your brain." The bottom frame is a still photograph of two eggs frying in a pan with the written text, "This is your brain on drugs." Teachers discussed the hard-hitting, in-your-face visual messages directed at adolescents and young adults, and how they perceived teens' response to such ads. After this discussion, we showed them several multimedia PSAs created by middle and high school students and teachers. With these demonstrations, teachers—in groups—designed, developed, and produced PSAs that addressed a social issue that was significant to their school and community.

Figure 12.5 shows the introductory frames of two PSAs; the first addressed pollution and the other the inhumane treatment and subsequent slaughter of chickens. What we found while we observed teachers in the process of designing PSAs was their fascination of how new literacies allowed them to communicate parts of the message across features of various platforms. For example, teachers found that their use of transitions such as fade to black or diamonds, and other special effects common to presentation software like PowerPoint and movie-making software such as iMovie and Windows MovieMaker2, more completely communicated their overall message. Some integrated film as part of their PSA, while others used digital images. Some used irony and surprise to convey their message, as was the case in Figure 12.5 (chicken frame). These teachers started out with "innocent" images of chickens with playful background music. After about 15 seconds, the music turned sinister, and a picture of Colonel Sanders of the Kentucky Fried Chicken chain of fast-food restaurants appeared, followed by images of crowded chicken pens and slaughterhouses.

The move toward digital media to communicate and change perspectives was not easy; some teachers found it challenging to insert images, sound, video, and timed transitions into their PSAs. They also found it disheartening when they created part of their PSA at home only

FIGURE 12.5. Introductory frames of two PSAs, created collaboratively and focused on social issues.

to find that when they brought this text to class, it would not play on a colleague's computer. We spent a great deal of time working with groups on individual issues regarding technology, software, and hardware. However, in the end, teachers appreciated the learning that came from this engagement and were more excited about integrating this project and these technologies into their classrooms. Sandy Sparks, one of the participants, shared in an e-mail weeks after the workshop ended that he had continued to blog and was integrating the use of podcasts in his elementary school teaching. He also stated that the workshop was the best one he had taken throughout his graduate program.

MOVING TO THE WORLDWIDE WEB

Having worked in the area of critical literacy for many years (Harste, Lewinsohn, Leland, Ociepka, & Vasquez, 1999; Vasquez, 1998, 2000) we were very aware of the different interpretations of critical literacy in the world and that many of these interpretations are of the sort that treat critical literacy as a topic of study rather than as lived experiences. One of our aims in the workshop was to make sure these teachers had an opportunity not only to learn about critical literacy but experience or "live" some strategies firsthand as well as to experience what it means to use texts to influence others and to contribute to change in some way. Specifically, we wanted the teachers not only to participate in the various activities but also to use what they had learned to take social action in the real world. We did not want them to come away with the idea that critical literacy is a program of study. What we wanted was for them to live a critical literacy experience and then use that experience to contribute to changing social inequities that were of interest to them.

To do this we introduced the Pecha Kucha, a video presentation format invented by Astrid Klein and Mark Dytham in 2003 as a way for young designers to meet and show their work in public (*www.pecha-kucha.org*). Using PowerPoint or similar software, a presenter is allowed 20 images, each shown for 20 seconds. Each presentation is, therefore, only 6 minutes and 40 seconds long. The slides are timed and the entire slide show is meant to run automatically. The result is the production of a video consisting of a series of slides with audio background in the form of music or narration. Given that we live in a sound-bite world, we thought that this format would be a good way of getting these teachers to get their messages across in a limited period of time. For our purposes, however, we did not adhere to the 20-seconds-per-slide rule, as this did not allow for the nuances that made the short video an effective tool for raising awareness.

We asked teachers to take stock of the previous activities and tease out a particular issue that stood out for them. They were then to take the issue and create their Pecha Kucha video as a way of raising awareness regarding their issue. The videos were then to be uploaded to You-Tube as a way of making it accessible to a broader audience and as a way of giving their work life beyond the time frame of the workshop. Their experiences in creating this final video were similar to their experiences in creating their PSAs, except that they had become somewhat more experienced at using the technology. Alongside the creation of their video they also were asked to create a blog from which to link their video and to post their thoughts regarding critical literacy and new literacies.

Figure 12.6 is an image from "Take Action," a video created by two workshop teachers (*www.youtube.com/watch?v=uwVH9Qt6QZ4*). The video is composed of a series of images with background music that creates space for viewers to reflect on inequities in the world. The second half of the video focuses on ways for taking social action and contributing to change.

Figure 12.7, 12.8, and 12.9 come from two other videos posted on YouTube by teachers. The video "Progress?" asks the question, "Progress at whose expense?" This video works to create opportunities for conversations around who benefits from the "progress" that we talk about in the world and who is disadvantaged by such progress (*www.youtube.com/watch?v=fcTHG7YWafs*). Figure 12.8 (*www.youtube.com/watch?v=qqUBd9ZBjcw*) and Figure 12.9 (*www.youtube.com/watch?v=qqUBd9ZBjcw*) are screen shots of a video that looks at homelessness. This video titled "The Comparison" focuses on positioning, advantage, and disadvantage.

FIGURE 12.6. YouTube video on taking action to contribute to change in the world.

FIGURE 12.7. YouTube video that problematizes the notion of progress.

FIGURE 12.8. YouTube video "The Comparison."

FIGURE 12.9. YouTube video on home-lessness.

MOVING TOWARD NEW LITERACIES AND NEW PERSPECTIVES

In this workshop, we found that teachers enthusiastically engaged with new literacies, especially once they recognized how new technologies can enhance the work they do. Framing their work from a critical literacy perspective helped them to come to this realization, as it was through engaging with critical literacies that they were able to better understand the importance for taking social action and focusing curricula around social issues such as race, class, or gender. They also came to an understanding that new literacies and new technologies in and of themselves are not critical literacies but are powerful tools to be used in carrying out critical literacy work.

By engagement with print and digital media initially, teachers experienced a "new ethos" (Lankshear & Knobel, 2006, p. 93), or an inner mindset about arts-based and digital media approaches to communication. They also began to develop a different mindset toward Web 2.0 tools and communication. Within this new perspective, they not only communicated between and among themselves, but with a worldwide audience, thrusting them into cyberspace and offering opportunities to join new affinity groups (Gee, 2004), in which meaning is collectively and actively constructed across people. This, of course, is a powerful way to recruit people to think, act, interact, value, and feel in certain ways, and to construct new identities. One teacher came into the class the morning following the posting of her PSA on her blog and informed us that she had already received several messages from others in cyberspace who had viewed her PSA. This teacher both experienced a new ethos and reshaped her identity to include Web 2.0 tools as part of her new communications, as did many of her co-participants.

Our teaching and curriculum were not without tension. Although teachers created PSAs around issues that were significant to their community, some of the images that they selected, the organization of written text around them, and the compositions, at some level reproduced the very stereotypes around culture, poverty, education, and other social issues of which we hoped we could make them consciously aware. As part of the workshop, a space was created to talk about the need to think about the positions of privilege from which we speak. Throughout the workshop, teachers were able to use language to question, interrogate, problematize, denaturalize, interrupt, and disrupt those issues and ideas that are often normalized or naturalized. They were able to take a step back to rethink, reinterpret, and redesign problematic "texts," including those they had created. In so doing they were able to extend the repertoires of literacy and communications practices for use in their classrooms and their everyday lives.

Imagine what might happen if policymakers were to take on similar perspectives and on an ongoing basis critically interrogate how their decisions support or fight against extant systems of meaning. They would likely be better able to interrogate the assumptions that underlie most educational decision making, from remedial education (who gets labeled "remedial" and why), to their responsibility in being accountable for their decisions. Accountability is, of course, something classroom teachers are charged with. However, policymakers also need to examine the ways in which they themselves are accountable for providing the support teachers need. After all, there is no innocent ground here, and as we said at the start of this chapter, no texts, including those created by policymakers, are neutral.

REFERENCES

Albers, P. (2007). Visual discourse analysis: An introduction to the analysis of school-generated visual texts. In D. W. Rowe, R. T. Jimenez, D. L. Compton, D. K. Dickinson, Y. Kim, Kevin M. Leander, & V. J. Risko (Eds.), *56th Yearbook of the National Reading Conference* (pp. 81–95). Oak Creek, WI: National Reading Conference.

Albers, P., Harste, J. C., Vander Zanden, S., & Felderman, C. (2008). Using popular culture to promote critical literacy practices. In Y. Kim, V. J. Risko, D. L. Compton, D. K. Dickinson, M. Hundley, R. T. Jiménez, K. M. Leander, & D. W. Rowe (Eds.), *57th Yearbook of the National Reading Conference*. Oak Creek, WI: National Reading Conference.

Beach, R. (2007, November). *Creating critical classrooms: Double standards and bringing consumerism home*. Paper presented at the annual conference of the National Council of Teachers of English, New York, NY.

Britzman, D. P. (1995). Is there a queer pedagogy? Or, stop reading straight. *Educational Theory, 45*(2), 151–165.

Burke, C. L. (2004, November). *Curriculum as inquiry*. Presentation at the annual conference of the National Council of Teachers of English, Indianapolis, IN.

Carr, J. (2000). From "sympathetic" to "dialogic" imagination: Cultural study in the foreign language classroom. In A. Lo Bianco, A. J. Liddicoat, & C. Crozet (Eds.), *Striving for the third place: Intercultural competence through language education* (pp. 103–110). Melbourne: Language Australia.

Comber, B., & Kamler, B. (1997). Critical literacies: Politicising the language classroom. *Interpretations, 30*(1), 30–53.

Comber, B., Nixon, H., & Reid, J. (Eds.). (2007). *Literacies in place: Teaching environmental communication*. Newtown, New South Wales, Australia: Primary English Teaching Association.

Doering, A., Beach, R., & O'Brien, D. (2007). Infusing multimodal tools and digital literacies into an English education program. *English Education, 40*(1), 41–60.

Gee, J. P. (1999). *An introduction to discourse analysis*. New York: Routledge.

Gee, J. P. (2004). *What video games have to teach us about learning and literacy*. New York: Palgrave Macmillan.

Harste, J. C., Albers, P., Felderman, C., & Vander Zanden, S. (2007, December). *Unpacking advertisements*. Presentation at the annual conference of the National Reading Conference, Austin, TX.

Harste, J., Lewison, M., Leland, C., Ociepka, A., & Vasquez, V. (1999). Exploring critical literacy: You can hear a pin drop. *Language Arts, 77*(1), 70–77.

Kress, G. (2003). *Literacy in the new media age*. New York: Routledge.

Kress, G., & van Leeuwen, T. (1996). *Reading images: The grammar of visual design*. New York: Routledge.

Lakoff, G. (2008). *The political mind*. New York: Penguin Books.

Lankshear, C., & Knobel, M. (2006). *New literacies: Everyday practices and classroom learning*. Maidenhead, UK: Open University Press.

Lasseter, J. (Director). (2006). *Cars*. Los Angeles: Walt Disney Studios.

Lewison, M., Leland, C., & Harste, J. C. (2007). *Creating critical classrooms: K–8 reading and writing with an edge*. Mahwah, NJ: Erlbaum.

Marsh, J. (2006). Popular culture and literacy: A Bourdieuan analysis. *Reading Research Quarterly, 46*(2), 160–174.

Robinson, A. B. L. (1997). *A street called home.* New York: Harcourt Brace.

Steinberg, S. R., & Kincheloe, J. L. (2004). Introduction: No more secrets—kinderculture, information saturation, and the postmodern childhood. In S. R. Steinberg & J. L.Kincheloe (Eds.), *Kinderculture: The corporate construction of childhood* (pp. 1–30). Boulder, CO: Westview Press.

Vasquez, V. (1998). Building equitable communities: Taking social action in a kindergarten classroom. *Talking Points, 9*(2), 3–7.

Vasquez, V. (2000). Our way: Using the everyday to create a critical literacy curriculum. *Primary Voices, 9*(2), 8–13.

Vasquez, V. (2004). *Negotiating critical literacies with young children.* Mahwah, NJ: Erlbaum.

CHAPTER 13

New Literacies, New Insights
An Exploration of Traditional and New Perspectives

ELIZABETH A. BAKER

Theory attempts to explain how a phenomenon came to be as it is. In turn, theory can be used to predict what might become of the phenomenon. As described in Chapter 1 of this volume, Darwin's theory of evolution explains how animals adapted and evolved over time to survive in the changing conditions of their environments and become what we currently know to be various species. We can then use the theory of evolution to predict how the animal kingdom will continue to adapt and evolve to survive over extended periods of time.

Taken together, perspectives and theories play fundamental roles in gaining insights into the phenomena of reading and writing. Theoretical perspectives assist with how to define literacy, identify the skills that are paramount to literacy acquisition, determine the environmental factors that are necessary to support literacy development, and establish the criteria to assess literacy abilities. For decades, scholars have explored literacy from multiple theoretical perspectives. Each perspective has contributed to our current understandings of literacy. Some common perspectives are: behavioral, semiotic, cognitive, sociocultural, critical, and feminist (Alexander & Fox, 2004; Baker, Pearson,

& Rozendal, Chapter 1, this volume; Pearson & Stephens, 1994; Tracey & Morrow, 2006). Within each of these perspectives there exists a wide range of sensibilities toward defining and understanding literacy. Some of these perspectives have been used for decades while others have been adopted more recently.

Many of these perspectives provide insights into what it means to read and write with electronic technologies. One such insight is that there are new literacies. In other words, many researchers from a range of perspectives conclude that the reading and writing skills of yesteryear are insufficient in our increasingly digital world. Leu (2006) states, "the Internet is a reading and literacy issue, not a technology issue" (p. 6). While the insights provided by traditional perspectives are invaluable and are making significant contributions, additional perspectives may provide insights heretofore not considered. The purpose of this chapter is threefold: to briefly review insights provided by traditional perspectives toward new literacies (see Chapters 2–12, this volume), propose a couple of new theoretical perspectives that may increase our abilities to grapple with the complexities of new literacies, and challenge those interested in literacy to expand current conceptions of new literacies by wielding traditional as well as heretofore nascent theoretical perspectives with regard to literacy and new literacies.

NEW LITERACIES:
INSIGHTS FROM TRADITIONAL PERSPECTIVES

The purpose of this book is to showcase multiple perspectives and how they can be used to gain insights into a particular phenomenon: new literacies. Commonly, researchers from multiple perspectives seek ways to contrast their views and articulate how their view provides insights that others do not. While such contrasts are valuable and needed, in this book, I seek to value a range of perspectives so as to provide an enhanced and nuanced understanding of the complexities of new literacies. As a jeweler examines the multiple facets of a diamond, the contributing authors and I examine the multiple facets of new literacies as revealed from a range of theoretical perspectives. While this chapter cannot capture the rich insights provided by the contributing authors (I refer you to Chapters 2–12 for in-depth discussions), I seek to highlight some basic tenets that emerge from each perspective. I venture into this brief synopsis so as to generate a gestalt, an overarching view of new literacies, as well as to discuss the potential of new perspectives.

Behavioral Insights

Researchers who define the ability to read and write in terms of discrete, isolated skills that can be assessed as accurate responses to given stimuli (e.g., correct response to stimulus *c-a-t* is *cat*) rely on behavioral theories of literacy (see Hasselbring, Chapter 2, and McKenna & Conradi, Chapter 3, this volume). In other words, reading and writing involve the ability to wield a man-made code that represents words. In many regions of the world this code is alphabetic. When a child is able to break the code he can establish the oral equivalent of the word, then a string of words, and thereby comprehend text. Hasselbring states:

> Difficulties with word-level reading become increasingly problematic as students get older. Problems with decoding and sight-word fluency result in poor comprehension and lower motivation, and as texts become increasingly advanced with each grade, struggling readers fall further and further behind. (p. 24, this volume)

Technology can be harnessed to help children practice traditional reading and writing skills. Technology can assess how proficient children are with specific skills and then provide multiple practice sessions to help children develop fluency and automaticity with those skills (e.g., *Read 180; System 44; Voyager*). From this perspective, technology can be used efficiently and effectively to provide practice with traditional reading and writing skills. Changes in the basic nature of literacy due to technology are not the focus of this lens.

McKenna and Conradi (Chapter 3, this volume) propose a model of the integration of literacy and technology as a scaffolded system that moves the user from behavioral, skills-based practice to constructivist, authentic engagement in reading and writing. Specifically, they discuss how technology can be designed to give children practice with traditional reading and writing skills in a behavioral manner and then gradually release responsibility from the computer program to the student. Similar to Hasselbring's discussion, technology is viewed as a tool to practice literacy skills. Given proficiency with decoding skills, and building on theories of constructivism, McKenna and Conradi propose that the software can step children toward independent and authentic uses of reading and writing.

Semiotic and Multiliteracies Insights

Researchers using a semiotic perspective argue that text has always been multimodal, so multimedia technologies simply reiterate the need to define literacy in terms of multiple sign systems (see Kalantzis, Cope, & Cloonan, Chapter 4, this volume; Labbo & Ryan, Chapter 5, this volume; Baker, 2001; Gee, 2003; Kress, 2003). Multiple sign systems are commonly used to facilitate communication (e.g., facial expressions, body gestures, choice of clothing and hairstyle). Traditional books and magazines include alphabetic text in conjunction with illustrations, maps, photographs, graphs, and other pertinent semiotic information. Technology allows readers and writers to employ the semiotic systems that are commonly used in face-to-face situations (e.g., gestures, voice inflections). Thus the semiotic systems are not new—rather, they are reprioritized because they are no longer limited to face-to-face interactions.

For example, users of Wikipedia readily encounter alphabetic text, hypertext, video, animation, sound effects, and narration. *Readers* need to know how and when to access each of these sign systems, what a video of Martin Luther King, Jr., provides that the alphabetic text might not offer, how to determine which hyperlinks are pertinent, as well as when and why they should select an audio file. *Writers* need to know how to use all of these sign systems to effectively create a website, blog, wiki, or other multimedia composition. When posting to Facebook or YouTube, they need to know how effective each of these sign systems might be for representing their intended meanings. When incorporating a video, they need to determine whether it should be serious, professional, silly, or satirical. When incorporating audio files, they need to decide the content, how it should be performed (e.g., professional voice, in character), as well as what musical accompaniment might be appropriate. From a semiotic perspective, reading and writing with multimedia embraces a rich array of new literacies.

Cognitive Insights

Researchers taking a cognitive perspective argue that new literacies require new cognitive and metacognitive abilities not currently considered in literacy education. Tracey, Storer, and Kazerounian (Chapter 6, this volume) describe four categories of cognitive processing perspectives: narrative theories, box-and-pointer models, computational models, and cognitive neuroscience. They discuss contributions and potentials of each category with regard to understanding new literacies. Hartman, Morsink, and Zheng (Chapter 7, this volume) review the incremental cognitive complexities of reading offline and online. As one example, they describe the metacognitive skills involved in not only declarative, procedural, and conditional knowledge but also identity knowledge, locational knowledge, and goal knowledge. Leu (2006) argues that conducting Internet searches requires new cognitive strategies. He states:

> there must be critical evaluation of information, synthesis of disparate information resources, and communication, as readers seek information from others or as they communicate what they have discovered to others. On the Internet, reading comprehension begins with a question and often ends with communication. This is different from reading a book. (p. 9)

Leu et al. (2005) report that no correlation was found between the abilities to read online and offline. In other words, students who performed well with offline, traditional reading tasks were no better or worse at comprehending online texts. Lawless, Schrader, and Mayall (2007) examined the impact of prior knowledge on Internet navigation. They found that prior knowledge allowed hypertext users to be nonlinear in their search for online information and that these proficient users were more likely to remain engaged online. Baker, Rozendal, and Whitenack (2000) found that students working in a technology-rich classroom had a fluid and dynamic relationship with their audience and that traditional notions of audience awareness need to be reformed to help writers of digital texts. Coiro and Dobler (2007) found that online readers used complex aspects of prior knowledge, inferential reasoning, and metacognition. For example, online readers actively set a purpose and evaluate online resources accordingly (see also Baker, Zhang, & Duke, 2008; Zhang & Duke, 2008). From a cognitive perspective, these and other studies indicate that new cognitive literacies skills are indeed needed to make sense of digital texts.

Gee (Chapter 8, this volume) provides a bridge between cognitive and sociocultural perspectives by taking a sociocognitive perspective. Specifically, he melds concepts of situated cognition with sociocultural views of language, literacy, and technology. Herein, he labels his perspective as "situated–sociocultural." Gee describes the goals we might have for a child learning to read. He highlights the need for traditional literacies such as phonemic awareness, decoding, and literal comprehension. Then he examines the complex literacies involved in gaming (which commonly incorporates technology)—even among very young children (e.g., *Pokemon, Yu-Gi-Oh!*) and describes implications for literacy instruction and assessment.

Sociocultural Insights

Researchers who examine new literacies from a sociocultural perspective argue that literacy changes as cultures change. In the mid-1500s you were considered literate if you could read familiar religious texts. In our culture, being literate goes beyond being able to read books and printed texts; you need to be able to effectively use e-mail, text messages, and the Internet (e.g., Google, Facebook, YouTube) for a range of purposes (see Gee, Chapter 8; Chandler-Olcott & Lewis, Chapter 9; Mikulecky, Chapter 10; all this volume). Studies focused on adolescents have found this population to be active users of social interaction technologies such as text messaging, Facebook, MySpace, and fanfiction (Alvermann, 2002; Black, 2008; Knobel & Lankshear, 2007; Lewis & Fabos, 2005). One area of this work has focused on identity development. Ito (2007) describes adolescents' use of anime, a Japanese animation form, in which adolescents create and take on identities of cartoon characters. Chandler-Olcott and Mahar (2003) examine adolescents' use of anime and fanfiction in which adolescents create alternative endings and additional episodes for popular books (see also Black, 2008). These adolescents take on identities of Harry Potter, Robin Hood, and thousands of other characters (see *fanfiction.net/book*). Kinzer and Thomas (2007) examine the complexities of identity, affinity, and agency in a virtual online environment called Second Life. Users create animated representations of themselves called avatars. Their avatars can be human-like or animal-like. They can be business owners, rock stars, and anime movie stars. Given anime, fanfiction, Second Life, and other online social interactions, authors can become someone new. Their new identity gives them access to new affinity groups. They might be considered low-achieving students at school but be rock stars who give live concerts in Second Life.

While adolescents explore identity development in various media they also actively move between media—they transmediate. The ability to follow plots and characters across media is also a significant new literacy in our digital culture (Ito, 2007; Lemke, 2007; Siegel, 1995; Suhor, 1984). Product placement across media can be pivotal in the success of a product. Coca-Cola utilizes the power of newspapers, magazines, TV, film, and the Internet to maximize its message. Arguably, the commercial success of a literary character is not how many books are sold, but how well the character is picked up across media (J. Bresman, personal communication, November 13, 2008). Adolescents readily read such books as in the Harry Potter series with an emphasis on alphabetic text; watch the corresponding movies with emphasis on video imbued with spoken performance, sound effects, and musical accompaniment; compose new plots and character development with fanfiction that utilizes alphabetic text; read and write blogs that incorporate alphabetic text, music, narration, and YouTube clips; and may even take on the persona of a character or create an avatar in Second Life. In other words, they actively move between various media as they read and write about Harry Potter and other literary characters. The ability to transmediate requires the ability not only to move between media but also to effectively select which media best communicate the intended meanings to their intended audience (see Kalantzis et al., Chapter 4, this volume).

From a sociocultural perspective, new literacies include the abilities to "fit in" to the social norms of the technology being used (Davies & Merchant, 2009). For example, ALL CAPS in e-mail may indicate emphasis (as with printed text), but more commonly is considered to be "shouting." Users who do not understand this social convention can readily offend their audience by misusing this simple textual feature. Users of text messaging demonstrate their prowess by how much of the txt lexicon they can use (e.g. lol, idk, plz; see *www.pbs.org/parents/childrenandmedia/mediaglossary-lexicon.html*). Understanding these social conventions are of paramount importance to proficiently communicate in online social environments. They entail an entire area of new literacies.

Shifting from the norms of adolescents' use of communicative technologies, Mikulecky (Chapter 10, this volume) examines the norms of the workplace. From a sociocultural perspective, he contends that it is paramount for new literacies to be taught in our schools so that children will be prepared to secure high-paying jobs and compete in the global market, which is highly dependent on information and communication technologies (ICT). Mikulecky traces the use of sociocultural theories in making sense of workplace literacies and encourages teachers and policymakers to value the complexities of new literacies required in a broad range of workplaces. While we cannot predict the new literacies of future workplaces, we must strive to prepare children for the new literacies that are evident as well as advance the dispositions (e.g., adapt to the social norms established within each community of ICT users) needed to wield the new literacies of the future.

Critical and Feminist Insights

From critical and feminist perspectives, literacy is examined to showcase policies and practices that limit access and opportunity (see Guzzetti, Chapters 11; and Vasquez, Harste, & Albers, Chapter 12, this volume). Critical studies advocate that students be taught how to explore digital texts critically. Vasquez et al. (Chapter 12, this volume) describe a workshop they designed to get teachers intimately involved with new literacies and critical literacies. Specifically, the teachers were asked to identify a social issue of importance in their communities. They collected a range of artifacts related to this issue (e.g., digital photos, sound bites, and interviews). Then they advocated for their cause via various social networks (e.g., Twitter, Utterz, and Blogger). Finally, they studied the use of media to advertise products and messages. All of these activities were designed to heighten awareness of the stereotypes and inequalities reified in our culture. Also from a critical perspective (as well as poststructural feminist theory), Wohlwend (see Baker & Wohlwend, 2009; Wohlwend, 2009) recently examined how preschool children reified gendered stereotypes by bringing to school and playing with Disney princess dolls. She found that the girls often transposed plots from books and movies that featured Cinderella, Pocahontas, and such into princess dolls who were empowered to solve their own problems. In summary, critical perspectives help us examine new literacies in terms of the power structures inherent in human cultures.

Insights revealed from a feminist perspective highlight the need to sensitize students to gendered and race-related text messages, e-mail, and websites as well as to the reification of stereotypes. Guzzetti and Gamboa (2004) found that adolescent girls who compose 'zines (pop culture online fanzines) can grow in their own awareness of feminist and gender issues. They state:

> Zines . . . have been referred to as an act of civil disobedience; a tool for inspiring other forms of activism; and a medium through which girls effect changes within themselves, including confronting their own weaknesses, such as racism, homophobia, and other forms of prejudice. (p. 411)

In a broader sense, Guzzetti (Chapter 11, this volume) states:

> One of the most important implications of the new literacies is to serve as a vehicle for raising young people's awareness of the ways in which gender interacts with other subjectivities such as social class and race to serve or disenfranchise particular groups. Students will be unable to change their behaviors and make informed choices until they are made aware of the issues of social justice that surround these new literate practices. (p. 259)

Herein, insights from a poststructural feminist perspective open avenues for critically evaluating the role of gender in empowerment and disempowerment to participate in our culture.

Using critical and feminist insights, it is argued that practices associated with such policies as No Child Left Behind disempower struggling readers (Baker, 2008; Leu, 2006). Ironically, this policy has potentially left more children behind. Teachers are held accountable by high-stakes tests that evaluate students' non-technology reading and writing skills (Leu, Ataya, & Coiro, 2002). Teachers are pressured to focus on traditional literacies and are likely to find it risky to take time to teach struggling readers and writers new literacies. Meanwhile, average and high-performing students might be given time at school to develop new literacies and are likely to go home and develop them even further. Certainly, those who develop new literacies will be better prepared for high-paying jobs than those who do not (Leu, 2006; Mikulecky, Chapter 10, this volume).

NEW LITERACIES: GLIMPSES INTO NEW PERSPECTIVES

In this section, I shift from the insights revealed by contributing authors that are derived from established and valued theoretical perspectives that have been used historically to make sense of reading and writing (e.g., behavioral, semiotic, cognitive, sociocultural, critical, and feminist; see Chapters 2–12, this volume) to the potential of new perspectives. In this section, I draw on perspectives used in astrophysics and engineering. Specifically, I examine new literacies in terms of time and space as well as the notion of autonomous agents derived from systems theory. Although my exploration of these theories is nascent, I offer these descriptions in an attempt to stretch the field of literacy and prime the pump for using alternative theoretical perspectives that may enrich our understanding and explorations of new literacies.

Astrophysical and Ontological Insights

What is it that demands we give credence to new literacies? Should new literacies be afforded the attention we give traditional reading and writing? Why should we invest the resources required to infuse new literacies into well-established pedagogical practices and school curricula? Socioculturalists contend that the nature of literacy is changing in our technological world. Critical and feminist theorists argue that a fundamental purpose of schools is to prepare students to be well equipped to engage in their culture and compete in a global market economy. Cognitivists contend that there are new thought processes involved in making sense of what is available online.

Semioticians help us understand that the nature of new literacies involves alphabetic as well as nonalphabetic sign systems (e.g., voice-overs, animation, video, sound effects, moods implied by music). None of these sign systems are new. Cave drawings predate alphabetic communication. Body language predates alphabetic communication. For centuries, schools have provided children with instruction in art and music. More recently, secondary and postsecondary education have offered courses as well as degrees in filmmaking. If new literacies are merely the incorporation of nonalphabetic sign systems into alphabetic curricula, and we already have venues for preparing children to be proficient users of nonalphabetic sign systems (e.g., art, music, and filmmaking classes), why should we incorporate them into the literacy curricula? My question is arguably an ontological one. What makes new literacies exist in the literacy world? What are the characteristics of semiotic signs that are new? Why are semiotic, nonalphabetic sign systems being birthed into the realm of literacy? In this section, I propose an astrophysical perspective to address this ontological question.

Astrophysicists contend that the fabric of existence is woven together by two components: time and space. They draw on theories of relativity to explain that all events take place at the intersection of time and space (Einstein, 1920; Ridley, 1995). If you meet someone for lunch, you must plan to rendezvous at a specific time as well as a specific place. If you choose the same time with unspecified place, you will miss each other. If you choose the same place but not the same time, you will miss each other. In this simplistic example, the coordinates of time and space are required to define the existence of an event. First, I explore the role of time and space in the ontology of alphabetic text. Then I consider whether time and space play a similar role in the ontology of digital semiotic texts.

The Role of Time and Space

The written word is significant to the human race. For example, prehistorical existence is defined in terms of the advent of the written word. Something is considered prehistoric if it existed before "history": before the written documentation of the human experience. The written word is so significant that people have been penalized and excommunicated for it. John Wycliffe was so despised for translating the Bible into English circa 1382 that 43 years after his death, his bones were dug up, burned and his ashes dumped into a river. With the advent of the printing press, the Bible was, for the first time, available to the general populace. This sparked the Reformation, a range of battles, and a drastic change in human history. In the history of American education, we commonly refer to the importance of the "three Rs." Due to the significance of the three Rs, you already know that two of the Rs are Reading and wRiting. Paramount to American education, from the inception of the country, has been the creation a literate citizenry who proficiently read and write alphabetic text. Why has the written word been so important to the human race so as to distinguish history from prehistory, inspire dissidents, cause battles, and be the impetus of the American education system for centuries? I propose that the written word derives the essence of its power to demand our recognition from two entities: its ability to travel through time and its ability to travel through space. In other words, because the written word is transtemporal and transpatial it is given exponentially greater credence than the oral word. Although time and space may not be an exhaustive list of the ontological constructs of reading and writing, they are the core of this discussion.

The spoken words of Socrates, Saint Paul, and Thomas Jefferson are long gone. There is no way of knowing the thoughts of peoples from long ago apart from what they wrote down. Cultures without written communication are largely unknown to us. Tens of thousands of years of human civilization are unknown to us because their written language is yet to be found or deciphered. Attempts are made to make sense of art, pottery, and other artifacts, but archaeologists are left to guess and superimpose meanings. Their cultures are lost because written expressions of these civilizations are yet to be uncovered. Their words did not travel through time.

Similarly, the oral words of Socrates, Saint Paul, and Thomas Jefferson would be unknown apart from their ability to travel through space. I was not in ancient Greece when Socrates spoke. I was not in Rome when Saint Paul spoke. I was not in Virginia or Pennsylvania when Thomas Jefferson spoke. Apart from the written word (or various technologies such as radio or TV), the only way to know what you orally spoke today is if I was within earshot of your voice. When you write down your thoughts, they are empowered to traverse beyond your geographical region. I do not have to be in Greece, Rome, Pennsylvania, or Virginia. The oral word is birthed into existence beyond its geographical space by being written down.

It is its ability to travel through time and space that creates and justifies the attention we give to the written word. One could argue, however, that art has the ability to travel through time and space—yet in our schools we do not afford it the same value as the written word. We have the sculptures of ancient Greece, the porcelain and statues of Chinese dynasties, the frescoes of Michelangelo, and the paintings of Rembrandt. However, many of these pieces of art would be unfamiliar to us apart from being transposed into photography or drawings. While they travel through time they do not readily travel through space.

Facial expressions and body language, while persistent forms of communication, are given little instructional time in our classrooms arguably because they cannot travel through time and space. With the advent of filmmaking, however, these sign systems have become transpatial and transtemporal. Indeed, actors and those who are involved in capturing meaning and communication via filmmaking actively study how to proficiently communicate with facial expression and body language. Again, it is the ability of these communication systems to travel through time and space that catapults them into an esteemed realm of communication and study.

With the advent of digital technologies, alphabetic and semiotic texts are readily empowered to travel through time and space. This is one reason that new literacies should be given heightened credence in our alphabetically based pedagogies and curricula. Text messages, e-mail, blogs, websites, fanfiction, YouTube, and Second Life all have unprecedented abilities to travel across space. We can communicate almost immediately with anyone in the world, even with astronauts in outer space. Furthermore, this communication is not merely alphabetic. We can engage in two-way video chats that can be captured and disseminated worldwide. As computer bandwidth, processing speed, and storage capacity increase, so do the multimodalities of communication and new literacies. As technology spreads throughout our culture and around the world, multitudes are able to capture and send semiotic expressions. Semiotic expressions are no longer limited to those who occupy the same time and space (e.g., ancient Greece) or have expensive equipment (e.g., filmmakers). Anyone with a relatively new computer and relatively fast Internet access can capture and send messages that incorporate alphabetic text, narration, music, video, animation, illustration, photos, and the like. Multiple modes we have long used to communicate face to face can now be captured, stored, and widely disseminated. The multiple modes we have long used to communicate face to face should be given attention in our school pedagogy and curricula because they are now transtemporal and transpatial—like the printed word.

Comparison of Transtemporal and Transpatial Qualities

While new literacies share transtemporal and transpatial qualities with the written word they are not equal in these qualities. The printed word is arguably less transpatial but more transtemporal than digital communications. For example, books must be transported by plane and truck to arrive in my local bookstore or library. I must then get in a car, drive to my local bookstore or library, and find the printed material I seek. On the other hand, digital communication quickly travels across space. E-mail, text messages, even digital books are instantaneously available in digital form. Digital expression travels across space much better than the printed word.

The printed word, however, still outperforms digital communication in temporal terms. Libraries and personal collections commonly include books that are more than 200 years old. On the other hand, my current computer cannot open files on my previous computer, which had a different operating system, that are only 5 years old. Herein, digital texts are currently low in transtemporal qualities. Arguably, it is the low transtemporal capacities of digital expression that minimize new literacies in schools that esteem traditional literacy. However, as more and more users create and store items online (e.g., blogs, Twitter, Google Docs, Facebook, YouTube) the more transtemporal digital communications become. Regardless of changes in my local operating system, the same files traverse time when stored on servers that are accessible simply by means of an online portal. Given an astrophysical perspective of new literacies, it seems predictable that as new literacies increase in transtemporal qualities they will increase in their importance to our society and schools.

In Chapter 1 (this volume), we argued that theory is valuable because it helps to explain how a phenomenon came to be as it is. In addition, theory fosters the ability to predict how phenomena may proceed. In these terms, an astrophysical perspective toward new literacies may provide significant insights into explaining how new literacies came into existence and how they may evolve. Specifically, new literacies should be esteemed because semiotic systems are now able to travel across time and space. In addition, the ability to be a proficient user of semiotic systems is likely to increase in importance and significance as technology enhances the ability to capture video, music, narration, animation, alphabetic text, and the like in such a way as to increase these systems' transpatial and transtemporal capabilities. Currently, new literacies have unprecedented transpatial capabilities, but comparably minimal transtemporal capabilities (e.g., it is yet to be determined whether my Facebook communications will be available in 200 years, as is the case for many printed texts that are hundreds and even thousands of years old). As technology acquires the ability to make communication transtemporal it is likely that new literacies will achieve even greater significance. Transtemporal and transpatial qualities appear to be needed in tandem to establish ontological viability in the literacy world. These are qualities that new literacies lack in full, but are quickly developing.

Future Research and Implications

Additional research needs to be done to explore the usefulness of an astrophysical perspective toward traditional and new literacies. Bakhtin (1930/1981) explores time and space in terms of the chronotope. His discussion focuses on the unique qualities of the novel and the need of the author to create temporal and spatial worlds that draw on his own realities. An astrophysical perspective may bridge notions of the chronotope from descriptions of the novel to reading and writing semiotic, multimodal, and digital expressions. Lefebvre (1974/1991) examines the social production of space. For example, he contends that the ancient world cannot be described merely as an account of people occupying space, but it must also consider how they created that space. An astrophysical perspective may be able to build on Lefebvre's work in terms of the social creation of virtual worlds. Additional work is being done to understand the ontology of virtual space (e.g., Bromage, 2004). An astrophysical perspective of new literacies may inform such efforts. Leander and colleagues (Leander, 2008; Leander & Lovvorn, 2006; Leander & McKim, 2003) effectively describe the importance of tracing literacy events through time and space. They highlight text as actants that cross temporal and spatial boundaries. Similarly, an astrophysical perspective examines how digital texts travel through time and space, as do the reading of digital texts. An astrophysical perspective, as described in this chapter however, seeks to explain why new literacies deserve the credence we give to printed text.

An astrophysical perspective toward new literacies may have implications for current conceptions of situated cognition (Brown, Collins, & Duguid, 1989; Lave & Wenger, 1991; Gee, Chapter 8 this volume). If human cognition is highly situated and semiotic systems that heretofore have been limited to the *here and now* can be transported through time and space, are new cognitive skills required? Are people who are able to situate their literacy and learning within the technology (e.g., e-mail), instead of their physical space (e.g., office), better able to maximize their literacies? What we have commonly referred to as multitasking may be better conceptualized as multisituating. We may not be doing more tasks simultaneously, but, rather, old tasks in new places (e.g., phone interview while at a coffee shop; teach online from the airport). Herein, those who situate their literacy within the technology may be empowered over those who situate their literacy within a physical space (e.g., the office is where I communicate with colleagues, the classroom is where I teach). Additional research is needed to explore cognition and multisituatedness.

As research refines the notion of literacy in terms of temporal and spatial qualities there will likely be significant implications for pedagogy and curricula. Pedagogically, there is already a boom with online learning. In 2009 the state of Pennsylvania enrolled more than 150,000 students in online K–12 programs (see *www.blendedschools.org*). Blackboard, Moodle, and Sakai are quickly becoming ubiquitous classroom management systems that allow students to take courses from anywhere in the world. Pedagogical understanding of new literacies in such environments is nascent. With regard to curriculum, there seems to be a looming necessity to incorporate new literacies into kindergarten through university classrooms. As digital texts increase and surpass print media in transtemporal and transpatial abilities so, too, will the importance of new literacies. Policymakers will need to change what is being deemed significant in literacy curricula. State testing will need to include new literacies. Materials for literacy instruction will need to incorporate new literacies. Based on an astrophysical perspective, it would appear that new literacies exist in the literacy world and will only increase in their importance.

Systems Theory and Autonomous Agents

The Need for a Systemic Perspective

Another perspective that may yield fresh insights into understanding new literacies is derived from engineering. This lens is known as an autonomous agents perspective. To make sense of this lens, I refer to the rich and varied complexities revealed about literacy from each perspective as a *system*. In other words, throughout this book and other volumes (e.g., Kamil, Pearson, Moje, Afflerbach, & Mosenthal, 2010; Ruddell & Unrau, 2004; Tracey & Morrow, 2006) literacy is understood from a range of theoretical perspectives. In this section, I refer to the revealed nature of literacy from each perspective as a system unto itself (e.g., cognitive system, sociocultural system, critical system, feminist system, semiotic system, cognitive system). When applied to literacy, an autonomous agents perspective may allow for the conceptualization of what it means to *orchestrate* multiple *systems* of reading and writing. From this perspective, I attempt to consider the relationship between multiple systems of reading and writing with technology.

Readers and writers of digital texts use sociocultural (e.g., proliferation of digital texts, online identities, online norms), semiotic (e.g., alphabetic, verbocentric, video, sound effects, narration, musical accompaniment), critical/feminist (e.g., empowerment), and cognitive systems (e.g., online navigation, synthesis across semiotic systems and range of sources, audience awareness). In other words, readers and writers are required to deal with new literacies as a holistic system that involves the ability to simultaneously utilize capacities revealed by sociocultural, critical, feminist, semiotic, and cognitive perspectives. While studies conducted from each perspective are valuable and need to continue, I contend that they overlook a vital element of new literacies. They overlook the fact that readers and writers are required to *orchestrate all of these systems*. In other words, online readers are not merely using cognitive systems but also sociocultural, critical, feminist, and semiotic systems. In addition, the use all of these systems occurs simultaneously.

One way to think about the orchestration of systems is as qualitative researchers think about grounded theory. Specifically, qualitative researchers conduct studies with the following goals in mind: describe a relatively unknown phenomenon, provide conceptual ordering of emergent characteristics of a phenomenon, and generate grounded theory to explain the origins and possible direction of a phenomenon (Strauss & Corbin, 1998). This last goal, grounded theory, commonly involves analysis of the relationships between the emergent categories and conceptual ordering of a phenomenon. For example, botanists provide rich descriptions of the plant world. Carl Linnaeus is known for conceptually ordering these descriptions into binomial nomenclature. I see parallels with the contributions made by the chapter authors of this book and a systemic perspective toward new literacies (see Figure 13.1). Specifically, the authors provide rich and nuanced descriptions of new literacies from multiple perspectives (Figure 13.1A, circles). These descriptions might be compared with categories of plants that emerge during botanical studies. These descriptions might also be compared with categories of findings that emerge during qualitative inquiry. These descriptions are valuable as we seek to understand this relatively unknown phenomenon some refer to as new literacies. Although descriptions from each perspec-

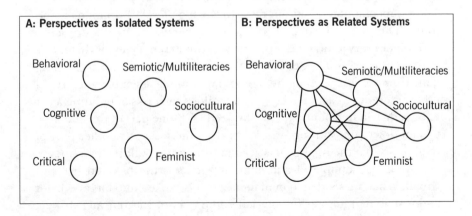

FIGURE 13.1. Perspectives as isolated and related systems.

tive make significant contributions in and of themselves, I seek to take the discussion a step further by calling for a systemic understanding of new literacies. I propose an examination of the interplay between these perspectives (Figure 13.1B, lines). Specifically, I encourage researchers to explore the usefulness of systems theory as a way to grapple with the complexities of new literacies and formulate a new model for conceptualizing new literacies. For digital readers and writers, all of these systems are one literacy system. Current theories used to understand new literacies isolate these systems. To address this dilemma and make sense of how these systems are orchestrated by digital readers and writers, I turn to the following type of systems theory: autonomous agents.

Description of an Autonomous Agents Perspective

The notion of autonomous agents comes from software development and the use of technology in electrical engineering (Green, Hurst, Nangle, & Cunningham, 1997). An autonomous agent is something or someone who does whatever is necessary to accomplish a task. Nwana and Woodridge (1996) state, "we define an agent as referring to a component of software and/or hardware which is capable of acting exactingly in order to accomplish tasks on behalf of its user." A software component is autonomous when it is designed to do what is needed to accomplish a specified task. The software programmer creates options within the software that allow the corresponding machine to complete the specified task.

Computers that run traditional assembly lines are set up in a pyramid structure. A mega-computer hands off tasks to subcomputers. These subcomputers send out tasks to the next level of computers, and so on. The pyramid expands as far as it is needed to turn every screw and solder every joint. One problem with this arrangement is that if one node of the pyramid goes down, the assembly comes to a screeching halt. However, if the computers of an automobile assembly line are set up as autonomous agents, the software allows the tasks of building a car to be redistributed along the line as needed. If one part of the line were to shut down, the software would reassign the tasks to another part of the line so that the final goal is accomplished: the building of a car.

Another example of autonomous agents is the bits and bytes of e-mail. When we send an e-mail message, it is broken into bits and bytes and distributed among the myriad computers of the Internet. If part of the Internet backbone is not working between the origin (e.g., Missouri) and the destination (e.g., New York) the bits and bytes are simply rerouted such that they reconvene at the destination in one coherent piece. In this way, the bits and bytes are made to act as autonomous agents. Regardless of obstacles, the bits and bytes accomplish their task: send an e-mail message.

Another way to think of autonomous agents is as a metaphorical example of a colony of hornets. If a colony of 500 hornets are left alone they will build a nest. If half of the colony is wiped out, the remaining hornets will redistribute the tasks and still build a nest, not half a nest. If half of those are wiped out, they will redistribute the tasks again and build a complete nest, not a fourth of a nest. In other words, the autonomous agents (e.g., software, e-mail, hornets) adjust to do whatever is necessary to accomplish the task (e.g., build a car, send a message, build a nest).

An autonomous agents perspective can be used to understand the reading process. Some models argue that readers use the following components to make sense of alphabetic text: syntax, semantics, graphophonemics, pragmatics, metacognition, affect, and automaticity (Ruddell & Unrau, 2004). From an autonomous agents perspective, these components are distributed and redistributed by accomplished readers until the purpose is accomplished: the comprehension of a given text. Such was the essence of Goodman's (1967) seminal work arguing that reading is a psycholinguistic guessing game. Readers orchestrate graphophonemic, syntactic, and semantic cues in complex ways to create meaning from text. When literacy is expanded from alphabetic texts to multimodal, semiotic, transmediated texts, as with new literacies, the process of reading and writing is made exponentially complex (e.g., Hartman, Morsink, & Zheng, Chapter 7, this volume). An autonomous agents perspective can be used to account for the rich and complex processes involved in new literacies.

Taking an autonomous agents perspective is useful because it provides a systemic perspective toward understanding new literacies. In other words, an autonomous agents perspective allows us to employ insights gained from sociocultural, critical, feminist, semiotic, and cognitive perspectives about new literacies into a larger, overarching framework. Readers and writers of new literacies use the insights identified by each of these perspectives. Just as a psycholinguistic perspective facilitates the ability to consider reading and writing as a complex and strategic use of multiple cueing systems I propose an autonomous agents perspective as a way to facilitate the ability to consider the complex and strategic use of new literacies.

An autonomous agents perspective indicates that learning to read and write is accomplished through a variety of means, and each individual may engage different tools, sensitivities, and strategies to arrive at the goal of communication and understanding. Proficient readers and writers orchestrate their literacy process by drawing on strengths to support weaker systems. In new literacies the range of available tools is significantly expanded and includes a greater range of communicative options. Researchers have made significant strides in identifying new literacies from sociocultural, semiotic, critical, feminist, and cognitive perspectives. When looking at new literacies from an autonomous agents perspective, however, important issues for research and pedagogy become apparent. No one set of insights (i.e., those revealed from sociocultural, semiotic, critical, feminist, and cognitive perspectives) constitute the whole of new literacies, just as traditional reading and writing cannot be defined by graphophonemic skills alone. Instead, it is the *orchestration* of sociocultural, semiotic, critical, feminist, and cognitive systems that enable proficiency in new literacies. Readers and writers of new literacies are engaged in a polysystems guessing game.

Autonomous agents, as a perspective that characterizes the entirety of processes involved in new literacies, provides some exciting opportunities for research and instruction. With regard to research, this perspective allows researchers to study how sociocultural, semiotic, critical, feminist, and cognitive systems are related to one another and are orchestrated by readers and writers as they become proficient with new literacies. The users of new literacies need to use these skills as an integrated system; therefore we need to research them as an integrated system. For researchers, an autonomous agents perspective reveals several questions that require further study. For example, what is the dynamic between these systems? When, why, and how do users depend on sociocultural constructs more than semiotic constructs? Behavioral? Cognitive? Critical? Feminist? When we use new literacies to read and write, do these systems relate to one another reciprocally, symbiotically, linearly, or in some other way? What contributes to this dynamic? When a *reader* seeks to make sense of a topic, how does he orchestrate his options? For example, I recently needed to learn how to clean the terminals of my car battery. I needed to find and read appropriate texts. I turned to YouTube, not Wikipedia, Facebook, or Twitter. I wanted not only a visual representation but a video-based demonstration. Alphabetic text, photos, and illustrations were insufficient for me. Conversely, how does a *writer* orchestrate a range of semiotic systems to communicate her desired meaning to a specific audience with genre-related expectations? These are but a few ideas for future research from a systemic autonomous agents perspective.

An autonomous agents perspective also has implications for educators. If we take an autonomous agents perspective toward new literacies, similar to strategy instruction based in cognitive perspectives, we not only need to teach students the necessary systems to be able to read and write with digital technologies, but we also need to teach students to flexibly use these systems to adjust as needed to accomplish their goal of reading or writing. This shifts the curriculum from simply teaching the skills of new literacies to also teaching students to *orchestrate* a range of systems and adjust as necessary to make sense of digital texts. Similarly, it reinforces the need to teach students a variety of literacy skills and strategies, since it is the complementary and flexible use of the entire domain of new literacies systems that enables literate activity. Flexible use of all domains of new literacies recognizes that within any individual a weaker system (i.e., cultural, cognitive, political, semiotic) can and should be bolstered by the systems with which an individual is more proficient. Therefore, not all readers will accomplish the desired outcome of comprehension in the same way. For example, background knowledge is known to influence comprehension. Readers with minimal background knowledge on the topic commonly struggle to make sense of the text. Coiro (2008) found that students who scored poorly on reading achievement and related background knowledge measures were able to find and use nonalphabetic texts in such a way as to quickly grasp comparable concepts as classmates with proficient reading skills and corresponding background knowledge. These students were then able to perform at much higher levels on reading comprehension tasks than scores measuring their reading abilities and background knowledge would indicate. Readers with minimal background on a topic can now access nonalphabetic texts to bolster their ability to make sense of alphabetic texts. Similarly in writing, new literacies enable an author to communicate messages in a variety of acceptable ways. Multiple systems are used to produce the desired result of comprehension and composition.

As teachers, curriculum developers, and researchers, we need to be careful that as we study and create pedagogies and curricula for new literacies, we do not develop a narrow pedagogical focus. Instead, as we develop new literacies curricula we need to ask how the entire range of domains work together to develop students' proficiencies. Similarly, assessment practices need to be developed for new literacies that reflect these integrated domains. Teaching cognitive, sociocultural, critical, feminist, and semiotic insights as separate domains would be similar to isolated instruction in graphophonemics, semantics, syntax, and pragmatics. Autonomous Agents provides a holistic approach to conceptualizing new literacies.

Autonomous agents is a useful perspective for understanding the complexities of new literacies. As a concept in electrical engineering, autonomous agents enables designers to orchestrate technology to accomplish a goal using a variety of integrated systems. These systems are able to overcome weaknesses in any part of the system itself to reach the desired outcome. If we think of new literacies as an integrated system of behavioral, sociocultural, semiotic, critical, feminist, and cognitive domains we understand that there is a greater set of traditional and new literacies capabilities at students' disposal to communicate meaning or develop understandings from digital texts. While new literacies are being researched in earnest, curriculum and pedagogical approaches that utilize new literacies in the classroom are still being developed. As we look to harness the potential of new literacies for school learning, we must remember to enable our students to become proficient in traditional literacy and new literacies as well as learn how to orchestrate these new literacies in a variety of ways to become autonomous agents of literacy.

CONCLUSION

In this chapter, I examined the role of divergent perspectives and theories in understanding any phenomena. Next, I briefly reviewed the insights provided by several well-established perspectives in understanding an emerging phenomenon: new literacies (see Table 13.1). In turn, I briefly described a couple of additional perspectives and how they may assist us as we grapple with the complexities of new literacies: astrophysical and autonomous agents. Finally, I close with a call for additional theoretical explorations of new literacies.

While traditional perspectives as well as astrophysical and autonomous agents perspectives may provide glimpses into understanding new literacies, so will additional perspectives. I encourage and invite increased dialogue regarding how these and other perspectives can shed new light on the nature of literacy in our digital world. For example, emergent

TABLE 13.1. Characteristics of New Literacies from Traditional and New Perspectives

Perspectives	Characteristics
Behavioral	Technology can be harnessed to assess individual's traditional literacy needs, provide targeted practice, and increase traditional automaticity and fluency.
Sociocultural	Literacy changes as culture changes. The abilities to read and write in our culture include many new literacies.
Semiotic and multiliteracies	Literacy includes the ability to read and write alphabetic text as well as nonalphabetic, non-verbocentric texts.
Critical and feminist	Students are being empowered and disempowered by verbocentric pedagogies and curricula. Students need to be aware of reification of oppressive stereotypes espoused via alphabetic as well as semiotic sign systems. Pedagogies and curricula need to be revamped to prepare students for the future instead of yesteryear.
Cognitive	There are reprioritized traditional cognitive strategies as well as new cognitive strategies involved in reading and writing digital texts that are semiotic, hyperlinked, and transmediated.
Astrophysical	New literacies gain credibility and viability that is traditionally given to printed texts as semiotic signs increase in their ability to traverse time and space via digital technologies.
Autonomous agents (systems theory)	New literacies involve the orchestration of new literacies identified by all perspectives. In the orchestration of multiple systems, analysis needs to be done to understand the relationship between systems. Readers and writers of digital texts engage in a guessing game that demands the simultaneous use of sociocultural, semiotic, critical, and feminist domains.

systems theory (Graves, 2007; see Ellis & Vanderbilt, 2008) may hold promise for understanding the cumulative role of multiple technologies in new literacies (C. K. Kinzer, personal communication, November 14, 2008). Self-determination theory (Deci & Ryan, 1985) as well as work from emotional and motivational perspectives (e.g., Guthrie & Wigfield, 1997; Lepper, 1988) will provide insights into online identity development and affinity participation. This is a significant time in the evolution of literacy theory. I know I am joined by all the contributors to this volume in the hope that this book advances the growing conversation about new literacies and fosters an increasing interest in understanding new literacies from multiple perspectives. We have vast opportunities to forge a new field of inquiry and influence how our children are prepared for the future.

REFERENCES

Alexander, P. A., & Fox, E. (2004). A historical perspective on reading research and practice. In R. B. Ruddell & N. J. Unrau (Eds.), *Theoretical models and processes of reading* (5th ed., pp. 33–68). Newark, DE: International Reading Association.

Alvermann, D. E. (2002). *Adolescents and literacy in a digital world.* New York: Lang.

Baker, E. A. (2001). The nature of literacy in a technology rich classroom. *Reading Research and Instruction, 40*(2), 153–179.

Baker, E. A. (2008). Support for new literacies, cultural expectations, and pedagogy: Potential and features for classroom websites. *New England Reading Association Journal, 43*(2), 56–62.

Baker, E. A., Rozendal, M., & Whitenack, J. (2000). Audience awareness in a technology rich elementary classroom. *Journal of Literacy Research, 32*(3), 395–419.

Baker, E. A., & Wohlwend, K. (2009). Play with Disney princess dolls and children's literacy development. *Voice of Literacy.* Podcast retrieved February 16, 2009, from *voiceofliteracy.org/posts/30565.*

Baker, E. A., Zhang, S., & Duke, N. (2008). The role of purpose when reading online. *Voice of Literacy.* Podcast retrieved November 3, 2008, from *www.voiceofliteracy.org/posts/28208.*

Bakhtin, M. M. (1981). *The dialogic imagination: Four essays.* In M. Holquist (Ed.) & C. Emerson & M. Holquist (Trans.). Austin: University of Texas Press. (Original work published 1930).

Black, R. W. (2008). *Adolescents and online fan fiction.* New York: Lang.

Bromage, A. (2004). Avatvistic avatars: Ontology, education and "virtual worlds." In D. S. Preston (Ed.), *Virtual learning and higher education.* Amsterdam: Rodopi.

Brown, J. S., Collins, A., & Duguid, P. (1989). Situated cognition and the culture of learning. *Educational Researcher, 18*(1), 32–41.

Chandler-Olcott, K., & Mahar, D. (2003). Adolescents' anime-inspired "fanfictions": An exploration of multiliteracies. *Journal of Adolescent and Adult Literacy, 46,* 556–566.

Coiro, J. (2008, December). *Exploring the relationship between online reading com-*

prehension ability, frequency of Internet use, and adolescents' dispositions toward reading online. Paper presented at the meeting of the National Reading Conference, Orlando, FL.

Coiro, J., & Dobler, E. (2007). Exploring the online reading comprehension strategies used by sixth-grade skilled readers to search for and locate information on the Internet. *Reading Research Quarterly, 42*(2), 214–257.

Davies, J., & Merchant, G. (2009). *Web 2.0 for schools.* New York: Lang.

Deci, E. L., & Ryan, R. M. (1985). *Intrinsic motivation and self-determination in human behavior.* New York: Plenum Press.

Einstein, A. (1920). *Relativity: The special and general theory.* (R. W. Lawson, Trans.). New York: Holt.

Ellis, L., & Vanderbilt, T. (2008). *Traffic: Why we drive the way we do.* Retrieved December 15, 2008, from *www.wfpl.org/CMS/?p=2901.*

Gee, J. P. (2003). *What video games have to teach us about learning and literacy.* New York: Palgrave Macmillian.

Goodman, K. S. (1967). Reading: A psycholinguistic guessing game. *Journal of the Reading Specialist, 4,* 126–135.

Graves, M. (2007). Peircean approaches to emergent systems in cognitive science and religion. *Zygon Journal of Religion and Science, 42*(1), 241–248.

Green, S., Hurst, L., Nangle, B., & Cunningham, P. (1997). *Software agents: A review.* Dublin: Trinity College.

Guthrie, J. T., & Wigfield, A. (Eds.). (1997). *Reading engagement: Motivating readers through integrated instruction.* Newark, DE: International Reading Association.

Guzzetti, B. J., & Gamboa, M. (2004). Zines for social justice: Adolescent girls writing on their own. *Reading Research Quarterly, 39*(4), 408–436.

Ito, M. (2007, February). *Amateur, matched up, and derivative: New media literacies and Otaku culture.* Paper presented at the meeting of the National Council for Teachers of English—Assembly for Research, Nashville, TN.

Kamil, M. L., Pearson, P. D., Moje, E. B., Afflerbach, P., & Mosenthal, P. B. (Eds.). (2010). *Handbook of reading research, Vol. 4.* New York: Routledge.

Kinzer, C. K., & Thomas, A. (2007, February). *Embodiment in virtual environments: Exploring literacies, identity, research, and community.* Paper presented at the meeting of the National Council for Teachers of English—Assembly for Research, Nashville, TN.

Knobel, M., & Lankshear, C. (2007). *A new literacies sampler.* New York: Lang.

Kress, G. (2003). *Literacy in the new media age.* New York: Routledge.

Lave, J., & Wenger, E. (1991). *Situated learning: Legitimate peripheral participation.* Cambridge, UK: Cambridge University Press.

Lawless, K. A., Schrader, P. G., & Mayall, H. J. (2007). Acquisition of information online: Knowledge, navigation and learning outcomes. *Journal of Literacy Research, 39*(3), 289–306.

Leander, K. M. (2008). Toward a connective ethnography of online/offline literacy networks. In J. Coiro, M. Knobel, C. Lankshear, & D. Leu (Eds.). *Handbook of research on new literacies* (pp. 33–65). Mahwah, NJ: Erlbaum.

Leander, K. M., & Lovvorn, J. F. (2006). Literacy networks: Following the circulation of texts, bodies, and objects in the schooling and online gaming of one youth. *Cognition and Instruction, 24*(3), 291–340.

Leander, K. M., & McKim, K. K. (2003). Tracing the everyday "sitings" of adolescents on the Internet: A strategic adaptation of ethnography across online and offline spaces. *Education, Communication, and Information, 3*(2), 211–240.

Lefebvre, H. (1991). *The production of space.* (D. Nicholson-Smith, Trans.). Oxford: Basil Blackwell. (Original work published 1974)

Lemke, J. (2007, February). *New media and new learning communities: Critical, creative and independent.* Paper presented at the meeting of the National Council for Teachers of English—Assembly for Research, Nashville, TN.

Lepper, M. R. (1988). Motivational considerations in the study of instruction. *Cognition and Instruction, 5*(4), 289–309.

Leu, D. J., Jr. (2006). New literacies, reading research, and the challenges of change: A deictic perspective. In J. V Hoffman, D. L. Schallert, C. M. Fairbanks, J. Worthy, & B. Maloch (Eds.), *55th National Reading Conference Yearbook* (pp. 1–20). Oak Creek, WI: National Reading Conference.

Leu, D. J., Ataya, R., & Coiro, J. (2002, December). *Assessing assessment strategies among the 50 states: Evaluating the literacies of our past or our future?* Paper presented at the National Reading Conference, Miami, FL.

Leu, D. J., Jr., Castek, J., Hartman, D., Coiro, J., Henry, L. A., Kulikowich, J., & Lyver, S. (2005). *Evaluating the development of scientific knowledge and new forms of reading comprehension during online learning.* Final report presented to the North Central Regional Educational Laboratory/Learning Point Associates. Retrieved February 10, 2008, from *www.newliteracies.uconn.edu/ncrel.html.*

Lewis, C., & Fabos, B. (2005). Instant messaging, literacies, and social identities. *Reading Research Quarterly, 40*(4), 470–501.

Nwana, H. S., & Woodridge, M. (1996). Software agent technologies. *British Telecommunications Technology Journal, 14*(4), 16–27.

Pearson, P. D., & Stephens, D. (1994). Learning about literacy: A 30–year journey. In R. B. Ruddell, M. R. Ruddell, & H. Singer (Eds.), *Theoretical models and processes of reading,* (pp. 22–42). Newark, DE: International Reading Association.

Ridley, B. K. (1995). *Time, space, and things.* (3rd ed.). Cambridge, UK: Cambridge University Press.

Ruddell, R. B., & Unrau, N. J. (Eds.). (2004). *Theoretical models and processes of reading* (5th ed.). Newark, DE: International Reading Association.

Siegel, M. (1995). More than words: The generative power of transmediation for learning. *Canadian Journal of Education, 20*(4), 455–475.

Strauss, A., & Corbin, J. (1998). *Basics of qualitative research: Techniques and procedures for developing grounded theory* (2nd ed.). Thousand Oaks, CA: Sage.

Suhor, C. (1984). Toward a semiotics-based curriculum. *Journal of Curriculum Studies, 16*, 247–257.

Tracey, D. H., & Morrow, L. M. (2006). *Lenses on reading: An introduction to theories and models.* New York: Guilford Press.

Wohlwend, K. E. (2009). Damsels in discourse: Girls consuming and producing identity texts through Disney princess play. *Reading Research Quarterly, 44*(1), 57–83.

Zhang, S., & Duke, N. K. (2008). Strategies for Internet reading with different reading purposes: A descriptive study of twelve good Internet readers. *Journal of Literacy Research, 40*, 128–162.

Index